## PRAISE FOR *TRANS PEOPLE IN HIGHER EDUCATION*

"Beemyn's advocacy and research on trans people in higher education is groundbreaking, and this edited volume is no exception. Through a mix of narratives and personal accounts, as well as the findings of research studies by major scholars in the field, the book paints a rich portrait of the variety of trans identities and experiences on college campuses today, along with recommendations for how campuses can create a more inclusive environment. The volume is an extraordinary resource for all who are committed to creating campus communities that are welcoming and affirming for trans students, faculty, and staff, and for those who simply want to learn more about the experiences of trans people on college campuses today."
— Kristin G. Esterberg, President, State University of New York at Potsdam

"For more than two decades, Genny Beemyn has been at the forefront of higher education research and policy advocacy regarding trans issues. Beemyn has given us yet another stellar contribution to those fields with this new anthology, which showcases an impressive cohort of emerging voices as well as a burgeoning body of high-quality scholarship. It's the best, most comprehensive overview to date on the timely topics it addresses."
— Susan Stryker, author of *Transgender History, Revised Edition: The Roots of Today's Revolution*

"*Trans People in Higher Education* combines the powerful accessibility of compelling personal stories with the complex and often harsh findings of qualitative and quantitative research to demonstrate the continued need for trans-affirming campuses, from policy to classroom engagement. Despite more than two decades of positive changes in academic institutions, trans and non-binary students, faculty, and staff continue to struggle for acceptance and equal access. This timely book shows that, in challenging the constricts of the binary gender system, helping others develop skills for culturally competent interactions, and expanding campus-wide policies, these individuals offer academia the best gift of all: learning opportunities and the inspiration to do better."
— Willy Wilkinson, author of *Born on the Edge of Race and Gender: A Voice for Cultural Competency*

# TRANS PEOPLE IN HIGHER EDUCATION

# TRANS PEOPLE IN HIGHER EDUCATION

Edited by Genny Beemyn

**SUNY** PRESS

Cover art: "Transition" by Yulonda Rios, mixed media.

Published by State University of New York Press, Albany

© 2019 State University of New York

For information, contact State University of New York Press, Albany, NY
www.sunypress.edu

**Library of Congress Cataloging-in-Publication Data**

Names: Beemyn, Genny, 1966- editor.
Title: Trans people in higher education / Edited by Genny Beemyn.
Description: Albany, NY : State University of New York Press, [2019] | Includes bibli-ographical references.
Identifiers: LCCN 2018009226| ISBN 9781438472737 (hardcover) |
    ISBN 9781438472744 (pbk.) | ISBN 9781438472751 (e-book)
Subjects: LCSH: Transgender people—Education (Higher)
Classification: LCC LC2574.6 .T73 2019 | DDC 378.0086/64—dc23 LC record available
    at https://lccn.loc.gov/2018009226

10  9  8  7  6  5  4  3  2  1

To the younger nonbinary trans people who helped create a world in which I could exist.

# CONTENTS

# INTRODUCTION

*Genny Beemyn*

DEPENDING ON ONE'S PERSPECTIVE, there has been either significant change or little change regarding the inclusion of and support for trans people in higher education over the past twenty years. On the positive side, many colleges and universities in the United States have taken at least some steps to address the needs of trans students, staff, and faculty and to create campus climates in which trans people can be out without having to face constant harassment and discrimination. Although there has not been any national research on the topic, it is safe to say that there are more out trans students, staff, and faculty on campuses now than ever before. On the negative side, there is not a single college or university that currently does enough to support their trans community members, and the majority of higher education institutions fail to ensure even the basic rights of trans people, such as by providing gender-inclusive housing options or a significant number of gender-inclusive restrooms. Many trans students, staff, and faculty are out today, but many more are not, or are open about their gender identity only to a select group of friends, because they do not feel safe or comfortable on campus. Thus, while the gains made by trans people at colleges in the last couple of decades are important and should be recognized, this progress is only the beginning of the changes that are needed for higher education to be a truly trans-welcoming and trans-supportive environment.

## EDUCATING ABOUT TRANS PEOPLE ON COLLEGE CAMPUSES

Works about the lives of trans students, staff, and faculty, especially by trans people themselves, can help create more trans-inclusive college environments by educating campus communities, and for this reason I accepted SUNY Press's invitation to edit this anthology. My hope is that the book will encourage cis students, staff, and faculty to learn more about the experiences of trans people in higher education and that the text will be used in undergraduate and graduate courses in LGBTQ+ studies, women's and gender studies, sociology, education, and other fields that have (or should have) the lives of trans people as a critical part of their curriculum. By including personal narratives and the findings of research studies, the anthology is especially well suited for current and future student affairs practitioners, many of whom are taught little or nothing about trans students in higher education programs.

While I envision people in higher education to be the principal audience for the book, I also hope it will be read by those with no connection to college campuses, who simply want to learn more about the experiences of trans people, especially younger trans people, today. In seeking to make the book accessible to this wider audience, I have not presumed a certain level of knowledge about trans people on the part of the reader. I included a glossary of trans-related terms that are used by the authors and by me in this introduction, and have edited the chapters to limit academic jargon. In addition, I asked many of the authors of research studies not to follow the standard academic journal format (i.e., literature review, theoretical framework, methodology, findings, discussion and implications, limitations, and future research needs) so as to make their work more readable to a general public. The minutia of research studies can be uninteresting (if not off-putting) to many general readers. Moreover, given the nearly total absence of articles about trans people in higher education until relatively recently, a literature review for every research-focused chapter would be highly redundant.

Some broader context is still needed. To enable readers to better understand the research-focused chapters, I review the history of studies of trans people in higher education in this introduction. The amount of material being published on trans college students, in particular, has grown phenomenally in the past few years, as demonstrated by this book. A decade ago, there would not have been enough new research for such a volume. I begin by providing a history of trans-inclusive campus policies. This history is important to review first because, without a more trans-supportive policy environment, fewer trans students would have felt comfortable coming out and been willing to participate in studies about their experiences. Thus campus policy changes made the current surge in research on trans students possible.

## TRANS-INCLUSIVE POLICIES ON COLLEGE CAMPUSES

The history of colleges recognizing and addressing the needs of trans people is relatively brief. In 1996, when I was a graduate student at the University of Iowa, I and a faculty member, Mickey Eliason, worked to add "gender identity" to the university's nondiscrimination statement. As a result, the University of Iowa became the first college in the country to have a trans-inclusive nondiscrimination policy and probably the first college to have any formal trans-inclusive policy. I had hoped that our success would lead other colleges to follow suit, but years went by before any other institution began to consider the needs of their trans students, staff, and faculty.

In retrospect, I should not have been surprised by the lack of immediate action elsewhere. In the mid-1990s, no college had an officially recognized trans student group and only a few dozen had lesbian, gay, bisexual, transgender, and queer (LGBTQ) centers, most of which were newly established and focused primarily on sexual orientation issues (Beemyn 2002). As a result, there were not institutional organizations in place that could advocate for such changes. In addition, few trans students, staff, and faculty were then out on college campuses—I was just beginning to identify as genderqueer myself—and in a position to challenge the hostile climates they experienced at their institutions and advocate for trans-supportive policies. Of course, most trans students, staff, and faculty did not disclose their gender identities because the environment at most colleges was so negative. Moreover, most cis campus community members failed to recognize, much less address, institutional genderism (the rigid adherence to the gender binary in practices, policies, and norms) because they were not directly affected by it.

It was not until the late 2000s and early 2010s that more than a handful of colleges started taking steps to support their trans populations, primarily in response to a growing number of students beginning to identify and be out as trans and requesting that their institutions become more trans inclusive. Since 2004, I have tracked trans-supportive policies at colleges, first for the Transgender Law and Policy Institute and then for Campus Pride as part of its Trans Policy Clearinghouse. When I began this work, fewer than twenty colleges had "gender identity" in their nondiscrimination policy; only one, Wesleyan University, provided a gender-inclusive housing option; and no college allowed trans students to use a name other than their legal name on campus records and documents or covered hormones and gender-affirming surgeries under student health insurance.

More than a dozen years later, the policy landscape has shifted significantly. For example, more than one thousand colleges now specifically include "gender identity" in their nondiscrimination policy; more than 250 have some form of gender-inclusive housing; about the same number enable students to use a chosen name, instead of their dead name (i.e., the name they were given at birth), on campus records and documents; and at least 75 cover hormone replacement therapy and gender-affirming surgeries under student health insurance (Campus Pride Trans Policy Clearinghouse 2017). A number of colleges have also created gender-inclusive restrooms across their campuses and stated publicly that trans people have the right to use facilities in keeping with their gender identity (e.g., Baker 2016; DesVergnes 2017; June 2017; Robles 2017), despite the federal executive branch allowing discrimination against trans students in access to school restrooms and some state governments seeking to require this mistreatment (National Conference of State Legislatures 2017).

Considering that there are more than 4,700 postsecondary institutions in the United States (US Department of Education 2016), this means that the vast majority of colleges still provide no institutional support to their trans students, much less to trans staff and faculty. Moreover, with the executive branch's withdrawal of the federal guidance on the inclusion of trans students under Title IX in 2017, it is unlikely that the colleges that have long failed to address harassment and discrimination against trans people will become motivated to do so without other pressures. Hopefully, as trans students continue to come out and advocate for themselves and are joined by trans staff and faculty, all colleges will be compelled to do much more to improve their campus climates for trans people.

## RESEARCH ON TRANS PEOPLE ON COLLEGE CAMPUSES

As recently as the early 2000s, there was almost no research on the experiences of trans people at colleges. Susan Rankin (2003) included trans people in a larger work on the campus climate for LGBT people; however, she did not separate trans individuals from cis LGB individuals in most of her analysis. Notably, she did include trans staff and faculty members. Since then, only one large research study (Rankin, Weber, Blumenfeld, and Frazer 2010) has similarly surveyed trans staff and faculty, and only the work of Erich Pitcher (2017, 2018) has addressed faculty members.

A handful of articles on trans students were published prior to the mid-2000s (Beemyn 2003; Carter 2000; Lees 1998; Nakamura 1998), but these articles relied largely on anecdotal evidence in suggesting ways that colleges could become more trans inclusive, such as by eliminating the gender binary in activities and facilities, providing services and resources for trans students, and educating the campus about gender identity. Subsequent articles that I wrote individually and in collaboration with others (Beemyn 2005a, 2005b; Beemyn,

Curtis, Davis, and Tubbs 2005; Beemyn, Domingue, Pettitt, and Smith 2005) provided more specific recommendations about the policies and practices that colleges need in place to support trans students.

The first published research studies on trans students were included in an issue of the *Journal of Gay and Lesbian Issues in Education* (Beemyn 2005c), now named the *Journal of LGBT Youth*. These studies included Rob S. Pusch (2005) on how trans students characterized the reactions of their family and friends when they disclosed their gender identity to them; Jeffrey S. McKinney (2005) on the campus experiences of trans undergraduate and graduate students; and Brent Bilodeau (2005) on the identity development processes of two trans students. Bilodeau's work was expanded into his dissertation, which became the first published book on trans people in higher education (2009).

In the 2010s, there has been a quickly expanding body of published work on trans students, which has been made possible by the growing number of college students identifying as trans and by a growing number of trans researchers, who bring an insider's knowledge and perspective to their work. Research on trans students has also been boosted by national surveys of college students adding questions that ask about gender identity, such as the Multi-Institutional Study of Leadership in 2006 (with expanded options in 2009, 2015, and 2018), the American College Health Association's National College Health Assessment (ACHA-NCHA) in 2008 (with expanded options in 2016), the National Survey of Student Engagement (NSSE) in 2014, and the Cooperative Institutional Research Program (CIRP) Freshman Survey in 2015. As a result of these changes, we now have large-scale data sets that can be used to consider the diversity of trans student experiences and make extensive comparisons between trans and cis students.

Most studies involving trans students over the past decade can be classified into five categories, based on their research methodology: single-campus studies of trans students, multiple-campus/national studies of trans students, national studies of LGBTQ students that separately address trans students, national studies of trans people that separately address college students, and national studies of college students that separately address trans students. All of these approaches can provide valuable insights into the lives of trans students and contribute to our small but growing body of knowledge about trans students who identify in different ways (e.g., gender, sexual orientation, race, class, religion) and who attend different types of institutions (e.g., public universities, liberal arts colleges, religiously affiliated colleges, women's colleges, historically Black colleges and universities, community colleges).

Studies of a single campus (e.g., Duran and Nicolazzo 2017; Pryor 2015) allow for an in-depth exploration of the experiences of trans individuals and the particular obstacles they encounter in a specific environment. Z Nicolazzo (2016b, 2017a) found that the nine trans students from one university whom ze interviewed over the course of one or more semesters practiced resilience as a strategy to cope with institutional and individual instances of genderism. Their use of resilience varied, depending on the context and their needs for self-care and self-protection. Some disclosed their gender identity in classes and other campus settings to affirm themselves, avoid being misgendered, and educate cis people, while others chose not to indicate that they were trans to avoid harassment and discrimination.

Studies of trans students on multiple campuses (e.g., Catalano 2015; Jourian 2017; Krum, Davis, and Galupo 2013; Seelman et al. 2012; Singh, Meng, and Hansen 2013; Wentling 2015) range in scope from research involving a few colleges to online projects that may include trans students from dozens to more than a hundred institutions. Building on hir work on resilience, Nicolazzo and colleagues (2017) focus on kinship as a framework for understanding trans college students' persistence and success. In interviewing eighteen trans students who attended a large, Midwestern LGBTQ student conference, they found that by establishing on- and off-campus kinship networks with other trans people and sometimes with supportive cis individuals, the students developed a sense of belonging that they often did not experience otherwise at their institutions. Kinship was developed in physical spaces, such as in LGBTQ and trans-specific student groups, the campus LGBTQ center, and LGBTQ student conferences; in virtual spaces, particularly social media sites; and through the emotional support systems the students had established for themselves. This study demonstrates that in seeking to create trans-inclusive and -welcoming campuses, college administrators must not only work to change policies and practices that exclude and marginalize trans students but also recognize the importance of peer networks.

Abbie Goldberg, Genny Beemyn, and JuliAnna Smith (2018) examine the trans-supportive policies and practices that are desired by trans students and provided by colleges. They surveyed more than five hundred undergraduate and graduate trans students and asked them to rank the importance of seventeen different trans-supportive policies and practices. The students rated gender-inclusive restrooms in most campus buildings as the most important policy, followed closely by a nondiscrimination policy that includes gender identity/expression, a college-recognized LGBTQ student organization, and the ability to change one's name on campus records without a legal name change. All seventeen policies and practices were viewed as at least somewhat important, but most of the students indicated that their colleges had few of them, especially if they were attending two-year or religiously affiliated institutions.

The trans-supportive policies and practices at women's colleges have come under particular scrutiny in recent years (e.g., Hart and Lester 2011; Nanney and Brunsma 2017; Weber 2016), as a growing number of their students do not identify as women (i.e., identifying as trans men or as nonbinary) and as trans women have sought admittance. In an especially insightful approach to this issue, Susan Marine (2011) conducted in-depth interviews with thirty-one student affairs administrators at five women's colleges to understand their reactions to how male-identified trans students are changing the nature of what it means to be a "women's" institution. Marine placed the participants into three categories: ambivalent toward, supportive of, or advocates for trans students. Some of the actions taken by the people in the latter two groups included using inclusive language, being accommodating to trans students and sensitive to their needs, equipping trans students for life outside of the college, and demonstrating departmental leadership on trans inclusion.

Other studies about trans college students over the past decade include them as part of larger research projects. The most extensive study to date of LGBTQ people in higher education, the *2010 State of Higher Education for LGBT People* (Rankin, Weber, Blumenfeld, and Frazer 2010), involved more than 5,100 students, staff, and faculty, 8 percent of whom identified as gender nonconforming, 3 percent as transmasculine, and 2 percent as transfeminine. The study found that the trans-identified participants reported higher rates of harassment, a greater fear for their physical safety, and more negative perceptions of the climate on their campuses than did the cis participants. For example, more than a third of the transmasculine and transfeminine students indicated that they had been harassed, and a majority did not disclose their gender identity for fear of being mistreated. Taken together, these figures suggest that students who are known or thought to be trans will likely experience harassment at some point at their institutions. The data from Rankin et al. has served as the basis for studies that consider the level of outness among LGBTQ students (Garvey and Rankin 2015a), the classroom experiences of LGBTQ students (Garvey and Rankin 2015b), and the campus climate for LGBTQ community college students (Beemyn 2012; Garvey, Taylor, and Rankin 2015).

The largest studies of trans people in the United States have been conducted in the past decade, and each of these works considers the experiences of trans college students. Recognizing that there had not been a national study that examined the identity development processes of both binary and nonbinary trans individuals, Sue Rankin and I (Beemyn and Rankin 2011; Rankin and Beemyn 2012) undertook this research to better understand the lives of trans people, particularly those who were traditionally college-aged. As I describe in my chapter in this book, we found similarities in experiences across various gender identities and significant generational differences.

Although not specifically focused on college students, the 2011 National Transgender Discrimination Survey (NTDS; Grant et al. 2011) and the 2015 US Transgender Survey (James et al. 2016) can offer insights into student experiences because of their large sample sizes (6,456 and 27,715 participants, respectively) and the ability to do cross-tabulations across a range of variables. For example, using data from the NTDS about the individuals who had attended college, Kristie Seelman (2014) found that trans women, trans people of color, younger trans people, trans people with a disability, and people who are more frequently perceived as trans are more likely than other trans individuals to be denied access to gender-appropriate campus restrooms due to being trans or gender nonconforming. The trans female participants were also much more likely than the other trans participants to have been denied access to gender-appropriate campus housing.

In another study, Seelman (2016) used the NTDS to consider the relationship between campus discrimination and suicidality. She discovered that individuals who had been denied access to gender-appropriate campus restrooms or housing or who had experienced harassment or assault from other students because of being trans were much more likely to have attempted suicide at some point in their lives than trans people who had not had these experiences. The NTDS did not ask when the participants had attempted suicide, so discrimination cannot be said to have caused suicidality, but these findings should still give pause to college administrators. Institutions that do not have written trans-supportive policies and do not actively ensure that these measures are followed risk causing irreparable harm to their trans students.

Arguably the most important development in research on trans students in the past decade has been the addition of gender identity questions to national surveys of college students. This change has made it possible to consider differences between trans and cis students on instruments like the ACHA's National College Health Assessment (Diemer et al. 2015; Griner et al. 2017; Oswalt and

Lederer 2017), the CIRP Freshman Survey (Eagan et al. 2017; Stolzenberg and Hughes 2017), the National Survey of Student Engagement (BrckaLorenz, Garvey, Hurtado, and Latopolski 2017), and the Multi-Institutional Study of Leadership (Dugan, Kusel, and Simounet 2012). The results of these studies demonstrate that, compared with their cis peers, trans students experience higher rates of verbal, physical, and sexual assault and have more negative physical, mental, and emotional health outcomes. But they are also more socially, civically, and politically engaged on campuses.

Using data from the ACHA-NCHA, Stacey Griner and colleagues (2017) discovered that the trans survey respondents were more likely than the cis female and male respondents to have experienced physical violence (physical assault and being verbally threatened), sexual violence (sexual touching without consent, attempted sexual penetration, and sexual penetration), and intimate partner violence (physical abuse, sexual abuse, and stalking). Another national study (Cantor et al. 2015) similarly found that trans students indicated the highest rates of sexual harassment, sexual assault, stalking, and intimate partner violence. At the same time, they were the least likely group to state that they would report an incident of sexual harassment or sexual assault to campus authorities because few had faith in the system at their colleges to support and protect the rights of trans people.

Sara Oswalt and Alyssa Lederer (2017) also used data from the ACHA-NCHA. They focused on the questions related to mental health conditions and found that the trans participants were more likely to indicate that they had been diagnosed or were under treatment in the previous year for attention deficit hyperactivity disorder, anorexia, anxiety, bipolar disorder, bulimia, depression, obsessive compulsive disorder, panic attacks, phobia, schizophrenia, and substance abuse/addiction. Anxiety and depression were especially widespread among trans students, with more than a third indicating they had been diagnosed or treated for each, which was about three times the rate of the cis students. This study points to the difficulties that trans students often face in trying to cope with the rejection and marginalization they commonly experience in college.

The results of the CIRP Freshman Survey (Stolzenberg and Hughes 2017) likewise show the psychological distress that many trans students experience when they are unable to find means to cope with the strains of discrimination, harassment, and violence. Compared with the survey participants overall, the trans students rated themselves as having poorer emotional and mental health, felt depressed more frequently, and were much more likely to state that they felt overwhelmed in the year prior to college. But on the positive side, the trans students were more frequently connected with others through socializing with friends and online social networks, were much more likely to be politically and socially involved, and more frequently stated that it was "very important" or "essential" to influence the political structure and social values, keep up to date with political affairs, and help promote racial understanding. Thus, while many trans students struggle with the emotional and psychological effects of mistreatment, they remain engaged with society, seeking to bring about change to improve their lives and the lives of others.

## ABOUT THE CHAPTERS

The essays in *Trans People in Higher Education* further existing research and take it in new, original directions. In compiling this book, I chose to include both personal narratives and research studies, recognizing that each approach offers different insights into the lives of trans people in higher education. Narratives can provide an up-close view of someone's reality and give the reader a glimpse of how that person sees the world, whereas research studies can present the big picture, considering trends and common themes in the experiences of a larger group. Both methods are particularly valuable in relation to trans people in higher education not only because of the limited amount of material that has been published to date but also because what has been published is limited in whom it covers. For example, there are few works by or about nonbinary trans undergraduates, trans graduate students, and trans faculty and staff—groups that are all discussed in this anthology.

I also wanted to bring together personal narratives and research studies because these approaches can inform each other. The narratives reinforce the findings of the research and ensure that the lives of individual trans people and the struggles they face at many colleges are not obscured by a lot of numbers. At the same time, the studies show that the negative campus climates experienced by the individual narrators are not an aberration; if you are a trans person in higher education today, you can expect to be frequently invalidated, marginalized, and made invisible because campuses were built on and still often reinforce a gender binary. The research articles, several of which involve large-scale, national studies, are also able to consider the diversity of trans people's lives in ways that a limited number of individual narratives cannot.

Because the literature on trans college students has too often relied on very small, nonrepresentative samples (e.g., Bilodeau 2009; Goodrich 2012;

Nicolazzo 2016a, 2017a; Pryor 2015) and thus could reach only tentative or limited conclusions, I wanted to include research that had relatively more participants and could "say" more. I also sought to include articles that address the experiences of nonbinary trans people and individuals who are just beginning to transition, as many personal narratives and studies of trans people involve trans women and men, especially binary trans people who have long since medically transitioned (for a recent example, see Cutler-Seeber 2018).

To provide different vantage points about being trans in higher education, I wanted the book to include works by and about trans people at various types of colleges and in various institutional roles: undergraduate students, graduate students, staff, and faculty members. At the same time, I wanted the majority of chapters in both the narrative and research sections to focus on the experiences of students, because they are the largest group of trans people in higher education, and many face relatively more difficult struggles to find personal and institutional support than do staff and faculty. I had sought to include more research articles on trans staff and faculty, only to be disappointed by the seeming lack of studies involving these groups, particularly examinations of the lives of trans staff members. I hope that this anthology inspires others to undertake a wide variety of research studies on trans people on college campuses; research involving trans faculty and staff is one area where such work is greatly needed.

Among the narratives in *Trans People in Higher Education*, four chapters are by students. Caden Campbell, with the help of Lisa Johnston, recounts his experiences as the first out trans man at his Southern women's college. Despite some difficulties with administrators and other students, Caden[1] found that he benefited from attending the school and was glad he went there. At the same time, the school benefited from him, as he argues that for women's colleges to remain relevant today, they must fully embrace trans students.

Three contributors discuss different aspects of being graduate students: taking classes, researching, and teaching. Annabelle Talia Bruno compares her experiences as a trans woman student in two different master's programs. In the first, she was misgendered and otherwise mistreated because of her gender, which caused her to question herself and her abilities. With more support and less need to have to defend herself, she was more academically successful in the second program.

While Annabelle recounts how her first graduate program failed her, Alandis Johnson considers how reconceptualizing failure as a positive outcome can be used to educate about gender inclusion in the classroom. As a nonbinary trans person, Alandis notes that they are disparaged for failing to adhere to the dominant gender system. By being what they describe as a "gender failure," they feel that they can better connect with the students they teach, many of whom also see themselves as failures in different ways and struggle to be understood. Moreover, Alandis argues that the "unintelligibility" of their gender broadens possibilities for others on their campus to see themselves in nonbinary terms and helps create a community of people who fail in their gender.

S. Simmons discusses their research on trans educators from the perspective of their own life as a Black trans person and an educator. Like Alandis, S. is able to relate to others by examining and being open about their experiences. In their case, they connected with their research participants, many of whom identified with S. because they saw themselves reflected in them. This affirmation from other trans educators, in turn, helped S. better understand themselves and the value of their work.

The remaining personal narratives are written by faculty and staff members. Although higher education is presumed to be a more welcoming environment in which to be trans than many other workplaces, both C. Ray Borck and Kei Graves describe mixed responses from co-workers when they came out to them as trans. Medically transitioning as a faculty member at a New York City community college, C. Ray encountered ignorant questions and stereotypes, particularly from colleagues, but as he increasingly fit others' perceptions of what a man should look like, he gained greater acceptance and began to be treated by other heterosexual male faculty members as "one of the guys." In contrast, Kei, a staff adviser and adjunct faculty member who identifies as agender and often presents in ways that are typically read as queer, embodies an ongoing challenge to dominant expectations for gender and sexuality. As a result, Kei found that many of their colleagues at the relatively conservative community college where they work were noticeably uncomfortable when they came out to them. But they did receive outward support from two staff members, one gay and one bisexual, and were surprised when a student whom they were advising reacted favorably to learning that they are trans, because the student's partner is trans.

Jackson Wright Shultz's narrative focuses on a particular advising experience. Like Kei, he worried when a student whom he had taught asked him if he is trans, fearing that the student would react harshly and file a complaint against him. But the student was looking for support in coming out as trans herself and seeking advice on how that might affect her future and career plans. The interaction led Jackson to think about his experiences as a queer undergraduate student and his struggles with how visible he should be as a trans person. The stories shared by Kei and Jackson demonstrate the importance of out trans staff and faculty.

The second section of the book consists of research on trans people, especially trans students, in higher education. These articles are groundbreaking for the populations they consider, the scale or scope of the studies discussed, or their methodologies. Together, the research chapters show the diversity of trans experiences and the commonality of discrimination and marginalization.

The chapters by Kasey Ashton and Tre Wentling consider trans students more generally. Kasey interviews trans students about how they developed, experienced, and made meaning of their gender identity. She garners further insights into their lives through the unique approach of having them bring in and talk about a visual or textual representation of how they perceive and understand their gender. Tre examines how trans students' experiences vary across campus spaces and how they respond to instances of institutional and personal discrimination. Contrary to the common depiction of trans students as victimized and defeated, he finds that many of the students are resilient and effectively advocate for themselves.

Three of the chapters consider particular groups of trans students. Abbie Goldberg addresses the experiences of trans and gender-nonconforming graduate students in the United States and a few other countries; I present the findings of a national study I conducted of nonbinary trans students; and Shannon Weber explores how two Western Massachusetts women's colleges have a "complicated relationship" toward the inclusion and support of trans students. The articles by Abbie and me are based on the first large-scale research projects involving trans graduate students and nonbinary trans undergraduates, respectively, and each work shows that group members face unique challenges in relation to other students and their institutions. Shannon undertook the largest study to date of trans students at women's colleges for her article, and her discussion of the struggles of trans men at these institutions speaks to Caden Campbell's experiences at his women's college.

While the other studies of trans students included here rely on trans-specific surveys and interviews done by the researchers, James DeVita and Katrin Wesner use a large, general data set on college student health to provide the first detailed analysis of the sexual health of trans students. They find that trans students have more negative sexual health outcomes than their cis peers, and that these sexual health disparities vary among trans students based on sexual orientation. James and Katrin call for more research to be conducted on the sexual behaviors and identities of trans students, but they argue that based on their findings, institutions should be providing trans support services now and not wait for additional studies.

The last three chapters cover a range of campus populations and themes. Erich Pitcher describes the experiences of trans academics, many of whom reported being misgendered, having to contend with institutional gender binaries, and needing to perform the extra labor of educating others. Similar to Shannon Weber's findings about trans men at women's colleges, many of the academics also described feeling hypervisible or invisible, depending on the situation. Erich's work here and in their recent book (2018) constitutes the first extensive research on trans faculty members and graduate student instructors.

While other studies have examined the treatment of trans students by staff, faculty, and other students (e.g., Garvey and Rankin 2015a, 2015b; Pryor 2015), Kristie Seelman takes a broader, more innovative approach by considering the interactions that trans students, staff, and faculty have with individuals who hold institutional power, such as supervisors, administrators, senior staff, and professors (in relation to students). She finds that these college leaders were largely a negative force in the lives of trans individuals and on the campus climate for trans people. In contrast, Matthew Antonio Bosch and Dana Carnes show how those with institutional power can make a positive difference on a campus. They discuss how their university became more LGBTQIA-inclusive, particularly more trans-supportive, through administrative leadership, institutional strategic planning, and providing resources to improve services and programs for LGBTQIA students. Their article can serve as a guide for other colleges that are looking to develop more welcoming campus climates for trans students, staff, and faculty.

## A NOTE ON "TRANS" TERMINOLOGY

Throughout the anthology, the term *trans* refers to individuals with both binary and nonbinary transgender identities. Although *trans** is sometimes used today, especially in academia, to signal the inclusion of all non–cis gender identities and to challenge the conflation of *trans* with "transsexual" (e.g., Nicolazzo 2017a, 2017b; Nicolazzo, Marine, and Galarte 2015), I believe the asterisk is unnecessary, inaccurate, and actually contributes to noninclusivity. In Latin, *trans* means both "across, on the other side of" and "beyond," so the term fits both binary and nonbinary transgender individuals, making the asterisk superfluous. Admittedly, many cis people and some members of the trans community ignore this fact and consider *trans* to be shorthand for "transsexual," applying the term only to individuals who are medically transitioning. But the use of the asterisk only encourages *trans* to be equated with "transsexual" and concedes the exclusion of nonbinary people from *trans*.

The asterisk also does not work from an operational perspective. When and how *trans\** began to be used is not well documented, but it seems to have been inspired by computing, where an asterisk is used as a wildcard in computer searches, producing results that begin with the letters before the asterisk (Ryan 2014). Thus a search for trans* would return "transgender" and "transsexual." But it would also yield words that have nothing to do with trans identities, like "translucent," "transcript," and "transfer." At the same time, most of the language that has been developed to describe nonbinary individuals, such as genderqueer, gender fluid, and agender, do not begin with *trans*, so would not be returned in a "trans*" computer search. Therefore, ironically, the identities meant to be forefronted in *trans\** are not even included. Supporters of *trans\** would presumably argue that their use of the asterisk is metaphorical, but the fact that it literally does not work undermines the concept and makes explaining what the asterisk means problematic.

Finally, I do not use the asterisk because it is often understood as having the opposite meaning to what was seemingly intended—that it was coined as a means to exclude nonbinary people as well as trans women (Diamond and Erlick 2016). The source of this interpretation is unclear, but like the advent of the asterisk, its supposedly exclusionary history was widely spread through social media, such that this narrative has often supplanted the original, inclusionary one. When, as director of the Stonewall Center at UMass Amherst, I began to use the asterisk in some of our online posts, I received immediate pushback from students who believed that its usage was furthering the cause of "trans exclusionary radical feminists" (TERFs). While TERFs apparently had nothing to do with creating *trans\**, I did not want anyone to misread our intentions, so I immediately stopped using the term. Similarly, I want to make it clear with the language of this book that nonbinary individuals and trans women are integral to the "trans" community, both literally and linguistically.

## NOTES

1. I refer to contributors by their first names here and in the list of contributors because I find the standard academic practice of using only last names to be clinical and distancing.

WORKS CITED

Baker, Mitzi. 2016. "UCSF Installs New Gender-Inclusive Restroom Signage." UCSF News, June 21. https://www.ucsf.edu/news/2016/06/403291/ucsf-installs-new-gender-inclusive-restroom-signage.

Beemyn, Genny. 2002. "The Development and Administration of Campus LGBT Centers and Offices." In *Our Place on Campus: Lesbian, Gay, Bisexual, Transgender Services and Programs in Higher Education*, edited by Ronni Sanlo, Sue Rankin, and Robert Schoenberg, 25–32. Westport, CT: Greenwood Press.

———. 2003. "Serving the Needs of Transgender College Students." *Journal of Gay and Lesbian Issues in Education* 1 (1): 33–50.

———. 2005a. "Making Campuses More Inclusive of Transgender Students." *Journal of Gay and Lesbian Issues in Education* 3 (1): 77–87.

———. 2005b. "Trans on Campus: Measuring and Improving the Climate for Transgender Students." *On Campus with Women* 34 (3). http://archive.aacu.org/ocww/volume34_3/index.cfm.

———, ed. 2005c. "Trans Youth." Special issue of *Journal of Gay and Lesbian Issues in Education* 3 (1).

———. 2012. "The Experiences and Needs of Transgender Community College Students." *Community College Journal of Research and Practice* 36 (7): 504–10.

Beemyn, Brett Genny, Andrea Domingue, Jessica Pettitt, and Todd Smith. 2005. "Suggested Steps to Make Campuses More Trans-Inclusive." *Journal of Gay and Lesbian Issues in Education* 3 (1): 89–94.

Beemyn, Brett [Genny], Billy Curtis, Masen Davis, and Nancy Jean Tubbs. 2005. "Transgender Issues on Campus." In *Gender Identity and Sexual Orientation: Research, Policy, and Personal Perspectives: New Directions for Student Services*, edited by Ronni Sanlo, 49–60. San Francisco: Jossey-Bass.

Beemyn, Genny, and Susan Rankin. 2011. *The Lives of Transgender People*. New York: Columbia University Press.

Bilodeau, Brent. 2005. "Beyond the Gender Binary: A Case Study of Two Transgender Students at a Midwestern Research University." *Journal of Gay & Lesbian Issues in Education* 3 (1): 29–44.

———. 2009. *Genderism: Transgender Students, Binary Systems and Higher Education*. Saarbrücken, Germany: Dr. Müller.

BrckaLorenz, Allison, Jason C. Garvey, Sarah S. Hurtado, and Keely Latopolski. 2017. "High-Impact Practices and Student-Faculty Interactions for

Gender-Variant Students." *Journal of Diversity in Higher Education 10* (4): 350–65.

Campus Pride. "Campus Pride Trans Policy Clearinghouse." 2017. https://www.campuspride.org/tpc.

Cantor, David, Bonnie Fisher, Susan Chibnall, Reanne Townsend, Hyunshik Lee, Carol Bruce, and Gail Thomas. 2015. *AAU Climate Survey on Sexual Assault and Sexual Misconduct.* Association of American Universities. https://www.aau.edu/uploadedFiles/AAU_Publications/AAU_Reports/Sexual_Assault_Campus_Survey/AAU_Campus_Climate_Survey_12_14_15.pdf.

Carter, Kelly A. 2000. "Transgenderism and College Students: Issues of Gender Identity and Its Role on Our Campuses." In *Toward Acceptance: Sexual Orientation Issues on Campus*, edited by Vernon A. Wall and Nancy J. Evans, 261–82. Lanham, MD: University Press of America.

Catalano, D. Chase J. 2015. " 'Trans Enough?': The Pressures Trans Men Negotiate in Higher Education." *Transgender Studies Quarterly* 2 (3): 411–30.

Cutler-Seeber, Andrew. 2018. *Trans\* Lives in the United States: Challenges of Transition and Beyond.* New York: Routledge.

DesVergnes, Abigail. 2017. "At Norton's Wheaton College, Restrooms Are Going Gender Neutral." *Sun Chronicle*, March 3. http://www.thesunchronicle.com/news/local_news/at-norton-s-wheaton-college-restrooms-are-going-gender-neutral/article_b3fe52ec-59bd-5671-b844-87b82208cb62.html.

Diamond, Danie, and Eli Erlick. 2016. "Why We Used Trans\* and Why We Don't Anymore." TSER: Trans Student Educational Resources. http://www.transstudent.org/asterisk.

Diemer, Elizabeth W., Julia D. Grant, Melissa A. Munn-Chernoff, David A. Patterson, and Alexis E. Duncan. 2015. "Gender Identity, Sexual Orientation, and Eating-Related Pathology in a National Sample of College Students." *Journal of Adolescent Health* 57 (2): 144–49.

Dugan, John P., Michelle L. Kusel, and Dawn M. Simounet. 2012. "Transgender College Students: An Exploratory Study of Perceptions, Engagement, and Educational Outcomes." *Journal of College Student Development* 53 (5): 719–36.

Duran, Antonio, and Z Nicolazzo. 2017. "Exploring the Ways Trans\* Collegians Navigate Academic, Romantic, and Social Relationships." *Journal of College Student Development* 58 (4): 526–44.

Eagan, Kevin, Ellen Bara Stolzenberg, Hilary B. Zimmerman, Melissa C. Aragon, Hannah Whang Sayson, and Cecilia Rios-Aguilar. 2017. *The*

*American Freshman: National Norms Fall 2016*. Los Angeles: Higher Education Research Institute, UCLA.

Garvey, Jason C., and Susan R. Rankin. 2015a. "The Influence of Campus Experiences on the Level of Outness among Trans-Spectrum and Queer-Spectrum Youth." *Journal of Homosexuality* 62 (3): 374–93.

———. 2015b. "Making the Grade? Classroom Climate for LGBTQ Students across Gender Conformity." *Journal of Student Affairs Research and Practice* 52 (2): 190–203.

Garvey, Jason C., Jason L. Taylor, and Susan Rankin. 2015. "An Examination of Campus Climate for LGBTQ Community College Students." *Community College Journal of Research and Practice* 39 (6): 1–15.

Goldberg, Abbie E., Genny Beemyn, and JuliAnna Z. Smith. 2018. "What Is Needed, What Is Valued: Trans Students' Perspectives on Trans-Inclusive Policies and Practices in Higher Education." *Journal of Educational and Psychological Consultation*. https://doi.org/10.1080/10474412.2018.1480376.

Goodrich, Kristopher M. 2012. "Lived Experiences of College-Age Transsexual Individuals." *Journal of College Counseling* 15 (3): 215–32.

Grant, Jaime M., Lisa A. Mottet, Justin Tanis, Jack Harrison, Jody L. Herman, and Mara Keisling. 2011. *Injustice at Every Turn: A Report of the National Transgender Discrimination Survey*. Washington, DC: National Center for Transgender Equality and the National Gay and Lesbian Task Force. www.thetaskforce.org/downloads/reports/reports/ntds_full.pdf.

Griner, Stacey B., Cheryl A. Vamos, Erika L. Thompson, Rachel Logan, Coralia Vázquez-Otero, and Ellen M. Daley. 2017. "The Intersection of Gender Identity and Violence: Victimization Experienced by Transgender College Students." *Journal of Interpersonal Violence*. doi: 10.1177/0886260517723743.

Hart, Jeni, and Jaime Lester. 2011. "Starring Students: Gender Performance at a Women's College." *NASPA Journal About Women in Higher Education* 4 (2): 193–217.

James, Sandy E., Jody L. Herman, Susan Rankin, Mara Keisling, Lisa Mottet, and Ma'ayan Anafi. 2016. *The Report of the 2015 U.S. Transgender Survey*. Washington, DC: National Center for Transgender Equality.

Jourian, T. J. 2017. "Trans*forming College Masculinities: Carving Out Trans* Masculine Pathways through the Threshold of Dominance." *International Journal of Qualitative Studies in Education* 30 (3): 245–65.

June, Sophia. 2017. "Trump or No Trump, Portland State University Is Keeping Its Transgender Bathrooms." *Willamette Week*, February 22. http://www.

wweek.com/news/2017/02/22/trump-or-no-trump-portland-state-uni
versity-is-keeping-its-transgender-bathrooms.

Krum, Tiana E., Kyle S. Davis, and M. Paz Galupo. 2013. "Gender-Inclusive
Housing Preferences: A Survey of College-Aged Transgender Students."
*Journal of LGBT Youth* 10 (1–2): 64–82.

Lees, Lisa J. 1998. "Transgender Students on Our Campuses." In *Working with
Lesbian, Gay, Bisexual, and Transgender College Students: A Handbook for
Faculty and Administrators*, edited by Ronni L. Sanlo, 37–43. Westport,
CT: Greenwood Press.

Marine, Susan B. 2011. " 'Our College Is Changing': Women's College
Student Affairs Administrators and Transgender Students." *Journal of
Homosexuality* 58 (9): 1165–86.

McKinney, Jeffrey S. 2005. "On the Margins: A Study of the Experiences
of Transgender College Students." *Journal of Gay & Lesbian Issues in
Education* 3 (1): 63–76.

Nakamura, Karen. 1998. "Transitioning on Campus: A Case Studies Approach."
In *Working with Lesbian, Gay, Bisexual, and Transgender College Students:
A Handbook for Faculty and Administrators*, edited by Ronni L. Sanlo,
179–86. Westport, CT: Greenwood Press.

Nanney, Megan, and David L. Brunsma. 2017. "Moving Beyond Cis-terhood:
Determining Gender through Transgender Admittance Policies at U.S.
Women's Colleges." *Gender & Society* 31 (2): 145–70.

National Conference of State Legislatures. 2017. " 'Bathroom Bill' Legislative
Tracking." http://www.ncsl.org/research/education/-bathroom-bill-
legislative-tracking635951130.aspx.

Nicolazzo, Z. 2016a " 'It's a Hard Line to Walk': Black Non-Binary Trans*
Collegians' Perspectives on Passing, Realness, and Trans*-Normativity."
*International Journal of Qualitative Studies in Education* 29 (9): 1173–88.

———. 2016b. " 'Just Go in Looking Good': The Resilience, Resistance, and
Kinship-Building of Trans* College Students." *Journal of College Student
Development* 57 (5): 538–56.

———. 2017a. *Trans* in College: Transgender Students' Strategies for Navigating
Campus Life and the Institutional Politics of Inclusion*. Sterling, VA: Stylus.

———. 2017b. "What's Transgressive about Trans* Studies in Education Now?"
*International Journal of Qualitative Studies in Education* 30 (3): 211–16.

Nicolazzo, Z, Susan B. Marine, and Francisco J. Galarte, eds. 2015.
"Trans*formational Pedagogies." Special issue of *TSQ: Transgender Studies
Quarterly* 2 (3).

Nicolazzo, Z, Erich N. Pitcher, Kristen A. Renn, and Michael Woodford. 2017. "An Exploration of Trans* Kinship as a Strategy for Student Success." *International Journal of Qualitative Studies in Education* 30 (3): 305–19.

Oswalt, Sara B., and Alyssa M. Lederer. 2017. "Beyond Depression and Suicide: The Mental Health of Transgender College Students." *Social Science* 6 (1): 20. http://www.mdpi.com/2076-0760/6/1/20.

Pitcher, Erich N. 2017. " 'There's Stuff that Comes with Being an Unexpected Guest': Experiences of Trans* Academics with Microaggressions." *International Journal of Qualitative Studies in Education* 30 (7): 688–703.

———. 2018. *Being and Becoming Professionally Other: Identities, Voices, and Experiences of U.S. Trans* Academics.* New York: Peter Lang.

Pryor, Jonathan T. 2015. "Out in the Classroom: Transgender Student Experiences at a Large Public University." *Journal of College Student Development* 56 (5): 440–55.

Pusch, Rob S. 2005. "Objects of Curiosity: Transgender College Students' Perceptions of the Reactions of Others." *Journal of Gay & Lesbian Issues in Education* 3 (1): 45–61.

Rankin, Susan R. 2003. *Campus Climate for Gay, Lesbian, Bisexual, and Transgender People: A National Perspective.* New York: National Gay and Lesbian Task Force Policy Institute.

Rankin, Sue, and Genny Beemyn. 2012. "Beyond a Binary: The Lives of Gender-Nonconforming Youth." *About Campus* (17): 2–10.

Rankin, Susan, Genevieve Weber, Warren Blumenfeld, and Somjen Frazer. 2010. *2010 State of Higher Education for Lesbian, Gay, Bisexual, and Transgender People.* Charlotte, NC: Campus Pride.

Robles, Alison. 2017. "Gender-Inclusive Bathroom Signs Installed across Campus." *Ionian*, January 26. http://www.ioniannews.com/gallery/article_89811f86-e40a-11e6-9ea3-27435cdc97bd.html.

Ryan, Hugh. 2014. "What Does *Trans*\* Mean, and Where Did It Come From?" *Slate*, January 10. http://www.slate.com/blogs/outward/2014/01/10/trans_what_does_it_mean_and_where_did_it_come_from.html.

Seelman, Kristie L. 2014. "Transgender Individuals' Access to College Housing and Bathrooms: Findings from the National Transgender Discrimination Survey." *Journal of Gay and Lesbian Social Services* 26 (2): 186–206.

———. 2016. "Transgender Adults' Access to College Bathrooms and Housing and the Relationship to Suicidality." *Journal of Homosexuality* 63 (10): 1378-1399.

Seelman, Kristie L., N. Eugene Walls, Kelly Costello, Karly Steffens, Kyle Inselman, Hillary Montague-Asp, and Colorado Trans on Campus

Coalition. 2012. *Invisibilities, Uncertainties, and Unexpected Surprises: The Experiences of Transgender and Gender Non-Conforming Students, Staff, and Faculty at Universities and Colleges in Colorado.* Denver, CO: Authors.

Singh, Anneliese A., Sarah Meng, and Anthony Hansen. 2013. " 'It's Already Hard Enough Being a Student': Developing Affirming College Environments for Trans Youth." *Journal of LGBT Youth* 10 (3): 208–23.

Stolzenberg, Ellen Bara, and Bryce Hughes. 2017. "The Experiences of Incoming Transgender College Students: New Data on Gender Identity." *Liberal Education* 103 (2). https://www.aacu.org/liberaleducation/2017/spring/stolzenberg_hughes.

US Department of Education, National Center for Education Statistics. 2016. "Fast Facts." https://nces.ed.gov/fastfacts/display.asp?id=84.

Weber, Shannon. 2016. " 'Womanhood Does Not Reside in Documentation': Queerness, Student Activism, and Transgender Women's Inclusion at Women's Colleges." *Journal of Lesbian Studies* 20 (1): 29–45.

Wentling, Tre. 2015. "Trans* Disruptions: Pedagogical Practices and Pronoun Recognition." *Transgender Studies Quarterly* 2 (3): 469–76.

# THE VOICES OF TRANS STUDENTS, STAFF, AND FACULTY

ONE

# An Unescorted Male
## Transcending Gender at a Southern Women's College
*Lisa N. Johnston and Caden J. Campbell*

### ONE STORY, TWO VOICES: LISA'S EXPERIENCES

When I arrived at Sweet Briar College as a new librarian in 1989, I was used to being out of the closet as a lesbian at work, and I was not going back in, despite being warned that central Virginia, just seventeen miles north of Jerry Falwell's Baptist Liberty University, was the buckle of the Bible Belt. I had attended college in Tennessee, and I was used to hiding my sexual identity when I was away from my friends and off campus. What I did not realize was that I would be the first openly queer faculty member at a school where most of the students were relatively conservative, particularly for students at a women's college. Within a year of my arrival, the college's feminist Episcopal chaplain had convinced me to sponsor a group for lesbian and bisexual students and their allies. That there could be trans people at Sweet Briar College was not mentioned, let alone considered to be a reality, in the early 1990s.

One of the questions parents often asked on admissions tours was "do you have a lesbian problem here?" Sweet Briar College had queer students, it always had, but the atmosphere for these students was hostile. Those who initially participated in the college's first official lesbian and bisexual group were mostly straight-identified women concerned about their queer friends. Because they were fearful about being outed, the queer students were reluctant to join if the group met in a campus building. When meetings were moved to my apartment, which was on the edge of campus, the queer students began to attend. We hosted guest speakers, read and discussed books, and watched films, but mainly the lesbian and bisexual students shared stories about their lives and the pain of being in the closet at college, where they expected to feel free

3

to express themselves. Twenty-five years later, the situation for queer students, faculty, and staff has improved greatly. For example, the college offered domestic partner benefits prior to same-sex marriage becoming legal nationwide, and queer couples can hold hands on campus without fear of harassment.

But just as it was for lesbian and bisexual people on campus twenty-five years ago, there is not much visibility and support for trans students, faculty, and staff today. Questions like who they are, what they need, and whether they would be permitted to attend the school had long been off of the radar as an institution. This all began to change in 2011, when CJ Campbell started to live openly as a trans man, becoming Sweet Briar's first out transmasculine student. I met CJ soon after he came out.

CJ's support from faculty and students varied, depending primarily on how much they knew about and were accepting of trans identities. At times, he encountered a tremendous amount of hostility. The women who lived in his dorm posted a sign on the men's restroom, stating that it was a space for their boyfriends, not him. Members of the first-year soccer team refused to refer to CJ as he/him, even after he spoke to them about his transmasculinity. Similarly, some faculty spouses continued to call him by his former, feminine name, despite being aware of his new name and his trans identity.

Along with these negative incidents were just as many positive interactions. CJ was not like the majority of Sweet Briar community members, but he was a community member nonetheless, and that could be seen in the overwhelming support he received from most faculty and staff and from many other students. Some of the opposition he encountered was simply because of ignorance, which would have been alleviated had the college intervened to educate students and established trans-inclusive admissions and community policies. After CJ graduated, more transmasculine students came out, but they encountered the same lack of overall institutional support, which is an issue throughout higher education, especially at women's colleges.

Thinking back on my experience as Sweet Briar's first openly gay faculty member, and thinking back on the conversations that the college's hidden bisexual and lesbian community had in my apartment in the 1990s, I cannot help but draw connections between CJ's experiences and my own. The anguish CJ experienced because he often felt invisible and ignored by the institution is reminiscent of the experiences of many bisexual and lesbian students, faculty, and staff twenty-five years ago.

This chapter represented a chance for CJ and me to work together to tell his story, with CJ being the wordsmith and me serving as the main researcher.

We wanted to examine the effects of the lack of trans-specific policies at Sweet Briar and address the need for changes in the missions of all women's colleges by establishing clear and inclusive trans student policies. These issues were explored through the narrative of Sweet Briar's first openly transitioning student, the story of the Sweet Briar man.

## ONE STORY, TWO VOICES: CJ'S EXPERIENCES

It was a mistake: I was not supposed to be at the talk. When I woke up on the morning of March 23, 2010, I had not known that it was going to take place. As I walked up the grassy hill that led to Sweet Briar College's library, I heard that author and trans educator Mara Drummond was giving a presentation. I remember an intense curiosity emerging within me. *What would she say?* I had known of one trans person in my life, and my experience of her had been that of an older student twirling across the cafeteria in high school. Going to Mara's talk was the first time that I had actually heard a trans narrative.

I listened as she described *transgender* as an umbrella term that encompassed many different people—those who felt estranged from the gender they had been assigned at birth. I became increasingly aware that she was talking about me. The realization that there was something very nonbinary about me was like taking my first breath: I felt awakened; it was my "a ha!" moment. Mara's presentation gave meaning to something that I had been feeling for so long but did not have the words to articulate.

As the presentation drew to a close, I approached her with a copy of her just-purchased book and, much to my surprise, suddenly found myself belching out a life-changing declaration, "I don't really know what I am." She looked up, and I began to feel that treacherous mouth go bone-dry. "That is okay, we are all on a journey," she said.

In her book, *Transitions: A Guide to Transitioning for Transsexuals and Their Families* (2009), Drummond writes that

> Once you declare to that first person or to yourself that you are transsexual, you start down a long, dark road, a road that has many hairpin turns and unknown hazards along the way, possibly without any sense of where you are truly heading. The journey that you then undertake may be one of the hardest passages you will ever make. (p. xi)

Truer words, it seemed to me at the time, could never be spoken. I had opened my mouth, as if slowly opening a heavy steel door, and admitted that I had no clue who or what I was, but I knew what I was not. My life prior to that moment had been filled with images of who and what I should be. I had been trapped in this hell-house of patriarchal and binary angst, a house that was plastered with images of the societal standards of gender: vagina = girl, penis = boy, pink versus blue, girl power, men are dogs, women are fragile, long hair, short hair, dresses, and pants. Once I opened that door, a road had been laid, brick by brick, before me and the only place I could step was forward. Little did I know that by choosing Sweet Briar College as the stage for my transitioning journey, I would find myself in a hotbed of the political and societal confusion, fear, and anxiety of Southern women's colleges that are in many ways still influenced by the Antebellum South.

## TRANS STUDENTS AT WOMEN'S COLLEGES

Given the increased visibility of trans students, colleges and universities across the country are now faced with the question of where trans students fit on their campuses. Women's colleges, in particular, "have experienced significant controversy around transgender issues" (Schneider 2010, 100). The most well-known historically women's colleges were the Seven Sisters in the Northeastern United States: Barnard, Bryn Mawr, Radcliffe (which has since merged with Harvard), Smith, Vassar (now coeducational), Mount Holyoke, and Wellesley. The five institutions that remain women's colleges have helped lead the way among single-sex institutions in addressing the presence of trans students with each having a written policy about trans inclusion.

The most far-reaching, trans-inclusive policy at a women's college was established at Mount Holyoke in September 2014. While the other four remaining Seven Sisters, along with Mills College and Simmons College, have policies that admit all qualified students who identify as women, Mount Holyoke goes a step further and considers applications from all trans-identified people, no matter their gender assigned at birth. In other words, the college is open to all gender minority individuals—everyone except those who are "biologically born male; identifies as man" (Trans Policy Clearinghouse 2016).

The South's answer to the Seven Sisters is a loose association of women's colleges informally referred to as the "Seven Sisters of the South": Agnes Scott College (GA), Brenau University's Women's College (GA), Hollins University (VA), Mary Baldwin College (VA), Salem College (NC), Sweet Briar College (VA), and Wesleyan College (GA). Unlike their Northern counterparts, the majority of the Seven Sisters of the South have yet to issue written policies that address the inclusion of trans students. In fact, the one college in the group to have enacted an official policy on the admission and graduation of trans students, Hollins, forces trans men who take steps to affirm their identities to leave the school.[1]

For decades, many women's colleges have had an unwritten policy that female students who subsequently identified as male could continue at the institution, if they chose, because they were a member of the campus community. This practice changed in 2007, when Hollins first began including the following policy in its student handbook:

> If a degree-seeking undergraduate student undergoes sex reassignment from female to male (as defined by the university below) at any point during her [sic] time at Hollins, the student will be helped to transfer to another institution since conferral of a Hollins degree will be limited to those who are women. In an effort to recognize and honor the choices of individual students, the university considers sex reassignment to have occurred when an undergraduate student "self identifies" as a male and initiates any of the following processes: 1) undergoes hormone therapy with the intent to transform anatomically from female to male; 2) undergoes any surgical process (procedure) to transform from female to male; or, 3) changes her name legally with the intent of identifying herself as a man. (Hollins University 2015, 7)

This policy has been widely condemned as "unnecessarily punitive ... You're forcing [trans men] to either uproot their life and leave school or suppress something that's really important and significant in their life." While Hollins has said that it is reconsidering the policy and has not expelled any trans students, at least five trans men have indicated that they had left the college on their own, and a hostile campus climate for trans students has been institutionalized (Troop 2011, para. 5).

Sweet Briar College is currently looking to create an official policy on trans students. It does include "gender identity" in its nondiscrimination policy and has had at least one out trans student at the college: me.

## THE DUALITY OF SOUTHERN WOMEN'S COLLEGES

I decided to attend Sweet Briar, a college far from my home in Arkansas, in part because of what I see now as deluded reasoning. Its overtly feminine advertising dazzled me: pink flowers, pearls, and ponies. I swooned under the misogynistic signs that read "think is for girls," and when I stepped onto the

campus and saw the rolling hills, stables, and plantation house, my precon-
ceived notions of Southern women's education painted a compelling picture
and transferred me back to a time where, as the old and vapid adage goes, "men
were men, and women were women." It felt like a place where I could truly embrace a kind of wholeness in my gender that I had not felt before, a wholeness
that could be placed in a neat little box topped with a pink and green satin bow.

Within my first few weeks as a student, I realized that Sweet Briar College
was a much more complicated mix. Like its advertising, "Think Is for Girls"
(Sweet Briar College's advertising campaign from 2005–9), there were things
that were fantastically empowering for women. Yet the culture of the school
and many of its deep-rooted traditions felt belittling and antifeminist, like referring to educated women as "girls." It was Hogwarts meets *Gone with the
Wind*, or a Jekyll and Hyde struggle between a feminist future and an arguably
misogynistic past. In my first year, there were times I hoped I would suddenly
emerge as a Xena Warrior Princess type, bursting forward to say, "I am woman,
hear me roar!" At other times, a secret part of me hoped to transform into a
Stepford wife, sweetly replying, "Yes, dear," as I fell into step with the chivalric
images of a delicate but fierce Southern rose.

There has been a sexist stereotype since the development of higher education for women that women's colleges were producing wives and mothers
over leaders and academics. It did not help that "the press sometimes portrayed
women's colleges as not academically serious but rather as places where women
could learn how to become refined partners of rich men—the 'finishing school'
image" (Miller-Bernal 2011, 223). Even today, Sweet Briar has not fully rid itself
of this stereotype, with snide jokes about its "MRS" degree, its vixen mascot,
long weekends at Hampden Sydney College for men, and Cinderella-like winter
balls with the cadets of the Virginia Military Institute. There has long been a
dualism at Sweet Briar and the other Seven Sisters of the South that is not seen
in other parts of the country: the refined lady of the Antebellum South versus
the educated feminist and independent global citizen. It is a dualism that is
both holding them back and struggling to propel them forward.

## SWEET BRIAR'S POLICIES

There is a policy at Sweet Briar stating that no male outside of faculty and staff
can be on campus without an escort. This policy became an instant inside joke
for many students, including me. "To Herald" was the name of the game, the
object being that whenever you saw an unescorted male, you would whisper to

someone else, "escort," and then that person would say a little louder, "escort," for someone else to repeat it even louder, and so on. Eventually, it would reach the point of yelling, and some people would be too embarrassed to participate. But there was always that person with brazen assurance who would announce the presence of a lone male to the whole campus. It was stupid, yet its stupidity made it even funnier. That changed for me during the fall of my sophomore year, when I realized that I would be considered that unescorted male—a lone man walking the halls of Sweet Briar College.

About seven months after my first encounter with Mara Drummond, following many desperate and heartbreaking conversations with her, and some very dark nights on the phone with the Trevor Project, I came out as transgender, not only to myself but also to a few of my family members, friends, and Sweet Briar College. My journey in coming out to the school began with English professor Tony Lilly. I was not entirely sure why I trusted Tony; I did not know him very well, but I did know that he was a strong advocate for LGBTQIA+ students. I called him and said, "Dr. Lilly, I am a trans man." His response carried a note of surprise: "Oh, I did not know you identified that way." Me neither. This conversation, the first of many, was the genesis of a friendship and mentorship that was paramount in those first few years to me as an out trans man undergoing hormone replacement therapy at a women's college below the Mason-Dixon Line and, as far as we knew, the first out transmasculine student Sweet Briar had known.

Tony and I found ourselves researching and asking questions about Sweet Briar's policies regarding trans students. The question of whether I would have a place at the college as I began to transition needed an immediate answer. Seeking the advice of the dean of the college at the time, Jonathan Green, we were assured that it did not matter what happened while a student was at Sweet Briar, just that they identified as a "woman" when they had been admitted. When I asked then college President Jo Ellen Parker about this informal policy a little over a year later, she wrote:

> Our practice is to admit students who identify as women at the time of admission. Admitted students who fulfill the academic standards and requirements will be awarded degrees. While "gender identity and its expression" was added this year to the statement of community values, you are correct that we do not have a written policy statement specifically on transgendered [*sic*] students—although as I think you know, senior staff has looked at various examples and has started the process

of determining the best way for Sweet Briar to develop policy on this matter as well as on some other similar matters. (J. E. Parker, personal communication, November 5, 2012)

I could stay at Sweet Briar; purely for the reason that I had checked the box when I applied indicating that I was a "woman." I felt selfishly relieved. I was happy that I would not have to leave the place in which I had come to recognize this part of myself. I did not take a moment to consider that there was no security in an unofficial policy; the school could easily ask me to leave as soon as I began hormone replacement therapy, changed my name, or undertook some other gender-affirming process. I also did not consider the other trans men who were not being considered for acceptance simply because they had acknowledged and accepted their transmasculinity prior to college, or the trans women who had accepted themselves as women but whom the school did not recognize as such. I felt like a boulder had been rolled off of my shoulders: they were going to let me stay.

I wanted to remain at Sweet Briar because I realized that it was where I felt the safest, not despite identifying as a trans man but because of it. When I studied in England within a coeducational program environment, many of my cis male peers would promulgate their feelings about my gender identity: from refusing to use my chosen name once they read my legal name on an instructor's list, threatening physical violence preceded with words like *bitch* when we had fallen into disagreement, and even drunkenly correcting me on my "lifestyle choices." I was fortunate that these verbal altercations did not evolve into physical violence like it does for many trans people, especially trans women of color, but the knowledge that their words did not result in physical violence on those particular days did not entirely ease the fear that it might happen at a later point. In those early years, I found myself constantly trying to somehow deal with this ever-present fear brewing deep inside me and engulfing me in anxiety. It was exhausting. Will today be the day that someone decides to hurt me?

## THE FUTURE OF WOMEN'S COLLEGES

Given the sense of safety I felt at Sweet Briar, I was devastated by the news on March 3, 2015, that the college would close after 114 years because of declining enrollment. In making the announcement, Sweet Briar President James F. Jones Jr. said:

The board, some key alumnae and I have worked diligently to find a solution to the challenges Sweet Briar faces. This work led us to the unfortunate conclusion that there are two key realities that we could not change: the declining number of students choosing to attend small, rural, private liberal arts colleges and even fewer young women willing to consider a single-sex education, and the increase in the tuition discount rate that we have to extend to enroll each new class is financially unsustainable. (Jackson 2015, para. 5)

Within hours of the announcement, alumnae began asking questions and raising money. These efforts, along with mediation provided by the office of the Attorney General of the Commonwealth of Virginia, gave Sweet Briar College another chance at life.

By July 1, 2015, alumnae, students, and faculty had raised over $12 million, enough to keep the college running for at least one more year, and by July 1, 2016, another $10 million had been donated. Sweet Briar had 325 students at the beginning of the academic year in August 2016; 175 of them will be in the class of 2020. College President Philip Stone described 2016 as a "rebuilding year," and in a written statement said, "We took over a mostly shuttered institution and could not start recruiting a new class until September of 2015, six months later than other institutions. The fact that we will have a student body of this size in such a short time is one more Sweet Briar miracle" (Svrluga 2016).

Given this resurrection, however, there is a fundamental question that needs to be raised now more than ever: if there has been a decrease in the enrollment of Sweet Briar and many other women's colleges and a subsequent weakening of institutional financial security, is it not time to redefine what a women's college looks like?

Over the past fifty years, there has been seen a steady decline in women's colleges across the United States and Canada. According to the Women's College Coalition (2018), there were 230 women's colleges in 1960, but that number had fallen to 47 in 2014. Of those remaining schools, fourteen are located in the Southeastern United States: the Seven Sisters of the South, Spelman College, Bennett College, Meredith College, Judson College, Converse College, and Columbia College.

If women's colleges want to remain relevant and financially secure today, they have to challenge the ways we see gender and support all people with minoritized genders. Since their inception, women's colleges have been

embracing and progressing ideas of gender that were considered radical for
their time. Women's colleges as places singularly for cis women can no longer
be supported, just as a segregated Sweet Briar student community was abandoned in 1967.

Discussing the continued need for women's colleges, Helen Drinan (2015),
the current president of Simmons College, wrote:

> Women's colleges in particular foster a space for young women to
> mature and develop as competent adults without fear of gendered
> social judgment or expectations. Women's colleges explicitly promote
> self-awareness and self-confidence so women can successfully navigate
> the very subtle (and not so subtle) gender issues that can arise in the
> workplace and society at large. (para. 7)

These societal "gender issues" include crises involving on-campus sexual violence; the shaming and lack of protection of women in coeducational environments; the reality that "female full-time workers made only 79 cents for every
dollar earned by men, a gender wage gap of 21%"[2] (Institute for Women's Policy
Research 2015); and the fact that 52 percent of women surveyed in the United
States have reported that they were victims of violence, predominantly male
violence (Tjaden and Thoennes 2000). Given these issues, Drinan's assertion
about the importance and relevance of women's colleges is certainly accurate,
but perhaps somewhat shortsighted.

Women's colleges are environments in which those who have been unfairly victimized by a patriarchal society have opportunities to become leaders
in an academic environment that challenges the notion that men are better
and valued more highly than women. However, it is not just cis female students who are in need of a nonpatriarchal environment that enables them to
succeed without the fear of repercussions. Trans youth experience extremely
high rates of discrimination, harassment, and violence. For example, a national survey of trans people (Grant, Mottet, and Tanis 2011) found that the
participants who expressed their trans identity or gender nonconformity
while in grades K–12 reported experiencing alarming rates of harassment (78
percent), physical assault (35 percent), and sexual violence (12 percent). Trans
students of color indicated experiencing even higher rates of harassment and
physical and sexual assault than did the white trans students. Research suggests that it does not get better in college. According to a large-scale study of
college students (Association of American Universities 2015), trans students
experience higher rates of rape, sexual assault, sexual harassment, stalking,

and intimate partner violence than do cis female students, and they are less likely to report incidents of assault and harassment. The prevalence of anti-trans harassment and violence underscores the need for trans students to have access to academic environments that nurture, rather than diminish, their individual gifts.

## CREATING A TRANS-INCLUSIVE ENVIRONMENT AT SWEET BRIAR

After successfully keeping the institution open, the community of Sweet Briar College installed President Stone in August 2015. In his inauguration speech and invocation for the new school year, Stone called for continued action and embracing new realities. He said that "making history means taking control of one's destiny and creating a new reality," and that the challenge now is "how do we not only save the college, how do we make it flourish and save it for noble purposes?" He concluded his invocation by stating that the college must "face the future boldly, creatively and with excitement" (Carey 2015, para. 1). The call for creativity appears to be making an impact at Sweet Briar. To date, the college has received a record number of applications, over 1,000—the largest it has seen in fifty years. However, if this momentum begins to die down, what will be the next step? Of these more than 1,000 applications, how many, if any, are from trans students, and will they be considered for admission?

When I addressed this issue with Sweet Briar College's Interim Chief Enrollment Officer, Steven Nape (personal communication, February 16, 2016), he spoke very confidently, and in agreement with Stone's message of creativity, that the new board of directors of Sweet Briar is tackling issues with new perspective and great vigor. In terms of trans inclusion, he expects that discussions will begin again at the college with the goal of having a formal policy in place after "appropriate deliberations" have occurred. Some of these deliberations have since started to occur. On April 8, 2016, Sweet Briar faculty voted unanimously to urge the board of directors to adopt an inclusive policy regarding the admittance and retention of trans and gender-nonconforming individuals. To date, there has not been a formal response from the board about creating a trans-inclusive student policy. As it stands, the unofficial policy remains in place, that as long as a student identifies as a "woman" on entering the school, whatever happens after that presumably does not matter—which is not very reassuring to trans male students.

I think that most college students feel a strong sense of anxiety as they move closer to graduation day. Did I take all of the required classes? Pay that last bill? Fill out the correct forms? Most students experience a mix of rational and irrational fears. My anxiety manifested as something else entirely; it was not whether I had returned my library books that plagued my thoughts, but the reality that at Sweet Briar, men can take classes but can never graduate. Well, I had attended, so now what? Would an overly enthusiastic campus safety officer bolt in front of the bagpipe-led processional with an order for me to leave? Or would they let me slip by unnoticed?

The lack of a policy indicating the college's stance on the admission and graduation of trans students instilled a very real fear in me. Fortunately, not only was I able to graduate, but then President Jo Ellen Parker allowed for my chosen name to be included in the program and to be announced as I crossed the stage. I actually did not receive my diploma on that day because I opted to wait until I had legally changed my name. But it was a small sacrifice to pay to have a document that reflected me.

My diploma came to me unceremoniously in a mail tube not long after the college successfully fought the board to stay open. As I unrolled the diploma, my first thought was whether the Latin was gendered correctly. Then it hit me: I am now officially a member of a very small group of Sweet Briar alumni—Sweet Briar men. After I graduated, I found out that while I was the first trans student to come out and transition as a student, two other graduates transitioned after college. Trans students have thus long been present at Sweet Briar, even if not acknowledged by the college.

Given the prejudices facing trans people in the world today, there is a desperate need for a space for us in higher education, including a visible space for us in women's colleges. If Sweet Briar and other Southern women's colleges are to continue striving for excellence, as well as continue to have relevance, they must fully embrace binary and nonbinary trans students, and this can only be done by creating clear and inclusive policies on the admission and graduation of trans students.

NOTES

1. While Agnes Scott College does not have a trans-inclusive admissions policy, it has issued a "Statement on Gender Expression and Gender Identity" (Agnes Scott College 2010), which reads in part: "We recognize and value individuals across the spectrum of gender and are proud of the trans women, trans men, and nonbinary individuals who have been admitted and/or graduated from Agnes Scott." The statement does not clarify if the students were out

as trans when they were admitted, and in the absence of a formal admissions policy, trans students do not know if they can apply to Agnes Scott.

2. The wage gap between women of color and white men is even larger. As a percent of white men's earnings, Hispanic or Latina women make 54 percent, African American women make 64 percent, Native Hawaiian and other Pacific Islander women make 65 percent, American Indian and Alaska Native women make 59 percent, and Asian American women make 90 percent (Fisher 2015).

## WORKS CITED

Agnes Scott College. 2010. "Agnes Scott College Statement on Gender Expression and Gender Identity." Revised November 2014. https://www.agnesscott.edu/president/presidential-committee-diversity/statement-on-gender-expression-and-gender-identity.html.

Association of American Universities. 2015. *AAU Campus Survey on Sexual Assault and Sexual Misconduct*. https://www.aau.edu/Climate-Survey.aspx.

Carey, Janika. 2015. "Sweet Briar Installs 12th President, Celebrates Founder's Day." *Sweet Briar College News*, September 25. http://oldweb.sbc.edu/news/academics/college-installs-12th-president-celebrates-founders-day.

Drinan, Helen. 2015. "Amid Sweet Briar Battle, Women's Colleges Remain Important and Relevant." *Huffington Post*, March 27. http://www.huffingtonpost.com/helen-drinan/amid-sweet-briar-loss-womens-colleges-remain-important-and-relevant_b_6953640.html.

Drummond, Mara Christine. 2009. *Transitions: A Guide to Transitioning for Transsexuals and Their Families*. Raleigh, NC: Lulu Press.

Fisher, Milia. 2015. "Women of Color and the Gender Wage Gap." Center for American Progress, April 14. https://www.americanprogress.org/issues/women/report/2015/04/14/110962/women-of-color-and-the-gender-wage-gap.

Grant, Jaime M., Lisa A. Mottet, and Justin Tanis. 2011. *Injustice at Every Turn: A Report of The National Transgender Discrimination Survey*. Washington, DC: National Center for Transgender Equality and the National Gay and Lesbian Task Force.

Hollins University. 2015. *2015–2016 Student Handbook*. https://www.hollins.edu/wp-content/uploads/2014/09/Student-Handbook.pdf.

Institute for Women's Policy Research. 2015. "Pay Equity and Discrimination." http://www.iwpr.org/initiatives/pay-equity-and-discrimination (accessed November 2015).

Jackson, Christy. 2015. "Sweet Briar College News: Board of Directors Votes to Close College at the End of 2014–2015 Academic Year." Sweet Brier College, March 4. http://sbc.edu/news/board-of-directors-votes-to-close-college-at-the-end-of-2014-2015-academic-year/.

Miller-Bernal, Leslie. 2011. "The Role of Women's Colleges in the Twenty-First Century." In *Diversity in American Higher Education: Toward a More Comprehensive Approach,* edited by Lisa M. Stulberg and Sharon Lawner Weinberg, 221–31. New York: Routledge.

Schneider, Wendy. 2010. "Where Do We Belong? Addressing the Needs of Transgender Students in Higher Education." *Vermont Connection* 31: 96–106.

Svrluga, Susan. 2016. "A Year after Sweet Briar Was Saved from Closing, School Leaders Celebrate Fundraising Growth." *Washington Post,* July 12. https://www.washingtonpost.com/news/grade-point/wp/2016/07/12/a-year-after-sweet-briar-was-saved-from-closing-school-leaders-celebrate-fundraising-growth

Tjaden, Patricia, and Nancy Thoennes. 2010. *Full Report of the Prevalence, Incidence, and Consequences of Violence Against Women: Findings From the National Violence Against Women Survey.* US Department of Justice, National Institute of Justice. https://www.ncjrs.gov/pdffiles1/nij/183781.pdf.

Trans Policy Clearinghouse. 2016. "Women's Colleges with Trans-Inclusive Policies." https://www.campuspride.org/tpc/womens-colleges.

Troop, Don. 2011. "Women's University to Reconsider Hard Line on Transgender Students." *Chronicle of Higher Education,* October 23. http://chronicle.com/article/Womens-University-to/129490.

Women's College Coalition. 2018. "Our History." http://womenscolleges.org/history.

# TWO

# Transitional Matriculation
## Losing (and Finding) Yourself in Higher Education

*Annabelle Talia Bruno*

A COLLEAGUE OF MINE, a trans man in the early days of his transition, recently asked me for advice. He wanted to know if anything in my experiences as a trans woman could help him navigate his own journey. I offered a few pieces of wisdom and told him that while every person's path through life is different, the lives of people who choose to transition are especially dissimilar. Nobody's experiences with transitioning will be like anyone else's, and by necessity we all embark on such a journey at our own pace and in our own ways.

Many trans people choose to never transition, and they should be acknowledged and respected for knowing and being true to themselves. For others, including myself, transitioning becomes essential. Some of us know we need to transition from a young age, whereas others come to such a realization later in life. I recognized that transitioning was a fundamental necessity for my health and well-being during the time between graduating from my undergraduate college and starting graduate school. To be precise, the onset of my transition—the inauguration of my most real self—occurred during a transatlantic flight from the US East Coast to Shanghai.

Despite knowing that transitioning is a gradual, lifelong process—that we do not simply "wake up trans" one day and never have to think about gender identity again—we nevertheless often index some time in our lives as a tipping point, the "no more" moment when not transitioning became intolerable. We also tend to talk about transitioning in terms that link the process to some specific era of our lives. We say things like, "well, I transitioned in 1997, although, of course, I had *known* I was going to transition for years before that," or "I was transitioning while I worked for such-and-such company," or, as in my case, "by the time I started graduate school, I had already transitioned."

Of course, there are many individual moments that someone could identify as vital to their process of transitioning. It could be the day someone started hormone therapy, or the day they started "couch therapy." The day someone came out to their family, or the day someone came to truly understand themselves. These individual moments are important, and some trans people celebrate them (for example, I annually mark the day I had my name legally changed to reflect my identity).

Although some of my earliest memories include moments when I did not feel comfortable in my own skin, I had neither the courage nor the language to articulate exactly why my body felt so foreign to me until I was in college. Perhaps because of my feelings of self-doubt, I do not recall being particularly social during my youth, and I spent a great deal of my childhood sequestered in my room. Being exceedingly shy and an only child, I never really had the opportunity to discuss my feelings or my questions about gender, sex, and bodies with anyone close to my own age, so I did not begin to have a strong sense of myself and my sexuality and gender until I started dating.

Being bisexual had always made a great deal of sense to me. But being a woman had not really sunk in—had not, in fact, really entered into the equation—until intimacy forced me to recognize that the uncomfortable feelings I had about my body went beyond the ordinary degree of inadequacy felt by many young people. As I tip-toed hesitantly into romantic relationships with my peers, it became harder for me to escape the sense that my perception of myself did not coincide with my physical body. Relationships, in the broadest sense, shifted my struggle with gender dysphoria from conceptual curiosity to cemented reality.

Even after I came to understand more about what it means to be trans, and specifically what it means for me, I was not certain that transitioning made good sense for my future. Like many young trans women, I feared that even if I did transition, I would always be only liminally female, that I would never come to see myself as I do today—as simply female. I had always been a "feminine" child, by which I mean that I exhibited attributes that are traditionally defined as female in nature. But accepting that I was "female" was a lot harder for me than accepting that I was "feminine," particularly because I did not (and still do not) believe that feminine qualities are necessary aspects of femaleness.

My undergrad career was therefore punctuated by a host of moments related to my internal transition, of coming to understand that I was more than just a "feminine bisexual-identified person." Ultimately, in my senior year, I made the conscious but private choice to start hormone therapy and began my personal journey toward womanhood.

During college, I had been seeing a friend off and on to whom I finally opened up about my identity. Looking back, I should not have been surprised that he was utterly unfazed by my gender identity, especially in contrast to how world-changing it had been for me (this goes to show that those around us often know us better than we know ourselves). After I began hormone replacement therapy and the changes to my body, presentation, and mood started to become apparent, he asked me the question that I had been asking myself: "When are you going to let other people see you for who you really are?"

I had been accepted into graduate school and was planning to move far away, so it seemed ideal to start my life there as my new/true self, unfettered by the baggage of everyone's history with the person I had been prior to transitioning. However, during my last semester at my undergraduate school, I accepted a scholarship to study in China for the summer with a group of students from my college whom I knew quite well. I sat down with my friend and explained that I had changed my mind about waiting until I started grad school, that I was tired of pretending to be someone else and wanted to go to China with my undergrad peers as *myself*. He said, not unsupportively, "You always have to take the hardest possible path, don't you?"

I packed my bags and left home, presenting as the person I had tried so hard to convince everyone, including myself, was me. I knew that I needed to land in China as my real self, for safety if not for the sense of desperation I was beginning to feel about my gender. About an hour into my overnight flight, I excused myself from my seat, took my backpack into the lavatory, and publicly transitioned (all I did was change clothes and put on a little makeup, but that sufficed). The clothes I had worn onto the plane were left behind, both metaphorically and literally, and I never looked back. From that point on, I told myself, I was going to present to the world as myself, unapologetically. But it was more than finally coming out to others. At that moment, in that airplane lavatory, I came to accept myself; it was the moment that I became me.

My time in China was not uneventful, filled as it was with all of the experiences one might expect during the first months of being out as trans. But it was complicated by cultural shock for me and for my hosts. Many of the Chinese people I met apparently did not know what to make of this six-foot-tall blonde girl blossoming (clumsily) into womanhood. But transitioning under these unusual conditions strengthened my resolve, and I became convinced that nothing I could possibly experience in the future would get under my skin. How very wrong I was.

When I applied to study Japanese literature in graduate school, I did not have a course of action in mind for my transition, nor did I know for certain whether I wanted to be out as trans. My focus was on getting admitted, so I was not thinking about what name and pronouns to use on my application materials. I did not broach the subject with my reference letter writers, none of whom knew then that I identified as trans, so they identified me in their letters by the name and pronouns that they had always used for me. Because the admissions application asked "sex," meaning "legal sex," I indicated the sex assigned to me at birth, which was the necessary response at that time in my life, even if it did not reflect who I was. My department later claimed that I gave "false information" on my application because they accepted who they thought was a male student and were not prepared for the young woman who entered their program.

I remember speaking to my therapist about my application right before departing for China, as I was lamenting the fact that the people who had admitted me into their graduate program were going to meet someone different from the person they had expected to meet. My therapist, who was always pretty even-keeled, simply shrugged and said, "Nothing you can do about that now." She was right. I was on a trajectory from which there was likely no course correction. This is a typical experience for trans people. We are afraid to transition because we know it will be difficult, know people will judge us, and know we will experience discrimination. But many of us feel we have no choice; we must transition in spite of these obstacles. The fact that we can never fully anticipate the forms or the severity of the struggles we will face speaks volumes about the bravery of those who transition. So it was with me, and in those early days I wore my bravery like a badge.

Within a week of returning from China, I moved into an apartment within walking distance of my new university, with classes set to begin one week later. When I look back and consider that I was starting graduate school, returning from an extended stay abroad, moving across the country, leaving my family for the first time, and transitioning all at once, I should have realized that I was setting myself up for more than I could handle. But it did not dawn on me then.

I do not know how other students prepare for meeting faculty members who will make up their thesis committee for the first time, but it was an agonizing experience for me. I did not fully comprehend that these people would be evaluating the caliber of my academic contributions in the months and years to come, but I did recognize that it was critical for me to make my best possible first impression—doubly so, as a trans person.

Meeting my academic adviser, who became the chair of my thesis committee, went the easiest. She did not bat an eye at my female appearance, nor seem taken aback when I introduced myself as Anna, rather than as the name on my records. In our first meeting, she told me that other people had often mispronounced her name in her youth, and as a result, she found it very important to refer to people by how they wanted to be named. This seemed like a good start.

Unfortunately, most of the other faculty members I met, including those from my program, were not at all accepting. Only a few weeks into graduate school, I was called in to a meeting with faculty from various departments, seemingly assembled for no reason other than to have me justify my gender. I was asked questions like, "How can we be sure you are who you say you are?" and "Why should we be required to respect your pronoun *choice* [emphasis mine]?" Although I did have some faculty and cohort members who were very supportive, they were also quick to make excuses for the faculty who treated me poorly, saying things like, "Oh, well she's just from a different generation," or "You can't expect to be accepted by people from other countries." This never sat well with me. I felt that if my personhood was important to people, they would respect my identity and all the nuances that went with it.

While I was being challenged about whether I was "really" female, I also began to feel that I was being devalued because I *was* seen as female—that the quality of my work and the level my intelligence were assumed to be inferior to that of my male peers. When I explained the situation to a female colleague in my cohort, she pointed out that to be judged unfairly because of one's gender is part of what it is to be a woman, and that in a twisted way, I should feel validated by their mistreatment, as it made me one of the group. Rather than improve my outlook, her response made me feel all the more bitter.

The hyperscrutiny and degradation heightened my self-doubt and sense of despair, which led to my grades falling, and I feared that I would fail out of the program. I raised my concerns with a professor in whose class I was struggling, and she responded harshly, "What did you expect to happen? This is grad school, not a place for finding yourself."

By the end of the first term, I had pulled it together enough to satisfy my own goals, receiving A's in my core courses, except hers, in which I was ecstatic to earn a B. I had never been a straight-A student, and I was exceedingly proud of the work I had done—to the extent that a professor later described me as "smug about it." I did not recognize then that the B would become the stain that followed me around for the rest of my time at the university. Although I was pleased about having pulled myself out of the gutter, professors in my department focused on the one low grade. Knowing none of this, I made an appointment with a faculty member in the Japanese program early in the winter term to discuss how I had struggled with my course work and to ask for advice going forward in the program. His response was to threaten me, stating that "if ever you earn anything less than an A in a graduate course again, I will personally escort you off this campus." Whether this was actually within his jurisdiction or not, I did not take it as an idle threat, which placed additional pressure on me to succeed in a way that I felt was unjust.

In my first year in the Japanese program, I had had to argue that my gender, my name, and my pronouns were valid and deserved the same consideration as any other student's. I eventually was able to get even the faculty members who were hostile toward trans people (one of whom once told me that he would never allow me around his children because of my gender identity) to use the appropriate name and pronouns consistently. However, in my second year, I began to notice a pattern developing in which professors would misgender me when I failed to live up to their expectations as a way to humiliate me. For example, if I got a question wrong, a faculty member might address the class saying, "No, and let me explain to you all why he is wrong." This was always jarring for me, but in the case of larger lecture classes, where I was not well acquainted with all of my classmates, it often caused some extremely curious glances, which made me feel even more embarrassed. Thankfully, I never experienced any harassment or violence as a result of being widely outed in this way, but given the prevalence of hate crimes against trans women, I could easily have been victimized.

The worst of these incidents, the one that still keeps me up at night, occurred during a graduate-level translation course. I was asked to read a passage in a language that I did not know well and provide a succinct translation. Not surprisingly, I faltered and stumbled over words. Exasperated, the professor slammed his hands down on the table and groaned, "Oh, my God, will somebody help him out." This was one of two times in my life that I had to leave a classroom because I could not stop crying (the other was the first day of kindergarten). The professor made the situation even worse by later telling members of my cohort that I was "overly hormonal."

Concurrently, I had to decide on the subject of my master's thesis. I approached my committee members individually early in my second year to ask for their suggestions to help me narrow down my topic. I knew that I wanted to write about the literature of a particular period in Japanese history and that I was interested in considering religion as one aspect of that history, but I had not yet selected a work to focus on or a question to drive my research. As can happen, the three members of my committee offered me pretty dissimilar advice. To their credit, two provided insightful comments about my research interests, while the third, whose advice I ultimately followed, suggested that I base my decision on job prospects, rather than on my passions.

According to the third committee member, I would be remiss if I did not think about what would actually get me a position in academia. There were not many jobs in Japanese, and, according to him, I would not be competitive when jobs became available, so he said that I should study something that touched on another, more popular field to make me more marketable. That was sound, practical advice, but then came the leap. He claimed that since I am trans, I should conduct research related to trans identities because I would thereby be more likely to get a job in LGBT studies. In retrospect, I should have walked out of his office right then and there and chalked up his advice to bias. What he said to me is hardly different from saying to any person from a minoritized group that they should study only "their own people."

Prejudices can be really difficult to detect because they are often not openly expressed. For example, a biased employer today will rarely state explicitly that they are not hiring or promoting someone because of their race, gender, sexuality, and so on. Instead, they may couch their prejudice in terms of the individual "not being a good fit," by which they really mean that the person does not match their assumption that the best person for the job is a white, heterosexual, cisgender man.

In my case, I ultimately recognized the prejudice of the professor who said that I should limit myself to studying trans people. But in other instances, I remain unsure which to believe more: that some of my professors put me through hell because I am trans or because I was not a superstar student. Even though many of my peers insisted that I was being mistreated solely on the basis of my trans identity, I tried to convince myself, all evidence to the contrary, that my program was simply one of those proving grounds in which all students are pushed to their breaking points as an academic initiation test. I half expected the abusive professors to show up at my graduation ceremony and proclaim, "We're not really unrealistic taskmasters! It was all to make you better! We don't actually hate you!" But none of my professors came to my graduation, and no such conversation ever happened.

My experiences speak to how trans people, especially trans women, are caught between a rock and a hard place. Even if we are not judged unfairly because of being trans, we know that at any time we could be, and so how we present ourselves to the world becomes a matter of self-preservation. We may obsess over our presentations to the point that we stress ourselves out, but we do so because we are afraid of what other people will think of us if we do not. This has long been the double bind experienced by cis women: care about your appearance too much and you are considered vain, do not care enough and you are regarded as unwomanly. However, for trans women, the cost of failing to be seen as womanly is often harassment and violence.

I gave up studying Japanese soon after graduating. In fact, I was so traumatized by my graduate school experience that I was afraid to speak Japanese with my friends. It took me years to heal from those scars, and some will never go away. Years later, after I accepted a job at a Japanese school, I realized that the limitations I had placed on my ability to speak the language were the result of being told by professors for years that I was not proficient. I now regularly engage in rich conversations with native speakers and have even taught Japanese at the university level. I cannot help but wonder how my life might be different today if I had heard encouragement more often than disparagement from the Japanese program faculty.

When I look back at my master's program and compare it to where I am now, studying linguistics at a different university, I notice some stark differences. Now that I have really come into my own, both academically and in terms of the level of comfort I have with my body, I find that I am challenged much less frequently about my abilities and am given respect and treated as a peer by faculty members. During my first master's program, I was constantly on the defensive, asked to prove my language ability, my analytical ability, my strength as a student, and, without fail, my femininity. I was a newly transitioned/transitioning girl who was unsure of herself, which made me especially vulnerable when I experienced mistreatment. Conversely, I was warmly welcomed into my current program and have never been made to feel that I need to justify my identity or my mastery of the subject matter. As a result, I have been able to focus on my studies, rather than on constantly defending myself.

There is a pedagogical lesson to be learned here. Although I have substantially less knowledge in the field of my second master's degree than my first, the confidence I have in my abilities within linguistics is much more developed. I have gained more in significantly less time studying linguistics, seemingly for no better reason than because I am now treated as a person. Having had mentors who constantly questioned my skills and judgment, I had questioned my selfhood and felt smaller. As I consider my own future as an educator, I cannot think of better evidence for the benefits of a positive and accepting learning environment than the markedly different experiences I have had. In my role as a teacher, I want to work hard to build students up.

It seems common among those of us who transition that we initially become hypervigilant about the perceptions of other people. I once told a partner that I wished I could have ESP for a day, so that I would finally know what others see when they see me. I would frequently ask my friends if they thought I "looked feminine enough" or if I "passed," which I have since come to see as culturally obligatory—a terribly unfortunate necessity for any trans person who wishes to avoid harassment. Looking back on the experience, I am not sure how I managed to read a hundred pages a night for four or five graduate courses each semester when my brain was already filled with thoughts like "Do I look okay?" "Do I sound okay?" "Did I dress appropriately?" or my worst fear, "Are people going to accost me today because I'm trans?" In describing my situation here, I am not trying to imply that trans people are unable to conduct exemplary graduate work, lead successful lives, or simply function each day with relative ease. But for me, in my circumstances, starting to transition and pursuing grad work simultaneously was overwhelming and meant that I struggled to do both effectively.

However, because of the difficulties I experienced in transitioning, I have had to find ways to persevere. Today, I am able to take an active role in my community and engage in activism because I am once again comfortable in my own skin. As I stated previously, I had a tremendous sense of self-esteem when I returned to the United States from China. My first graduate school program shattered that self-worth, but not irreparably, and in the process of rebuilding it, I discovered my inner strength.

As a trans woman, I have sometimes been afraid to show strength. We are falsely taught as children that certain qualities exemplify one or the other binary gender. Blue is for boys, pink is for girls. Boys are strong, girls are delicate. Many trans women, myself included, try too hard to distance ourselves from those aspects that we were taught are "masculine," and by doing so, we inadvertently accept the conventions that bound us in the first place—we perpetuate how gender is socially constructed. While I am hesitant to show the world my strength, it is nevertheless a part of me, a beautiful part of which I am proud. These days, I think a lot about coming out as *strong*. We often talk about the phrase "coming out" as if it is the sole domain of LGBT communities, but I view coming out as something that all people do on a daily basis in many different contexts. I look at the process of coming out as letting someone see one layer deeper into the tapestry that is my identity.

I increasingly find that I need to come out as trans so as not to be assumed as cis by people who do not know me. Having become accustomed to feeling that I was the elephant in the room wherever I went and being treated by members of the academic community as if my identity did not deserve to be respected, I am taken aback by the realization that I am now often seen as cis, though still as queer. I have said to my peers that not everyone is cut out to be an activist, that identifying as LGBT should not necessitate being out, especially given the hostile climate that still exists in many places for LGBT people. For me, however, the experience of not being read as trans is as jarring in some ways as coming out and suddenly being seen as trans had been on my trip to China.

Even though I no longer need to justify who I am, the work I had to do for years to validate myself to others has led me to feel comfortable with myself today. When you have no choice but to repeatedly tell those around you that you are a person deserving of respect, it sticks. You convince yourself, if not them.

What I obtained from my graduate study was not the mastery of any specific field, but rather a mastery of myself, a feeling that I can conquer anything because I managed to make it through on my own merit. Despite the trial by fire that was transitioning during grad school, and despite the abuse I received from some professors, those experiences ultimately made me stronger in my own skin than I had been before. I will not say that any greater good was served by my mistreatment or that I am particularly thankful for those harrowing, emotionally tumultuous years. The irony is that because I had to fight to legitimize my identity, I have become a more confident woman, a better teacher, and, I like to think, a better person all around.

# THREE

# Read between the Lines
## Teaching and Learning while Nonbinary Trans

*Alandis Johnson*

I LOOK DOWN AT MY watch, and it reads 12:55. Students are still coming into the classroom and finding a seat. I wait patiently for the last five minutes. Finally, the clock strikes one, and I begin class by stating:

> Hello, everyone. This is WGS 202: Introduction to LGBT Studies, so hopefully, you are all here for that. Before we begin, I think it's important that we get to know who is in the room. Likewise, I have provided name cards, so that we can get to know one another over the course of the semester. When you introduce yourself, could you please tell us all what you like to be called by for your name, the pronouns that you use, and something fun you did this summer?

The students have a look of confusion on their faces as they hear my request, so I say, "I'll go first. My name is Alandis Johnson, and I use 'they/them/their' pronouns. I'll be your instructor this fall, but I hope to learn from you as much as you learn from me. Something fun I did this past summer was go kayaking." There are some looks of relief from the crowd of faces, and they begin introducing themselves. Surprisingly, the class has more diversity within it than I expected—some white, US-born, cis, queer students; some US-born students of color of various sexualities; some straight international students; and a couple of white, US-born nonbinary trans students. I can tell that this is going to be a great learning environment.

After the students finish introducing themselves, I ask a simple but pointed question: "How many of your previous classes have ever asked what pronouns you use? If you've had this happen in any of your other courses before, raise your hand." No one raises their hand, and this does not surprise me. None of my professors throughout my undergraduate, master's, or doctoral programs has asked this question on the first day of class.

The process of asking chosen name and pronouns should be common in higher education classrooms, but institutional structures are largely unsupportive of this change. Relatively few colleges enable students to have their chosen name on class rosters, and only a handful provide a means to add pronouns as well (Campus Pride Trans Policy Clearinghouse 2017). This failure is indicative of how deeply ingrained the gender binary is within higher education and how colleges and universities continually render trans people, particularly nonbinary students, marginal and invisible. Refusing to respect someone's gender identity is an expression of gender violence and can be considered a form of harassment, so why are chosen names and pronouns rarely asked for in classes and other spaces in higher education to ensure that students can be treated as how they identify?

Acknowledging and respecting identity within the classroom is necessary and important, no matter the type of class, as doing so validates students and invites them into safer learning spaces. My personal teaching philosophy is built on what bell hooks (1994, 21) calls "a holistic model of learning," which is deeply tethered to identity, both mine and the students'. In this approach to education, hooks states that

> students are not the only ones who are asked to share, to confess. Engaged pedagogy does not seek simply to empower students. Any classroom that employs a holistic model of learning will also be a place where teachers grow, and are empowered by the process. That empowerment cannot happen if we refuse to be vulnerable while encouraging students to take risks. (21)

I believe that engaged pedagogy should be practiced by students and teachers, and this engagement needs to start on the first day of class by the instructor recognizing and validating students' identities by simply asking their names and pronouns. Of course, it is not that simple, and I struggle with a host of questions about the binary ways the dynamics of student and teacher are often navigated. What power exists in this tension between student and teacher? What things can we garner from being both student and teacher simultaneously? What do we forgo as educators if vulnerability surrounding identity and experience is not practiced? What if your whole existence on a college campus is risky? What happens if your gender is seen as a "failure" by others and the whole system of higher education?

I see the concepts of risk and failure as not necessarily negative, because failure can serve as a means for higher education to rethink policies, practices, and procedures. Here I share my personal experiences related to my gender-queer identity as both an instructor and student to elucidate how gender failure can be considered productive and necessary and how we can continue to (re) think gender possibilities on college campuses.

Graduate student instructors generally pose an interesting predicament to institutions of higher education. We are typically positioned as student *or* teacher, not student *and* teacher, even though we often occupy both positions simultaneously. This failure to capture the complexity of the lives of graduate student teachers compounds the situation faced by instructors like me whose gender identity is nonbinary, for we are rarely seen and respected as our complete selves.

Failure is not so straightforward if the binary logic that underpins the concepts of failure and success is deconstructed. In *The Queer Art of Failure*, Jack Halberstam examines and dismantles the assumptions behind failure and success, arguing that "Under certain circumstances failing, losing, forgetting, unmaking, undoing, unbecoming, not knowing may in fact offer more creative, more cooperative, more surprising ways of being in the world. Failing is something queers do and have always done exceptionally well" (2011, 2–3). I contend that higher education largely fails trans, and more specifically nonbinary, students and educators, but this failure has the potential to radically transform higher education. Moreover, defining failure as not necessarily negative can broaden possibilities for inclusion. In this sense, failure is not deficient, just a different way of being.

*Failure* can be a scary word. I certainly learned that personal failure, whether it was failing college classes, failing your friends, or failing at achieving your goals, came with negative repercussions. As a nonbinary trans graduate student, I have also experienced failure as a lack, such as when friends, faculty, administrators, and other students disavow my right to exist by referring to me with incorrect pronouns or when colleges do not provide gender-inclusive restrooms and the ability to have a chosen name on campus records and the appropriate gender marker in institutional databases. Even the colleges that do relatively better to accommodate nonbinary individuals still fail to achieve true inclusion by continuing to operate largely on a gender binary.

At the same time, failure can be reframed in more positive ways. My gender is considered a failure because it is outside of a binary, but that means it is different and unique. By failing to adhere to the dominant gender system, I broaden possibilities for others on campus to see themselves in similar nonbinary terms and help develop a community of people who fail in their gender. Moreover, in knowing that my institution has and will continue to fail me as a nonbinary person, I can be prepared and at times use this failure to bring about change.

From this perspective, the misgendering and stereotyping of trans people are not solely negative, as failure can accommodate many types of experiences simultaneously; in this case, failure can lead to education about gender inclusion. Most of the students in my Introduction to LGBT Studies course—and, I would argue, most cis people on college campuses—have not considered what it means to be seen as a "gender failure." By learning how they fail at gender, in the sense of not understanding the experiences of trans people, my students are able to recognize how they are affected by the binary gender system and how they can challenge it.

Still, it is tough when I hear students misgendering me or other trans students in the classroom and other campus spaces. It never feels good to have pronouns applied to you that you have rejected and then having to decide how you will respond. I do my best not to let it bother me, but sometimes it does. Being a gender failure is not easy. Getting students and staff to learn new pronouns for me while unlearning others can be extremely difficult. I find it especially hard to navigate these issues as a graduate student instructor, because I feel that I lack credibility for not yet having a Ph.D. However, my role as an educator demands that I push my students to learn, sometimes at the price of my own comfort.

The challenging nature of my situation was made evident to me one day toward the end of the semester in the Introduction to LGBT Studies course. I had allotted some time for students to work on their group projects, and as I was listening in on the conversations, I heard a cis gay male student refer to me as "she" in speaking to the rest of his group. "If we have questions, *she* is more than happy to answer them," he said. I cringed at his words. I told myself that I should take comfort in being seen as a source of support for the group, but I could not get past his use of incorrect pronouns, especially so late in the semester. I was so distraught that I decided to stick close to my desk at the front of the room and did not engage him or other students. I chose not to correct the student for fear of shaming him in front of his peers, but that meant I censored myself and missed an opportunity to educate him on this failure. I still think about ways that I could have intervened, and how confronting this student might have been valuable to his and other students' learning.

In retrospect, I realize that for many of the cis, heterosexual students in the course, this was the first time they had met people who openly identified not only as trans but also nonbinary. I felt fortunate to have two other out trans students in my class, as I had always been the only one in any of my courses since I had started my doctoral program. But the cis students did not respond to them any differently than they did to me. The other trans students were similarly often misgendered, which they too found difficult to confront.

In thinking back on my gender education, I recognize that much of it came from meeting and getting to know other trans people. In fact, I spent years trying to figure out my gender before I met another trans person who helped me understand my identity. I was thus happy to have trans undergraduates in the class, who, by presenting gender in complex, nuanced ways, offered new gender possibilities to the other students. I hoped that meeting nonbinary trans people would help the students who needed to find such a community at the college and in the small town where the institution is located. To my knowledge, I am the only nonbinary graduate student at my midsized public university. I find it quite terrifying that there is no community of nonbinary trans people near my age directly around me for support, but I am glad that undergraduates do not have to be as isolated.

As I have grown more comfortable in my role as an instructor and as a nonbinary person, I have been more willing to take risks in the classroom and present my gender in ways that challenge a gender binary and frequently confound others. My aim is for my gender to be unintelligible—a visual marker and badge of honor of my queerness. The effect on students has been similar to my disclosure of being nonbinary, in that they might be more apt to bring up the perspectives of trans people, but they also struggle because for most of them, my course is the first one they have taken that addresses the topic of identity, and certainly the first to consider trans identities.

Recently I taught an introductory women's studies course. As in the LGBT studies course, I asked the students to introduce themselves and share their pronouns. Most of the students looked confused throughout this process, and they had a hard time articulating their pronouns. I was the only person who said that they went by "they/them" pronouns, and from what I could gather from the reactions of the other students, I was the only trans person in the class.

I introduced myself with a very honest and upfront disclosure of my nonbinary identity as well as my identity as a recent cancer survivor. It has been strange to see how the intersections of queerness and (dis)ability function to make my body unintelligible, and how students respond to my illness. The failure of my body to function while harboring cancer made me unrecognizable even to myself, and now that I am beginning to regain some of the aspects of my appearance that I lost because of chemotherapy and radiation, I can be intelligible to myself again, while still being unintelligible to others as a nonbinary individual. I imagined that the students in the class would respond to my announcement of having cancer with many questions, like they do when I disclose my trans identity, but they did not ask me about it. Unlike the LGBT studies course, the students in this class were mostly white and straight, as well as cis, which is reflective of the student population of the university as a whole. Despite the relative lack of diversity in the class, these students seemed to be more understanding of my gender, as my trans identity was seemingly easier for them to grasp than my being a cancer survivor. I noticed that the students were particularly attentive to trans issues and perspectives, and I believe they were more engaged because I chose to disclose my multiple positionalities on the first day of class.

The curriculum of the course also incorporated readings that addressed intersectionalities, including being trans and having a disability. One reading in particular, Eli Clare's "Gawking, Gaping, Staring," struck a chord with the students and reified the importance of considering multiple identities. The closing lines of the essay powerfully speak to the difficulties and the possibilities of unintelligibility:

> I am looking for friends and allies, for communities where the gawking, gaping, staring finally turns to something else, something true to the bone. Places where strength gets to be softened and tempered, love honed and stretched. Where gender is known as more than a simple binary. Where we encourage each other to swish and swagger, limp and roll, and learn the language of pride. Places where our bodies begin to become home. Gawking, gaping, staring: I can't say when it first happened. (Clare 2003, 261)

As a nonbinary trans instructor, I feel that unintelligibility and failure have allowed me to connect on a deeper level with undergraduate students, as we all face struggles to be understood and need to learn how to support each other. Failure creates the possibility for me to share my story and foster a greater sense of humanity among my students.

However, as a graduate student, my gender failure has placed me in some very difficult and uncomfortable positions. In some classes, I felt that my gender was tokenized and fetishized; in others, it was completely ignored. Even the four courses that I took for a graduate certificate in women/gender/sexuality studies did not consider the gender identities of the students, and most of the professors failed to include any material by and about trans people in the curriculum. I was sorely disappointed that classes that teach about gender did little to recognize and educate about gender outside of a binary.

My graduate program in Student Affairs in Higher Education (SAHE) focuses on equity and inclusion, student learning, and identity development. Yet cis students in the program are rarely knowledgeable about gender beyond a binary and often reject or marginalize trans people, whether subtly or not so subtly. Even students who have some understanding of trans perspectives disavow or exclude trans individuals at times. One particularly egregious example involved a master's student who uses "they/them" pronouns for themselves but identifies as a cis queer woman. This student, who preached about the importance of using correct pronouns and respecting gender difference, was one of the worst perpetrators of genderism in the program. They often disparaged my clothing choices, as I did not dress "trans enough" in their mind, and regularly misgendered me, despite my efforts to correct them. Yet this student was often lauded by SAHE faculty and other students as an example of someone deeply committed to social justice and inclusion. Clearly, there is more work to be done, not just in my program, but throughout higher education.

My college's SAHE program also fails in its ability to engage students in dialogue across difference. In my experience, trans, queer, and many other minoritized identities often get tokenized and fetishized for those who are in the majority to learn. One particular instance occurred in a doctoral seminar on identity development that I took. Throughout the semester, students (including me) shared stories related to our identities and the impact of our identities on our experiences as students and our worldviews. I was the only one who openly identified as trans and queer and asserted many minoritized identities. As a result, the instructor continually expected me to educate my classmates, rather than facilitating these conversations herself. I do not believe that the faculty member fully recognized the extent to which my marginalized positionalities affected my willingness to share in the class.

Having to constantly educate others is the reality for many visibly trans people in higher education, whether they are students, staff, or faculty members. For me, it is never easy to have to speak about my experiences all the time. But I do so because I am passionate about and invested in the liberation of trans people and feel that I have a responsibility to use my relatively privileged position to try to make a difference. Moreover, if I do not educate others about nonbinary trans people, who will?

At the same time, I long for the day when I am not practically the only grad student on my campus capable of educating others about gender identity. In reflecting on my graduate college experiences, I wonder what would have happened had my instructors included the voices of trans people in their curricula and actually been knowledgeable about trans issues, and not relied on me to address the inevitable questions about gender identity from other students. Expecting emotional labor from me to teach others when I was there to learn made me resentful and not able to focus on myself as a student.

I also resent being placed in positions where I am expected to speak for all trans people. My experiences are in no way representative, as many trans people do not have the opportunity to attend college, much less pursue a doctorate. As a white, somewhat able-bodied grad student, I recognize that I have privileges that are denied to most other trans people, who are disproportionately affected by poverty, unemployment, violence, and other negative life experiences (James et al. 2016).

Suffice it to say, navigating student and academic life as a graduate student, an instructor, and a nonbinary trans person simultaneously have been a daily struggle. But these challenges are well worth it, because only through confronting the invisibility and marginalization of trans people in higher education will there be institutional change. I will continue to fight and push forward, seeking to have others develop a more fluid understanding of gender and help dismantle gender binary systems. I hope that my and others' gender failures and "unintelligible" genders can lead to greater gender possibilities.

## WORKS CITED

Campus Pride Trans Policy Clearinghouse. 2017. "Colleges and Universities that Allow Students to Change the Name and Gender on Campus Records." https://www.campuspride.org/tpc/records.

Clare, Eli. 2003. "Gawking, Gaping, Staring." *GLQ: A Journal of Lesbian and Gay Studies* 9 (1–2): 257–61.

Halberstam, Jack. 2011. *The Queer Art of Failure*. Durham, NC: Duke University Press.

hooks, bell. 1994. *Teaching to Transgress: Education as a Practice of Freedom*. New York: Routledge.

James, Sandy E., Jody L. Herman, Susan Rankin, Mara Keisling, Lisa Mottet, and Ma'ayan Anafi. 2016. *The Report of the 2015 U.S. Transgender Survey*. Washington, DC: National Center for Transgender Equality.

FOUR

# "I Am Because We Are"
## Holding a Mirror as a Trans Educator

*S. Simmons*

A COMMON AND ALL TOO TRUE NARRATIVE among trans people is one of invisibility, harassment, being questioned about their identities and existence, and being misunderstood. Examples of these experiences are everywhere, from media coverage to familial relations. In fact, thousands of trans people have died by suicide or murder since I began my research on the experiences of trans educators in fall 2014. For example, on December 11, 2014, a twelve-year-old who had been assigned male at birth killed themselves[1] because of the bullying they received for their perceived gender nonconformity—they were a cheerleader (Gremore 2014). A few weeks before that, individuals and organizations paid tribute to the hundreds of trans people, mostly transfeminine people of color, who were reported to have been murdered across the world that year by participating in the International Transgender Day of Remembrance ("Memorializing" 2014). In the United States, twenty-three trans people were known to have been murdered in 2015 and twenty-six in 2016, almost all of whom were women of color. These are the deadliest years on record for the country's trans population (Ring 2016; Tourjee 2015). Many other trans and gender-nonconforming people in the United States and around the world have experienced physical assault and verbal harassment, including me. Recently, when leaving a public bathroom on the campus where I work, I was confronted by someone who waited for me to exit so that they could snap a picture of "the guy" in the women's bathroom.

These unfortunate narratives flood my Facebook timeline and illuminate issues of bias, discrimination, and binary gender assumptions. I wanted to counter these narratives with my research on trans educators. What I discovered is that trans educators' stories can expand notions and conceptions of gender through their experiences and through analyses that use multiple gender lenses. Each and every day, trans people, including educators, are excluded, ignored, minimized, marginalized, bullied, and killed. And still we thrive, live, love, and educate. The purpose of this piece, which is drawn from my dissertation, is to help make more visible the lives of trans educators by using my own narrative. My dissertation examined fourteen trans educators' experiences within higher education and how they expand notions of gender, in the hope that people of all genders can live, learn, and work in affirming, safe, and healthy environments. Specifically, I considered how Bronfrenbrenner's bioecological model (1999) and intersectionality (Crenshaw 1989), along with Lawrence-Lightfoot and Davis's (1987) portraiture methodology, offer insights into how educators navigate institutions and environments that are laced with interlocking systems of oppression, including racism, sexism, genderism, ableism, and xenophobia. I found that despite such oppressions, trans educators are thriving in many ways and changing institutions, which will ultimately change higher education.

## WITNESSING AND MIRRORING

When I began my research, I did not know the impact that talking to other trans educators would have on my life. The ideas of witnessing and mirroring other trans people, which are the basis of Devor's (2004) model of transsexual identity formation, have allowed me to explore my own narrative as a Black, queer, trans educator. Though not an easy process, witnessing and mirroring are instrumental in trans identity development. Devor (2004) described witnessing as being seen by others for who we are, whereas mirroring means having people whom we see as like ourselves also see us as like them. The concepts of witnessing and mirroring demonstrate the influence of other's perceptions on one's own trans identity.

While conducting my research, I identified myself as a trans educator to potential participants. Throughout the processes of observing and interviewing, I believed that the other trans educators saw me in many of the same ways that I see myself and saw me as like them. In particular, I found myself reflected in and by two of the participants, Austin and Kyle London.[2] Both identified as Black and genderqueer and had strong connections to being Black even before they navigated their trans identities, an experience that resonated with me. Throughout my interviews with them, there were many verbal "uh huhs," "yeses," and "I feel yous" between us. They definitely held up some mirrors for me and held space to see me. Devor (2004) described this experience when he said:

> Each of us has a deep need to be witnessed by others for whom we are like. Each of us wants to see ourselves mirrored in others' eyes as we see ourselves. Each of us needs to know that people who we think we are like also see us as like them. (46)

Although Devor's model is not inclusive of nonbinary trans people and may not be applicable to all segments of the trans population,[3] the concepts of witnessing and mirroring were instrumental in my identity development process as I engaged in this research project. For me, witnessing and mirroring are a valuable source of affirmation to counter the disempowerment that occurs from feeling, and literally being, invisible (not seen for who I am) or hypervisible (targeted for bias, harassment, or murder) because I do not conform to social expectations of one of the binary genders. Seeing myself in and being seen for who I am by the other trans educators was life-giving and lifesaving.

## METHODOLOGY

Using portraiture methodology, a form of qualitative research developed out of blending other qualitative methodologies such as ethnography, autoethnography, critical race theory, oral history, narrative inquiry, and phenomenology (Lawrence-Lightfoot and Davis 1997), I set out to highlight the experiences of trans educators. Because the theme of community was present in the experiences and reflections the educators shared with me, I presented the results as a semi-fictional fishbowl dialogue to put the educators in conversation with each other, even if only in my writing. Identifying as trans, I also embarked on "me-search" (Nash and Bradley 2011). In me-search, "The researcher brings [their] own history—familial, cultural, ideological, and educational—to the inquiry" (Lawrence-Lightfoot and Davis 1997, 95). Building on one of the elements of portraiture, "voice as autobiography" (Lawrence-Lightfoot and Davis 1997), I constructed the parts of my own story that are connected to my gender identity development and my interest in the topic. Through this process, I wanted to situate myself, while also setting myself aside. Many feminist and trans activists and academics find situating themselves in their writing to be one of the most important parts of making positive change through their work (Feinberg 1996; Hesse-Biber, Leavy, and Yaiser 2004; Zimmerman 2005). By discussing myself and my experiences, I hope for trans lives to be further known, respected, and valued. As I describe in the next section, my gender journey has led me to believe firmly that a crucial way for us to realize our full potential and make a difference in the world is to witness and mirror people who share some of our experiences (Devor 2004).

## MY LIFE

Today, I identify as transgenderqueer. Usually when I tell people that, they look confused and unsure, and sometimes they ask questions like "What is that?" I welcome thoughtful, sincere inquiry. I start by explaining that for me, it means that I do not identify as a man or woman, trying to put my feelings into terms they know first. Then I build on that and describe how I feel that I embody some aspects of masculinity, femininity, and androgyny and how I reject other aspects of these social constructions often connected to gender. But sometimes their confusion does not dissipate; they still do not understand, partly because of genderism—the cultural belief that there are only two genders (Bilodeau 2005; Catalano and Griffin 2016; Wilchins 2004). Admittedly, I still do not fully understand what it all means myself. I just know how I feel, and I try, with limited language and success, to describe and express it. I see my gender journey as a process of ongoing negotiations with myself and others, involving exploration, brave decisions, uncertainty, and self-determination— testing different witnesses and mirrors. My experiences represent a challenge to the monolithic, bleak trans narrative of disownment, despair, and death and contribute to a greater understanding of gender identity development.

## BEGINNINGS

I was born "a girl." As I write these words, something does not feel right. Was I born a girl or was I encouraged to be a girl because of what was (not) between my legs? I was born on May 28, 1983, in Chicago Heights, Illinois. My mom says I did not give her much trouble coming through the birth canal. I imagine that the doctor pulled me out, took one look between my legs, and proclaimed, "It's a girl." I was named Symone. I was a chocolate, round baby with a lot of jet-black hair. Looking back at pictures of my childhood, I am reminded of some of the ways my parents presented me to the world as their "girl" child.

Old pictures of me include a head full of hair in various styles: one or more ponytails, curls, and an afro. Seeing the ponytails reminds me of the times I spent with my dad while he combed my hair. I enjoyed spending time with him. My dad was something of a "Mr. Mom," a way I heard others refer to him. In addition to parting my hair perfectly for those ponytails, he cooked and cleaned. These are some of my earliest experiences of gender nonconformity. Also in these pictures, I was in various outfits: dresses and bows, jeans and sweatshirts, frilly socks and shiny shoes, earrings, and other adornments that signaled to onlookers that I was a girl, their daughter. As a kid, I did not mind the clothing and accouterments. I was spoiled. I was an only child for seven years, so I often got anything I wanted, and surely had everything I needed.

## TOMBOY

As I grew older and started making decisions for myself about how I wanted to present to the world and who I wanted to be, which included choosing my clothes, activities, and friends, I started hearing the label "tomboy." This label, which felt to me as an accusation, usually came up because of an activity in which I was engaged (e.g., basketball, football, hanging with the "boys") or something I was wearing or not wearing. Initially, I did not want to accept "tomboy" as a descriptor. However, because of the label, and the expectations that went with it, I was able to participate in the activities I loved, wear the clothes I wanted, and show up as me. Over time, I embraced the identity to some degree.

## CHOCOLATE SKIN

I am considered dark-skinned because of my complexion. When I was growing up, people close to me, like uncles and family friends, used to describe me as "smooth black," "chocolate drop," and "dark and lovely." But sometimes my skin color has had negative social connotations. In many communities of color, and specifically in some communities that include Black or African American women, light skin is preferred and dark skin may be perceived as ugly and undesirable (Jones and Shorter-Gooden 2003). However, my family made me feel beautiful and accepted in my chocolate skin, which gave me great pride in and love for my Black identity.

Regardless of my pride, I have still encountered situations that posed a threat to me because I am Black. When I was around six years old, my dad's job relocated him, and our family to Lancaster, Pennsylvania. Lancaster is a majority white city with a large Amish community. When we moved there, I was one of only two Black kids in the elementary school. I noticed this fact, but I am not sure I made much meaning of it at first. However, one day when I came home from school, as I got off the bus at my stop, an older white kid spit on me out of the window. My grandmother, who was visiting us at that time, tells me that when I returned home from school that day, I was particularly quiet. This was not necessarily unusual, but she picked up that something was bothering me. After much persuasion, I told her what had happened. I have always viewed my mother, aunts, and grandmother as protective, independent, smart, funny, no-nonsense, and strong Black women—in many ways, gender nonconforming themselves. So when my grandmother told me she would walk me to the bus stop the next morning, I felt safe. I do not remember all of the details, but my grandmother asked me to point him out. She approached him and asked about the incident. I do not remember what he told her, but no matter what he said, she told him if anything like that happened again, she would be back from Chicago Heights. I did not have any more problems with him.

## KIDS

We only lived in Pennsylvania for two years. After that, we moved back home to Chicago Heights. But the effects of that time in Lancaster lingered. In addition to memories of the bus incident, I also brought back with me a different dialect; my cousins would tell me, "You talk white." I knew what they meant, but at the same time, did not fully know. I noticed that we talked differently, but I am Black, so how could I "talk white?" I have since often grappled with this idea of "talking white," which has gone beyond talk to things like dancing, advanced education, and more liberal perspectives. I think labeling these things as "white" has significant effects on people's choices. For example, what if I had internalized what folks said and went to an extreme to reject these so-called white activities and experiences to prove my Blackness? I might have clung to binary gender expectations, opting to fall in line and grow up to be the Black woman everyone expected. I imagine my life today might look very different.

Growing up in Chicago Heights, I remember diverse schools in which I interacted with all kinds of people. We shared classroom time and let loose together on the playground. I do not remember many other trans or gender-nonconforming kids around me. But one of the people closest to me, a male-assigned cousin, was gender nonconforming. It seemed that he and I did the activities that people thought the other should do. While he perfected his double Dutch jump rope moves, hair styling, and sashaying, I was called double-handed (which essentially meant that I did not turn the rope correctly) and preferred basketball, math, and science, which are often coded as male interests.

My perspective today on being trans is much different from my conception of it as a kid. I thought of trans as being confused and as binary, in the sense that one wanted to change from "one" sex/gender to the "other." At the time, I did not think I knew any openly trans people. But I did know people who were queer in their sexual orientation and/or presented in gender- non-conforming ways.

## EXPLORING SEXUALITY, OR GENDER, OR BOTH?

Once I got to high school, I continued to challenge expectations around gender. At this time, I was gaining more independence, and I shopped for my own clothes and shoes, had diverse friends, and explored different romantic attractions. For my clothes, I only shopped in the boys or men's section, except for things like underwear, although I had also started wearing boxer shorts around this time. Though I wore traditionally men's clothes and presented in masculine ways, people did not question my sexuality, or my gender for that matter, at least not to my face. I did not either. I assumed I was heterosexual and behaved accordingly. As far back as I can remember, I "went with" boys. At one point, I even called myself "strictly dickly," meaning I wanted to be with only boys/men, which I equated with wanting to be with someone with a penis. For a long time, I dated boys and then men and did not think much about it. I liked them well enough. However, when it came to sexual encounters, I just did not feel comfortable. It did not feel right to me. I thought it was the way I was supposed to feel and I would get used to it. I eventually decided that I did not want to get used to it.

Around this time, I spent most weekends at the local roller skating rink, where I met Angela,[4] a great skater who frequented the rink. I went skating every week, hoping to see Angela there. She was also gender nonconforming, mixing her gendered appearance, so that on a given day she could have her hair in cornrows, be wearing traditionally men's clothing, such as oversized jeans and a shirt, and have on long fake nails and make-up. Angela was female-assigned, but presented and had a presence that transcended gendered limits. Angela was respected and well regarded. I could not figure out if I wanted to date her or be like her. I did not spend much time with her because she was several years older than me. However, watching Angela over the years supported my development. I believe Angela's confidence and the way she moved through the world helped me find my own confidence.

Prior to going to college, I divulged to my mom that I was bisexual. My disclosure was not completely voluntary, because someone saw me kissing a girl and told my family, which prompted the conversation. My disclosure was also not accurate, because at the time I was attracted only to women. But I thought it was safer to claim a bisexual identity because it would give my mom hope that I could be with a man in the future. She was pretty distraught when she found out that I liked and dated women.

In grappling with this situation with my mom, I remember a vivid desire to change my gender. I wanted to be a man because I believed I was meant to be a man and would feel more like myself. To express this desire, I presented myself through clothing and accessories in hypermasculine ways: sagging my pants and wearing all kinds of hats, walking with a lean/dip, and sitting with my legs wide open. I also stifled any aspect of myself that could be seen as feminine because I thought it did not match who I was. To be a man or masculine meant not embracing femininity. In my mind, men had to be entirely masculine.

This belief influenced my relationships with women, in that I subscribed to and reinforced heteronormative expectations about what relationships were supposed to be like. I thought there needed to be a masculine and a feminine partner, and I was playing the masculine part. This meant I opened doors, drove us around, and took out the trash, and she was supposed to cook and clean. By acting in this way, I was assuming an inherent link between gender roles, gender presentation, and sexual orientation. I embraced a masculine role because masculinity was already a part of who I wanted to be and how I presented myself. I felt comfortable. I felt like myself. My desires also meant possessing certain physical and nonphysical attributes I equated with men, namely, a penis, no breasts, and being in charge.

## GROWING AS AN EDUCATOR

Throughout graduate school and into my professional journey, I continued exploring and expanding my understandings and conceptualizations of myself and challenging gender assumptions. For example, when I worked as an admissions counselor, we had to wear matching shirts, which came in men's and women's versions. On more than one occasion, I defied gender expectations by requesting men's shirts. I would hear statements like, "the cut of the women's would fit better" or "the men's shirts are too big." They were making an assumption about how I wanted my shirt to fit or how it should fit. Regardless of these biases, I knew what I wanted and ordered accordingly. In most instances, I made my own choices, but early in my career, I was sometimes afraid to express who I was to people I did not know because I feared hostile or discriminatory responses. This was especially the case during a job interview at a university in Georgia.

I had been on a professional interview before. But it was at the institution where I had spent more than six years as an undergraduate and graduate student and in the department where I had completed a graduate assistantship. I was comfortable there. They knew me and I knew them. We had negotiated through some of their gender expectations. They knew I was dating a woman and that I performed my gender in nonconforming ways. For that interview, I did not worry about whether to wear a dress shirt and tie, but what color and type.

This time, I was interviewing at an unfamiliar place, several hundred miles from where I lived. I was anxious about how my gender presentation would be perceived and received. Although the person who would be my supervisor already knew I was queer, I had not disclosed anything about my gender, and they assumed I was a woman. I talked to different folks, including Facebook friends, colleagues, and mentors, about whether I should disclose my queer identity in the interview. After all, my wife was the reason we were moving to Atlanta, to complete her doctoral internship. The overwhelming sentiment was that I should not disclose because it did not matter. One of my mentors strongly discouraged it, which I found surprising, because I see this mentor as gender nonconforming and queer, even though she has not come out to me. But I also see her as conservative and discreet about her gender and sexual orientation, regardless of context. I did not listen to her reservations. I could not. It would not have been me. I was becoming more comfortable in my queer and gender-nonconforming identities and did not want to enter the position withholding parts of me that are central to who I am. So in my first conversation with my future supervisor, I told him about my wife. He asked me to repeat that I have "a wife." I did, and we moved on with the interview.

Genderqueer and trans people are sometimes told that we are not professional because we do not adhere to societal expectations around gender presentation. For the on-campus interview, I sought to be professional, but I also wanted my masculinity to be apparent. I needed them to know that this was a part of me. I also wanted them to know that if I was hired, I would be wearing slacks, button-down and polo shirts, ties, and suits to work. So I went back and forth about the tie I purchased for the interview. I put it on. I took it off. I put it on again. I even bound my breasts for the first time the day of my interview. I am not sure what I was trying to convey by doing this, or why I wanted a flatter chest that day. To say that I was uncomfortable, bound in the Georgia heat, is an understatement. I was sweating, and since it was my first time binding, I was not familiar with the feeling. I was not accustomed to something being wrapped around me restricting my movements. Though I bound, I chose not to wear the tie. That day, I was wrestling with how I wanted to show up and be seen by others in a professional context, and literally wrestling with my garments. In the end, my interview went well and I was offered the position. I had shown up as me, and my education, experience, and skills demonstrated my qualifications.

## EFFECTS ON CAMPUS

I had become increasingly comfortable in my queerness and in disclosing that identity to others. Yet my genderqueerness remained a deeply personal experience. When I started my new job, I disclosed my queer identity to pretty much everyone with whom I worked, including the students in the McNair program, for which I was the educational program specialist. I was still discerning my gender identity and how or whether to disclose it publicly. Since my wife also worked on campus, she often visited me in the office. We were very open about our relationship, which I believe allowed others to explore, understand, and disclose parts of themselves. I became a friend and mentor to many of the students in the program because of some of our shared identities (i.e., queer, Black, first-gen, low-income), and I had the honor and privilege of "giving away" one of my scholars to another at their wedding. They are Black, Muslim, queer womyn who met through the program. I know my wife's and my role modeling contributed to an affirming environment in which they could be out and share aspects of themselves. The student I "gave away" remembers a conversation with me in which they said that they must be "crazy," since they were attracted to another womyn. I spoke to them with care and expressed that there was nothing wrong with them; they were just in love.

As I write this, I am proud to identify openly as a Black transgender-queer educator and use it in my work in a gender and sexuality center, where I provide education to students, faculty, staff, and community members about identities and issues connected to gender and sexuality, with a specific focus on LGBTQIA+ identities. In doing this work, I often share parts of my journey to connect some of the abstract concepts around the binary construction of gender to real people and bodies. An example might be how I was presented to the world by my parents as a girl, or an experience at a department store, where I was told that women could not use the men's dressing room, even though I was purchasing clothing in the men's section. I also encouraged others to think about how the construction of gender applies to their own lives, as these concepts affect us all.

One of the ways that gender constructs most affect my life and experience currently is through pronouns. For me, pronouns mean so much more than "they," "she," "he," "hir," "ze," and others. Asking people to refer to me a certain way makes me feel like I have power over my own identity. Being called by my first initial (S), first name (Symone), and "they," "them," and "their" make me feel recognized. Even if others do not quite see me as how I see myself, they may see how important my identity is to me. Out in the world, it takes great effort and persistence to be acknowledged for who I am. This is particularly challenging in relationships. My wife has been journeying with me, and we still experience challenges with my identity, including pronouns.

JOURNEYING IN RELATIONSHIPS

I was assumed to be a girl at birth, but like many others, I have challenged that designation and its associated implications. I am constantly negotiating and sometimes I still struggle, but I think that is the point. Identity development is ongoing, complex, and challenging. Furthermore, my gender journey has not been mine alone, and it has not only been about gender. This relational, intersectional process has helped me get comfortable with myself and allowed me to open and share spaces with others on their journeys, such as the participants in my study. If I was asking others to share themselves with me through interviews and observations, I believed it was important for me to explore parts of myself through my study and situate myself in my work. By hearing aspects of the participants' life histories, I became acutely aware of my own.

Throughout my gender journey, I have wanted to portray on the outside (and have others see and respect) how I feel about and see myself. But I am aware that other trans and genderqueer people may not be able to do so, as they are differently affected by larger systems, laws, and policies in how they navigate the world. I have been fortunate, maybe privileged, to be in positions to be affirmed, validated, and celebrated in my identities. Even identifying as trans, I still experience privilege in a number of ways, which has been difficult for me to admit because I have clung to my marginalized identities for community and connection. But the advantages I have had are hard to ignore once I recognize them.

In terms of societal expectations of someone who is assigned female at birth, I still express and embrace certain aspects of myself that are read by others as "female" and often as "woman," even if my gender presentation and identity challenge their assumptions. In the past, as I have mentioned, I rejected femininity. I have since come to realize that I was trying to be who I thought I should be because of my rigid gender perspectives, instead of being true to myself.

Additionally, my identities and experiences are wrapped up in and intersect with each other. Although I pulled out experiences and stories for this piece and connected them specifically to my queer and trans identities, I recognize that there are many more identities, experiences, and stories I did not share here that contribute to my life. Constructing myself the way I want to be and the way I see myself is an ongoing process involving multiple identities, including gender, race, and sexual orientation, that are influenced by interactions within and across various contexts and environments, such as with family, in school, and at work (Bronfenbrenner 1999; Crenshaw 1989; Du Bois 1984).

Mine is just one story of a trans educator. By reflecting on my own stories and experiences, I was able to connect with myself and other educators. Developing a greater awareness of my own history has allowed me to recognize my biases. For example, understanding myself helped me be open to stories different from mine and not judging the participants in my study whose ideas and actions may still align with binaries of sex and gender.

## SEEING MYSELF

Over the course of the year I spent observing, interviewing, and immersing myself in research, I reflected intently on gender and my own gender journey. During the research process, I also experienced physical changes as a result of hormones and chest reconstructive surgery, which changed how I navigated the university and other gendered spaces. Hearing from other trans educators about how they perceived and navigated their universities helped me see the value of trans educators like myself, as well as how campuses support and encourage us while also marginalizing us. I used the mirrors of the other educators to see the strength and resilience in my narrative and how I could use these assets in my social justice work. I see the world beyond the binaries that have been constructed to keep people in their place. I value and encourage others to be who they want to be. I share more and more with my family about my identities to help them understand the issues that affect queer and trans communities.

I am grateful to the many people who have held space for me as mirrors and witnesses. I believe we all need mirrors and witnesses to become who we are. I am me because of my family. I am me because of Angela and others. I am me because of my friends. I am me because of the trans educators in my study. "I am because we are."

## NOTES

1. I do not know what pronouns this young person used, but "he/him" were used in the coverage. I use "they/them" to be inclusive.

2. Kyle London was the only participant who included a last name. Both of zir names had special meaning.

3. The study mostly incorporated the experiences of trans women, and the examples used to demonstrate each stage are mostly from the lives of white trans-identified people

4. This name is a pseudonym.

## WORKS CITED

Bilodeau, Brent. 2009. "Beyond the Gender Binary: A Case Study of Two Transgender Students at a Midwestern Research University." *Journal of Gay & Lesbian Issues in Education* 3: 29–44.

Bronfenbrenner, Urie. 1999. "Environments in Developmental Perspective: Theoretical and Operational Models." In *Measuring Environment across the Life Span: Emerging Methods and Concepts*, edited by Sarah L. Friedman and Theodore D. Wachs, 3–28. Washington, DC: American Psychological Association Press.

Catalano, D. Chase J., and Pat Griffin. 2016. "Sexism, Heterosexism, and Trans* Oppression: An Integrated Perspective." In *Teaching for Diversity and Social Justice*, edited by Maurianne Adams and Lee Anne Bell, 183–213. New York: Routledge.

Crenshaw, Kimberlé. 1989. "Demarginalizing the Intersection of Race and Sex: A Black Feminist Critique of Antidiscrimination Doctrine, Feminist Theory and Antiracist Politics." *University Chicago Legal Forum* 1: 139–67.

Devor, Aaron. 2004. "Witnessing and Mirroring: A Fourteen Stage Model of Transsexual Identity Formation." *Journal of Gay & Lesbian Mental Health* 8: 41–67.

Du Bois, W. E. B. 1984. *The Souls of Black Folk*. New York: Oxford University Press.

Feinberg, Leslie. 1996. *Transgender Warriors: Making History from Joan of Arc to Dennis Rodman*. Boston: Beacon Press.

Gremore, Graham. 2014. "Bullied to Death: 12-Year-Old Male Cheerleader
    Commits Suicide Because of Classmates." *Queerty*, December 5.
    http://www.queerty.com/bullied-to-death-12-year-old-male-cheerleader-c
    ommits-suicide-because-of-classmates-20141205.
Hesse-Biber, Sharlene Nagy, Patricia Leavy, and Michelle L. Yaiser. 2004.
    "Feminist Approaches to Research as a *Process*: Reconceptualizing
    Epistemology, Methodology, and Method." In *Feminist Perspectives on
    Social Research*, edited by Sharlene Nagy Hesse-Biber and Michelle L.
    Yaiser, 3–26. New York: Oxford University Press.
Jones, Charisse, and Kumea Shorter-Gooden. 2009. *Shifting: The Double Lives of
    Black Women in America*. New York: Harper Collins.
Lawrence-Lightfoot, Sara, and Jessica Hoffmann Davis. 1997. *The Art and
    Science of Portraiture*. San Francisco: Jossey-Bass.
"Memorializing 2014." 2014. *International Transgender Day of Remembrance*.
    http://tdor.info/memorializing-2014-2 (accessed October 30, 2016).
Nash, Robert J., and DeMethra LaSha Bradley. 2011. *Me-Search and Re-Search:
    A Guide for Writing Scholarly Personal Narrative Manuscripts*. Charlotte,
    NC: Information Age Publishing.
Ring, Trudy. 2016. "Two More Transgender Deaths
    Reported; Possible Homicides." *Advocate*, November
    15. http://www.advocate.com/transgender/2016/11/15/
    two-more-transgender-deaths-reported-possible-homicides.
Tourjee, Diana. 2015. " 'He's Not Done Killing Her': Why So Many Trans
    Women Were Murdered in 2015." *Broadly*, December 15. https://broadly.
    vice.com/en_us/article/hes-not-done-killing-her-why-so-many-trans-wo
    men-were-murdered-in-2015.
Wilchins, Riki. 2004. *Queer Theory, Gender Theory: An Instant Primer*. Los
    Angeles: Alyson Books.
Zimmerman, Bonnie. 2005. "Beyond Dualisms: Some Thoughts about
    the Future of Women's Studies." In *Women's Studies for the Future:
    Foundations, Interrogations, Politics*, edited by Elizabeth Lapovsky
    Kennedy and Agatha Beins, 31–39. New Brunswick, NJ: Rutgers University
    Press.

# FIVE

# "Do You Get to Choose How Big Your Penis Will Be?"

## Transitioning as Faculty

*C. Ray Borck*

MY COLLEAGUE STACEY[1] sidled up to me in the noisy Manhattan bar, "So do you get to choose how big your penis will be?," she asked in a titillated tone. We were at the departmental holiday party—the once-a-year get together at the close of the fall semester, just before winter break. It was December, cold outside, and toward the end of the night. Faculty with small children or early classes the next morning had gone home; the rest of us were staying for another drink. Two historians were standing in the corner, arguing about Foucault, while others were making unwise late-night disclosures about their personal relationships and private troubles.

I was halfway through my second academic year working as a sociology professor in an unusually large social sciences department at Borough of Manhattan Community College (BMCC) in New York City. The department employs more than seventy full-time faculty in the various subdisciplines of sociology, psychology, political science, history, anthropology, and criminology. Like me, Stacey is a sociologist, but she is tenured and has worked at the college for over a decade. I was a junior colleague, recently out of graduate school.

Through the vodka fogging my brain, I had so many thoughts at once. In the short six months since I had come out as trans, I had learned that people were going to ask these types of bizarre, inappropriate questions. Each time, I would have the opportunity to respond, and different styles of response would accomplish different goals. Would I use this opportunity to educate Stacey on the current state of the science and technology of phalloplasty? Would I shame her for inappropriately asking about a colleague's genitalia? Would I shut her down by curtly replying that I would not be acquiring a penis? Or would I wax postmodern and evasive by asking her what she meant by "choice," "size," or "penis?"

Her question was not completely out of the blue. Some of my colleagues knew that I was having surgery over the winter break. I was not having bottom surgery, though; I was having top surgery.[2] Even as the testosterone I was taking had begun to cause small changes in the shape and texture of my face and body, I was still usually read as female because of my protruding chest. There at the bar, I wondered to myself, "She thinks I'm getting a penis over break? She thinks I'm keeping this chest and adding a penis?" As queer as I am, I was not going for a large-breasts-plus-phalloplasty look. I was conforming to the well-worn protocol for how to become a trans guy—testosterone and top surgery.

Stacey's question about my would-be penis reveals a set of assumptions about trans bodies that are fairly common. Humans almost always assign gender at birth on the basis of genitalia and ascribe whole sets of gendered expectations to bodies; infants get imagined as future football players or ballerinas. This enduring cultural practice produces strong associations between gender and genitalia. Many well-educated adults have assumed that my transition is primarily about my genitals. The assumption that I am on my way to achieving a penis exposes the supposed inseparability of "man" and "penis" in the apprehension of my gendered body. It also reveals some ignorance about the state of phalloplasty. One cannot very easily walk into a hospital and get a penis. Phalloplasties exist, but they are far from exact replicas of cis male penises, and most trans men do not get them.

Transitioning has required me to regularly manage other people's thoughts, feelings, and assumptions about my gender and body. Often this management includes explaining or defending myself, or in the language of Judith Butler, "giving an account of oneself." Butler (2003) writes,

> When the "I" seeks to give an account of itself, it can start with itself, but it will find that this self is already implicated in a social temporality that exceeds its own capacities for narration; indeed, when the "I" seeks to give an account of itself, [that] account must include the conditions of its own emergence. (7–8).

It is compulsory that I make myself intelligible to others and I can only become intelligible within already established frameworks for making sense of gender. When my interlocutor fails to possess a framework for my intelligibility, I become required to provide it or sink into invisibility, incomprehensible.

Trans people perform the emotional labor of helping the people in our lives comprehend our transitions. Good-intentioned cis[3] people (perhaps especially academics who make their living portraying themselves as competent about things) want to seem like they get it. But gender is complicated and pervades every area of our lives, so each trans person's transition and understanding of themselves as trans is unique, layered, and sometimes seemingly contradictory. Any trans person has thought painstakingly about their gender identity and is embodying and performing many aspects of their gender quite deliberately.

In some ways, this essay could be characterized as the trivial complaints of a very privileged trans man. I am a white, transmasculine sociology professor with health insurance that has paid for most of my medical transition-related costs, living in New York City in 2016. As far as transitioning circumstances go, it probably does not get much easier than this (for the time being). What follows is a sociological reflection on the entanglements of academic and gender practices, using my gender transition in the context of a university setting as an occasion for analyzing how the microdynamics of gender performance are informed by larger hegemonic cultural discourses, the politics of becoming a man, pedagogical uses of the body, and emergent embodied understandings of heteromasculine privilege.

## SOCIOLOGY AS QUEER HOME

There has always been a close relationship between my queerness and my academic, professional, and career trajectories. I am not the kind of trans person who "always knew" I was trans or would transition, but I am the kind of queer person who has always struggled with gender as a social and personal construct. As long as I can remember, I have experienced the gender and sexual norms of my culture as constricting and suffocating, always looking for communities and spaces where I could take more expansive breaths in my body and desire.

In high school and early college, I was initially drawn to sociology because it created intellectual space for me to explore so much of what I found to be intolerable about life—gender expectations but also classism, racism, sexism, capitalism, nationalism, and all of the other -isms that cause so much human suffering. Sociology was a place where I could deconstruct and reconstruct many of the concepts that make our lives intelligible and meaningful to ourselves and each other.

As a kid envisioning myself as an adult, I always imagined myself as a man, typically a writer and father. Much of the time, I did not like being a girl, but changing my gender was not particularly urgent, as it often is for trans children. I did not know transitioning was possible until I was sixteen and met a trans man named Jay, who made the future seem bright and possible in an unprecedented way. I was a lesbian with a genderqueer presentation and, for many years, I felt ambivalent about medical transition, made materially impossible due to financial limitations. I continued to lack the urgency to transition that many other trans people feel. I hated being a woman, but I could usually tolerate it.

Feminism, genderqueer communities, and body positivity got me through college and graduate school. In 2014, I finished my Ph.D. and got my current tenure-track job in New York City (providing me with job security, permanent residence in a relatively trans-inclusive city, and stable health insurance). At the same time, New York Governor Andrew Cuomo issued regulations mandating New York State health insurers to cover trans care.[4] With these shifts in the financial stability of my life and access to health care, transition became immediately inevitable for me.

Throughout my first year as a BMCC professor, I spent most evenings researching hormonal and surgical treatments for trans men. By the end of that school year, I was meeting with the medical providers who would help me change my body. I decided on the timing of my medical transition (when I would begin taking testosterone and schedule my chest surgery) almost entirely based on concerns about my job. I started taking testosterone in June after the spring semester had ended. At the time, I fantasized that I could fully transition to living as a passing man over the summer. I referred to my transition as my "summer project." Realistically I knew this was unlikely, but it was a story I told myself to manage the anxiety of having an unintelligible gender in my everyday life, especially in front of my students. I love queer, androgynous genders, but personally—and especially in professional settings—having a gender that confuses people is stressful.

I waited until June to start taking testosterone because I did not want to change too much in front of my students. In retrospect, I think of that decision as kind of cute and certainly naïve—two months on testosterone would not have changed anything enough for my students to notice, and three months was not going to change me that much either. Logically I knew this, but I created a fantasy about how my transition was going to unfold so that I did not have to think about how uncomfortable I would feel having my body change in front of my students.

A gender transition is simultaneously private and public. In my role as professor, I find it unfortunate that I have to have a body at all, much less a body that is changing. I think of a *New York Times* article about New York City fashion that I read years ago. In it, the author described professors as people who think of their bodies as mere carts for carrying their brains around from place to place. I related to the characterization. Teaching is a performance. I stand in front of a group of thirty-five people who are all looking at me, and I am supposed to facilitate a classroom space and be authoritative about a subject. I like to come across as put together, and there are consequences if I do not.

## ERASURES OF A PAST SELF

Just as there are cultural codes of conduct, behavioral norms, and rituals of regard about how to treat cis men and women, so too are there expanding proliferations of discourse about how to treat trans people, due in part to increased media attention to trans people and issues. For example, more and more people are aware that they should not "dead name" a trans person (call them by the name they were assigned at birth, rather than their chosen name) or use the wrong pronouns to refer to them.

Many of these rules of regard emerged as responses to highly transphobic and trans-exclusionary environments where trans people were being called by the wrong name and pronouns with malicious intent. In response to these microaggressions, new norms developed. For example, in some college classrooms and activist circles, it has become common for people to introduce themselves by giving their chosen name and gender pronouns. These new norms, paired with the fact that it is common for trans people to never have identified with their assigned name and gender, and the ongoing reification of the gender binary within both cis and trans communities, accounted for the effort on the parts of my colleagues to pretend like I was never a woman, never a lesbian, and never Cathy (my former name). I appreciated the intention, but I also became fascinated by how these erasures were produced and why.

I prefer to keep my history intact. I am not a woman any more, not a lesbian, and not Cathy, but I was, for thirty-two years. I am only beginning to be a guy—a neophyte man with some ineptitude and unfamiliarity. I occupy the liminal space between my past and my present, where names, pronouns, organic and synthetic hormones, uncut and scar tissues meet and blur. Like everyone else, I am continuously coming into being as a gendered subject.

Before the fall semester began (after my "summer project"), I sent an email to the faculty in my department, telling them that I was transitioning and what my new name and pronouns were. "C. Ray" and "he/him" would replace "Cathy" and "she/her." I tried to keep the tone casual—no big deal. The various reactions of my colleagues were always well meaning, but reflected how little linguistic and cultural room there is for genders that are not stable and continuous. Because of medicalization and the dominance of biomedical and psychoanalytic power over defining the terms of trans experience, trans people are supposed to always have been trans and always have known it. Pasts are expected to be erased. Maleness and femaleness are produced as mutually exclusive.

On one of the first days of the semester, when the campus was buzzing with fresh, back-to-school energy, a colleague stopped by my office. She gave the door frame a quick knock as she passed by and said in a celebratory, congratulatory tone, "I never thought of you as a Cathy!" She was trying to affirm my new name, pronouns, and transition, but I felt sad, even as I smiled and waved, "Thanks!"

I do not need my transition to erase my past. Cathy was awesome. I love(d) Cathy. I do not need to pretend she did not exist. Cathy made it possible for me to become C. Ray. At the same time, I am still new in my transition and expect this to shift. I was much more comfortable being accidentally called "Cathy" a few months into my transition than I am now. Perhaps the more time I accrue as my male self, the more comfortable I will be leaving Cathy behind.

One evening after class, a small group of faculty and I went to a bar near campus. Five of us sat around a table sharing carrots and hummus—me and four cis women. One colleague had just come out as lesbian after living a substantial portion of her adult life married to a man. She was talking about the joy and excitement she had found in her new relationship with a woman, and in a cheersing sort of gesture proclaimed, "Who needs penises!" and then nudged me and said in earshot of everyone at the table, "Sorry C. Ray, I know you want one." Throughout the night, this colleague made various comments that were dismissive of men, and each time she did so, she punctuated them with, "Sorry, C. Ray!" as though I—a man—would be offended by her comments.

This colleague lumped me into the category of men, as though there were nothing unique or different about me, except my lack of a penis. I have never shared with her if I want a penis, and desire for a penis is not what makes or breaks my trans guy status. That is, I may or may not want a penis, but there is no way for her to know whether I want a penis, just because I am trans. Furthermore, I was raised and socialized as a girl, and lived as a woman for thirty-two years; those are facts about my gender history. Many of her comments about men were actually what I would describe as lightweight critiques of patriarchy. She apologized to me for her "antimale" comments because there is a tacit assumption that if I have joined men, then I embrace and aspire to emulate all men and have quickly become the kind of man who takes offense at lamentations about the daily struggles of putting up with male dominance.

## FEMINISM AND MASCULINITY

Many colleagues (not only at my college, but in my larger academic networks, which also include my closest personal friendships) have had a difficult time reconciling my decision to transition with their and my feminisms. When I told my best friend from graduate school—also a sociologist—that I was going to transition, she cried all day. She lamented her loss of a dyke best friend and worried that I would become like men in her life who had harmed, discounted, or devalued her. Initially, I worried, too. If women are the vanguard of the feminist revolution, why be a man? If men are the oppressive class, why join them? If gender is a social construct, why acquiesce to the binary? These are difficult questions because there are politics to having a gender, but gender is not only political. In practice, my personal feminist politics have been much more about living my feminist values in everyday life than they have been about marching in the streets (although I have done plenty of that, too). For me, living a feminist praxis in everyday life has meant everything from being hypervigilant and critical of unequal divisions of power, resources, and labor, to prioritizing women's voices and experiences, to loving my body.

For many years, I felt a deep and profound ambivalence about transitioning because I felt like I should want to be a woman. There was a period of time when I forced myself to femme up my wardrobe because I was critical of my own butchness. Somewhere along the line I had internalized the notion that butchness was immature—something that rebellious teenagers do, not grown adults.

Female masculinity has long been viewed with skepticism by some feminists. As a teenager, I first began to display signs of masculinity at the same time that I first began to display signs of feminism. I remember my mother—a second-wave feminist—asking on many occasions, "If you hate men so much, why do you want to look like one?" It was a question I was only beginning to achieve the personal, intellectual, and political tools necessary to answer. Over the course of my life, she and other women wondered out loud if my butch self-expression meant that I judged more femme-presenting women as weak or inferior. I wondered, too. It has always felt like a cop-out to say that misogyny plays no part in my gender identity and expression. Misogyny is such a dominant part of culture; I do not see how anyone could escape from it unaffected.

From eating disorders and beauty pageants to sex work and trans guys, I believe that we are all negotiating the harmful internalized messages that we have received about gender, living within hegemonic patriarchy.

Due to the experience of having breasts (and all of their attendant social meanings), more so than my gender identity per se, I considered top surgery (irrespective of transitioning) on and off throughout my twenties. I always found my breasts to be cumbersome and resented that I was required to manage them in public. I either had to wear some kind of bra or binder or be subject to the leering and harassment of men. At the same time, I existed in feminist, body-positive social, political, and academic circles. I felt like I should love my breasts because they were part of me. I felt that whatever negative associations I had about them was the result of "The Patriarchy," and that it was my responsibility to liberate myself from those negative associations while somehow keeping my body intact.

For a long time, I was able to prevent myself from transitioning by telling myself that gender was a mere social construct. It was compulsory and unfair, but ultimately meaningless and untrue. In college, I tagged "No Gender" on bathroom walls and newspaper stands in Sharpie and longed for a genderless utopia.

Political and theoretical analyses of gender aside, it is mandatory and compulsory that I live my life inside a body that is gendered. I spend the majority of my time taking the subway, teaching my classes, buying groceries, and seeing friends. Before transitioning, it was in these mundane moments that I felt my yearning for a different self the most. Politically, intellectually, and practically, I thought that I should be a woman. I did not transition because I did or did not feel like a woman (or a man). I have never felt that a gender identity is something that I am or am not. Rather, gender is an overdetermined and hyperconsequential requirement for my social intelligibility. It was not the facts of my body that felt wrong, but that people treated me like a woman, and this treatment felt wrong. This distinction is important. My gender transition is not about my "self" or my "identity"; it is about how I want to move through the world. Now that I am a man, people treat me like a man, and I prefer this treatment—it is the way I feel I should be treated.

INCITEMENT TO GENDER ORDER

There is some social pressure (or wish) for our transitions to be tidy, and I have internalized this wish. At the same time, I feel like I should take some kind of queer pride in traversing the liminal space between man and woman. In some instances, that movement is easier than in others. Performing an ambiguous nonbinary gender presentation is not particularly comfortable in my role as a professor at a community college with no gender-inclusive restrooms and no liberal arts–style gender-inclusion practices and policies. By and large, BMCC students are poor and working-class immigrant youth of color who do not have access to white, educated, middle-class discourses where a thousand genders bloom.

In the context of the dominant cis culture, trans people are most intelligible when their genders conform to the before-and-after logics of talk show television, switching seemingly overnight from one neat and partitioned-off gender category to the other—a Venn diagram where the circles never intersect.

In reality, this is rarely (if ever) how a gender transition works. The trans narratives that are readily available in the media suggest that all trans people's genders are continuous and stable, with a simple conflict between "the inside" and "the outside" of a person, as though inside and outside exist as clear, embodied binary truths that are easy to navigate, compartmentalize, and medicalize. This is a vestige from the early- and mid-twentieth-century gender clinics, where trans people who wanted access to hormonal and surgical treatments were required to provide personal gender narratives describing themselves as having identified unwaveringly as the "other" gender (Meyerowitz 2002).

Transitioning and teaching are vulnerable contexts for me, and the intersection of them is particularly vulnerable and feels very much like I am transitioning in front of my students. Furthermore, students (being young and curious as they are) can be unpredictable, unkind, and intrusive. All teachers' bodies are on display to be read and interpreted by students, a site where corporal expectations, meanings, and anxieties are projected and affixed.

For reasons likely related to internalized transphobia and binary-supremacy, I wanted to hide my transition from my students. I did not want to confuse them. In general, part of my transition has included feeling guilty for bothering other people with my gender. I was apprehensive about changing my name and pronouns because I knew that it would be hard for people to adjust to. "Not wanting to confuse them" is, however, fairly ungenerous to my students and their intellects; they are certainly capable of understanding a gender transition. Unhappiness and discomfort are affects that are typically hidden in professional and academic cultures, and a gender transition exposes gender unhappiness and discomfort.

I did not want to have to expose so much of myself to my students. I did not want pity from them and I did not want them to know that I was so unhappy in my previous gender that I needed to change my name, my pronouns, and my body. I wanted them to perceive me as self-actualized and confident. For these reasons, transitioning in front of my students (and in general) has sometimes felt embarrassing. Testosterone is changing how I look, which is simultaneously exciting and uncomfortable. I am a thirty-four-year-old adult, and during the first year of my transition, my voice would sometimes crack while I lectured. I have the tiny mustache of a teenage boy—it is adorable, which is not the look I am going for in my role as a professor. There is some incongruence between my identity, my body, and the embodied identities that students learn to expect from their teachers.

## TRANSITIONING WITH STUDENTS

In a class last semester, I was teaching Susan Stryker's "An Introduction to Transgender Terms and Concepts" chapter of *Transgender History* (2008) in a class, when I suddenly became overwhelmed by dizzying panic, feeling the immediate urge to grab my backpack and run out of the room. I was being observed—the once-a-semester class period when a senior faculty member comes to watch me teach and then writes an evaluative report that goes into my personnel file, to be reviewed alongside other materials in several years when I am being considered for tenure.

The culture around teaching observations at my college is generally heartening. Junior faculty members are told that they should not feel too anxious about being observed and should teach how they always do. Unless something really troubling occurs, the evaluation will be descriptive and positive, with a few constructive suggestions for improvement.

Although I have been teaching at BMCC for only two years, I taught as an adjunct professor throughout graduate school, and so I have been teaching in college classrooms for about a decade and have been formally observed many times. Going into these class sessions, I usually feel a bit nervous, which I work to counter by making sure I am well prepared and by reassuring myself that I am a competent, good teacher.

It was in this spirit that I had begun the class period. I did not know the woman who was observing me well—we had been present at some of the same meetings, but had never had a one-on-one interaction. She seemed nice and I had no real reason to fear her presence in my classroom.

At BMCC, I teach between two and five sections of the same course—Introduction to Sociology—every semester. This has allowed me to see the extent to which the group dynamics of individual classes account for so much of the mood, tone, and affect of individual classrooms. As a group, BMCC students are typical community college age—eighteen to twenty years old, with a few older students in each class, especially evening classes, when those working day jobs can attend. Most students have recently finished high school, having attending New York City public schools. They are incredibly racially diverse students of color and either immigrants themselves or the children of immigrants—a reflection of the city's poor and working-class populations. They do not have a lot of educational capital and are beginning to be socialized into college life, often possessing some teenage-style rebellion, aloofness, and/or disaffectedness.

My classes are not authoritarian spaces. I do not have an authoritarian bone in my body. I am a nice and warm person, sometimes more than I wish to be. On the rare occasion that I am blatantly disrespected or threatened, I can become very serious, but in general, I am not the kind of professor who has a bunch of rules that I enforce all the time. This is probably less about my pedagogical values than my personality. What I personally loved about my own college experience was getting to read and think while having an expert who cared a lot about the material there to help me process it, and that is what I try to pass forward to my own students. So many of them have experienced schools as authoritarian, disciplinary spaces, and I work to transform that, trying to cultivate a safe(r), creative space for thought and exploration.

The particular class of students that I was teaching on observation day was a group who had clicked well with each other. I could see that they were carrying on friendships outside of the class. In addition, this particular group liked me a lot and viewed my transness as "cool" and interesting. We had developed a rapport over the course of the semester where they felt they could ask me anything, and I had come to trust our dynamic enough to answer them honestly.

In general, students have been very curious about my transition, which has been tricky to navigate and manage. My usual approach to teaching is to try to maximize the educational value of every classroom interaction. Although student curiosity is sometimes misguided, intrusive, or even mean-spirited, I believe it is ultimately a good thing, and I try to mobilize it for educational purposes.

Because I teach sociology, some of the conceptual topics we cover in my classes involve identity, presentation of self, gender, sexuality, socialization, norms, conformity, rebellion, subcultures, and so on—all topics that trans perspectives can speak to and illuminate. Due to this and my openness, there are days when students ask a lot of questions about my transition, about trans people in general, or about various aspects of the medicalization of trans bodies—surgeries, hormones, and so on. For example, more than one young man has asked me if, since I have taken testosterone and grown facial hair, they could take extra testosterone to grow extra facial hair or extra muscles. I usually find these types of interactions charming and constructive.

Even when questions like, "Do you have a penis?" detract from the centrality of whatever lesson I am working through that day, I often take the time to turn it into a teachable moment, and welcome such questions as a tactic for disarming students who try to say controversial things in classrooms as a way to buck professors' authority (something that many young cis women and trans professors deal with regularly). When students ask such questions, part of me thinks, "That is inappropriate and intrusive and I am tired of these stupid questions." Another (usually more prominent) part of me thinks, "Fine. If no one else is going to teach you about phalloplasties, I will." I use these student questions to steer us into the more sociological terrain of the cultural importance of "the Penis," the relationship between genitalia and gender, or the medicalization of bodies. I take pride in my ability to turn the musings and commentary of provocative nineteen-year-olds into sociologically interesting questions.

My teaching observation was occurring in this context, with all of these dynamics. It was a coincidence that the observation was on the single day I had assigned a reading on trans history and thought. A lot of what Stryker does in that chapter is to define some basic concepts, such as transvestite, intersex, and body morphology. As we were going through the concepts—I was eliciting definitions and examples—the students began to use me and my body as a case study. This made sense, both because of our rapport and because of my status as trans. For many if not all of the students, I am the only trans person they know, and so my identity and body make sense as a site where they would land the concepts covered in the chapter.

As this conversation was occurring, I wondered what the observer thought. Every time I looked over at her, she was concentrated on her large legal pad, quickly writing notes. Suddenly I became very worried that this senior faculty member had come to observe a Sociology 100-level class and the transsexual junior faculty member was discussing his own hormones and body morphology openly with students who were rapid-firing questions, such as, "Would a lesbian date you?" and "Did Caitlyn Jenner cut his [sic] penis off?"

It was a slightly out-of-control class period, which is not what I prefer when I am being observed. I could feel the blood rushing to my face and could see my panic reflected back at me in the concerned expressions of some of my more hypervigilant students. I quickly put them into small groups to do some activity while I fished around in my pencil bag for half a Xanax.

I got through the class period, and a few weeks later I met with the professor who had observed my class. She wrote a positive review and favorably described the class. She did not characterize me as a wildly inappropriate, overly disclosing teacher, as I had feared she might. I came away from the meeting realizing I had projected my own fears about being a trans teacher onto the class and the experience of being observed.

I tell this story as an example of the complexities of managing the intersections of course material and teacher/student identities. As a lesbian woman, I had encountered similar types of classroom dynamics, but I had been an out lesbian since I was sixteen, and by the time I was in the classroom at twenty-four, I had a lot of experience with people's bizarre questions about lesbians (e.g., "How *do* they have sex?"). But being so new in my transition, I am still learning how to verbalize myself in the face of student curiosity.

MY TRANS COLLEAGUE

I feel fortunate that throughout my transition, I have had a trans colleague I could look to as a role model and adviser.

I earned my Ph.D. at the CUNY Graduate Center—CUNY's doctoral-granting institution—and during my time as a graduate student there, I taught as an adjunct at several of the four-year CUNY colleges. One of these jobs was teaching in the Political Science department at Brooklyn College, where trans man, trans advocate, and trans scholar Paisley Currah was the department chair. Paisley and I had been acquaintances over the years, but had not known each other well. His very existence—as a trans man who had transitioned while a CUNY professor—was a great source of reassurance for me.

Coincidentally, Paisley was teaching a graduate-level course titled "Trans Theories, Practices and Politics" at the Graduate Center during the first semester of my medical transition. I asked Paisley if I could sit in on the class, figuring it would be useful to me because I could begin to learn about the field of transgender studies, which I was only marginally familiar with, while in the company of a trans professor and trans students who were navigating their genders in academia.

Sitting in on that class was personally and professionally nourishing for me because it provided an academic community of trans people and texts that I could physically and intellectually inhabit once a week. Because I am a sociologist and academic, I think hard about all of the facets of my identity, so at the beginning of my transition, I needed a space to engage academically with that part of myself. The supportive narratives that are available in the larger culture did not always resonate with me, but I felt visceral excitement when, for example, I read sentences like, "we can seize upon the textual violence inscribed in the transsexual body and turn it into a reconstructive force" (Stone 2006, 230), which made me feel understood and self-actualized. Seeing how useful the class was to my emotional health, my therapist began referring to it as my "support group."

It was instructive for me to watch Paisley teach trans material while being trans himself, and with so much experience doing both, as I was navigating the territory for the first time. His personal and teaching styles are calm, warm, and reserved. He is not self-righteous or personally disclosing (as I can be). He inhabits his trans body and teaches trans materials like those are completely normal, average, and even sometimes boring things to do. Because I was experiencing so much anxiety trying to do it myself, it was assuring and encouraging to watch Paisley teach. For example, when we were covering theoretical perspectives on genital surgeries, he unabashedly projected images of surgically reconstructed genitalia on the gigantic screen, taking up the majority of the wide, high-ceilinged wall. I later joked during a phone conversation with my mother that Paisley was able to talk about genitalia as though no one within at least twenty miles possessed any genitals at all. His presence and teaching style normalized trans bodies for me and helped me feel confident in myself and my work. A few times over the course of the semester, we went out for a beer after class. I shared some of my anxieties about teaching, and he always responded with the perspective that transitioning does not need to be a big deal. He was never dismissive, but he was able to disarm the titillation, fascination, and curiosity that everyone else in my life possessed about my transition.

## THE PLEASURE OF MALE PRIVILEGE

Throughout this essay thus far, I have focused on aspects of transitioning that have been uncomfortable, confusing, or alienating. I have likely internalized the expectation that this is the kind of narrative trans people should produce. The mainstream discursive landscape is saturated with stories about restroom access (*New York Times* Editorial Board 2016), the tally of year-to-date trans murders (Associated Press 2016), and Caitlyn Jenner as spectacle (Bissinger 2015), all within the larger transphobic, transmisogynistic, and cis-supremacist culture.

Part of my recent socialization as trans has included learning to view my trans status as primarily a site of struggle, labor, exhaustion, and vulnerability. What risks eclipse here—in the larger cultural discourse and reflected in this essay—is how enjoyable I find it to be a man, and not in the sense of being seen for who I truly am (I have never experienced my gender as "truth"). Being a man is enjoyable for me because the global culture is patriarchal, and male supremacy is a near-totalizing worldview that is rarely challenged. Importantly, not all men are privileged, and any man's experience of his maleness is significantly modified by intersections of race, class, citizenship, ability, age, and other social statuses. My ability to access male privilege is not just determined by my recent transition to male but also by my whiteness, my economic security, my US citizenship, my able body, my health, and my young adulthood.

During one of the first discussions in Paisley's class, a cis man who was fairly unfamiliar with trans, queer, or feminist concepts, was thinking aloud the way that confident, heterosexual, cis male graduate students are wont to do. We had read Harold Garfinkel's article "Passing and the Managed Achievement of Sex Status in an 'Intersexed' Person," which chronicles the medical history of Agnes, a trans woman who had begun taking her mother's estrogen pills at the age of twelve, developed feminized secondary sex characteristics, and presented at a gender clinic as intersex (although she was not, by any authoritative measure, intersex) to get genital confirmation surgery. Agnes did not originally disclose to her doctors that she had been taking her mother's estrogen pills for seven years, telling them that she had developed the feminized sex characteristics "naturally" (without pharmaceutical intervention). She was thus characterized by her doctors as a manipulative liar—as have many trans people who have lied to access the desired medical treatment (myself included).

During the class discussion, the pontificating student was trying to work out for himself the circumstances under which he believed people should be allowed to transition. He settled on his answer: "As long as they are doing it because of who they really are and not because they are going to benefit from it." I suppressed my urge to rejoin that I had decided to transition exactly because I would benefit from it.

I have never been able to relate to people who experience their gender irrespective of its social meanings. When people talk about their gender as being "who I really am," or "who I am on the inside," I do not relate. I believe them; it is just not the way that I experience my gender.

I view my gender and many of my decisions about it in fairly practical terms. Cultural legibility makes one's status as either a man or a woman compulsory. When our gender is unintelligible, we are made to name and account for it immediately. We can personally shirk gender with all our might, but in everyday life we will be gendered whether or not we consent to it. There are perceived to be only two genders, and I am required to live as one.

My decision to transition was not primarily about feeling as though I was truly a man with the wrong body (even though I have felt that way at times). I transitioned because I found living as a woman intolerable and wished to live as a man. These feelings had absolutely everything to do with the differential treatment of men and women in our society. As a girl and woman, I was socialized to be quiet, deferential, receptive, supportive, passive, domestic, and vulnerable (not bad characteristics, but certainly devoid of power). As a girl and woman, I was also sexually assaulted, sexually harassed, shushed, sexualized, overlooked, excluded, teased, and discounted.

My line of argumentation here could easily lend itself to the perspective that all women who choose to live as women and enjoy their femininity and subjectivity—even some of these qualities and experiences that I have listed—are mere dupes of patriarchal gender, or that being a man is only ever enjoyable. False consciousness is not what I am arguing. There are certainly things to be enjoyed about being a woman and disadvantages to being a man. However, having recently transitioned and begun to "pass," there is so much about being a man that I find to be so comfortable, secure, and leisurely. In public space, I am accommodated and allowed, even expected, to take up physical space. When sitting at a bar alone, no one tries to talk to me. I am not hit on by strangers. My authority is questioned far less. People ask me for help. I am viewed as capable and knowledgeable. The world has become truly safer. I experience more accessibility to my own time, space, mobility, respectability, and worth.

My students are more attentive, treat me with more deference, and follow my instructions more readily, and they do not even view me as a "real" man! My male colleagues are warmer to me, more likely to strike up a conversation and ask me for my input and opinions. Part of this shift is also because before transitioning, I was a lesbian, and men often shy away from lesbians, assuming they are man-haters or at least want nothing to do with men. As a trans man, though, I am seen by other men as wanting something they possess, or as trying to imitate, rather than intimidate, them.

## TESTOSTERONE MADE ME HETEROSEXUAL

Importantly, it is in the context of my emergent heterosexuality that I am able to most fully access male privilege. Thus far in my life, my sexuality has been women-oriented. As a woman, I was a six on the Kinsey scale; as a man, I am a zero.[5] It is striking to me how insidious my new (straight, white) male privilege is. During a conversation with a couple of colleagues who are women, they pointed out the extent to which this new privilege is significantly bound to my sexuality. If I were a gay trans man, they reminded me, my masculinity would be read very differently. But because I am sexually oriented to women—concretized by the fact that my usual object choices tend to conform to fairly normative modes of femininity—my masculinity is culturally legible, even celebrated and hegemonic. In the context of my heterosexual masculinity, my colleagues find a way to interact with me, extending to me whatever usual interactional style they use with other straight men. The fabric of these interactional dynamics is subtle and ephemeral, and thus difficult to describe, but perhaps because my maleness is so new, I am hyperaware of it. A few recent homosocial interactions come to mind as I try to capture the *je ne sais quoi* of heteromasculine regard.

By the end of my second semester after coming out, I had had top surgery, testosterone had rearranged my face and body enough that I was beginning to pass regularly, I was using the men's restroom, colleagues had made the adjustment to my new name and pronouns, and I was finally settling into my male identity with fewer and fewer daily linguistic and interactional snags. One afternoon, I was sitting at my desk in my office that is situated in a busy hallway where faculty are constantly coming and going between their offices and classrooms. I was tired, having finished teaching for the day, and I was leaning far back in my chair with my legs crossed at the ankles, perched at the heel on my desktop, as I flipped through an unsolicited book that a publisher had sent me to consider for course adoption.

My colleague Charlie stopped by to "shoot the shit." Charlie is a sixty-something white, heterosexual, cis man whose warm, collegial orientation toward me has not changed one bit over the course of my transition. He integrated the changes seamlessly, an unusual capacity I attribute in part to his two genderqueer, respectively lesbian and bisexual grown children. Charlie is the senior-most faculty member in the department. He is very active in our faculty union and a great mentor and advocate for all faculty. As such, everyone loves him. He came into my office and sat on my absent officemate's desk. I do not remember what we were talking about, but I remember taking mental note of both of our stereotypically masculine splaying postures. It was a busy, in-between-class-periods time, and soon several other male colleagues were crowded into my office, talking loudly over each other in comradely tones, making jokes, and laughing. As this was happening, I had a meta-level experience of this unfamiliar male homosociality, part of which was pure joy. I cannot express how validating and safe it feels for men to treat me as an equal and a friend, rather than as a lesser-than interlocutor in "the heterosexual matrix."[6] After they had shuffled off to their respective offices and next classes, I swiveled my legs off my desk, lunged forward to grab my phone, and texted a close friend: "A BUNCH OF MEN JUST HUNG OUT IN MY OFFICE. THIS HAS NEVER HAPPENED TO ME BEFORE," to which she comically replied, "cool story bro."

My masculinity is also legible via my heterosexuality in the classroom. As a lesbian, my sexuality was hidden, awkward, questioned, and scolded. Even though my personal style incorporated many of the usual trappings of a white, middle-class lesbian, many of my students read me as straight. I was constantly making choices around remaining closeted or coming out. When I did come out, male students regularly sexualized my lesbianism; they asked how I had sex, asked me to explain butch/femme sexual dynamics, told me never to have children, or said that I was going to hell. The occasional gay student sent warm and thankful emails and came to my office hours for support.

In contrast, around the same time that Charlie and the other colleagues gathered in my office for brief homosocial camaraderie, I was teaching a class where my heterosexuality bolstered my masculinity. One class period, my students and I were discussing gender, class, and criminalization, using the example of sex work, after having viewed the documentary *Live Nude Girls Unite*, which chronicles the union organizing efforts of dancers and support staff at the peep show venue Lusty Lady in San Francisco. One student mentioned the film *Pretty Woman* during the course of her comments, to which I had intended to reply, "I love *Pretty Woman*!" But I accidentally misspoke and said, "I love pretty women!" to which the whole class erupted into laughter, as one student blurted out, "I bet you do!" It was a hilarious moment, breaking up the serious academic manner with which I was attempting to discuss peep show politics with a room full of college students. I laughed and blushed a little, as another student asked, "Professor, do you have a pretty woman in your life?"

My sexual orientation is the same as it has always been; only my gender has changed. Even though my students know that I am trans, this gender shift has totally transformed the way that they understand me as a sexual subject.

Through the change in my gender, my sexuality has become intelligible, something they imagine that they can understand, given their general familiarity with heterosexuality as a cultural framework.

## COOL STORY BRO

Working through a gender transition provides an instructive site for thinking through the social organization and operation of gender, its requirements for intelligibility, and the ways that these intelligibilities are structured in the classroom, with colleagues, and with all manner of microinteractional dynamics. All trans people must navigate their transitions within the contexts of their work and life, and although the academy is often a more generous place for incongruent bodies than other locales, it is no utopia. It requires trans subjects to find each other and create and hold trans-inclusive spaces, where we can breathe and think outside of the day-to-day work of explaining our identities to others (even as this labor, if and when we choose it, can be very valuable for our students and colleagues). Transitioning in the classroom can be messy, disorganized, confusing, and anxiety-producing, but it can also be a site of privilege, self-actualization, learning, pedagogical innovation, and vulnerable rapport. Our bodies are doing the important work of queering spaces and perspectives, sometimes with and sometimes against our wills.

## NOTES

1. This name is a pseudonym.
2. In trans vernacular, "top" surgery refers to various chest surgeries, such as breast augmentation, mastectomy, and male chest reconstruction; "bottom" surgery refers to genital reconstruction surgeries, such as vaginoplasty, metoidioplasty, and phalloplasty.
3. "Cis" is shorthand for "cisgender" and refers to people whose gender identity matches the gender they were assigned at birth, that is, not trans. The cis/trans binary is not always useful, but it can be descriptively helpful in a crude way.
4. At the same time, Cuomo was attempting to make deep cuts to the City University of New York (CUNY)'s funding. BMCC is a college within the CUNY system.
5. The Kinsey scale, developed in 1948 by Alfred Kinsey and his colleagues (1998), is a zero-to-six scale used to describe a person's sexual orientation, where

zero means "exclusively heterosexual," six means "exclusively homosexual," and the range between one and five describes various bisexualities.

6. Judith Butler (1990) uses the concept of "the heterosexual matrix" to describe the intersections of heterosexuality, whiteness, male masculinity, and wealth in the production of hegemony, superiority, and dominance.

### WORKS CITED

Associated Press. 2016. "Murder of Trans Woman in Baltimore Nearly Ties Grim National Record." *LGBTQ Nation*, September 16. http://www. lgbtqnation.com/2016/09/murder-trans-woman-baltimore-ties-grim-national-record.

Bissinger, Buzz. 2015. "Caitlyn Jenner: The Full Story." *Vanity Fair*, July. http://www.vanityfair.com/hollywood/2015/06/caitlyn-jenner-bruce-cover-annie-leibovitz.

Butler, Judith. 1990. *Gender Trouble: Feminism and the Subversion of Identity*. New York: Routledge.

———. 2003. *Giving an Account of Oneself*. New York: Fordham University Press.

Garfinkel, Harold. 2006. "Passing and the Managed Achievement of Sex Status in an 'Intersexed' Person." In *The Transgender Studies Reader*, edited by Susan Stryker and Stephen Whittle, 58–93. New York: Routledge.

Kinsey, Alfred C., Wardell Baxter Pomeroy, and Clyde E. Martin. 1998. *Sexual Behavior in the Human Male*. Bloomington: Indiana University Press.

Meyerowitz, Joanne J. 2002. *How Sex Changed: A History of Transsexuality in the United States*. Cambridge, MA: Harvard University Press.

*New York Times* Editorial Board. 2016. "Transgender Bathroom Hysteria, Cont'd." *New York Times*, April 18. http://www.nytimes.com/2016/04/18/opinion/transgender-bathroom-hysteria-contd.html.

Stone, Sandy. 2006. "The Empire Strikes Back: A Posttranssexual Manifesto." In *The Transgender Studies Reader*, edited by Susan Stryker and Stephen Whittle, 221–35. New York: Routledge.

Stryker, Susan. 2008. *Transgender History*. Berkeley, CA: Seal Press.

SIX

# Typing My Way Out of the Cisheteronormative Closet at a Community College

*Kei Graves*


AN INTRODUCTION TO KEI

My name is Kei Graves, my pronouns are "they/them" or "he/him," and here are bits of my story. I currently work at the community college from which I graduated, which is in a suburb of a large city in Ohio. My primary role there is as a student success coach, meaning that I do advising, along with a hodge-podge of other projects. I am also an adjunct faculty member, teaching College 101. In my personal life, I am an agender queer who has been happily married to a genderqueer person for the past five years. For me, identifying as agender means that I see myself as having no gender or as being gender neutral.

My gender expression is masculine, and I tend to wear what would be considered "men's clothing." I am also multiracial (African American, German, and some other heritages) and sport visible piercings and tattoos. Over the course of the years that I have worked at this particular institution, I have often appeared in ways that are typically read as queer and have been open about being in a same-sex relationship. However, it was not until May 2016 that I decided to be out about my gender identity at work, which is where the story I tell here begins.


HERE, QUEER, AND SLIGHTLY UNCOMFORTABLE

I had been out about identifying as agender to friends and a few close coworkers since 2013, but I had not formally told others in my office about myself and my pronouns, even though I had worked with them since I had been an undergraduate student. I was reluctant to be more open at work because "gender

identity and expression" were not covered in my institution's nondiscrimination policy and LGBT people are not protected from employment discrimination in Ohio. But after having been working at the college for several years,
I felt that I was being untrue to myself to let others assume I was cis. I was
open about and accepted for being nonbinary outside of the office; I wanted
that same level of understanding and respect at work.

On that day in May, I was alone in the office, as most people in my section
had left for the day; it was about 6 p.m. Having the time to myself, I typed
up a short email to send to coworkers in which I briefly stated that I do not
identify as a woman and want to be referred to by "they/them" or "he/him"
in the future. I also said that I would understand if people continued to misgender me for the next few weeks and directed them to some online educational resources, including an article that I had written about the experiences
of LGBTQIA+ college students. I did not want to sound critical of the people
who were misgendering me, as they did not know what pronouns I used for
myself (although they also did not ask).

Rather than sending the email message when I was done, I kept reading
it over and making changes to ensure that I did not come off as demanding (I
even titled the email "An Unimportant Request"). I wanted the recipients to
have a sense of me and my feelings, and hopefully shift their behavior to be
more inclusive as a result. I sought to ensure that the email did not provoke ill
feelings toward me, as I feared that a negative backlash would get me fired. I
sent the email message to my partner, who was also struggling with whether
to come out in their workplace, and asked them, "Do you think that this is too
much? Do you think that this will be ok? What should I do?" Their response
was "It will be fine."

By this time, it was about 7:30 p.m., which is closing time for the office.
Out of time, I set my email message to "low importance" and sent it off to the
people I work with on a daily basis in my department and through serving on
various committees. I then quickly shut down my computer and briskly walked
from the office as if someone was chasing me. I drove home filled with anxiety.

The next day, I was shocked to discover that I had no reply emails and
no notes had been left on my desk. It was as if nothing had changed, except
that everything had.

I noticed that some people began to be uncomfortable around me. They
were not outright mean, but when I would walk in and greet them, they would
shy away or hesitate before responding. Other people avoided me altogether
and would not speak to me. I found their silence to be harder to take than

if they had been verbally confrontational. I stopped by some people's offices and asked if they had questions or if there was anything that I could do to help them. They shrugged it off, saying "No, I am good," or "No, I have no questions." At the time, I was satisfied with this response, because I thought it meant that they understood me and would be accepting. I realize now that they probably just did not know what to say.

My first real conversation was with a staff assistant. She pulled me into one of the empty student worker cubicles, and putting her hands on her hips, inquired, "So, you wanna be a man?"

My immediate response was to chuckle, as her question is usually the first one that cis people ask, especially when a trans individual changes the pronouns they use for themselves. Collecting myself, I answered, "Not at all. I am nonbinary; I do not identify as a male or female, but I am okay with he/him/his as my pronouns."

She was silent for a moment before following up with, "So what should I call you? How should I treat you now?"

I was slightly taken aback by these questions because it was very simple in my mind. I had explained in my email that all people had to do was shift the language that they used in referring to me. I had done this for the nonbinary people in my life without much difficulty, so I was surprised by her seeming lack of understanding. I told her, "As if you would for anyone else, I just don't go by she/her/hers or feel comfortable with terms like 'ladies' and things like that."

She shrugged and responded only with "Oh, okay" before walking away. I was not sure what to make of this reaction, but I heard later that she was concerned about which gendered bathrooms I would be using.

The following day, two of my colleagues brought me into their offices to talk about my email. The first was a woman who resides in a very liberal college town. I had a feeling that she would be accepting of my identity, and when we sat down to talk, she indicated that her main concern was why I had waited so long to tell everyone, as I had been working there for three years at that point. I explained that given the institution's lack of visible support for LGBTQIA+ people, I had been worried about being fired or other possible negative consequences, especially during my first couple of years at the college. I also noted that I had been met mostly with silence and discomfort even in coming out now, when people knew and seemingly liked me.

The second colleague was also supportive. She admitted that it would be difficult for her to make the transition from using "she/her" to "they/them" or "he/him" to refer to me, but she promised me that she would do her best, and that has turned out to be true. When I told her that I had received a chilly reception from most people in the office, she nodded and with a smile said, "Well, if anyone messes with you, I'll take care of them!" I found that reassuring.

It has now been six months since I told people at my community college that I identify as agender, and it feels as if I never stop having to come out, which seems to be a common situation among openly LGBTQIA+ people. Compared to what some trans individuals face when they come out, I cannot say that I have had a terrible experience, but it has also not been easy. Even though my coworkers are aware of my identity, many still misgender me on a regular basis by not using the appropriate pronouns. I correct them, so that they are cognizant of what they are saying, which leads some to become visibly frustrated with me. I do not like having other people upset with me, but I know that if I do not raise the issue, they will continue to misgender me, which I find even more hurtful. I take it a step at a time and use my position as the only out trans employee at the college (at least that I and others are aware of) to educate other staff members and try to bring about change on a personal level on my campus.

## "I NEED A HAND": A COWORKER'S RESPONSE

Soon after I came out at work, I received an email from a coworker I barely knew. The email was titled "Pronouns," so it immediately piqued my interest. I clicked on it and began to read.

> I need a hand, and I am hoping you could help me out. I am relatively uneducated on transgender/gender fluidity/nonbinary gender identity, etc. As a gay person, I do not think it is acceptable for me to be lacking this kind of knowledge, especially how important it is becoming lately. I bring this up to you because I have heard a couple of people make a kind of "joke" about your chosen pronouns . . . I spoke up and said "I think it is okay, doesn't bother me."
>
> It is bothering me that I have heard these "jokes" or comments, but it is also bothering me that I have not had more to say. While I'm going to spend some time educating myself on the importance of pronouns . . . I think it's important to reach out to people more personally when trying to learn and grow about issues we might not fully connect with.
>
> I do not believe that anyone means any harm by these "jokes" and I consider these people my friends . . . How do I help educate others, take

a stand, and also be respectful? I am hoping you can share a bit here—
we cannot make the workplace better by saying little or nothing at all.

At first, I was completely dumbfounded and admittedly a bit hurt. I knew the
people in the department fairly well, having worked with them for years, and
did not expect them to be making cruel remarks about me. I eventually chalked
it up to ignorance and focused on the positive aspects of the email—that I
now knew someone else in student affairs who was a part of the LGBTQIA+
community, and that he wanted to better understand me and others like me.
I forwarded him some resources from GLAAD and Wikipedia information
on pronouns and offered to meet him for coffee to explain myself better, to
which he agreed.

That meeting led to us developing a friendship and working together to
advocate for a college-sponsored training to educate others about LGBTQIA+
people. By taking just a few minutes out of his day to be kind, this person
sought to create a more inclusive work environment for me, and then demonstrated his commitment by becoming involved in efforts to further trans inclusion on campus.

"ARE YOU TRANS?" A STUDENT'S RESPONSE

Registering for classes at my community college is always a stressful time for
students and academic staff, as students have to wait in line for an hour or
more to speak with an overburdened staff member. The positive aspect for me
is that I have the opportunity to meet a wide range of incoming students who
need last-minute advising.

One of the students seeking support was interested in pursuing a general
associate of arts degree; these are my favorite students to work with because
they have so many different options available to them. I called him back to my
cubicle and went through my normal process—discussing placement scores,
grades, what classes he wanted to take, and so on. When we reached the final
portion of the appointment, where I sign him up for classes, I saw that he was
looking at some of the cultural diversity and LGBTQIA+ safe space images
that I have hung in a visible area of my space.

"Are you trans?," he asked. It felt like my heart nearly stopped as I was entering the numbers into my computer to pull up the courses for his schedule.
I breathed deeply and with a smile said, "Why, yes, I am." I hoped that my
disclosure would not lead to an argument or worse. The last thing I needed,
only two months after I had come out to my coworkers, was to have a student

complain about the "weirdo adviser who is imposing their sexual orientation and gender identity on innocent students."

"Oh, cool," he responded, and perking up, declared, "My boyfriend is trans." I nearly laughed with relief. "Really! That is awesome," I said. He then proceeded to tell me all about his partner, including how his boyfriend had come out when they had gotten together and how his boyfriend was worried that my student would not stay with him. My student stated that he was happy to be with his partner and was proud of him. I made a real connection with the student, such that he came back for a second appointment a few weeks into the semester. Because our community tends to be conservative and not many here are vocal supporters of LGBTQIA+ rights, I did not think I would ever have such a positive reaction from a student about my gender identity. I was very glad to have been wrong.

## "I HAVE YOUR BACK": A COLLEAGUE'S RESPONSE

In the days following the massacre at the Pulse nightclub in Orlando on June 12, 2016, I felt even more isolated and fearful. My institution was silent on the tragedy, and there was no public statement of condolence from the administration. The flags on campus were not even lowered to half-staff until it became a federal mandate. At the same time, people at work were still misgendering me without seeming to care. I corrected them politely, to which they would often huff in frustration or say that they were sorry in a way that felt more sarcastic than genuine. I had had enough.

Seeking support, I popped into a colleague's office and asked if she had a few minutes. When she invited me in, I immediately confessed to her that "I feel like I am in the wrong field." She was surprised and asked me to explain, so I told her that with the recent tragedy and coworkers still not respecting my identity, "I just feel like I do not belong right now." It was easy to speak freely with her and she always responded with warmth. She nodded to what I had said and looked at me before speaking.

"You know, I have never told you this but I trust you. There are few people I trust here with this information but I know you, and you will not share it with anyone else," she said. "My partner is a woman, and I am bisexual. You probably already knew. I know you have friends where she works." Indeed, I had already known, but I was surprised that she was telling me directly. I nodded in response and said, "Yes, but it means a lot that you would trust me with that information."

She explained that she and her partner live together and that she is out to her family and friends, but that she is afraid to be out at the college because she feels that if her coworkers knew, they would make her life hell. She praised me and other young people for being out in nonaccepting environments and fighting for what we believe in, and said that we would be the ones to bring about change. "I may not be able to be on the front lines with you," she stated, "but I am 100 percent your ally, and I have your back."

I swallowed back some tears and vowed at that moment that I would do all that I could to make my campus more welcoming to and inclusive of LGBTQIA+ people. I know of only five staff people at my college who openly identify as LGBTQIA+ besides me. I am sure that there are others, but they do not feel that they can be out at work. This fact saddens me as much, if not more, than my own plight and battle for respect.

## A LACK OF ACCESS TO RESTROOMS

Besides being misgendered, I struggle daily with which restrooms I should use. Currently, my campus has only two gender-inclusive restrooms, neither of which is near where I work. The college plans to add more in the future, and all newly constructed campus buildings will include gender-inclusive restrooms. In the meantime, I have to make do with what is available.

Although there are no gender-inclusive restrooms in buildings near my workplace, the library, which is a short distance away, has single-user men's and women's restrooms, so at least I am not faced with having to navigate multiuser spaces. The library restrooms function as gender-inclusive restrooms to a certain degree, as most people will use whichever one is available, ignoring the gender indicated on the sign. For me, it remains a no-win situation. Even though I am not sharing the space with anyone else, I feel too uncomfortable in the women's restroom to use it, except as a last resort, and while I commonly use the men's restroom, I do not feel that I fit there either. I find it especially difficult to enter the men's room when there is a man standing near it, as I fear that I will be stared at, confronted, or worse.

When I put my hand on the handle to enter a restroom, regardless of whether it is a men's or women's room, I am making a statement to the people who see me and to myself. The fact that higher education remains rooted in a gender binary is most evident to me at this moment, when I have to choose to be one or the other in a world where I am neither.

## THE EQUATING OF SEX WITH GENDER IDENTITY

When I consider my experiences as a trans person of color, I think about the Men of Color Committee on which I currently serve. Nationwide, there are numerous initiatives designed to assist Black and Latino men to enter and graduate from college, which I think is particularly true of Ohio schools, as institutions in the state are funded based in part on graduation rates.

While I fully support such recruitment and retention initiatives, at times I feel uncomfortable in the committee's meetings because everything is so binary. We look at the data on students whom we assume to be cis males of different races and use that information to determine the services we provide. I wonder how many of the "men" included in these numbers actually identify as men or if trans men and nonbinary individuals who were assigned male at birth are simply excluded from the research. Either way, trans people are erased, which likely skews the data. If colleges were to ask students to indicate their gender identity and not just their sex on applications and forms, institutions would have more accurate information to use in developing support programs. I doubt this will become a regular practice nationally any time soon, and I am not sure if the Men of Color Committee would be willing to advocate for this change at our college.

The committee's discussions about Black and Latino male representation among the college's staff and faculty likewise presume that all employees identify as cis. I often feel invisible in these meetings as a nonbinary staff member, and I am not sure how I can personally help when they consider student retention strategies, such as having male staff and faculty members of color serve as mentors to minoritized students. I feel that I am not the kind of staff person whom the other committee members have in mind as a mentor, but in treating me as nonmale, they, in effect, see me as female.

## BRINGING ABOUT INSTITUTIONAL CHANGE

After I came out, I became involved in trying to develop more campus programming and resources for LGBTQIA+ students, faculty, and staff. At the time, our Human Resources Department was planning an introductory "LGBT" training that would define terms and provide some basic information about the issues that LGBT people face. I was interested in helping with the training, but I was also hesitant to do so because I did not think the one-hour event they were organizing was enough. If my experiences were any indication, our campus needed much more.

After I sent my coming out email, I arranged a meeting with a staff person in human resources to discuss my concerns about the training. The HR person, who was very open minded and wanted to be supportive of LGBT people, said, "I see where you are coming from, if you feel that we need more, help us do it." That was how I became involved in developing a series of proposals to increase education about and resources for LGBTQIA+ people on my campus.

Initially, I was assisted in my efforts by a good friend who often works with me in my department and by the staff assistant who coordinates the LGBT campus pride group. We were soon joined by our part-time Diversity and Inclusion coordinator, another student affairs professional, and the gay coworker who had emailed me for information about the trans community. We met every other week during our lunch hour, as we could not meet during work time because our group was not formally recognized by the college. From these meetings, we developed a proposal that we submitted to the college's Operations Council, which consists of the president, provost, faculty and staff council presidents, and a representative from the campus foundation. In the proposal, we requested official standing as a committee, the creation of more gender-inclusive restrooms, the implementation of safe zone training for faculty and staff, the inclusion of an expanded diversity statement on the college's webpage, and a place on the website where the diversity of our campus community would be recognized and celebrated.

As we were writing and revising the proposal, I realized that whether I would ever feel included, welcomed, and safe at work and at the college more generally rode on the approval of the items in the proposal. The importance of these issues for me sometimes made it difficult to speak about the topic with others, who might not understand how critical these changes were for me and likely for other trans and gender-nonconforming people on campus. I do not know what I would have done had the proposal been rejected.

Fortunately, I did not have to find out, as the proposal received a very positive response from the Operations Council. The college president in particular was thrilled to see all of the suggestions; she immediately gave our committee official recognition and began to implement the other priorities from the proposal. One of the first changes was that my institution held its first ever LGBT safe zone training. The training was limited to faculty and staff, and about a dozen people attended. In addition, another forty staff members, faculty, and students expressed an interest in being trained, and our LGBT committee that started as three people suddenly grew to more than twenty, as others wanted to be involved in efforts to create a more LGBT-affirming campus climate. I am thrilled by this level of support from people within my college and feel that we will continue to make progress toward LGBT inclusion.

## SUPPORT AT WORK

Following the safe zone training, I received emails from many people on campus who wanted to be involved or attend the next training. One email caught my eye. It was from a newer employee in the division in which I work. I did not know her well, but she had told me in passing that she is a strong LGBT ally. She emailed me to learn more about the training, and at the very end of her email, she asked a simple question, but one that deeply moved me: "Would you mind if I correct people about your pronouns?"

I was stunned for a moment. The struggle to have others use the correct pronouns for me had become less difficult in the previous few months, but it was still a challenge. Thus to have someone with whom I was barely acquainted ask for permission to correct others who misgendered me felt incredibly validating. I happily typed "yes" in all caps and sent it off, along with some information about pronouns. I am curious to see how her support will affect my workplace. Even if I continue to be regularly misgendered, I know that at least one person in my space is working to build a more supportive and inclusive environment for trans and gender-nonconforming people like me.

While the political and social climate nationally for LGBTQIA+ people has grown significantly worse because of Donald Trump's candidacy and election as president, there has been more done at my institution this past year to support LGBTQIA+ people than ever before. These changes are far more than I could have imagined and give me hope that one day I will be able to feel included, welcomed, and safe at work and on my campus.

# SEVEN

# On Being (In)Visible in the Academy
## A Trans Scholar's Narrative

*Jackson Wright Shultz*

AS I WAS PREPARING to leave my office one spring afternoon, a former student of mine appeared in my doorway. My door is always open, but he hesitated and knocked on the doorframe. I stifled the urge to sigh as I glanced at the clock: 3:27. My goal had been to avoid rush hour and finish grading midterm papers at home.

I abandoned my efforts to shove my far-too-large stack of ungraded papers into my far-too-small messenger bag and forced a smile. "Hi, Sam. Come on in!"

I gestured to a chair and he sat, fingering the sleeve of his shirt and staring at the floor. Sam was normally calm, cheerful, and attentive to social conventions. His lack of eye contact concerned me.

"What can I help you with?" I inquired.

His eyes flitted briefly toward the doorway, then back to the ground.

"Ah," I thought, "one of those conversations." I stood, closed the door, and repeated my question.

Sam took a deep breath and, still not meeting my gaze, said quietly, "Tony told me that you're trans."

I faltered on the way back to my desk. My gender identity was not really private information: I had disclosed to Tony the previous semester when he voiced his frustration with a lack of trans faculty on campus. However, Sam's blatancy caught me off guard. "Where on Earth is he going with this?" I wondered.

"That's correct," I said slowly, settling myself back into my chair and giving up all hope of beating rush hour traffic.

"Well, that's a problem," Sam said, momentarily looking up from his sleeve to glare at me.

I immediately second-guessed the closed door. "What is this about?" I thought wildly. "Is he blackmailing me? Didn't he do well in my class? What grade did I give him? I can't remember. I'm going to be on the evening news. It will make the headlines: 'Student Accuses Trans Professor of Grade Bias.' No, the media never handles this well; it will be: 'Student Accuses a Transgendered of Grade Bias.' My mom will see it. I'll be fired. I've got to call the ACLU."

Before I could articulate a coherent thought, he continued, "Because . . . before I knew that you were trans, I could pretend that everything was fine. But now I can't stop thinking about transitioning. I . . . I think I'm a girl."

I thanked several gods in which I did not believe. Although I had the overwhelming urge to hug Sam, I was still wary of making the news. "Transgendered Caught Hugging Student: Acceptable Conduct or *Trans*ient Affair? You Decide."

I shunted my internal monologue to the side and smiled. "You know, I have a friend who likes to say that denial is single use."

Sam glanced up and gave me a small smile.

"Thank you for sharing this with me, Sam."

We spoke at length about various options for social, hormonal and non-hormonal, and surgical and nonsurgical transitions. We discussed the impact that transitioning might have on Sam's education and the resources available on campus. We talked about the appropriate pronouns for her, and when and in what contexts she would like me to use them (the answers were "she/her/hers" and "right now"). Sam's questions were mostly excited inquiries about medical matters, but after a long while, her queries turned to apprehensions.

"I'm in school so that I can get a degree and get a job, you know?," she said. "But if I transition, I'm afraid it will put me back at square one. I want to be able to be out and visible. What if I graduate with $40,000 of student loan debt and no one will hire me 'cause I'm trans?"

I sighed deeply. No amount of professorial support or advice could make the answer to those questions any easier. I wanted to be able to tell her unequivocally that transitioning would not be a problem. I wished I could promise that she could be as open as she wanted about her gender identity and no employer or potential employer would ever give her a moment's grief. I would have liked to say that decisions around disclosure and visibility were straightforward and easy to make. Instead, I told her the truth.

WHEN I WAS AN UNDERGRADUATE, a well-meaning professor told me that I should remove all references to LGBTQ activities, awards, and publications from my curriculum vitae. She said that including these references could potentially bar me from fair consideration for scholarships, graduate school admissions, and employment opportunities. I was not shocked by the suggestion—I had heard it before. I was, however, surprised to hear this recommendation from a professor of women's studies. I had come to understand the women's studies department as one of the few places on campus that provided shelter from these sorts of microaggressions, so I was somewhat startled by her proposal.

As part of a senior internship, students in our department were required to write both a general résumé and an academic CV. At the beginning of the term, she critiqued our documents, giving us the opportunity to make revisions before handing in our résumés and CVs again as part of our final portfolio. I knew the exercise was well intentioned, but her suggestion posed a serious problem: my leadership positions had primarily been in LGBTQ organizations, most of the grants and scholarships that I had received were contingent on my involvement in LGBTQ communities, and the handful of publications I had were centered in the emerging field of transgender studies. I contemplated her advice for a moment, and then told her, "If I remove all of the queer references from my CV, there will be nothing left."

She nodded sympathetically, but persisted. "It's something you need to think about before handing in the final draft."

Following her advice, I thought about my CV intently. In fact, I could not stop thinking about it. I contemplated which items were palatable enough to leave in and concluded that the list was dreadfully short. "I could list my major (women's studies) but not my minor (queer studies)," I thought. "I could include that diversity scholarship, as long as I'm ambiguous as to why it was awarded to me." For weeks I obsessed over a document that, in actuality, I rarely had cause to use.

Concerned as I was about the realities of applying to graduate school, my CV fixation persisted throughout the term. *"If I abandon my position with the Gay-Straight Alliance, it would free up enough time for me to join clubs that look better on my CV,"* I mused. I perused a campus directory of student organizations, but somehow putting "President of the Satanic Alliance" or "Treasurer of the Feminist Emancipation of The Uterus Society" (FETUS for short) on my CV did not seem any more agreeable. I briefly considered joining the College Republicans, but the effort involved in scraping the Obama bumper stickers off my car dissuaded me. In the flurry of organized chaos that came with the arrival of midterm papers and exams, my CV concerns were put on the back burner.

When the end of the term loomed near, I was forced to revisit my CV in preparation for the final portfolio. Aside from brief attendance at a film club meeting (to snag a slice of free pizza), I had not managed to join a single "respectable" student organization and had nothing new to add to the document. The night before the portfolio deadline, I sat in front of my computer screen. Deciding I should at least attempt to follow my professor's advice, I deleted all LGBTQ references from the document. I played with the font and margins for a while, but finally concluded that if I removed all hints of queerness from my CV, the only thing left would be my name at the top. On the heels of that thought, I realized that if my CV were going to be truly queer-free, that as a queer person, I would have to remove my name as well.

In the stubbornness of youth, I printed the page, blank but for a small page number, which I assumed could stay, since I had printed it in the straightest of fonts. "No italics for this guy," I thought facetiously. I wrote "Queer-Free CV" on a sticky note, slapped it onto my blank page, and stapled the recently gentrified CV to the back of my portfolio. I printed my actual CV, replete with queerness, and added it to the portfolio as well. I was resolute in my refusal to contribute to my own erasure as a trans scholar. My (perhaps naïve) hope was that any graduate school that would be willing to hire me with the words *transgender* and *queer* plastered all over my CV would be more likely to be supportive of my gender identity and expression. I knew that these may not have been the words admissions committees wanted to see, but when all was said and done, I figured they were probably still less controversial than "FETUS Treasurer."

When the time came to apply for graduate school, I fearlessly used my so-called lavender CV. In that moment, I did not pause to consider how privileged I was to be able to do so. The trans, gender-nonconforming, and allied students, staff, faculty, and administrators who came before me had carefully paved my way to graduate school. Each institution that offered me admission was clearly willing to embrace (or at least overlook) my blatantly queer track record. The battles to add "gender identity and expression" to nondiscrimination policies, to establish recognized LGBTQ student organizations, or to begin building a handful of gender-inclusive bathrooms on campuses had been waged before my time. Others' blood, sweat, and tears laid a foundation for me to obstinately and haphazardly reject respectability politics when filling out admissions applications with little concern about the results.

Over time, I began to recognize and push back on the privileges that had allowed me to so arrogantly assume that my presence as a queer person in academia was unalienable and permitted me to superciliously take my place in the ivory tower for granted. I began to understand that my own privileges as a formally educated, able-bodied, white, male-presenting individual allowed me to move through the world as a queer trans person with relative immunity to violence and discrimination that many trans women, especially trans women of color, are rarely afforded.

As I studied the movements of trans and gender-nonconforming students, I became increasingly appreciative of the efforts of the scholars who had come before me. Inspired by their activism, I decided to do my small part in continuing their legacy. Through this work, I learned to check the unabashed and frank attitude I often had as an undergrad, and I began to recognize how the areas in which I was privileged often trumped those in which I was not, effectively affording me substantial freedoms and considerably more undeserved space and power within academia than many of my peers. More important, I started to learn how to leverage these privileges for good. Gone were the days when I felt it my duty to print off a completely blank CV to demonstrate my unwillingness to take a professor's well-intentioned suggestion. Instead, a more calculated and (usually) less flippant form of activism took root.

As an undergrad, my preferred method of activism had been organizing or participating in loud, raucous protests, and it took me many years to realize that my personal activism could occur in myriad other forms. Do not get me wrong: I am always down for a hearty picket at a capitol building, and I love a good megaphone, but I have come to embrace a broader concept of activism. The queerer I get, the more my focus turns to intersectional activism, and the older I get, the more my focus turns to everyday activism. In grad school, I began mentoring trans and gender-nonconforming youth, realizing that my visibility as a trans person was often more powerful than any rally I ever attended. The importance of making myself visible to my students was solidified following the suicide of Leelah Alcorn, when the hashtag #RealLiveTransAdult first surfaced on social media, as many trans youth had never seen someone like me in the course of their education. Being able to fulfill that role propelled me forward in my activism and my research.

Unfortunately, activist fatigue is debilitating, particularly when your very existence is a revolutionary act. I would like to say that my commitments to trans and gender-nonconforming students have always been stalwart and unwavering, but the wear and tear of being a #RealLiveTransAdult has caused me my fair share of exhaustion. In fact, at the junctures of beginning both my master's and doctoral theses, I had small existential crises. Maybe it was because the rationale behind my former professor's advice was starting to sink in, or maybe I was growing fearful about starting my career, but I felt increasingly forced to operate within a set of proprieties to which I did not normally subscribe. Faced with questions of respectability politics, I briefly contemplated refocusing my research away from trans studies to make my work more appealing to future hiring committees. By pursuing the research interests that were the most meaningful and intriguing to me (read: all things trans), I risked raising suspicions about my own gender identity. The cyclical argument resounding through my head consisted of two conflicting points: "If all of my research is in trans studies, who will realistically hire me? If I'm not focusing on trans studies, why am I even researching?" After all, my educational pursuits were based in a desire to advance the causes of trans and gender-nonconforming communities.

When I discussed my concerns with a professor in my doctoral program about my research and about having a queer CV that, like a good cheese, only seemed to get more potent with age, his response was startlingly different from that of my undergraduate professor. Maybe the country had changed enough in the better part of a decade between the two conversations, or maybe his often obnoxious optimism informed his answer, but he said, "Your dissertation topic should be the thing you most want to be an expert on. The only question you need to answer is this: What do you want to be a doctor of? Pursue your passion and the rest will fall into place."

I was momentarily relieved by his answer. I wanted to do research in trans studies, but I was afraid of the consequences this could inevitably have on my career. He told me to ignore the potential penalties and "pursue my passion." Being a man of substantial privilege himself, he undoubtedly considered this solid advice. Unlike the advice I had received so many years before, his guidance did not come from a place of concern for me or of an awareness of the often harsh realities of having a lavender CV in a genderist and heterosexist world. Despite the potential consequences, his question resonated with me, and by answering it honestly, I realized I would have to sacrifice certain aspects of my privilege if I were going to complete the work I had set out to do.

I wanted my students to be able to identify me as a #RealLiveTransAdult and as someone to whom they could look for support. To do that, I had to consider the ways I made myself visible to them as a trans person. We live in a society that assumes everyone is heterosexual and cis until proven otherwise. I am frequently presumed to be cis by those I encounter, which affords me the immense privilege of deciding whether to disclose my status as a trans person in a given situation. Having the option of being stealth is undeniably an incredible advantage, and it has provided me with a sense of safety on many occasions. But because I am presumed to be cis, my trans identity is erased and I am sometimes rendered invisible against my will. As though negotiating visibility were not complicated enough on my own terms, I have learned that the privilege of being read as cis can be stripped away at any moment should anyone around me discover the not-at-all terrible, not-at-all-secret "terrible secret" that I am a trans person.

Alas, the Internet exists.

As an academic, the adage of "publish or perish" rules my career. The conundrum is that publishing research on trans and gender-nonconforming communities could well lead to my eventual perishing. Even now, despite the fact that my presumed-cis body is not automatically associated with queerness, my name already is, and this information is easily accessible online. While many trans individuals in generations past transitioned and disappeared into the background, the anonymity they were able to achieve is difficult, if not impossible, for a generation raised on the Internet. My online presence is hardly stealth and comes with calculated risks. By publishing and blogging without using a pseudonym, I hazard that coworkers, supervisors, or students to whom I have elected not to disclose could put two and two together, and the consequences for me could be dismal—particularly as a non–tenure-track faculty member working in a state wherein I can be fired on the basis of my gender identity.

Sometimes my work precedes me, so my status as a trans person is assumed before I arrive. At other times, new colleagues or students trip across my research or writing and their attitude toward me suddenly and unmistakably shifts. When those who had incorrectly assumed my gender identity discover my work, I am confronted with an array of reactions from open hostility to inappropriate inquiry about the state of my genitalia to affirmation that the person in question is "okay" with my "life choices." In the latter circumstance, I am often bombarded with an odd assortment of announcements about the person's numerous prior interactions with trans people and an avowal that they support my transition. "Thanks for your permission," I cannot help but think, "How did I ever live without it?"

In my attempts to mediate my level of disclosure, I have slowly learned that visibility is not a binary of visible and invisible. Like most things queer, it exists along a spectrum. I am visible as a queer academic to all because I am open about my sexuality. I am visible as a trans academic to some of my students and colleagues because I choose to actively and openly disclose to them. I become visible to others because they have elected to research (or have accidentally stumbled across) my work. Sometimes others disclose on my behalf. Sometimes they do this with hostile intent. If my college had a tabloid, I am sure I would make a regular appearance, as each new wave of students unearthed my writing: "English 257 Taught by Transsexual! See page 7 for exclusive details."

I cannot know what my life will look like in the future or what the eventual consequences of being visible will be on my career. Thus far, I have been grateful to have a semi-visible presence on campus. Colleagues and other students to whom I have disclosed know they can point students, like Sam, in my direction. At other times, these students find me on their own and show up at my office with an article I wrote in hand as a transparent segue to coming out or asking for help navigating academia as a trans or gender-nonconforming person. I am fully aware that there is only a thin curtain that divides me from those colleagues and students who I would rather not find out that I am trans, those who could make my life and my job even more difficult if they decided to do so. I proceed with an awareness that I can be outed faster than you can say "Google search." However, aside from the occasional spurt of gossip on campus, I have yet to have any major problems related to my visibility.

At times, I have fears about whether my visibility in my writing, on my CV, and on campus will eventually sabotage my career. Nevertheless, it is crucial that my students have identified faculty and staff members to whom they can turn for support, and it is essential that they have access to academic role models that students in my generation often lacked. For trans and gender-nonconforming students whose experiences are also compounded by intersectionality with other marginalized identities, the ability to distinguish supportive faculty is even more critical. Most of the time, I can lay my fears aside because I want to be a role model and mentor for my trans and gender-nonconforming students. That said, I am not interested in martyrdom. Successfully finding and maintaining the visibility/invisibility balance as a trans scholar is proving to be a lifelong endeavor.

THE EVENING SUNLIGHT poured through the dusty window of my office, casting long shadows throughout the room. Sam watched me expectantly, chewing on her bottom lip, awaiting my answer. I thought about the conflicting advice I had been given through the years, from encouragement to pursue research in trans studies to the suggestion that I scrub all things queer from my CV.

"If you really want a good answer to those questions, seek advice from many," I suggested. "But do what's right for you. My personal answer is this: There's not a singular trans experience. You may or may not have the option of being stealth and you will have to decide whether and to what extent you wish to disclose in countless contexts every day: in relationships, to friends and family, to acquaintances, and to employers. Sometimes that decision is easy, sometimes it's really difficult, and occasionally it's out of your hands entirely."

She nodded thoughtfully.

"I wish I had a better answer for you," I continued. "But I'll let you in on a secret that I wish someone had told me: visibility is usually negotiable and it's definitely not binary."

Sam smiled and thanked me for talking to her. I wrote down the contact information for a trans colleague who had given me permission to hand her name out like candy to any queer student in need and gave it to Sam. She paused at the door and assured me that she would be back with several hundred more questions at a later date. True to her word, she and I have had many more conversations since.

As I resumed packing the stack of ungraded papers into my bag, I replayed our conversation. I do not know that I was the best person to answer her questions, and I am sure others could have provided significantly better career advice. But what she needed at that moment was someone who had navigated their career as an intermittently visible trans person, and if nothing else, I was certainly that. I glanced at the clock again as I zipped my bag closed: 5:02. "Well, I'll definitely be caught in traffic," I thought, "but at least I won't be on the seven o'clock news."

# RESEARCH ON TRANS PEOPLE
# AND TRANS INCLUSION
# ON COLLEGE CAMPUSES

# EIGHT

# How I See Me, How You See Me
## Trans College Students Navigating Gender Outside the Binary

*Kasey Ashton*

TRANS COLLEGE STUDENTS are often an invisible minority on college campuses. This invisibility occurs for myriad reasons that are both systemic and personal. Colleges are built around and consistently reinforce a male/female binary through housing assignments, gender-specific bathrooms and locker rooms, institutional forms, and various other ways. To the extent that campuses provide trans-related programs and services, these activities are often based on the assumption that all trans students want to transition medically and socially from one gender extreme to another (male to female or female to male), ignoring students with nonbinary genders (Bilodeau 2007). As a result, trans students who are not seeking to transition or who want to transition socially but not medically (such as by changing their name and pronouns) receive little support.

At the same time, research focusing on trans college students is growing, but it largely concentrates on student perceptions of programmatic interventions, campus climate, and support services (Beemyn 2003; McKinney 2005; Miner 2009). The current study adds to the higher education literature by exploring how both binary and nonbinary trans college students self-author gender. The focus of the research was less on how college students experience campus climate and policies/procedures and more on the development of their gender identities. Because this study was primarily concerned with personal journeys, self-authorship theory was used to provide a unique perspective into how trans students construct, experience, and make meaning of gender. A deeper look into how gender is self-authored helps illuminate how gender privilege negatively affects students who do not fit easily within a male/female binary. Gender is not constructed nor understood within a vacuum; it is therefore essential to consider how personal cognition intersects with and is influenced by an internal sense of self and by relationships with others when exploring how trans college students understand gender.

## THEORETICAL FRAMEWORK

Marcia Baxter Magolda's theory of self-authorship (2009a, 2009b, 2010) served as a theoretical lens for this study. Self-authorship is the internal capacity to define one's own values, opinions, and beliefs and is a holistic perspective on development that includes epistemological, intrapersonal, and interpersonal dimensions (Baxter Magolda 2009a). Development in one dimension encourages growth in the other dimensions. Self-authorship is a cyclical journey that is informed and influenced not only by these intersecting dimensions but also by the personal and social contexts of an individual's daily life (Baxter Magolda 2009b; Boes, Baxter Magolda, and Buckley 2010). Self-authorship theory thus provides insights into how individuals deconstruct external gender messages to construct and redefine their gender identities.

Research has demonstrated that catalytic events, such as encountering racism, negative stereotypes, or harassment, can lead marginalized students to question what Baxter Magolda (2009b, 629) calls "external formulas"—social norms about "appropriate" gender roles and behaviors—prior to and after entering college (Abes, Jones, and McEwan 2007; Torres and Baxter Magolda 2004; Torres and Hernandez 2007). It follows, then, that trans college students may experience "ruptures [to] key structures," bringing gender issues to the fore and catalyzing change (Hines 2007, 55). While minoritized students may exhibit self-authored behavior upon entering college, they may fall back into external formulas for success to navigate college systems, which underscores the cyclical nature of self-authorship (Pizzolato 2004).

## METHODOLOGY

Narrative inquiry was used to explore the meaning-making process of gender identity. Stories provide a glimpse into how trans-identified students construct and understand their internal sense of self (Abes 2004). The process of telling one's story is empowering, especially for those whose voices have been largely silenced. Valentine (2008) noted that silence leaves room for stereotypes, discrimination, and fear, whereas storytelling has the power to imbue confidence and a sense of identity. Trans people have experienced the silencing and marginalization of their stories within both gender and LGBT research.

To delve sufficiently into participants' gender stories, two in-depth, in-person interviews were conducted with each participant. Between interviews, the participants were asked to reflect on their gender and bring to the second interview a visual or textual representation of how they perceive and understand their gender. The item could be anything they felt was an accurate reflection of their gender, including photographs, drawings, quotes, poems, or selections of prose. The second interview focused on the significance of the object to the participant. The personal items provided a unique look into how participants experience their gender, and their discussions of the items were analyzed as part of their overall narratives. Each participant's story was considered individually and as part of a larger story. The analysis focused on the content of a person's narrative (what the story communicates) and less on the structure (how the story was put together) (Riessman 2008).

## PARTICIPANT INTRODUCTIONS

Seven individuals were selected for the study: five current college students and two alums who had graduated within a year of the beginning of data collection. The participants self-identified as white/Caucasian ($n = 5$) or African American/Black ($n = 2$). The majority of the participants were nontraditional students. Because they had taken time off from school, transferred from a two- to a four-year institution, or changed majors, five of the interviewees were in their mid- to late twenties. Being older, these participants were often able to think critically about their lives and how their experiences have affected their gender. Four identified their gender as nonbinary (genderqueer or gender-fluid) and three as binary (male, trans man, or trans woman). Table 8.1 provides a brief overview of each participant's gender identity, pronouns, age, and race. The names are pseudonyms selected by the participants.

The study was conducted at a large, public research university considered to be one of the more trans-welcoming schools in the Southeast United States. The university includes "gender identity and expression" in its nondiscrimination policy, covers hormones for students who are transitioning under its student health insurance plan, and recently implemented a chosen name policy. The campus also has a professionally staffed LGBT center, which regularly sponsors trans-specific programming, and out trans students participate in these and other activities.

TABLE 8.1 Participants

| Name | Gender Identity | Pronouns | Age | Race |
|------|-----------------|----------|-----|------|
| Barry | Male | He/Him/His | Mid twenties (recent graduate) | White |
| Cee | Genderfluid | He/Him/His | Traditional age | African American |
| Jane | Queer | She/Her/Hers | Mid twenties | White |
| Leigh | Genderqueer | He/Him/His | Late twenties | African American |
| Mallory | Trans Woman | She/Her/Hers | Mid twenties | White |
| Mark | Trans Man | He/Him/His | Traditional age (recent graduate) | White |
| Page | Genderqueer | He/Him/His | Mid twenties | White |

## EMERGENT THEMES

Three overarching themes emerged from the data analysis: power in self-definition (how do I identify?), navigating gender roles (who am I?), and negotiating connections (what relationships do I want with others?). The themes weave together and influence each other as the participants self-author their gender.

## POWER IN SELF-DEFINITION

Individuals create a sense of self and identity and feel empowered by claiming specific labels for themselves. For many cis people, gender is not a matter of self-labeling; it simply "is." It is inherent and does not need to be examined or questioned. In contrast, the participants, whose gender identities challenge the binary and who question assumptions linked to biological sex, viewed gender as an identity to be explored, claimed, and expressed. What quickly became clear in their gender stories is that for them, gender could rarely be expressed in a one-word response, and their journeys were winding, sometimes circuitous, and intensely personal. Mallory, a white trans woman in her mid-twenties, described her gender journey as "being homesick for something you don't know. That kind of just longing and feeling that something's missing."

The way the participants understood and explained their genders was filtered through a lens of societal norms and expectations (Dragowski, Scharrón-del Río, and Sandigorsky 2011). Jane, a white, queer woman in her

mid-twenties, described notions of appropriate masculine and feminine behaviors as being so pervasive that "you can't really get away from it." Leigh, an
African American nontraditional student who identifies as genderqueer, acknowledged that for those who "cross those boundaries … there's all hell to pay."
Several participants cited the penalties imposed on those who do not adhere to
traditional gender roles or who step outside of a gender binary as the reason relatively few people do so. Mark, a recent graduate who is white and identifies as a
trans man, believed that most people are uncomfortable taking a deep look into
themselves because they find it scary to face aspects of themselves that are in conflict with dominant cultural norms and with how they want to see themselves.

Each of the participants grew up in a world where their gender was defined and limited by their families, peers, and larger societal expectations. As
they have gotten older and obtained the relative freedom offered by college,
they have taken the power of labeling and self-definition into their own hands
to create and strengthen their gender identities.

Queering the Label

For most participants, expressing and naming their gender identity was a mul-
tifaceted process. Barry, a white graduate in his mid-twenties, was the only participant who described his gender with a single word; he was male, and stated
that he was "male from the beginning." For the rest, expressing their gender
identity was more complicated. Leigh described himself as genderqueer, but
struggled to articulate how that particular label described his gender:

> I consider myself to be genderqueer … I was born male, but I feel like
> that's too strict or too confining. … Oftentimes I find myself wanting
> to … explore kind of female roles and typical female behavior, typical
> female things. My words are failing.

Cee, an African American student in his mid-twenties, also indicated that describing his gender to others was challenging because his identity did not fit
neatly into a single category. He explained, "Like for the most part I present as
male, but I don't think I necessarily identify as completely male … I mostly use
gender-fluid … it's not concrete and not necessarily male, not necessarily female."

The participants were also frustrated by the pressure to claim a label.
Jane used several terms to describe her gender, but preferred not to have to
pick a specific label. Although she sees herself as a woman, she feels a stronger
connection to other identities: "I would say like trans, queer, lesbian-type

person. . . . I feel like *queer* fits pretty well. It's kind of like a catch-all label for people who don't like labels, which is kind of like what I am."

As Mark transitioned, he struggled with pressure from friends to claim a label. Active within the LGBT center and the LGBT student organization on the campus, Mark found a strong and supportive group of friends who embraced his gender journey. However, members of this community were also the cause of stress and frustration at times because of their need to know Mark's gender label. He noted that he did not always have a label to share with them:

> I didn't identify as anything and that's really hard because it makes people uncomfortable and they don't know what to do with it. They really honest to God have no idea what to do with it. How do I identify? I don't identify. I don't. Because I was uncomfortable with the boxes. I didn't know where I wanted to be. I didn't know who I was and I was tired of people asking me to put a label on myself that I didn't understand.

Interestingly, the participants' refusal to self-label seemed to cause consternation for both LGBT and cis heterosexual individuals on campus. Mark's queer friends wanted to know how he identified, perhaps to see if he was similarly a member of the community. In contrast, he and other participants indicated that they were rarely asked about their gender identity or the pronouns they use by their cis heterosexual classmates. Instead, classmates would stare and whisper to each other if they could not readily identify someone's gender. Page, a white student in his mid-twenties who identifies as genderqueer, related how his appearance was very androgynous prior to taking hormones, and as a result people often did not know what gender label to use. But no one was willing to approach him. There was "just a lot of talking to each other about it and a lot of staring," which he found "awkward." When he began taking testosterone, the whispers stopped, as his male gender expression led others to assume he identified as male. But now that he is off hormones, he finds that the odd looks are back, "but still no one has specifically asked me [about my identity]."

Confusion about someone's gender, like other forms of confusion, is something that people typically find uncomfortable and seek to clear up as soon as possible. The collage that Cee created for this study, which included a big question mark with the word *confusion* below it, demonstrates that confusion does not need to be clarified or eliminated. He described the image as "*Confusion*, because my gender identity is a very confusing thing. Not that I mind. It's not a problem. It's just confusing to me, but it's a good kind of confusion. I just enjoy things not being straightforward and explainable."

Cee no longer lets a predefined gender label determine how he expresses his identity. When he first transitioned, he "tried to do the whole very binary like male-type things," but he realized that trying to conform to masculine stereotypes was not an accurate representation of his gender. Rather than suppress various aspects of his gender identity, he

> just kind of gave up on that and just realized people are gonna see me how they see me regardless really of what I do, so I was like, "I might as well do what I'm comfortable doing and present in a way that I'm comfortable presenting." I guess the more confidence I built in myself, the more I realize it's okay if I don't necessarily identify as 100 percent male. Like it's not a bad thing that I'm not super like binary identified.

In embracing gender confusion, Cee allows himself to accept his femininity and the fact that he spent the first eighteen years of his life as a woman. As a result, he is comfortable with both the person he used to be and the person he is becoming.

Whereas Cee has faced a struggle to reclaim his female past, Leigh seeks to escape from the societal expectation that he be male simply because he was assigned male at birth. For Leigh, his gender assignment is "not really a mandate on who I should be, but more so a template . . . to base my life around." He is "drawn to femininity" and feels that he has "a right to explore that and embrace that to whatever degree" he chooses. At the same time, he acknowledges that he is still at a questioning place in his gender journey and not ready to make lasting changes to his body.

In response to being asked to bring in a visual or textual representation of his gender, Leigh shared lyrics from the song "Reflections" from the Disney film *Mulan*: "When will my reflection show . . . who I am inside? Who is that girl I see staring back at me?" In explaining why he chose this representation, he said: "I resonate with that a lot because it's kind of like the same situation with me. It's from the point of a female trying to figure out her place and who she wants to be and how she can break gender roles and still kind of fit in."

Self-labeling is further complicated and confusing because language is constantly changing, as words come into or pass out of favor or take on new meanings. Labels, especially those related to gender, carry cultural and historical subtexts, which many of the participants took into consideration before adopting specific words to describe themselves. Mark shared that he grappled with the distinction between *transsexual* and *transgender* as he was coming out:

> One of the things I find really complicated—and this is probably partially because of when I came out—there's a shift between *transsexual* and *transgender* and more people are moving towards *transgender*, and also *transsexual* has some really strict boundaries around it that are troubling to me because . . . I don't fit neatly into a gender box. Because I mean especially when being trans was just starting to being a thing, *transsexual* was very strictly like, you . . . like unequivocally want to be the opposite . . . which is another thing that's problematic for me because I don't think that there are only two choices.

Mark struggled with the implied binary of a transsexual identity, the idea that to transition automatically meant switching from one gender extreme to the other. He found that he "feel[s] good being a masculine feminine person." While Cee embraced identity confusion, Mark was relieved to find a language that accurately reflected how he sees himself and leave confusion behind.

### Evolving Gender Identities

Just as the language around gender is fluid, so are the specific labels someone may choose for their gender, as identities often change over time to reflect lived experiences. These experiences are not always positive. For example, Page had dreamed of transitioning from female to male for years, but the reality was not what he expected, which forced him to reexamine his sense of self. He stated:

> I transitioned hormonally for a year from December of 2011 to December of 2012 and then decided it was not right for me. I didn't recognize myself in the mirror. I missed myself. I was very sad that I had to essentially kill the person that I was to [give] society the right presentation so they would give me the pronoun I wanted. It was a very sad process so I decided to end that.

Medically transitioning was something that Page had always wanted, but he found it "horribly disappointing to learn that I am not going to be the perfect whole guy." He mourns that he "missed a year of myself aging . . . I didn't see myself in the normal process of aging. But I do feel happy again when I look in the mirror." Although testosterone was not the "magic pill" he expected, the process helped him realize "that it's okay to be both genders, or neither gender, or a fluid gender ... I think all of that has brought me to the realization that I don't believe in gender."

The catalyst for changing/modifying identity labels is not always hardship or challenge. As life circumstances change, old identities may become cumbersome and ill-fitting. Mark, for example, initially referred to himself as transgender, but decided over time that this label did not adequately describe his identity. He explained:

> There was a time when saying the whole word *transgender* was important to me because my experience was so transgender, and I'm not [transgender] everywhere that I go now and it's not as big a part of my life. So it's almost like as it became less ... absorbing.... A part of my life kind of dropped off that—the transgender part—get rid of the gender part.... Now I'm just a trans man.

For others, physical transformation played a part in the development of their gender identities. Jane and Mallory acknowledged that their gender identities were not immediately reflected in their gender expressions, as they waited for their bodies to begin to change with hormones. Jane shared that her decision to transition was abrupt, and she immediately shifted from thinking of herself as a straight man to viewing herself as a lesbian woman. But she felt that she "couldn't advance mentally or emotionally" until her body began to resemble her internal sense of herself. Her physical transition occurred over the course of a year, as she began seeing a therapist, started hormones, and legally changed her name. A particularly significant and empowering moment for Jane happened the first time she looked into a mirror and "saw a girl instead of a guy."

Seeing herself in a mirror or in pictures has also been exciting and validating for Mallory because she is early in her transition and still envisions herself as male. Her physical transformation has bolstered her confidence in her gender identity and expression. At the time of our interviews, Mallory was planning to present as female in her classes in the next semester. Although physical transformations are not necessary for the development of gender identities, Jane's and Mallory's experiences illustrate that physical changes can help bridge potential gaps between a trans person's gender identity and their gender expression.

The participants experience and construct their gender in a culture that does not readily acknowledge gender identities outside of a binary and sets limits and expectations on appropriate gender behavior (Dragowski, Scharrón-del Río, and Sandigorsky 2011). Through self-labeling and defining for themselves what gender means, the participants are disengaging from the dominant cultural norms for "gender-being" and taking control of their identities, rather than allowing external formulas to define and restrict them to a binary (Regales 2008; Saltzburg and Davis 2011). Self-definition creates a foundation for them to tell their stories and understand themselves as individuals and as part of a larger social context. They have developed complex ways of knowing and are able to construct self-definitions based on their lived experiences and personal beliefs, instead of conforming to gender expectations (Baxter Magolda 2010).

## NAVIGATING GENDER ROLES

Self-authorship theory stresses that cognitive development does not happen in isolation but occurs in conjunction with the intrapersonal and interpersonal dimensions (Baxter Magolda 2009b, 2010). The intrapersonal dimension, where individuals ask questions such as "Who am I?" and "What do I value?" reveals the "influence of identity on epistemology" (Pizzolato 2007, 34). As the participants become less influenced by external expectations related to gender, they rely more on an internal foundation to determine their values and how they interpret their own gender (Baxter Magolda and King 2007; Kegan 1994).

### Gender Expectations and Stereotypes

All but one of the participants were raised and socialized as a gender with which they no longer identify, which meant that they struggled to navigate the gender expectations associated with how they identify today. At times they felt caught between the gender assumptions of others and honoring their own experiences. Dealing with stereotypes related to their gender identity was particularly troubling for several of the trans male participants who can pass. They were regularly expected by other, presumably cis men to join them in chauvinistic behavior, and cis women often questioned or feared their actions, seeing them as a potential threat to women and children. Mark explained:

> I feel like because of all my socialization as a woman and this is how women should behave, I really couldn't fill the role of a man because it requires a very different concept of how you're going to interact with the world in it. It almost requires resocialization or reconfiguring of what it means to be a man.

The participants' lack of "gender-appropriate" knowledge arose in multiple settings. Shopping for "women's" clothing posed challenges for Mallory, partly because "at that point I still didn't really know clothes in general 'cause I've never been shopping for myself before, period, much less for clothes I knew nothing about." Being raised as male, she did not receive the feminine socialization that girls tend to absorb from female family members, friends, peers, and celebrities and from media sources like movies, TV shows, fashion magazines, and targeted advertising. To help illustrate the unique situations that trans women can face while shopping, Mallory shared a blog post titled "The Young Man's Guide to Wearing and Shopping for Women's Clothing for the First Time" (Plett 2011) as part of the representation of her gender. In a comedic manner, the guide highlights how to navigate women's clothing options and dressing rooms.

By comparison, Cee, raised female, lacked knowledge about the aspects of Black culture "that [are] central to a lot of identity and becoming male." In the Black community, barber shops are "heavily masculine," and Cee finds them intimidating, explaining, "I still don't know how to be like in such a heavily male environment." Even though he had been going to barber shops for years prior to transitioning, the way he interacts with the space now, as a Black man, is different from when he was perceived as female. He commented, "I hate going to the barber shop so much . . .'cause they expect me to know what I want." Had he been raised as male, he would not only have learned how to navigate this space via regular haircuts but also more about what it means to be a man in Black culture. Cee sees it as "having to learn how to navigate two communities [Black and male] at one time and it's really interesting and kind of difficult."

Not all of the participants felt out of the knowledge loop. Barry, who has always felt male, could not understand being dressed like a girl as a child. He remembered being in kindergarten and wondering, "Mom, why did you put me in a freaking dress? . . . Like I'm a boy." He said, "I don't think I had a really big roller coaster trying to figure out who I am. It was just always male." Transitioning to a male identity and presentation was a natural fit for Barry; it was trying to "be a girl" before transitioning that was far more bewildering. Labeled a tomboy growing up, he wore traditionally male clothing in high school, and others seemed to accept it. Barry recalled, "It was kind of something I always did, so everyone saw it as me."

Along with expectations from cis individuals about common gender knowledge, several of the participants encountered expectations related to behavior, specifically the ways cis men often talk about women. Being read and accepted as male by other men was an important moment for Page, Cee, and Mark. At the same time, they were raised and socialized as women, and deciding how to respond to sexist behavior from other men was challenging.

Page had greatly looked forward to hormone therapy so that he would be treated as "one of the guys," but he often found the reality of that experience to be uncomfortable. He stated that "the way the guys started talking to me was very different. They started . . . degrading women to me in conversations and they were talking about body parts that I still have." Now that Page is no longer taking testosterone, his appearance has begun to change, and he is no longer included in so-called guy talk.

Cee, who describes himself as a "Southern gentleman," has also struggled with how to deal with sexism. On one hand, he is uncomfortable "trash talking" about women; on the other, he is concerned that refusing to do so could bring his masculinity into question. He explained:

> I work with a lot of guys and . . . like we always talk about girls, which is a thing I've always done. But they have this habit of doing it in a way . . . I don't like it. It's very stereotypically masculine. I'm like, "I don't want to join in with you," but . . . it's going to be seen as really weird if I don't join in because these are things that most guys do.

As Cee continues to grow in confidence in his masculinity, he is taking steps to match his behavior with his internal values system. He noted that in "changing these habits, I'm just like further pushing myself away from society's view of what masculinity means and kind of really making it my own."

### Challenging Gender Expectations

In response to being asked to bring in a visual or textual representation of his gender, Barry created a collage that reflects different aspects of his personality, not just his gender. Through the clippings he picked, he defined for himself what it means to be a man. For example, Barry included in his collage the quote, "He's a tough guy," because it reminded him of the documentary *Tough Guise: Violence, Media and the Crisis in Masculinity* (dir. Sut Jhally 1999), which makes the argument that violence and misogyny are directly linked to how society defines masculinity. He resonated with the concepts in the movie, saying, "You can either be a tough guy in the most respectful way of maybe even just respecting women and doing things that make yourself proud versus being a tough guy like, 'oh, I'm going to puff out my chest and be an ass about it' sort of thing."

For Jane, transitioning has meant the freedom to abandon behaviors associated with her biological sex. She feels that she does not "really act a lot differently than I did before I transitioned … the way that other people interact with me has changed." She has found a more authentic sense of self by letting go of the "masculine" behaviors she felt pressured to engage in but which never felt natural.

As a woman, Jane feels that she has more freedom to exhibit both traditionally masculine and feminine traits without others questioning her gender, "compared to if you were like a man who is gay or who acts effeminate." She is not interested in acting like a "stereotypical woman," but instead finds inspiration and role models in female athletes, which was reflected in the visual representation of her gender. Jane brought in a Gatorade commercial featuring Abby Wambach, a professional soccer player and two-time Olympic gold medalist. The commercial's nontraditional depiction of a female athlete appealed to Jane. Rather than focus on Wambach's femininity, the ad celebrates her athleticism, showing her sweaty, focused, and determined to win. What really stood out to Jane was a particular image, "where they actually zoom in on her face and you can see like the little hairs." The fact that the commercial does not downplay Wambach's "imperfections" resonated with Jane because she sees herself as being imperfect, too. By acknowledging herself as a woman, Jane has been able to embrace both her strengths and faults.

Clothing is another way some participants challenge gender norms. Mark, in particular, likes to "queer" his clothing, mixing masculine and feminine elements. He chose the outfit that he wore to the second interview, which included a kilt and red and yellow leggings, as the visual representation of his gender, and described his daily thought process about what to wear this way:

Well, if the thing that's going to be the most comfortable for me today is my kilt, how is that going to influence the people that are looking at me and the messages that I'm sending out about my gender? I explore the ramifications of a lot of it, especially the dressing choices that I make, the clothes that I put on my body, because they really change the way people see or interact with me…. And then some days I'm like, "Fuck it. I'm going to go out in the world and I'm going to screw with people's heads because that's fun, too." Like my outfit today is my "screw with people's heads" outfit.

Mark noted that he does not always look to push the boundaries of so-called gender-appropriate clothing. At work, he presents as male and chooses outfits that fit a male gender expression. But when he is out with his queer-identified friends, he often selects clothes that contain both masculine and feminine elements because he knows that his friends "will respect my gender, no matter how I present to them."

In contrast to other participants, Leigh has not socially or medically transitioned, because he is afraid of how others in the Black community will react if he presents in a way that is not considered typically male. "One of my biggest hang-ups right now towards just like fully embracing [my gender] identity," he indicated, "is how it will affect my standing in the African American [community]." At least for now, his fears outweigh his desire to be himself. But he is hopeful that the more he becomes comfortable with his identity, the more he will be able to express his gender in ways that feel authentic.

Experiencing Emotions

Because of the different societal limits placed on how men and women express their feelings, Jane and Cee found that they had more freedom to display certain emotions after transitioning. Jane explained that she feels "like I'm allowed to do more things because I feel like women have a little bit more leeway in how they want to act." She believes that people are generally more accepting of her displays of positive emotions, like love and sympathy, because she is seen as female.

In contrast, Cee finds that it is now more culturally acceptable for him to show negative emotions, particularly anger, than when he was perceived as female. Within Black communities, Black women are supposed "to be strong, you're supposed to hold everything down," Cee stated. "You're that anchor ... in a Black family." These expectations lead to suppressing emotion and putting up a brave front to keep the family together in the face of adversity. Now that he is seen as a Black man, Cee indicated he has had the opposite experience:

> While that expectation to be strong is still there, it's not as prevalent anymore. Like I'm allowed to be angry and be loud and be mad and express the fact that I'm upset and it's fine. Like it's not seen as normal, but it's not as big of a deal as trying to express those things as a Black woman.

Cee's role reversal illustrates the intersections of race and gender and how gender expectations function differently in different cultures.

Page's experiences around emotions are perhaps the most poignant and powerful. When asked to share a representation of his gender, Page brought in a glass jar containing a crumpled tissue. The tissue holds the tears that Page cried the night he came out to his parents about his gender identity. He explained:

[I] gave my parents my coming out video. I had waited years and years for this moment. And so I was crying and she [Page's significant other] was holding me and she was wiping my tears away with that tissue and she saved it on the windowsill . . . and several months later she put it in a glass jar . . . the tears on this tissue are significant because my whole life I felt like I couldn't be a real guy because I always had a really sensitive heart and I've always cried fairly easily. . . . I'm always very compassionate; I'm very empathetic. But I saw the guys around me, and especially my father, were not like that. I thought that in order to be a real guy you had to not cry. So I've kind of always hated that part of me all my life, that I was very sensitive enough to cry over . . . something like that.

When he came out to his parents, Page was six months into hormone therapy and taking the highest dosage of testosterone that he could. During that time, he found that his reaction to emotional situations had dramatically changed; where he once would have cried, he now reacted with anger. Being on testosterone made him feel "that I didn't need to or want to cry because I thought I was in control of everything." However, as he continued to move through his transition, he began to lose his need for control and "started being able to cry again." In the process of relearning how to access and display emotions besides anger, he had to challenge expectations of appropriate masculine behavior. The tissue preserved in the jar is a reminder that "it is okay to cry. No one has a right to tell [someone] that they can't cry or that they can't be emotional."

The participants who have transitioned now generally find that they have much more freedom to explore the range of their feelings and are better able to challenge gender stereotypes related to the display of emotions. In navigating gender norms and expectations, they have developed a greater sense of what gender means to them and how they want to express their gender.

NEGOTIATING CONNECTIONS

As individuals gain a better understanding of how they see and define themselves, there is often a shift in how they relate to others (Baxter Magolda 2009a; Kegan 1994; King 2010). In this case, the students' relationships matured from valuing other people over themselves to "negotiat[ing] multiple perspectives, and engag[ing] in genuinely mutual relationships" (Baxter Magolda and King 2007, 492). Although all of the participants discussed the importance of relationships with others, the ways they approached these relationships varied depending on where they were in their gender journeys.

### Changes in Family Relationships

Coming out as trans had a direct and immediate impact on relationships, especially with parents. The majority of the participants had at least one parent who did not react well to the news. For Barry, Cee, Mark, and Page, who already had tumultuous relationships with their parents, coming out caused a further deterioration in familial ties. Barry described his relationship with his mother as controlling and stunted. Throughout high school, he and his mother clashed over the clothes he wore, the activities he was involved in, and his nonfeminine behavior. Barry related, "We just never agreed on anything. She signed me up for prom dress catalogs. I'm like, 'Mom, I'm not going to prom. I'm not doing this, that's not me.'" As he has gotten older, their relationship has worsened, with his mother making negative comments about his appearance and calling him a "dyke." Barry realized that he did not have to tolerate her abusive behavior and made the decision to end all contact with her.

Cee also remembered fighting with his mother over his appearance throughout most of his school years because he was not "girly enough." When he came out as lesbian in high school, his mother was hostile, appalled that her child was "different." Cee shared that he was very depressed in high school and often felt suicidal, at least in part because of the lack of support from his mother. Their relationship is still contentious, and Cee has been taking steps to limit contact. He loves his mother because she is family, but he admits that he does not like her. While coming out to her as trans was less traumatic than coming out as lesbian, the experience had not been pleasant. His mother still engages in controlling behavior and is overly concerned about what other people will think about Cee's actions and appearance. Although he knows that cutting his mother out of his life may hurt, he has reached a point where he is unwilling to share his life with people who are not accepting of all aspects of himself.

Page has already limited contact with his parents, who refuse to call him by his chosen name or use the correct pronouns. He is letting them work through their emotions and "have their own journey." Mark made a similar decision after a significant fight with his parents. His mother wants him to change how he behaves at home, including how he dresses, so as not to make others in the family uncomfortable. Mark is frustrated by his mother's actions, feeling that she values other people's comfort over his own. He understands that his transition is not what his parents expected for his life and that "to go from having a sister to a brother or from a daughter to a son is really difficult." Still, he is not willing to take on their "angst and all of their discomfort."

Mallory's mother has been less than supportive, but she has found an ally in her stepmother, and her father is slowly becoming more understanding. A particularly significant and empowering moment in Mallory's gender journey happened over an Easter holiday. She went home for the school break and discovered that her stepmother had purchased some new blouses and a pretty bra for her. She says that knowing her stepmother "was willing to get stuff for me really meant a lot so I called her into my room and started crying for like two hours." During that same trip, Mallory was treated to a new haircut by her father, which was a powerful experience because it felt like a major step in gaining her father's acceptance. Familial approval of her gender identity has also been empowering for Jane. She noted that her mom "is awesome about it. My grandparents are really cool about it. . . . My dad has not been great about it, but recently he's shown more . . . acceptance of it."

Leigh has not come out to his parents yet because he wants to have a better understanding of his gender identity first. He worries that right now they would dismiss his gender identity as a phase, "to be like, 'Oh well, he's questioning, but he's not fixated or settled on certain things so maybe there's still hope.' I want to say, 'This is really my [gender].'" Leigh is hopeful that when he does come out, his parents will support him.

### Changes in Intimate Relationships

All but two of the participants were in intimate relationships. Many acknowledged that it can be difficult to transition while in a relationship(s), but it can also bring partners closer together. Barry began his transition while dating his now fiancé. When he told her that he felt male and wanted to transition, she was understanding and supportive. Her own sexual identity was not called into question because she does not "necessarily consider herself gay or straight . . . she just loves the person." Mark's partner is a trans woman who transitioned prior to their meeting. She encouraged him to explore his gender identity and have his gender expression fit his internal image of himself. She was also a main source of support when his parents reacted negatively to his coming out.

In contrast to Barry's and Mark's experiences, transitioning was hard on Page's relationship with his partner. Although his partner was fully in support of Page's need to transition, she struggled to reconcile her lesbian identity with dating a man, especially as he began to physically change and became more masculine in appearance. She was newly out as lesbian when they began dating and was still exploring her identity, which made the situation even more challenging. Page had appeared boyish prior to beginning hormones, but his partner was attracted to his femaleness, which was no longer possible when he began taking testosterone. Page recalled:

> She was not attracted to me any more almost immediately. She had to go through all the stuff over again that she didn't get to go through before we met, which is, "I'm a lesbian. I'm attracted to women. I love the female part of you, but I'm not allowed to address it or recognize it because I feel like I'm disrespecting you. I'm a lesbian with a man. I don't know how to reconcile that. I'm not attracted to you, but I love you."

They broke up for a time, before deciding that their feelings for one another outweighed gender and sexual identities. Page is now off hormones, and his physical appearance has become less masculine as the testosterone in his system has decreased. He still presents as male and uses "he/him" pronouns but is more comfortable identifying as genderqueer. At the time of data collection, both were working on how to honor each other's needs.

Cee describes himself as polyamorous (open to having more than one romantic relationship at a time, with the knowledge and consent of all partners). He noted that being poly and trans makes dating difficult because it can be challenging to find individuals who are supportive of both identities. He was excited about his current relationship because his significant other is also trans and poly-identified.

Mallory did not date much pretransition but now finds herself interested in potentially pursuing a relationship. In her mid-twenties and older than the majority of her peers on campus, she has looked to online dating as a way to meet other people. While she likes the ability to interact with a variety of people in a relatively safe environment, she noted that online dating as a trans person can be difficult because many cis people will "immediately reject you." When she discloses her gender identity to someone online, "most of the time they just stop talking to me. I always tell someone before I meet them, for safety reasons if nothing else." Mallory identifies as pansexual (a person who is attracted to others regardless of their gender identity or biological sex); she is more concerned about a person's personality than "their bits." She feels that being honest about herself and how she identifies is a must but wishes that others could be less focused on her biology and more on who she is as a person.

### Campus Experiences

The participants had varied perspectives on the climate for trans people at their university overall and in its different colleges and disciplines. Jane believes the location of the university in the Southeast plays a large part in how her gender is perceived there because "it's obviously going to have some more conservative perspectives on it than if we're in the Northeast or California or something. I would say it's very traditional." Page feels that the campus may be "a little more accept[ing], that there's room for androgyny . . . [and] growing acceptance . . . for people who live in the gray area." Despite the relatively more supportive atmosphere, he regularly encounters pockets of animosity and hate. He and other participants identified campus bathrooms in particular as hostile places. "I go into, you know the men's bathroom, even just today, and see gay slurs and 'faggot' written on the wall," Page said, "so I know that there's a large community here that does not accept it." Overall, he believes that the climate at the university is "very mixed, but it's getting better."

Five of the study participants are stealth (do not publicly disclose their trans identity) at the university, and they indicated that they feel relatively comfortable navigating campus spaces. Mallory still presents as male in classes, but has recently begun living openly as female in the off-campus apartment that she shares with three other students. She plans to begin presenting as female in classes next semester, when she will be further along in her transition and not have to be as concerned with her safety on campus. She commented, "I don't think anyone's going to like murder me horribly for what I am. But like comfortable—sometimes yeah, sometimes no. I mean I'm still a little iffy on going out as a girl by myself."

### Interactions with Faculty

Ironically, the participants who did not want to be out in the classroom had to out themselves to their professors each semester to ensure that the instructors used the correct name on the first day of class because at the time of data collection, the university did not enable students to have their chosen name on course rosters. The five participants who approached their professors indicated that it was a stressful experience, as there was no guarantee that the faculty members would honor such a request. But they found that most professors were supportive. Cee stated:

> That was one thing I was really, really anxious about, was having your teacher be like, "No, I'm not going to and you cannot make me." I've been prepared like ever since I started transitioning for that to happen and it hasn't yet ... and that just helped me realize that even though this campus as a whole is very conservative ... that there are certain people who understand how important it is ... to have affirmation [about] your identities.

Jane's experiences were similar, but she did encounter a professor who did not fully understand the importance of using her chosen (and now legal) name in class: "she was like, 'Oh if I mess up, just correct me.'" Feeling that it would be a constant struggle, Jane chose to drop the course. Page also had a professor who was ignorant about the desire of many trans people not to have their gender identities disclosed, as the faculty member said to her, "You can just tell me what your preferred name is when I call your name in class." Being outed in class is potentially dangerous for trans students because other students might harass or discriminate against them. The start of each semester was thus an anxious time for many of the participants, as they were forced to place their safety and sense of comfort in the hands of strangers.

Many of the participants also faced obstacles in online classroom environments, which were a component of some of their courses. Because these sites automatically used their birth name instead of their chosen name, the participants were essentially outed to their classmates. Page has dropped classes with a heavy online component because he does not feel safe in these environments. Being outed online would negate the work he has done with his professors to ensure that his correct name and pronouns are used in the actual classroom.

### Interactions with Peers

The participants' connections on campus were varied. Mallory, Jane, Barry, Leigh, and Page mentioned their age and living off campus as barriers to connecting with classmates and peers. Mallory, who is in her mid-twenties, explained that most of her friends live elsewhere or have already graduated and have jobs. Going to campus only when she has classes, Mallory does not have many interactions with other students. As transfer students, Page and Leigh have not felt a strong connection to the university. Page has not been involved in any campus organizations, which further limits the contact he has with other students. Leigh is trying to make connections by being active in the campus LGBT student organization and is considering reaching out to the college's minority support program as another avenue for meeting peers.

Although they do not have significant connections on campus, Jane and Barry have strong support networks in the local community. Jane plays soccer in several different adult leagues, both single-sex and co-ed, and works off campus. Many of her friends are other soccer players or coworkers. She has found her workplace to be very supportive and encouraging, noting that she is not the first person to have transitioned there. Barry, who recently graduated, has a wide network of friends, some from work or through his partner and more from the intramural athletic teams he played on when he was in school. Like him, these friends have graduated, and many now have jobs in the area.

Interactions with Campus LGBT and Trans Communities

Of all the participants, Mark and Cee described having the strongest connections to the university, especially to its LGBT and trans communities. Mark became involved with the campus LGBT center and LGBT student group early in his first semester and maintained these relationships until he graduated. Through this involvement, he developed a support network and a friend group that he described as being like family. Among these friends was another trans man who served as a role model:

> [He was] a really important person in my transition because he did a lot of the things that you think of when you think of transition like name change and hormones and like living full-time. He did a lot of those things before me and I got to watch him do it, [and] I knew . . . that this was a direction that I should be taking.

Cee has found the campus LGBT center to be incredibly helpful as well. The director helped him in obtaining a single room in a residence hall to avoid having a female roommate (the university does not enable students to change their gender marker on campus records and does not provide gender-inclusive housing). As a result of his campus involvement, Cee described his friend base as consisting almost completely of LGBT people, which he feels is "really nice, but makes for a semi-jaded life that you forget straight people exist."

For Mark and Cee, being trans is a critical aspect of their identities, and being a part of the trans community at the university was very important to them. Both found role models and support networks through the college's trans community and felt welcomed and embraced by the campus LGBT center. Leigh indicated that he too benefited from the LGBT center and the LGBT student organization on campus. He has regularly attended the student group's meetings as a way to meet new people and learn more about the LGBT community. He noted that through hearing a genderqueer person speak as part of a trans panel discussion sponsored by the center, he became more comfortable identifying as genderqueer himself.

Not all of the participants have looked to or sought a home in the LGBT or trans community on campus, particularly Barry. At least for now, Barry is not out as trans to most of his friends because he wants to develop relationships based on similar interests, without his gender identity being a factor. He said, "I want to meet people on my own terms . . . I want to be seen as [Barry] . . . So it's male first and then we go from there." Barry and Jane have occasionally attended programs offered by a local trans support group, but neither feels a strong connection to the group or its members. In contrast to Mark and Cee, they do not see being trans as a primary identity.

Self-authorship theory recognizes that relationships play a large part in becoming a self-authored individual (Baxter Magolda 2008, 2009a, 2009b, 2010). All but one of the study participants are in the process of transitioning, which has necessitated renegotiating their relationships with almost everyone in their lives. As the participants have gained a better sense of themselves, they have become better able to redefine and change interactions with family, significant others, and peers.

CONCLUSION

Much of the higher education research on trans college students assumes a common trans experience, and the recommendations for practice tend to take a one-size-fits-all approach (Alexander 2009; Beemyn 2003, 2005; Bilodeau 2007; Carter 2000). This study demonstrates that even among a small group of trans people at one university, how they experience and understand their gender identities are varied, complex, and ever-changing as they age and as many transition.

Each participant had to interpret and redefine for themselves what masculinity and femininity mean outside of social norms and deconstruct external messages of what it means to be a "real" man or woman. For many, this required challenging gender expectations and the assumption of a gender binary.

## WORKS CITED

Abes, Elisa S. 2004. "The Dynamics of Multiple Dimensions of Identity for Lesbian College Students." PhD diss., Ohio State University.

Abes, Elisa S., Susan R. Jones, and Marylu K. McEwen. 2007. "Reconceptualizing the Model of Multiple Dimensions of Identity: The Role of Meaning-Making Capacity in the Construction of Multiple Identities." *Journal of College Student Development* 48: 1–22.

Alexander, Jordan E. 2009. "Implications for Student Affairs of Negative Campus Climates for Transgender Students." *Journal of Student Affairs* 18: 55–61.

Baxter Magolda, Marcia B. 2008. "Three Elements of Self-Authorship." *Journal of College Student Development* 49: 269–84.

———. 2009a. "The Activity of Meaning Making: A Holistic Perspective on College Student Development." *Journal of College Student Development* 50: 621–39.

———. 2009b. *Authoring Your Life: Developing an Internal Voice to Navigate Life's Challenges.* Sterling, VA: Stylus.

———. 2010. "The Interweaving of Epistemological, Intrapersonal, and Interpersonal Development in the Evolution of Self-Authorship." In *Development and Assessment of Self-Authorship: Exploring the Concept across Cultures,* edited by Marcia B. Baxter Magolda, Elizabeth G. Creamer, and Peggy S. Meszaros, 25–43. Sterling, VA: Stylus.

Baxter Magolda, Marcia B., and Patricia M. King. 2007. "Interview Strategies for Assessing Self-Authorship: Constructing Conversations to Assess Meaning Making." *Journal of College Student Development* 48: 491–508.

Beemyn, Brett [Genny]. 2003. "Serving the Needs of Transgender College Students." *Journal of Gay and Lesbian Issues in Education* 1: 33–50.

———. 2005. "Trans on Campus: Measuring and Improving the Climate for Transgender Students." *On Campus with Women* 34 (3). http://archive.aacu.org/ocww/volume34_3/feature.cfm?section=2.

Bilodeau, Brent. 2007. "Genderism: Transgender Students, Binary Systems and Higher Education." PhD diss., Michigan State University.

Boes, Lisa M., Marcia B. Baxter Magolda, and Jennifer A. Buckley. 2010. "Foundational Assumptions and Constructive-Developmental Theory: Self-Authorship Narratives." In *Development and Assessment of Self-Authorship: Exploring the Concept across Cultures*, edited by Marcia B. Baxter Magolda, Elizabeth G. Creamer, and Peggy S. Meszaros, 3–24. Sterling, VA: Stylus.

Carter, Kelly A. 2000. "Transgenderism and College Students: Issues of Gender Identity and Its Role on Our Campuses." In *Toward Acceptance: Sexual Orientation Issues on Campus*, edited by Vernon A. Wall and Nancy J. Evans, 261–82. Lanham, MD: University Press of America.

Dragowski, Eliza A., María R. Scharrón-del Río, and Amy L. Sandigorsky. 2011. "Childhood Gender Identity . . . Disorder? Developmental, Cultural, and Diagnostic Concerns." *Journal of Counseling and Development* 89: 360–66.

Hines, Sally. 2007. *Transforming Gender: Transgender Practices of Identity, Intimacy and Care*. Bristol: Policy Press.

Jhally, Sut, dir. 1999. *Tough Guise: Violence, Media, and the Crisis in Masculinity*. Media Education Foundation.

Kegan, Robert. 1995. *In Over Our Heads: The Mental Demands of Modern Life*. Cambridge, MA: Harvard University Press.

King, Patricia M. 2010. "The Role of the Cognitive Dimension of Self-Authorship: An Equal Partner or the Strong Partner?" In *Development and Assessment of Self-Authorship: Exploring the Concept across Cultures*, edited by Marcia B. Baxter Magolda, Elizabeth G. Creamer, and Peggy S. Meszaros, 167–85. Sterling, VA: Stylus.

McKinney, Jeffrey S. 2005. "On the Margins: A Study of the Experiences of Transgender College Students." *Journal of Gay and Lesbian Issues in Education* 3: 63–76.

Miner, Jack. 2009. "How to Make Your Office and Institution More Transgender Friendly." *College and University* 84: 69–72, 74.

Pizzolato, Jane Elizabeth. 2004. "Coping with Conflict: Self-Authorship, Coping, and Adaptation to College in First-Year, High-Risk Students." *Journal of College Student Development* 45: 425–42.

———. 2007. "Assessing Self-Authorship." In *Self-Authorship: Advancing Students' Intellectual Growth: New Directions for Teaching and Learning*, edited by Peggy S. Meszaros, 31–42. San Francisco: Jossey-Bass.

Plett, Casey. 2011. "The Young Man's Guide to Wearing and Shopping for Women's Clothes for the First Time." *McSweeney's Internet Tendency*, January 31. https://www.mcsweeneys.net/articles/column-7-the-young-mans-guide-to-wearing-and-shopping-for-womens-clothes-for-the-first-time.

Regales, Jackie. 2008. "My Identity Is Fluid as Fuck: Transgender Zine Writers Constructing Themselves." In *Queer Youth Cultures*, edited by Susan Driver, 87–104. Albany: SUNY Press.

Riessman, Catherine Kohler. 2008. *Narrative Methods for the Human Sciences*. Thousand Oaks, CA: Sage.

Saltzburg, Susan, and Tamara S. Davis. 2010. "Co-Authoring Gender-Queer Youth Identities: Discursive Tellings and Retellings." *Journal of Ethnic and Cultural Diversity in Social Work* 19: 87–108.

Torres, Vasti, and Marcia B. Baxter Magolda. 2004. "Reconstructing Latino Identity: The Influence of Cognitive Development on the Ethnic Identity Process of Latino Students." *Journal of College Student Development* 45: 333–47.

Torres, Vasti, and Ebelia Hernandez. 2007. "The Influence of Ethnic Identity on Self-Authorship: A Longitudinal Study of Latino/a College Students." *Journal of College Student Development* 48: 558–73.

Valentine, James. 2008. "Narrative Acts: Telling Tales of Life and Love with the Wrong Gender." *Forum: Qualitative Social Research* 9(2): art. 49. http://www.qualitative-research.net/index.php/fqs/article/view/412/895.

# NINE

# Trans College Students' Experiences
## Institutional Discrimination and Empowered Responses

*Tre Wentling*

IT HAS BEEN MORE THAN FIFTEEN YEARS since the National Gay and Lesbian Task Force Policy Institute published Susan Rankin's (2003) groundbreaking report, *Campus Climate for Gay, Lesbian, Bisexual, and Transgender People: A National Perspective*. The report found that the out student, staff, and faculty respondents experienced high rates of harassment, discrimination, and violence. At the time, it was the largest study of LGBT people on college campuses, and it was the first multiple-college study to intentionally include trans people; of the 1,669 respondents, 68 (4 percent) identified as transgender (Rankin 2003).

Much of the literature on trans college students published since the *Campus Climate* report has similarly focused on their experiences of discrimination, harassment, and marginalization (McKinney 2005; Seelman 2016; Vaccaro 2012). This established, albeit limited, research illustrates the multilayered, institutional obstacles that trans undergraduate and graduate students often encounter in sex-segregated spaces (e.g., campus housing, bathrooms, and locker rooms), support services, counseling and health care services, and records and documentation (Beemyn et al. 2005; Beemyn and Brauer 2015; McKinney 2005; Singh, Meng, and Hansen 2013). These studies indicate that most colleges lack resources and supports for trans students and fail to educate cis students about gender identity, contributing to unsafe and hostile campus climates (Beemyn and Rankin 2011; Johnston 2016).

There are more out trans students on college campuses today than ever before (Beemyn and Rankin 2011; Bilodeau 2009), yet there is little research on their experiences beyond how they are treated by institutions (Catalano 2015; Dugan, Kusel, and Simounet 2012; Johnston 2016). To add to this scholarship, this chapter considers how trans students' experiences vary across campus spaces and how they respond to instances of institutional and personal discrimination. Contrary to the common representation of trans students as victimized and defeated, I found that many are resilient and effective advocates for themselves.

## DATA AND METHODS

The stories that fill this chapter are from a larger, mixed-methods research project that explores trans citizenship. People who were at least eighteen years old and identified as trans in any way were invited to complete an online survey (September 2011–December 2011) and participate in a follow-up interview (October 2011–June 2012). The survey was completed by 882 people, of whom 50 were randomly selected for a semi-structured, follow-up interview (26 college students and 24 nonstudents). I used snowball sampling (Cromwell 1999; Rubin 2003; Schilt and Connell 2007) to recruit survey participants by sending email invitations to personal and professional networks, 113 US-based community organizations, support groups, and the 175 institutional members of the Consortium of Higher Education LGBT Resource Professionals. Interviews were completed by telephone and online communication methods (e.g., Skype) and were audio recorded with participants' written consent.

The survey design included many opportunities for the respondents to describe their experiences. Participants were asked what compelled them to sign up for an interview, along with questions concerning their level of outness, campus involvement, the general climate for trans people at their college, and how chosen name, pronouns, and other gendered aspects of identity are addressed at their institution.

Using open, axial, and selective coding (Creswell 2007), I read through the interview transcripts and survey comments. I flagged responses in which participants referenced experiences that related to higher education and then made note of the different ways participants spoke about their gender-embodied identity management, interactions with institutional actors and student peers, and involvement in campus life. Inspired by Johnston's (2016) use of narrative analysis in his research with trans college students, I paid specific attention to the participants' use of "I" statements in their stories. Focusing on these first-person narratives honors participants' voices and provides insights into how they see themselves, their relationship to campus spaces, and their respective social relations on campus (Johnston 2016). Two major themes emerged from the participants' written comments and interviews. The first concerns intentional and unintentional changes to students' identification data and the uneven recognition of their identities across campus spaces and within social interactions. The second relates to their empowered responses to avoid or minimize misrecognition, which not only bettered their own experiences but also improved their campus climates.

This chapter is based on the twenty-six interviews with students and qualitative data from the online surveys. At the time of our interviews, twenty of the students were undergraduates and six were graduate students, and they attended a wide range of institutions, from small, private liberal arts colleges to large, public research universities. Two participants self-identified their ethnic/racial heritage as Black, two as Asian, and the rest as white. The students were eighteen to thirty-four years old, and all identified as trans, with fifteen specifically identifying as "man," six as "genderqueer," four as "woman," and one person as "part-time as man and woman." Recognizing such differences in gender identity labels is critical to understanding how trans students navigate within the binary gender systems of higher education (Beemyn and Rankin 2011; Bilodeau 2005, 2009; Nicolazzo, Marine, and Galarte 2015).

NAMING AND MISNAMING ON COLLEGE CAMPUSES

Naming practices are often based on sex assigned at birth (Bohm and Mason 2010; Elias 1991; Finch 2008), and because sex category assignment is presumed to be the same as gender (Lucal 2008; West and Zimmerman 1987, 2009), an individual's name is typically expected to reflect their gender identity. A mismatch between one's first name and one's gender identity can be especially stressful for trans people (Factor and Rothblum 2008). Many trans people alter their names, formally and informally, but not all who want to legally change their names are in a position to do so. Students in particular are often not able to change their names officially because of their age, the cost involved, or unfamiliarity with the process (Beemyn and Brauer 2015). This fact makes it imperative that colleges enable students to have a chosen name on all campus records that are not considered legal documents.

Institutional Records and Student Information Systems

Colleges use the information on admissions applications to create campus records for students. Once students matriculate, elements of their personal data are distributed across campus (e.g., to academic departments, residence life offices, health centers), so that this information resides in multiple software systems controlled by different offices and departments (Beemyn and Brauer 2015). As a result, trans students who want to have a chosen name, instead of their legal first name, on campus records face a tremendous challenge making this change on all of their records, even at the colleges that provide an option to do so. A twenty-two-year-old Black trans male student related this experience:

> When I first attended school, I began with my name given to me at birth. When I signed up to create an account in order to have computer and internet access within the school, they linked an account to my ID number. So when I returned with my new name, I had to use the same account that had my previous name on it, despite having had my name changed on all other school records. One of my instructors noticed the mismatch and she asked if I had a name change, then told me she already put in a request to have my name changed in the system.

The instructor recognized his name mismatch on the class roster, inquired about his name change, and used her institutional position to ensure that the appropriate name appeared. This example illustrates the inability of different software systems to "talk" to each other and the time it can take for changes to occur through administrative processes.

Other students encountered resistance from faculty members when they sought to have their chosen name respected. A white, thirty-four-year-old genderqueer law school student shared this experience:

> A professor changed the name I had listed on a class list, which everyone in the school would see, to a more "formal" version of my chosen masculine name, which I had never claimed or used. The message I received from that incident was that being myself was not allowed. I could request others view me as male, but I had to be a male "all the way" and in a manner that was acceptable to the school and the profession I was to enter. It seems trivial, but the incident rattled me quite a bit.

He felt disciplined by the faculty member, both as a student in the class and as a future member of the profession. His experience supports previous research that connects the campus climate perceived by LGBT graduate students to their understanding of what it means to be a lawyer, social worker, or other professional (Vaccaro 2012).

Another white, genderqueer student, who went by a nickname derived from his legal name, had some of his social work professors correct his name on papers "as if [he] had made a mistake." He felt insulted whenever this happened. Similar to the experiences of the law student, his professors believed they knew better than him about his gender.

Certain disciplines (e.g., humanities and social sciences) and professional degree programs (e.g., social work) are presumed to be more open and affirming, including of trans people (Linley and Nguyen 2015; Pryor 2015). As a result, trans students can be confused and disappointed if they enroll in a program they expect to be welcoming and find that it is not so, like the department described by the graduate social work student. When faculty members disregard or dismiss trans graduate students' gender identities, especially in professional disciplines, they further transphobia among cis students and contribute to these areas of study being less than inclusive spaces for trans students.

Although a growing number of colleges are using software systems that allows students to include a "chosen" or "preferred" name on campus records[1] (Beemyn and Brauer 2015; Beemyn and Rankin 2011), the implementation of this process can be inconsistent. The experiences of a white, twenty-two-year-old trans male student illustrate how campus records do not always reflect one's chosen name. He stated:

> My housing records my sophomore year of undergrad were changed without my request. This was because I went in and requested a single on a co-ed floor specifically (that housing complex typically has single-sex floors). I didn't even find out that this was a change in that entire record system until another year later when I applied for a job and went to go get a nametag, requested my preferred name, and had someone ask, "Is that not your legal name? Do we need to change our files?" Similarly, I changed my school email and such, and at one point I discovered my legal name email had been deleted, so I had to request to be put back on to my major listserv so I would get advising emails.

Although he had updated his campus records to reflect his chosen name, the failure of different software systems to talk to each other meant that his department continued to use his former, "dead" email address.

Some colleges have a chosen name policy, but do not adequately describe how it works or where the changes will appear. A white, twenty-three-year-old trans man discovered this fact when he became employed at his school before he legally changed his name. He explained:

> When I became employed with my school before my name change, I filled out a form which included specifying my "preferred name." I hadn't expected that would be for anything other than their own records, but it ended up being changed in several of the most-used computer systems at school (notably email and the enrollment website). I'd thought it was a mistake (most records at my school can only be changed via court order) . . . I wish they'd made the policy clearer.

This student had to visit multiple offices to address the situation, which meant he had to out himself to different staff members and hope they would be helpful and supportive. For trans students to avoid these kind of obstacles, colleges need to have a clearly defined chosen name policy and provide ongoing training to administrative staff about the policy.

### Social Interactions across Campus Spaces

Campus spaces and the social relations cultivated within them are never static. Academic disciplines and administrative and student affairs departments are unique and operate within localized contexts (Vaccaro 2012). Trans students must navigate multiple campus spaces, carefully negotiate social interactions within each, and manage these relationships over the duration of their degree program(s). Consider the stories shared by a senior white trans male student about his interactions with different faculty members and his supervisor. In one case, he related an experience that happened during his sophomore year after he missed a class session. When he was not there, the professor teaching the course asked the other students, "What's [student's] real name again? I need to send her an email." The misgendering and attempt at misnaming got back to the trans student, who confronted the professor:

> I was like, "Well my real name is [name], um, it's really all—that's really the only name that you need to know and you have my email address on your class roster. So, I don't think you really needed to bring it up to the class." She [the professor] was like, "I'm sorry maybe I shouldn't have done that." I was like, "Okay but can we at least agree like you shouldn't bring it up in class again?" She agreed, but I think it was like a week or two later she basically did the same thing, but

this time with me in class! She was like, "You know, I need to send you something can you tell me your name again?" I was like "[name]." She's like, "No, no your real name. Like the one that the class or that the school has you as."

Such negative interactions in the classroom, in front of student peers, can be especially devastating and lead to alienation (Linley et al. 2016; Vaccaro 2012). The student met with the department chair to discuss the repeated incidents of misnaming and misgendering and to ask that the faculty member be reminded about the university's nondiscrimination policy. According to the student, the department chair chose not to speak with the faculty member, based on a belief that the student was the only trans person on campus and that the university did not protect the rights of trans people. In fact, the university does have a nondiscrimination policy that is inclusive of gender identity/expression, because the student, as president of the campus LGBT student group, had worked with university officials to add this language. This example demonstrates the need for faculty to be required to attend periodic training sessions on campus policies that support trans students.

He shared another experience that took place during his junior year, this time with a faculty member from a different department and resulting in a fundamentally different outcome. Indeed, this example illustrates the importance of faculty offering both formal support through classroom practices and informal support through personal advising (Linley et al. 2016). He stated:

I was talking to her [professor] one-on-one about wanting to do a research project about LGBT people coming out. She was like, "While we're on the topic, you know, I've always meant to ask you . . . I use your name because it's on the roster and I use female pronouns because I'm just assuming, but I was just wondering, are you by any chance transgender?" I was like, "Yes!" (*laughs*) And the next day in class, [she used] male pronouns [for me], and the second I told her, "Oh, you know, I actually prefer the name [name]," she immediately switched.

After that, she was involved in my life [in] a positive way. She would ask how my family was taking things, but not in a curious way, more like, "Are you doing okay?" way. My family actually didn't deal with it okay and she—this is probably breaking boundaries with teacher-student, but she—was like, "Do you need a place to stay, are

you okay, are you going to be able to buy groceries this month?" ...
She was always willing to talk about anything, which was really cool,
and she helped me with my name change because I didn't understand
the paperwork.

These two faculty members took antithetical approaches to working with
a trans student. The faculty member from his sophomore year prioritized
name and sex assigned at birth and the institutional processes that regulate
student data, whereas the faculty member from his junior year honored his
gender identity, regardless of the name and gender marker on his campus records. He experienced the first faculty member and her department chair as
barriers to implementing trans-supportive policies and developing a campus
climate that is inclusive of trans students, while in the second faculty member
he found a compassionate, understanding person interested in his well-being
and overall development.

A final experience that he shared concerned his campus supervisor. He
works for the university's security department, and he told me that the director of residence life had outed him to the director of security, who also
happened to be his supervisor. Fortunately, she was supportive and sought to
understand his identity:

> She [his supervisor] was like "Will you tell me more about what this
> transitioning thing is because I heard this word and I just want to
> know" ... She tries a lot to use the right name and the right pronoun
> and everything. Every once in a while she slips up with pronouns.
> She has not called me my birth name since I came out to her, which is
> amazing. But every time she slips [on pronouns], she just looks at me
> and she's like, "I don't know why I do it. I don't. I look at you, I see male
> and know you're male ... it's just hard sometimes." [I told her,] "At least
> you're trying and you recognize it."

Being outed can lead to the person feeling embarrassed, uncomfortable, or offended at best and encountering discrimination, harassment, or violence at
worst. In this case, though, his supervisor was genuinely interested in learning
more about trans people, and he graciously took on the role of educator.
Although these stories represent one student's experiences, they exemplify
how trans students' experiences can vary in different campus spaces with different institutional actors and can change over the course of students' undergraduate or graduate careers (Pryor 2015).

PROACTIVE RESPONSES TO AVOID OR MINIMIZE DISCRIMINATION

Anticipatory Management

Trans students commonly experience misgendering and misnaming, but how they respond to these acts of discrimination vary. In some cases, they anticipate the situation and take steps to prevent possible negative outcomes, or at least to manage them. For example, a white, eighteen-year-old trans man shared this experience about his first-year housing assignment:

> Before the gender-neutral housing that will be coming this next year, you could email them and talk about special housing requests for LGBT students. Since I was—I think I'm the only trans freshman—they didn't have anybody to put me in a room with. So, it would have either been, be assigned a random roommate . . . of the same sex or whatever, or live in a single room, and single rooms are really expensive! So, I think I was gonna end up with living with a female roommate no matter, you know, how it turned out.

The student was proactive in contacting the residence life staff. However, recognizing that they were unlikely to be able to help and that he would be assigned a female roommate, he waited until he was given a roommate and then contacted that student. He explained: "Well, my roommate I told before we even moved in together 'cause I wanted to give her the option of not rooming with me if she didn't feel comfortable. But she's really cool and has other trans friends. So it wasn't a problem." While the university's residence life staff should have done more to arrange appropriate and comfortable housing for him, the trans male student's actions exemplify the empowered agency that I heard in many students stories. He addressed his needs to the best of his abilities in a binary gender system.

Another way that trans students demonstrate agency is through changing their gender expression to avoid negative consequences. A white, nineteen-year-old trans man who works in residence life at his college used this strategy when he hosted students' parents during parents' weekend. He stated:

> Especially with meeting my proctees' parents on parents' weekend, I definitely try to be as normal of a girl as I could because I just knew that I wasn't going to be read as male by these parents. And I didn't want to have the conversation with them at all. I don't really know the

exact ways that I played that up, but I definitely tried. One of the parents asked me what the origin of my [masculine-sounding] name was and I kind of answered that I didn't really know. (*laughs*) I didn't really have an answer for them, but then realized that in Hebrew [name] kind of sounds like [name] . . . So I was like, "In Hebrew it means paradise." [I was] compromising what my name actually means to me for them because they recognized it as non-normative.

His decision to manipulate how he presents himself to others demonstrates the need for trans people to try to be stealth at times, as well as the importance of temporal and spatial dynamics. Recognizing parental and institutional expectations, he briefly compromised both the gendered meaning of his name and his gender identity. Such embodied gender performance (Butler 2004; West and Zimmerman 1987, 2009), especially in the context of recognition by state agents, is what Kelly (2012, 28) calls "strategic normativity" and what Currah and Mulqueen (2011, 573) describe as trans people being "forced to contort their gendered selves to appear as conventionally gendered as possible." Although parents are not quite agents of the state, they wield power over students who are working for the college, expecting these students to serve their interests.

This same student shared another example of anticipatory management when he discussed his interview for the proctor position:

Now I know the residential life office and they're great and understanding of me and my gender, but when I was applying to be a proctor, they asked me if there was anything about myself that I think would scare my proctees away from connecting from me. And I kind of freaked out in the middle of that question and said, "Oh yeah, because I'm queer they might, you know, be afraid of me if they're homophobic or if they just don't understand that queer people exist" . . . But I wasn't comfortable enough, even within my own school, that I've had great experiences with, to say like, "Yeah, I'm trans and that might be really hard for my proctees to understand," because it was an interview and it felt more serious. We are adults, and most adults in my life haven't really gotten that, so I've been more reluctant to talk to adults.

He anticipated that the interviewers would be more accepting of a student who identified as queer rather than trans and strategically did not disclose his gender identity. This response was based on his experiences to that point, which were that older adults rarely understood or respected him as a trans man. However, as indicated by his subsequent praise of the residence life staff and their support, the student developed a more nuanced perspective on the attitudes of other adults through working in that position.

A fourth example of anticipatory management was shared by a white, twenty-two-year-old trans female student, who was a student ambassador at her college. In this job, one of her responsibilities was to provide campus tours to potential students and their families. However, at the time of our interview, she had yet to lead a tour. When asked why, she explained:

> I've had to miss work a couple of times because I was having issues regarding my trans problem, per se. I've went and spoken with my boss, saying that I have a medical psychological problem that's been keeping me from working those days. For the most part, they've been understanding, and they haven't tried to pry and ask for proof or what it was or anything. From what I know, I know that they have also had other students in the past that worked at my job with my or with this issue. . . .. I know that that individual was a female-to-male transgender and not a male-to-female transgender. So I wonder how much of a difference that will have . . . I don't think it will be either my superiors or my colleagues that will have an issue with it. I'm thinking it will be more the people I encounter. They will have problems with it.

Like the previous participant, she found her supervisor and coworkers to be supportive of her identity but feared how others would react. She was unwilling to risk interacting with people who did not know her because she anticipated that anyone with whom she did not have an established social relationship would be hostile toward her. Implicit in her response was that, as a trans woman, she would be read as trans and rejected by others—a situation she thought would likely be different for a trans male student employee. Indeed, this difference is reflected in the participants' experiences: the trans male student who worked for residence life mainly had to hide the gendered meaning of his name, but as a trans woman, she felt she had to hide herself.

Part of the difference in the experiences of trans women and trans men relates to the effects of hormones. In transitioning, trans men will typically find it easier to be stealth, if they want to, than will trans women, whose builds and voices will not change and who will also have to undergo a process of facial hair removal. As a result, trans women are often more visible in society and more likely to be targets of discrimination, harassment, and violence.

The mistreatment of trans women is also rooted in what Julia Serano (2007) called "trans-misogyny," the intersection of the hatred of trans people and the hatred of women. Trans women are singled out for attack because, despite being assigned male at birth and inheriting male privilege, they give up their superior position in society to be female. At the same time, trans men benefit from this system because maleness and masculinity are culturally valued. The intersections with other forms of oppression, such as racism, classism, and ableism, also effect trans people's social status (Coston and Kimmel 2017; de Vries 2012; Dozier 2005; Schilt 2006), which is reflected, for example, in poor trans women of color being the overwhelming majority of trans people killed each year in the United States (Boylan 2015). Thus trans students' experiences have to be considered within the larger sociocultural power dynamics that are manifested through both personal interactions and institutional practices.

## Contributions to Campus Communities

As Beemyn and colleagues (2005, 50) appreciated some time ago, "transgender students offer unique contributions to the campus community." Such contributions include raising trans visibility, educating other students about gender identity, and advocating for trans-inclusive institutional policies (Johnston 2016; Pusch 2005). A number of the students I interviewed had been or were currently leaders of the LGBTQ student organization on their campus. For example, a twenty-two year-old, Chinese American trans woman, who attends a college in West Virginia, became active in the school's LGBTQ student group soon after arriving on campus. Recognizing the lack of trans awareness among group members, she started a trans committee to educate other students, as well as faculty and staff. This initiative was especially important because, as she noted, "we're in the Bible Belt . . . in a very conservative area." While she says that faculty members may not have become more accepting as a result, they seem to be "more accommodating."

Another participant, a twenty-one-year-old, Korean and white genderqueer student, similarly realized that the LGBTQ student group at hir Midwestern college was failing to speak to the experiences and needs of trans students. When sie was elected president of the organization in hir junior year, the student advocated for more trans-focused programming, which led to the group sponsoring a presentation by genderqueer speakers. Sie said that the event was well received, which "was really validating and fulfilling" for hir.

These students created space and visibility for trans people and educational programming about trans experiences because they felt invisible in their LGBTQ groups and on their campuses more generally. Instead of feeling isolated and segregated from the student organizations and their colleges (Linley and Nguyen 2015), they sought to make them more inclusive. Their stories support the need for members of campus groups, even those that serve minoritized students, to be educated about trans identities and experiences (Pusch 2005).

Many trans students serve in campus leadership roles and speak on educational panels during their college careers (Pryor 2015; Renn and Bilodeau 2005). A white, thirty-four-year-old trans male student I interviewed was among the participants to have done both as an undergraduate. Now a graduate student, his activism today revolves around his scholarship on trans people. Because there are not faculty members at his college who conduct research in trans studies, he said that "a lot of students come to me for help and advice." He serves as a resource for them and for his campus more broadly.

CONCLUDING THOUGHTS

Colleges and universities are complex, dynamic entities that are shaped by a variety of factors, including institutional actors and the political and cultural contexts within and outside of the campus. Students' experiences can thus vary greatly at different colleges, as well as within a college, as different academic disciplines, workplaces, residence halls, and other campus spaces have their own cultures. Any in-depth examination of the lives of trans students must therefore consider institutional factors, in addition to accountability structures (e.g., campus nondiscrimination policies, state laws) and the dominant cultural ideologies that reinforce a gender binary (Butler 2004; Connell 2010; Currah and Mulqueen 2011; Namaste 2000).

Trans students' campus experiences are complicated by the binary gender structures of higher education institutions (Bilodeau 2005, 2009). As participants in this chapter discussed, their formal relationship to a college is established through an application process that often relies on their birth-assigned name, providing no opportunity to indicate a chosen name. Even where they can indicate the name they go by, it is not always recognized in different social interactions across various campus spaces, such as in classrooms, residence halls, and workplaces. Trans students must therefore find ways to navigate these spaces on their own, which often means acting in anticipatory ways to attempt to prevent or minimize misrecognition.

Some trans students feel empowered to try to change the culture of some campus spaces, such as LGBTQ student groups, when they notice a lack of trans inclusion. In some cases, trans students participate in speaker panels and training sessions, but they can grow tired of constantly having to educate others (Pusch 2005). Moreover, changes to student-led spaces can be short-lived, as the cis students who have become more trans-inclusive graduate.

The climate for trans students in different campus spaces depends on the institutional actors within that space. Whereas some faculty and staff members are informed about and sensitive to the needs of trans students, many are not, which means that trans students are often misrecognized and discriminated against in campus departments, organizations, and policies. Without a much greater concern for trans students' well-being and their overall campus experience, institutional spaces and processes will never consistently affirm and support them. Colleges need to require ongoing trans awareness trainings for all faculty and staff members, rather than offering one-time, optional workshops, as many institutions do now (Dugan, Kusel, and Simounet 2012; Garvey and Rankin 2015; Pryor 2015). In addition, colleges should intentionally recruit a diverse range of trans faculty and staff (Seelman 2014) and ensure that they are supported by their departments and offices (Vaccaro 2012).

Institutional and personal commitments to trans inclusion can mitigate negative campus spaces and foster the expansion of positive ones. I believe that the investment in resources, including hiring trans-identified institutional actors and requiring ongoing trans educational workshops for all staff and faculty, will positively affect the climate for trans students across all campus spaces in higher education institutions.

## NOTES

1.  See both Beemyn and Brauer (2015) and Wentling (2016) for a discussion on the problematic use of *preferred*.

## WORKS CITED

Beemyn, Genny, and Dot Brauer. 2015. "Trans-Inclusive College Records: Meeting the Needs of an Increasingly Diverse U.S. Student Population." *TSQ: Transgender Studies Quarterly* 2: 478–87.
Beemyn, Genny, and Susan Rankin. 2011. *The Lives of Transgender People*. New York: Columbia University Press.

Beemyn, Brett [Genny], Billy Curtis, Masen Davis, and Nancy Jean Tubbs. 2005. "Transgender Issues on College Campuses." *New Directions for Student Services* 111: 49–60.

Bilodeau, Brent. 2005. "Beyond the Gender Binary: A Case Study for Two Transgender Students at a Midwestern Research University." *Journal of Gay and Lesbian Issues in Education* 3: 29–44.

———. 2009. *Genderism: Transgender Students, Binary Systems and Higher Education.* Saarbrücken, Germany: VDM.

Bohm, Nicholas, and Stephen Mason. 2010. "Identity and Its Verification." *Computer Law and Security Review* 26: 43–51.

Boylan, Jennifer Finney. 2015. "Trans Death, White Privilege." *New York Times*, August 21. http://www.nytimes.com/2015/08/22/opinion/trans-deaths-white-privilege.html.

Butler, Judith. 2004. *Undoing Gender.* New York: Routledge.

Catalano, Chase. 2015. " 'Trans Enough?' The Pressures Trans Men Negotiate in Higher Education." *TSQ: Transgender Studies Quarterly* 2: 411–30.

Connell, Catherine. 2010. "Doing, Undoing or Redoing Gender? Learning from the Workplace Experiences of Transpeople." *Gender and Society* 24: 31–55.

Coston, Bethany M., and Michael Kimmel. 2017. "Seeing Privilege Where It Isn't: Marginalized Masculinities and the Intersectionality of Privilege." In *Sex, Gender, Sexuality: The New Basics*, edited by Abby L. Ferber, Kimberly Holcomb, and Tre Wentling, 21–29. New York: Oxford University Press.

Creswell, John. 2007. *Qualitative Inquiry and Research Design: Choosing among Five Approaches.* Thousand Oaks, CA: Sage.

Cromwell, Jason. 1999. *Transmen and FTMs: Identities, Bodies, Genders and Sexualities.* Chicago: University of Illinois Press.

Currah, Paisley, and Tara Mulqueen. 2011. "Securitizing Gender: Identity, Biometrics, and Transgender Bodies at the Airport." *Social Research* 78: 557–82.

de Vries, Kylan Mattias. 2012. "Intersectional Identities and Conceptions of the Self: The Experience of Transgender People." *Symbolic Interactions* 35: 49–67.

Dozier, Raine. 2005. "Beards, Breasts, and Bodies: Doing Sex in a Gendered World." *Gender and Society* 19: 297–316.

Dugan, John P., Michelle L. Kusel, and Dawn M. Simounet. 2012. "Transgender College Students: An Exploratory Study of Perceptions, Engagement, and Educational Outcomes." *Journal of College Student Development* 53: 719–36.

Elias, Norbert. 1991. *The Society of Individuals*. New York: Oxford University Press.

Factor, Rhonda, and Esther Rothblum. 2008. "Exploring Gender Identity and Community among Three Groups of Transgender Individuals in the United States: MTFs, FTMs, and Genderqueers." *Health Sociology Review* 17: 241–59.

Finch, Janet. 2008. "Naming Names: Kinship, Individuality and Personal Names." *Sociology* 42: 709–25.

Garvey, Jason C., and Susan R. Rankin. 2015. "Making the Grade? Classroom Climate for LGBTQ Student across Gender Conformity." *Journal of Student Affairs Research and Practice* 52: 190–203.

Johnston, Matthew S. 2016. " 'Until that Magical Day . . . No Campus Is Safe': Reflections on How Transgender Students Experience Gender and Stigma on Campus." *Reflective Practice* 17: 143–58.

Kelly, Reese C. 2012. "Bodies That Matter: Trans Identity Management." PhD diss., State University of New York at Albany.

Linley, Jodi L., and David J. Nguyen. 2015. "LGBTQ Experiences in Curricular Contexts." *New Directions for Student Services* 152: 41–53.

Linley, Jodi L., David J. Nguyen, G. Blue Brazelton, Brianna Becker, Kristen Renn, and Michael Woodford. 2016. "Faculty as Sources of Support for LGBTQ College Students." *College Teaching* 64: 55–63.

Lucal, Betsy. 2008. "Building Boxes and Policing Boundaries: (De)Constructing Intersexuality, Transgender, and Bisexuality." *Sociology Compass* 2: 519–36.

McKinney, Jeffrey S. 2005. "On the Margins: A Study of the Experiences of Transgender College Students." *Journal of Gay and Lesbian Issues in Education* 3: 63–76.

Namaste, Viviane K. 2000. *Invisible Lives: The Erasure of Transsexual and Transgendered People*. Chicago: University of Chicago Press.

Nicolazzo, Z, Susan B. Marine, and Francisco J. Galarte. 2015. "Introduction." *TSQ: Transgender Studies Quarterly* 2: 367–75.

Pryor, Jonathan T. 2015. "Out in the Classroom: Transgender Student Experiences at a Large Public University." *Journal of College Student Development* 56: 440–55.

Pusch, Rob S. 2005. "Objects of Curiosity: Transgender College Students' Perceptions of the Reactions of Others." *Journal of Gay and Lesbian Issues in Education* 3: 45–61.

Rankin, Susan R. 2003. *Campus Climate for Gay, Lesbian, Bisexual, and Transgender People: A National Perspective*. Washington, DC: National Gay and Lesbian Task Force.

Renn, Kristen A., and Brent L. Bilodeau. 2005. "Leadership Identity
    Development among Lesbian, Gay, Bisexual, and Transgender Student
    Leaders." *NASPA Journal* 42: 342–67.

Rubin, Henry. 2003. *Self-Made Men: Identity and Embodiment among
    Transsexual Men*. Nashville, TN: Vanderbilt University Press.

Schilt, Kristen. 2006. "Just One of the Guys?: How Transmen Make Gender
    Visible in the Workplace." *Gender and Society* 20: 465–90.

Schilt, Kristen, and Catherine Connell. 2007. "Do Gender Transitions Make
    Gender Trouble?" *Gender, Work, and Organization* 14: 596–618.

Seelman, Kristie L. 2014. "Recommendations of Transgender Students, Staff,
    and Faculty in the USA for Improving College Campuses." *Gender and
    Education* 26: 618–35.

———. 2016. "Transgender Adults' Access to College Bathrooms and Housing
    and the Relationship to Suicidality." *Journal of Homosexuality* 63: 1378–99.

Serano, Julia. 2007. *Whipping Girl: A Transsexual Woman on Sexism and the
    Scapegoating of Femininity*. Berkeley, CA: Seal Press.

Singh, Anneliese A., Sarah Meng, and Anthony Hansen. 2013. " 'It's
    Already Hard Enough Being a Student': Developing Affirming College
    Environments for Trans Youth." *Journal of LGBT Youth* 10: 208–23.

Vaccaro, Annemarie. 2012. "Campus Microclimates for LGBT Faculty, Staff,
    and Students: An Exploration of the Intersections of Social Identity and
    Campus Roles." *Journal of Student Affairs Research and Practice* 49:
    429–46.

Wentling, Tre. 2016. "Critical Pedagogy: Disrupting Classroom Hegemony."
    In *Teaching Gender and Sex in Contemporary America*, edited by
    Kristin Haltinner and Ryanne Pilgeram, 229–38. Switzerland: Springer
    International.

West, Candace, and Don H. Zimmerman. 1987. "Doing Gender." *Gender and
    Society* 1: 125–51.

———. 2009. "Accounting for Doing Gender." *Gender and Society* 23: 112–22.

TEN

# Higher Educational Experiences of Trans Binary and Nonbinary Graduate Students

*Abbie E. Goldberg*

TRANS AND GENDER-NONCONFORMING (TGNC or trans for short[1]) college students have been the focus of little empirical research (e.g., Bilodeau 2005; Dugan, Kusel, and Simounet 2012; Garvey and Rankin 2015; Pusch 2005; Rankin and Beemyn 2012), and even less work has focused on the experiences of TGNC graduate students (McKinney 2005). Furthermore, the little work that exists has mainly addressed the experiences of trans students who claim binary trans identifications (i.e., trans women and trans men). There is evidence that an increasing number of young adults under the trans umbrella endorse nonbinary gender identities—that is, they do not identify exclusively with maleness or femaleness and may identify as both genders, a third gender, or outside the gender binary (e.g., as genderless; Bilodeau 2005). Thus research on the experiences of trans binary and nonbinary students in higher education, particularly those in graduate school (McKinney 2005), is greatly needed.

This study uses data from ninety-one graduate students who responded to a survey focusing on TGNC students' experiences in higher education. Students who asserted nonbinary gender identities (e.g., genderqueer) were explicitly encouraged to participate in the call for participants. The primary questions this study seeks to answer are as follows. (1) To what extent and in what ways do TGNC graduate students experience misgendering by faculty and other students? (2) To what extent and in what ways do trans binary students versus trans nonbinary students encounter different challenges in relation to misgendering? (3) How and in what ways do TGNC students expect their gender identities to shape their career goals and possibilities?

## REVIEW OF LITERATURE

### TGNC Youth and College Students

Trans high school students often face victimization on the basis of their gender identity and expression, as well as their sexual orientation (Greytak, Kosciw, and Diaz 2009; Kosciw et al. 2014). A large-scale survey of more than 7,000 LGBT middle and high school students in the United States, which included more than 1,800 trans students, found that more than 42 percent of the trans participants had been prevented from using their affirmed name (i.e., the name they used for themselves; Kosciw et al. 2014). Furthermore, trans students, compared with cis LGB students, generally "faced the most hostile school climates" (85). For example, more than 73 percent of the trans binary students and more than half of the trans nonbinary students reported verbal harassment related to their gender expression, and more than 32 percent of the trans binary students and more than 21 percent of the trans nonbinary students reported physical harassment related to their gender expression (Kosciw et al. 2014). Such victimization has implications for educational outcomes in that trans students are much more likely to indicate missing school due to feeling unsafe and to indicate having lower grade point averages and lower educational aspirations (Greytak, Kosciw, and Diaz 2009; Kosciw et al. 2014). Importantly, the presence of institutional supports (e.g., gay-straight alliances, antibullying policies that explicitly include gender identity and sexual orientation, supportive school staff) can buffer the negative effects of victimization on educational outcomes (Kosciw et al. 2013) and increase the likelihood that LGBT students pursue higher education (Kosciw et al. 2014).

TGNC students may experience a more trans-affirming climate in college, compared with high school, given that they presumably have some choice in where they attend college—although this choice is shaped by cultural, social class, geographic, and other factors. As Beemyn (2003) and others have noted, college is often the first opportunity that many students have to question, explore, and sometimes actively resist their assigned gender. Young adulthood is a time of identity exploration in general (Arnett and Tanner 2006), and colleges are often open to and may provide resources for such introspection (e.g., via LGBTQ offices and groups; Garvey and Rankin 2015). However, students who are specifically examining their gender identity may encounter a more heightened level of ignorance and stigma than those who consider other aspects of their identities (Beemyn 2016).

Research indicates that trans college students report greater exposure to harassment and discrimination on campuses and a lower sense of belonging in comparison to cis students (Dugan, Kusel, and Simounet 2012; Garvey and Rankin 2015; Rankin and Beemyn 2012). For example, a study of sixty-eight trans-identified students, faculty, and staff from fourteen colleges found that 41 percent of the respondents had experienced on-campus harassment (Rankin 2003). Derogatory remarks were the most common form of harassment (89 percent); other types included verbal harassment or threats (48 percent) and pressure to be silent (38 percent). Similarly, a study by Dugan, Kusel, and Simounet (2012) compared the experiences of ninety-one trans-identified students with matched samples of cis LGB and heterosexual students and found that trans students described more frequent encounters with harassment and discrimination and a lower sense of belonging within the college community.

Within the classroom, interactions with faculty and peers have the potential to be uncomfortable and stressful, if not outright threatening, for trans students, especially for graduate students, as they tend to have closer relationships with faculty, attend smaller classes where they are more visible, and have personal and academic lives that are more strongly tied to their classwork and interactions with faculty and other students (Tompkins et al. 2016). In particular, misgendering in classes by faculty and other students can be profoundly distressing. Pusch (2005), who interviewed trans male and trans female college students, found that the classroom was a particularly salient site of potential misgendering, observing that trans students often felt vulnerable in classes when, for example, rosters did not reflect their chosen names. To circumvent discomfort, trans students sometimes avoided coming out in classes, thus masking their identities (Bilodeau 2009) and rendering themselves invisible. Pryor (2015) studied five trans students (four undergraduates and one graduate student), two of whom identified as trans men, two as trans women, and one as genderqueer, and found that the students experienced a great deal of anxiety about revealing their chosen name and pronouns.

Students who do not assert a binary gender identity or whose physical presentation is not clearly gendered male or female may encounter unique challenges (Rankin and Beemyn 2012). In his study, Pusch (2005) observed that the participants who identified themselves as pretransition and who were living part-time as their self-identified gender described more negative reactions by others, which reinforced their sense of being different. In contrast, the participants who were living full-time in their self-identified gender described a greater sense of normalcy in their lives. Thus, although this study did not aim to explore the experiences of nonbinary students, the findings hint at the distress that trans students may experience when others do not "read" them as unambiguously male/female.

### Graduate Students: Unique Experiences and Needs

Graduate students are uniquely dependent on faculty members, particularly their thesis/dissertation advisers and mentors, for various personal and professional resources, including formal and informal networking opportunities, research/job opportunities, and letters of recommendation (Thomas, Willis, and Davis 2007). Faculty mentors play a major role in graduate students' training, program completion, research collaborations, career advancement, and job placement (Noy and Reay 2012; Trask et al. 2009). In addition to academic and professional support, faculty mentors provide emotional support to graduate students, which can considerably enhance their quality of life and well-being (Malik and Malik 2015). Indeed, relationships with faculty and other students significantly affect graduate students' program satisfaction and life satisfaction (Tompkins et al. 2016). Yet importantly, minoritized students (e.g., students of color, LGBTQ students) are vulnerable to inadequate and ineffective mentoring, insensitive supervision, and isolation (Fletcher et al. 2015; Girves, Zepeda, and Gwathmey 2005).

Despite their susceptibility to cis-normative beliefs within classroom settings and inadequate mentoring by supervisors and other faculty (Bilodeau 2009), the experiences of graduate students who identify as TGNC have rarely been studied. In one of the only studies that included both trans undergraduate students ($n = 50$) and trans graduate students ($n = 25$), McKinney (2005) found that none of the students considered faculty and staff to be trans-supportive, with some noting that professors frequently made hostile or ignorant comments about trans people in class. Graduate students were particularly likely to describe insensitive remarks made by faculty and staff members; although some tried to educate professors and staff, they generally felt that such efforts were useless. The graduate students also reported a lack of support elsewhere on campus. Few were aware of a trans-specific group at their college, and many did not want to join LGBT student groups, which consisted mainly of undergraduates. Those who did become involved in an LGBT organization often felt marginalized because of their trans identity. Whereas all knew cis LGB graduate students, they typically did not know other trans graduate students.

## Inclusion of Nonbinary Gender Identities

Studies of trans college students have historically overlooked the experiences of nonbinary students—that is, those whose gender identities challenge the assumption there are only two genders and that they are "opposites" (Beemyn 2003, 2016). However, with more and more nonbinary trans students coming out today, there is growing awareness that individuals with nonbinary gender identities (i.e., genderqueer, gender-fluid, agender) are a part of the broader category of transgender (Burdge 2007). Moreover, the rise of postmodern conceptions of gender is encouraging the recognition of fluidity in gender identities and gender roles, which arguably benefits trans students (Dugan, Kusel, and Simounet 2012).

Nonbinary students seemingly encounter unique challenges, but their experiences have not been the subject of much formal investigation. In general, trans students face pressure to "mask" their identities on college campuses, which tend to be fairly cis-normative settings (Baker and Boland 2011; Bilodeau 2009). Yet trans students who actively seek to express their gender identities must also navigate pressures to conform to stereotypical gender norms, such as in terms of appearance and dress (Chang, Singh, and Rossman 2017). These pressures may affect students who espouse binary and nonbinary identities differently. Namely, students with trans binary identities may experience pressure to present as hypermasculine or hyperfeminine to be effectively "read" as male or female and thus avoid questioning. Students with trans nonbinary identities, by definition, do not fit into the binary gender system and are confronted with the ongoing challenge of presenting themselves in a way that is consonant with their gender identity but does not draw unwanted scrutiny from others (Bilodeau 2009). As a result, the experience of misgendering is likely different for trans binary and nonbinary students. Although both may not be recognized as their true gender and may face confusion, humiliation, and harassment, nonbinary students may be vulnerable to particular scrutiny in that they are not seeking to conform to or be recognized as either gender extreme and thus can be seen as more fundamentally challenging cisnormativity (Oswald et al. 2016).

## Theoretical Framework

This study draws from microaggression frameworks. Much theoretical and empirical work on microaggressions has focused on racial microaggressions (Sue 2010; Sue et al. 2007), but recently, such work has been extended to specifically address the experiences of LGBT people (Nadal, Rivera, and Corpus 2010; Nordmarken 2014). Microaggressions are defined as everyday "othering" messages related to a person's perceived marginalized status, which often reflect and perpetuate stereotypes and reproduce and instantiate oppression at interpersonal and societal levels (Nordmarken 2014; Sue et al. 2007). Microaggressions are often invisible to both senders and recipients, which makes them difficult to pinpoint, acknowledge, and confront.

Sue et al. (2007) categorized microaggressions into several forms: microassaults: conscious, intentional actions or slurs (e.g., use of trans-negative language, such as a cis student calling trans people "freaks" when learning about trans identities in a class or when encountering a trans person on campus); microinsults: verbal and nonverbal communications (e.g., facial expressions, body language) that convey insensitivity and demean a person's gender expression or identity (e.g., asking a person if they have had "the surgery"); and microinvalidations: communications that subtly exclude or negate the thoughts, feelings, or reality of TGNC people (e.g., misgendering through the use of incorrect pronouns or former names ["dead naming"]; Nordmarken 2014). Microinsults and microinvalidations are of special interest because they can be difficult to recognize and address, yet their cumulative impact over time on mental health and personal well-being is significant (Nadal et al. 2015).

Microaggressions against trans individuals have their root in and serve to maintain, cis-normative notions about gender as binary and as tied to biological sex. The lack of accurate representations of trans people, especially nonbinary individuals, means that many cis people, including faculty and students, do not understand TGNC individuals' gender identities and expressions and engage in misgendering (Nadal et al. 2015). It is also common for cis people, particularly those who believe they possess some knowledge about trans experiences, to (over)apply the "wrong body" narrative (i.e., the notion that all trans people feel "trapped in the wrong body" or want to alter their bodies via hormones and surgery) to trans people who do not experience their gender in such a way (Nordmarken 2014). When TGNC people address others' misgendering them or misunderstanding their particular trans experience, they may meet a range of responses, including confusion, disgust, skepticism, or overapologizing, which can create further discomfort (Nadal, Rivera, and Corpus 2010; Nordmarken 2014).

## METHOD

### Participants

The data for this study were drawn from a larger survey of TGNC students' experiences in higher education, which was approved by the Human Subjects

Board at Clark University. A total of 340 students completed the survey between June 1 and October 1, 2016, of which 93 (27.4 percent) were graduate students. Two of these students responded to less than half of the questions and were removed from the final sample, leaving 91 participants.

The graduate students ($M$ age = 27.9 years) reported a range of academic disciplines. The largest number were pursuing degrees in psychology/social work/counseling ($n$ = 18; 20.2 percent); lesser numbers of participants were in other social sciences (e.g., sociology, anthropology; $n$ = 11; 12.1 percent), gender/women's studies/LGBTQ studies ($n$ = 6; 6.6 percent), education ($n$ = 6), English/literature ($n$ = 6), computers/information technology ($n$ = 5; 5.5 percent), law ($n$ = 5), and business ($n$ = 4; 4.4 percent). Three or fewer respondents were in programs in public health, divinity/religion, medicine, math, architecture, and engineering.

Not all of the participants chose to report where they attended graduate school, but most did ($n$ = 84; 92.3 percent). Sixty-nine of the respondents were in colleges in the United States, in the states of New York ($n$ = 10), Texas ($n$ = 6), California ($n$ = 5), Illinois ($n$ = 5), Michigan ($n$ = 5), Mississippi ($n$ = 5), Georgia ($n$ = 4), Massachusetts ($n$ = 4), Iowa ($n$ = 3), New Jersey ($n$ = 3), Ohio ($n$ = 3), Virginia ($n$ = 3), Colorado ($n$ = 2), and Oklahoma ($n$ = 2). One respondent each resided in Florida, Indiana, Kentucky, Nebraska, Oklahoma, Oregon, Pennsylvania, Vermont, and Washington. Fifteen respondents lived outside of the United States, in Germany ($n$ = 6), Austria ($n$ = 3), the United Kingdom ($n$ = 3), and one each in Australia, Canada, and Sweden.

The participants were able to select multiple racial/ethnic categories. Eighty-two percent ($n$ = 75) identified as white/European American, 4.4 percent ($n$ = 4) as Latino/a/x/Latin American, 4.4 percent as mixed race, 4.4 percent as Black/African American, 3.3 percent ($n$ = 3) as Asian/Asian American, 3.3 percent as Middle Eastern, 2.2 percent ($n$ = 2) as Native American/American Indian/Aboriginal, and 1.1 percent ($n$ = 1) as Native Hawaiian/Pacific Islander.

Data Collection

Data were collected using an anonymous online survey. Focus groups with seven TGNC students helped inform the development of the survey, and it was pilot tested for ease of use and technical functionality by four TGNC students. Feedback was also sought from several scholars who study TGNC populations. The survey was revised based on the suggestions of both groups.

The survey included several questions that assessed aspects of the participants' gender identities and gender expressions. For example, they were asked,

"What gender identity label or labels do you feel best describes you? (What best matches your internal gender identity?)," and were given fifteen response options, plus the option to write in identities that were not listed. Other questions concerned the participants' sense of physical and emotional safety on campus, their perceptions of the level of trans sensitivity and trans awareness among classmates and faculty, misgendering by classmates and faculty, and trans-related advocacy.

### Data Analysis

Cross-tabs and analyses of variance were used to examine differences between the quantitative responses of the binary and nonbinary students. Qualitative analysis (i.e., thematic analysis; Bogdan and Biklen 2007) was used to consider the responses to the open-ended portions of the survey, which ranged from several sentences to several pages of text, with most students providing responses of three to five sentences per question. This mixed-methods approach (Creswell and Plano Clark 2011) provided for a deeper understanding of the students' experiences, as the qualitative data both amplified and provided nuances to the quantitative data.

## FINDINGS

### Graduate Students' Gender Identity and Expression

Students were allowed to select multiple gender identity options. More than half of the participants (51.6 percent, $n = 47$) identified as trans/transgender; 44.0 percent ($n = 40$) identified as nonbinary; 35.2 percent ($n = 32$) identified as genderqueer; 19.8 percent ($n = 18$) identified as gender-nonconforming; 19.8 percent identified as a transgender man; 18.7 percent ($n = 17$) identified as gender fluid; 14.3 percent ($n = 13$) identified as androgynous; 12.1 percent ($n = 11$) identified as agender; 11.0 percent ($n = 10$) identified as a transgender woman; 9.9 percent ($n = 9$) identified as masculine of center; 7.7 percent ($n = 7$) identified as demigender; 5.5 percent ($n = 5$) identified as feminine of center; 2.3 percent ($n = 2$) identified as questioning or unsure; and 1.1 percent ($n = 1$) identified as pangender. No students chose bigender, which was the other option provided. Fourteen participants (15.4 percent) selected "another identity not listed here." Two respondents each identified as man, woman, butch lesbian, and FTM (female-to-male), and one each identified as trans guy, demiguy, gendernull, FTMTX (female-to-male-to-x), transmasculine, and third gender. More than 60 percent of the participants ($n = 57$) indicated that they had previously identified as trans in a way that is different from how they see themselves today.

While recognizing the problems inherent in collapsing categories and reducing the complex array of gender identities to a dichotomous variable, I wanted to compare the experiences of trans students with binary and nonbinary identities. I created binary/nonbinary categories whereby all the participants who selected transgender, trans, trans woman, trans man, MTF (male-to-female), FTM, woman, man, or trans guy and who did not select any of the nonbinary options were categorized as "gender binary," and those who selected at least one nonbinary option (nonbinary, genderqueer, gender-nonconforming, gender fluid, androgynous, agender, demigender, gendernull, third gender, masculine/feminine of center, demiguy, butch lesbian, FTMTX, transmasculine, or questioning/unsure) were categorized as "gender nonbinary."

Of the binary-identified students ($n = 27$; 29.7 percent of the larger sample of graduate students), two-thirds ($n = 18$) were assigned female at birth (AFAB) and one-third ($n = 9$) were assigned male at birth (AMAB). Of the nonbinary-identified students ($n = 64$; 70.3 percent), 76.6 percent ($n = 49$) were AFAB, 21.9 percent ($n = 14$) were AMAB, and 1.6 percent ($n = 1$) was born intersex and AFAB. There were no significant differences in birth sex distribution across binary and nonbinary participants. On average, the students had used their current gender identity label for 4.4 years and had started to explore their gender identity when they were 16.3 years old. There were no differences in these domains by binary/nonbinary status. The binary and nonbinary students did differ in their current level of security in their gender identity (0–100), such that binary students reported significantly greater security ($M = 88.7$) than nonbinary students ($M = 76.7$).

The participants were asked to identify their gender expression on campus and could choose multiple options. Binary and nonbinary students did not differ in the frequency by which they chose feminine, masculine, feminine of center, or masculine of center, but nonbinary students were significantly more likely to select gender-nonconforming (62 percent versus 4 percent), androgynous (47 percent versus 13 percent), and genderless (25 percent versus 0 percent).

Of the ninety-one graduate students, 94.5 percent ($n = 86$) wore clothes that matched their gender identity in social situations, and 85.7 percent ($n = 78$) also wore clothes that matched their gender identity to classes or jobs. Endorsement of these items did not differ by binary/nonbinary status. Forty-five percent ($n$ = 41) said that they had taken hormones; binary students were significantly more likely to be or to have been on hormones than nonbinary students (85 percent versus 28 percent). Twenty-one percent of the respondents ($n$ = 19) had undergone nonsurgical cosmetic procedures such as electrolysis; there were no differences by binary/nonbinary status. Thirty percent ($n$ = 27) had completed nongenital surgery (e.g., breast implants/reductions); binary students were significantly more likely to have pursued this option than nonbinary students (63 percent versus 16 percent). More than 5 percent of the participants ($n$ = 5) had undergone genital surgery; there were no differences by binary/nonbinary status. Finally, 71.4 percent ($n$ = 65) had adopted a first name different from what they were given at birth, which they used in one or more settings (e.g., school, job, with family); binary students were significantly more likely to go by a chosen name than nonbinary students (96 percent versus 61 percent).

In terms of sexual orientation, 46.2 percent ($n$ = 42) of the students identified as queer, 15.4 percent ($n$ = 14) as bisexual, 8.8 percent ($n$ = 8) as gay, 7.7 percent ($n$ = 7) as lesbian, 7.7 percent as pansexual, 6.6 percent ($n$ = 6) as asexual, 2.2 percent ($n$ = 2) as heterosexual, and 5.5 percent ($n$ = 5) as another identity (e.g., gay but open; only attracted to masculine people regardless of birth sex). Nonbinary students were significantly more likely to identify as queer than were binary students (57 percent versus 22 percent).

### Graduate Students' Concerns about Safety on Campus and Gender Presentation

Sixty-seven percent of the students ($n$ = 61) indicated that concerns about physical/emotional safety affected how they presented their gender on campus. Such concerns did not differ by binary/nonbinary status. Participants were asked to elaborate on their responses (i.e., how concerns about safety did or did not affect them), and eighty-five of the ninety-one students (93 percent) offered an explanation.

*Concerns about Safety Do Not Affect Gender Presentation.* Among those who indicated that such concerns did not affect their gender presentation ($n$ = 30; 11 binary and 19 nonbinary), half stated that they "passed" fairly well (usually as a cis man) and thus were not concerned for their safety. One participant, who identified as a trans man, noted, "I present male and in our society, this can make one safe." Several students ($n$ = 4), all of whom were AFAB, believed that gender nonconformity was more acceptable among AFAB persons and thus they felt that they could present in a more masculine manner without safety concerns. A few participants ($n$ = 3) described their college campuses as "very LGBTQ-friendly," which contributed to their sense that they did not need to modify their gender expression. Finally, a few participants ($n$ = 3) noted that they "dressed however [they] want[ed] to," despite feeling "not fully comfortable because of others' judgment."

Concerns about Safety Affect Gender Presentation.   Among the participants who expressed safety concerns ($n$ = 61; 16 binary, 45 nonbinary), many shared that they were worried that their trans (typically nonbinary) status might invite rejection, ridicule, or even harassment and violence—the likelihood of which some ($n$ = 7, all nonbinary) felt was enhanced by the religious/political conservatism of their graduate institution or the area in which it was located. Many nonbinary students indicated that such concerns had led them to alter their appearance to be more stereotypically gendered (e.g., very masculine or very feminine) than they would prefer ($n$ = 24). These students spoke to the academic and professional risks of dressing in a way that was less clearly gendered and/or that deviated from their birth sex. A student who identified as gender nonconforming and questioning stated, "I tend to lean more cisgender on campus just for fear of what some professors would think. Especially since I will be depending on them for letters of recommendation." A few students ($n$ = 4) who espoused binary gender identities also expressed resentment at having to comply with highly gendered expectations for appearance. For example, a trans woman received "disparaging" remarks from faculty members, who suggested that her dress was too "ambiguous" (i.e., it did not adequately signal their gender to others). She felt pressured to wear feminine suits to fit in with the professional (and highly gendered) environment.

Misgendering on Campus by Other Graduate Students and Faculty

When asked to what extent the other students in their classes were trans-affirming, 12 percent said they were "very affirming," 32 percent said they were "somewhat affirming," 35 percent said they were "neutral," 16 percent said they were "not very affirming (somewhat trans-phobic)," and 5 percent said they were "not at all affirming (very trans-phobic)." The distribution of responses did not differ by binary/nonbinary status.

Misgendering by other students in their classes occurred more often for the nonbinary-identified (e.g., genderqueer) students than for the binary-identified (e.g., trans woman, trans man) students. Forty-five percent of the nonbinary students said that student misgendering happened "often," 33 percent said it happened "sometimes," 14 percent said it happened "rarely," and 8 percent said it "never" happened. Among the binary students, the percentages were reversed: 4 percent said that student misgendering happened "often," 12 percent said it happened "sometimes," 32 percent said it happened "rarely," and 52 percent said it "never" happened.

When asked to what extent faculty members were trans-affirming, 16 percent reported that they were "very affirming," 37 percent said that they were "somewhat affirming," 25 percent said that they were "neutral," 19 percent said that they were "not very affirming (somewhat trans-phobic)," and 3 percent said that they were "not at all affirming (very trans-phobic)." Responses did not differ by binary/nonbinary status.

Similar to their experiences with other students, the nonbinary students also tended to report significantly higher frequencies of misgendering by faculty members. Forty-four percent of the nonbinary students said that faculty misgendering happened "often," 33 percent said it happened "sometimes," 13 percent said it happened "rarely," and 10 percent said it "never" happened. Among the binary students, 8 percent said faculty misgendering happened "often," 12 percent said it happened "sometimes," 32 percent said it happened "rarely," and 50 percent said it "never" happened.

The participants were asked to provide examples of misgendering by faculty members and to elaborate on their experiences with transphobia in graduate school more broadly; seventy of the students (77 percent) offered responses.

Effect of Misgendering in Graduate Programs.  Consistent with the data presented here, the nonbinary students more often provided examples of misgendering and negative treatment. Because their gender expressions were, as reported, more likely to be androgynous, they were seemingly more likely to be read as gender ambiguous, which rendered them uniquely vulnerable to unintended misgendering. Many of the nonbinary students related their misgendering to the fact that "nobody knows nonbinary is a thing." A student who identifies as agender noted, "Because I am nonbinary, it is impossible for them to gender me correctly unless I have informed them of my gender and/or pronouns." Likewise, another nonbinary participant wrote, "All the focus is on transitioning from one gender to another, making nonbinary gender incomprehensible." Consistent with evidence that microinvalidations are especially difficult to confront (Sue 2010), the students sometimes felt uncomfortable correcting others or asking them to use "they/them" or other gender-neutral pronouns. As one AFAB genderqueer participant stated:

> I now appear masculine of center, so I am almost always gendered male and people use he/him pronouns for me automatically. This bothers me a lot, as I am not comfortable with any binary pronouns. However, I have a very hard time asking people to use they/them pronouns, as it rarely leads to an easy situation to deal with so I most often say nothing.

Many participants ($n = 26$) stated that even though they informed faculty in their program of their pronouns and chosen name, the professors continued to misgender and misname them, as well as used cis-normative language within the classroom (e.g., referring to students as "ladies and gentlemen"). For example, one genderqueer student wrote that their professors have "repeatedly referred to me as 'her' even after pronouns were stated (at my request) during introductions, and even when I have had a name badge with my pronouns on it." Students expressed frustration that some faculty members would "ask for pronouns, understand them, but never use them." They felt it was "really disheartening" that professors solicited and acknowledged students' gender identities but failed to change their behavior or language.

In some cases, instances of misgendering are perhaps better understood as examples of microassaults, insomuch as the speaker seemed to be consciously seeking to negate or challenge participants' gender identities, sometimes appearing to reflect their belief that trans identities, particularly nonbinary identities, were not legitimate or real (Nordmarken 2014). As one nonbinary student shared, a professor had asked them "if he should call [me] 'it.'" Another participant, who identifies as genderqueer, described having told their boss and coworkers

> multiple times that I am nonbinary and to call me they/them. My coworker tries but mostly complains or makes a joke out of it. My boss straight up refused to call me "they" because "that's multiple people." I tried to laugh it off, joking that maybe I would start using the imperial "we" to make it easier, but on the inside I just felt defeated.

When participants did approach faculty to "invite [them] to consider that not all [their] students were binary identified [and] talk a bit about proper pronouns," their actions tended to be met with confusion, invalidation, and/ or dismissal. As a consequence, the stress of continually educating others was often regarded as "not worth it" (Nadal et al. 2010).

Participants who were binary-identified (e.g., trans woman, trans man) less frequently experienced misgendering, but they often found these experiences to be quite distressing, in part because they were more invested in being perceived by others as female or male. Indeed, although all trans people must navigate cis-normativity, coming out as trans may pose different challenges for trans binary and nonbinary students. As Zimman (2009) notes, when a person first comes out as trans, that person is "asserting a self-experienced gender identity that is different from the gender he or she [sic] is perceived to be by others," and thus "an invisible gender identity is being claimed," whereas "when a transgender person has assumed a gender role matching their identity, coming out does not involve asserting a hidden gender identity, but rather revealing the fact that they formerly occupied a different gender role" (60). For example, one participant, a trans man, wrote about how he came out as trans to a faculty member at a social gathering and how that "faculty member began messing up my pronouns and misgendering me. This had never happened before I shared my trans status with him. I didn't say anything because I was scared to make a scene." Another participant, a trans man, described how one of his professors

> who I was really close to, misgendered me after I had been out for over a year and had been on testosterone for six months. I was very hurt, disappointed, and shocked at the time because I considered her one of my biggest supporters. It was probably an accident, but I worried at the time that the slip-up revealed what she really thought of me (that I was actually a woman, that my identity was invalid).

Misgendering by Advisers and Supervisors.   A number of participants ($n = 16$) reported experiencing misgendering by immediate supervisors and advisors, and in all cases it was experienced as quite hurtful, perhaps because students expected more from them (e.g., based on prior conversations about names/pronouns) and worked closely with them, rendering such incidents especially personal and upsetting (Tompkins et al. 2016). Well aware of the power differentials between themselves and their supervisors and advisers, the participants were often "scared" to address being misgendered, as the costs of speaking up seemed too great. One genderqueer participant shared: "My dissertation advisor, who is aware of my gender identity, refers to me exclusively using the wrong pronouns. It's upsetting and frustrates me, but I haven't corrected her yet because I don't feel comfortable doing so [because of the] culture [within] my department." Even when participants made efforts to inform their supervisors and advisers of their pronouns and chosen names, such efforts often seemed to go unheard. For example, in meetings with their adviser and graduate committee members, one agender participant found that the faculty members

> would often misgender me when speaking to each other about me (e.g., "Oh, she did this much this week") or to me (e.g., "You go girl!") despite the fact that I had introduced myself to and in front of them several times with my pronouns and had worn a large pin with my pronouns to our meetings, which one of them … had commented on. It always felt like a kick to the gut, like they didn't care about or respect me, and like they don't care about trans students despite their vocal assurance that they do. I usually [don't] say anything though because I had seen one of them grade my peers lower on assignments after they disagreed with her in class … I felt unsafe correcting someone who could and likely would seek some sort of vengeance.

Such incidents were upsetting, yet students rarely felt that they had the power to confront their advisers' and supervisors' poor treatment. In sum, "fatigue, lack of support, fear of reprisal, and professional uncertainty" kept them from speaking up. "I can't ask more vociferously or more often because it will endanger my [future]," said one genderqueer student.

Positive Experiences with Advisers and Supervisors.   Nine participants explicitly described positive experiences with advisers and supervisors. These faculty members were not necessarily well educated about TGNC issues or identities, but they made a strong effort to learn from and respond compassionately to the trans students. The participants expressed appreciation for advisers and supervisors who tended to "apologize" or "correct themselves," if they accidentally misgendered them, and who demonstrated a commitment to learning and "doing better." As one genderqueer participant noted, "My PhD adviser uses they/them for me or at least beats themselves up about if they slip. It is great." Another genderqueer participant stated, "My adviser checks in with me in person and via email," and held a "private meeting with me [and the administration] to understand trans issues better and my personal needs."

## Trans Advocacy on Campus

The respondents were asked to what extent they were active in trans-related campus advocacy (e.g., bringing in speakers, advocating for trans resources). More than a fourth (26 percent) were "not active," 30 percent were "not very active," 24 percent were "somewhat active," and 20 percent were "very active." There were no differences by binary/nonbinary status. The types of activities pursued by students included advocating for staff/faculty trainings on TGNC issues; conducting TGNC-related trainings for students, staff, and faculty; hosting trans events on campus; seeking to promote more inclusive teaching practices (e.g., "incorporating preferred names and pronouns into introductions"); helping "map the gender-neutral restrooms on campus"; recommending that gender identity be asked on admissions forms; and serving on university committees to represent TGNC perspectives.

All of the students ($n = 51$) who said that they were "not active" or "not very active" provided a reason(s) for their lack of involvement in TGNC-related advocacy. Most commonly cited ($n = 14$) was a lack of time because of the demands of being a graduate student; some noted that they would be involved if they were not so busy. Many participants ($n = 13$) also mentioned their fears about being visible on campus, as they worried about the consequences of "standing out in this way." In some cases, students were not entirely out as TGNC within their departments or programs and were concerned about how faculty or peers might react if they were to "assert" their "transness." Other students, particularly some trans male participants, "passed" or were "stealth," and they "[did] not want to be forced into coming out," since graduate school was one of their first opportunities to be in a space with people "only knowing me as male." Some students ($n = 8$) rarely engaged in advocacy because these efforts were led on their campus by LGBTQ groups that were dominated by undergraduates, and they felt disconnected from or unable to relate to them. Other students ($n = 5$) noted that LGBTQ activism on their campus was primarily focused on LGBQ issues, so that there were not TGNC advocacy efforts they could join.

Less frequent reasons provided for not being involved in activism included mental and physical health issues ($n = 5$), finding advocacy efforts "tiring" and "exhausting" ($n = 3$), a lack of interest ($n = 3$), and concerns about balancing professional boundaries and roles ($n = 3$).

## DISCUSSION

This is one of the first studies to address the experiences of TGNC graduate students (McKinney 2005), and it breaks new ground by including and highlighting the experiences of nonbinary graduate students. Hopefully the findings of this work can serve as a platform for future studies. For example, the research shows that TGNC graduate students, on average, had begun questioning their gender identities when they were in high school, suggesting that colleges and universities can play a pivotal role in validating gender identity exploration and providing support related to this process (Marine and Nicolazzo 2014). The nonbinary students felt less secure in their current gender identity, which could reflect a lack of societal understanding and affirmation of nonbinary identities (Rankin and Beemyn 2012); it could also be that the nonbinary students in the sample were at an earlier stage in their gender identity exploration process than the binary students.

The findings highlight the often difficult climate that TGNC graduate students face in higher education and, in particular, the challenges encountered by students who identify as nonbinary. They do not "fit" the dominant (i.e., "wrong body") narrative of trans people (Nordmarken 2014), and thus may be misunderstood by others. As indicated by the descriptive data, the nonbinary students were less likely to have taken hormones or have had nongenital surgery and often described themselves as presenting as gender ambiguous. Their gender expression seemed to create some uncertainty (for others) and anxiety (for themselves) in terms of navigating issues of pronouns and names; indeed, they were more likely than binary students to report being misgendered by peers and faculty. Yet out of concerns related to emotional and physical safety, some presented in ways that were more stereotypically masculine or feminine than they would have preferred. These efforts may have reduced anxiety in one domain (e.g., they were less likely to be stared at by a professor), but increased anxiety in another (e.g., their clothes did not match their internal gender identity). The challenge of confronting misgendering was also often intensified for nonbinary students, as they were more likely than binary students to raise the subject of gender-neutral pronouns with faculty and thus challenge cis-normative practices and ways of thinking. Moreover, even when faculty members seemed, on the surface, to be open to and aware of nonbinary gender identities (as evidenced by asking students to indicate their pronouns on the first day of classes), they typically did not hold themselves or cis students accountable for actually using these pronouns consistently.

The findings related to TGNC graduate students' experiences with their mentors and advisers are particularly important to consider, as such relationships have powerful professional implications (Malik and Malik 2015). Some participants described their adviser as misgendering them repeatedly, even after they had educated the faculty member about their name and pronouns. Such behavior represents a harmful form of microinvalidation, in that even if these actions were unconscious, they were perpetuated by a person in power and had a detrimental impact on the participants, as evidenced by their expressions of helplessness in the face of such disregard (Smith, Shin, and Officer 2012; Sue 2010). Aware of their advisers' evaluative role and dependent on faculty members for various forms of professional capital (Thomas et al. 2007), the students were more likely to stay silent than to question their advisers' behavior.

Some positive study findings are also worth noting. First, some faculty members were characterized as wanting to learn and sincerely trying to use students' correct pronouns, and such affirming experiences meant a great deal to participants. In this way, the data present a somewhat more optimistic portrait of TGNC graduate students' experiences than McKinney (2005), whose study participants did not describe any faculty as particularly trans-affirming. Second, the students in the current study indicated a fairly high level of self-advocacy, with many noting that they had spoken to faculty and peers about their pronouns and names. In contrast, Pryor (2015) reported that the five trans students in their sample expressed considerable anxiety about disclosing their names and pronouns. Of course, the current study's positive results in this area are diminished by the fact that many faculty members either refused or forgot to use the correct names and pronouns, reflecting ongoing issues of trans-negativity in higher education. Such findings point to the need for in-depth faculty trainings on the needs of TGNC students. It is insufficient to suggest to faculty that they simply "ask for pronouns." Without appropriate context for this guidance and follow-through on the part of faculty members, such advice is likely to be poorly executed.

In terms of trans-related campus advocacy, McKinney (2005) found that many trans graduate students were uninterested in joining LGBT organizations, and those who tried often felt excluded because of their gender identity. The current study extends this research, finding that many trans graduate students have no desire to participate in an LGBT group because of the risks associated with being visibly trans on campus and their perceptions that these groups are dominated by undergraduates and focus solely on LGB issues, ignoring TGNC concerns. Thus graduate students who might otherwise become involved do not do so because of feeling marginalized as both graduate students and trans individuals. To address this situation, colleges should encourage the creation of student organizations geared toward TGNC graduate students, and departments and programs should seek to promote these groups as excellent opportunities for activism and support.

## CONCLUSIONS AND FUTURE DIRECTIONS

It is important to emphasize that for TGNC students, especially nonbinary students, trying to convey their gender identities amid dominant cisnormative discourses can be frustrating and limiting (Smith, Shin, and Officer 2012). Higher education should seek to become more inclusive of trans students' experiences and identities, with particular attention to including those who identify outside the gender binary, by acknowledging the limitations of existing terminology and considering alternative, gender-neutral language, particularly in disciplines like law and business that rely heavily and unnecessarily on the gender binary in professional discourse (e.g., use of terms like "sir" and "madam").

Exploring one's gender identity can be an ongoing process, so a person's identity may vary depending on when researchers survey them. Future studies should explore the ways that nonbinary people navigate graduate school and the beginning years of their chosen field. This type of longitudinal research can help shed light on the variety of challenges that nonbinary individuals encounter and the ways they meet these obstacles through personal and community resilience.

## ACKNOWLEDGMENTS

Some of these data are reported in a manuscript under review, along with original data not provided in that manuscript. This study was funded by a Dean of Research grant. The author acknowledges, with gratitude, the contributions of several TGNC college students at her institution who assisted with the development of this study. The author is also grateful to Genny Beemyn, Katherine Kuvalanka, and lore dickey for their assistance with the development of this project.

## NOTES

1. I use the terms *TGNC* and *trans* interchangeably to refer inclusively to individuals with both binary (e.g., trans men, trans women) and nonbinary (e.g., gender-fluid, genderqueer) gender identities. I have not chosen one term over another to acknowledge that terminology use varies greatly among TGNC/trans individuals (Simmons and White 2014).

## WORKS CITED

Arnett, Jeffrey J., and Jennifer L. Tanner. 2006. *Emerging Adults in America: Coming of Age in the 21st Century*. Washington, DC: American Psychological Association.

Baker, Kerri, and Kathleen Boland. 2011. "Assessing Safety: A Campus-Wide Initiative." *College Student Journal* 45: 684–99.

Beemyn, Brett [Genny]. 2003. "Serving the Needs of Transgender College Students." *Journal of Gay and Lesbian Issues in Education* 1: 33–50.

———. 2016. "Transgender Inclusion on College Campuses." In *The Sage Encyclopedia of LGBTQ Studies*, edited by Abbie E. Goldberg, 1226–29. Thousand Oaks, CA: Sage.

Bilodeau, Brent. 2005. "Beyond the Gender Binary: A Case Study of Two Transgender Students at a Midwestern Research University." *Journal of Gay and Lesbian Issues in Education* 3: 29–44.

———. 2009. *Genderism: Transgender Students, Binary Systems, and Higher Education*. Saarbrücken, Germany: VDM.

Bogdan, Robert, and Sari Knopp Biklen. 2007. *Qualitative Research for Education: An Introduction to Theories and Methods*, 5th ed.. New York: Pearson.

Burdge, Barb J. 2007. "Bending Gender, Ending Gender: Theoretical Foundations for Social Work Practice with the Transgender Community." *Social Work* 52: 243–50.

Chang, Sand C., Anneliese A. Singh, and Kinton Rossman. 2017. "Gender and Sexual Orientation Diversity within the TGNC Community." In *Affirmative Counseling and Psychological Practice with Transgender and Gender Diverse Clients*, edited by Anneliese A. Singh and lore m. dickey, 19–40. Washington, DC: American Psychological Association.

Creswell, John W., and Vicki L. Plano Clark. 2011. *Designing and Conducting Mixed Methods Research*, 2nd ed. Thousand Oaks, CA: Sage.

Dugan, John P., Michelle L. Kusel, and Dawn M. Simounet. 2012. "Transgender College Students: An Exploratory Study of Perceptions, Engagement, and Educational Outcomes." *Journal of College Student Development* 53: 719–36.

Fletcher, Joan, Claudia Bernard, Anna Fairtlough, and Akile Ahmet. 2015. "Beyond Equal Access to Equal Outcomes: The Role of the Institutional Culture in Promoting Full Participation, Positive Inter-Group Interaction and Timely Progression for Minority Social Work Students." *British Journal of Social Work* 45: 120–37.

Garvey, Jason C., and Susan R. Rankin. 2015. "The Influence of Campus Experiences on the Level of Outness among Trans-Spectrum and Queer-Spectrum Students." *Journal of Homosexuality* 62: 374–93.

Girves, Jean E., Yolanda Zepeda, and Judith K. Gwathmey. 2005. "Mentoring in a Post-Affirmative Action World." *Journal of Social Issues* 61: 449–80.

Greytak, Emily, Joseph G. Kosciw, and Elizabeth M. Diaz. 2009. "Harsh Realities: The Experiences of Transgender Youth in our Nation's Schools." *A Report from the Gay, Lesbian, and Straight Education Network.* http://www.teni.ie/attachments/c95b5e6b-f0e6-43aa-9038-1e357e3163ea.PDF (accessed November 28, 2016).

Kosciw, Joseph G., Emily A. Greytak, Neal A. Palmer, and Madelyn J. Boesen. 2014. *The 2013 National School Climate Survey: The Experiences of Lesbian, Gay, Bisexual, and Transgender Youth in our Nation's Schools.* New York: Gay, Lesbian and Straight Education Network.

Kosciw, Joseph G., Neal A. Palmer, Ryan M. Krull, and Emily A. Greytak. 2013. "The Effects of Negative School Climate on Academic Outcomes for LGBT Youth and the Role of In-School Supports." *Journal of School Violence* 12: 45–63.

Malik, Shahab Alam, and Shujah Alam Malik. 2015. "Graduate School Supervisees' Relationship with Their Academic Mentors." *Journal of Applied Research in Higher Education* 7: 211–28.

Marine, Susan B., and Z. Nicolazzo. 2014. "Names that Matter: Exploring the Tensions of Campus LGBTQ Centers and Trans* Inclusion." *Journal of Diversity in Higher Education* 7: 265–81.

McKinney, Jeffrey S. 2005. "On the Margins: A Study of the Experiences of Transgender College Students." *Journal of Gay and Lesbian Issues in Education* 3: 63–75.

Nadal, Kevin L., Kristin C. Davidoff, Lindsey S. Davis, Yinglee Wong, David Marshall, and Victoria McKenzie. 2015. "A Qualitative Approach to

Intersectional Microaggressions: Understanding Influences of Race, Ethnicity, Gender, Sexuality, and Religion." *Qualitative Psychology* 2: 147–63.

Nadal, Kevin, David P. Rivera, and Melissa J. H. Corpus. 2010. "Sexual Orientation and Transgender Microaggressions: Implications for Mental Health and Counseling." In *Microaggressions and Marginality: Manifestation, Dynamics, and Impact*, edited by Derald Wing Sue, 217–40. Hoboken, NJ: Wiley.

*Nordmarken, Sonny. 2014. "Microagressions." Transgender Studies Quarterly 1: 129–34.*

Noy, Shiri, and Rashawn Ray. 2012. "Graduate Students' Perceptions of Their Advisors: Is There Systematic Disadvantage in Mentorship?" *Journal of Higher Education* 83: 876–914.

Oswald, Ramona Faith, Jenifer K. McGuire, Katherine A. Kuvalanka, Jory M. Catalpa, and Russell B. Toomey. "Transfamily Theory: How the Presence of Trans* Family Members Informs Gender Development in Families." *Journal of Family Theory and Review* 8: 60–74.

Pryor, Jonathan T. 2015. "Out in the Classroom: Transgender Student Experiences at a Large Public University." *Journal of College Student Development* 56: 440–55.

Pusch, Rob S. 2005. "Objects of Curiosity: Transgender College Students' Perceptions of the Reactions of Others." *Journal of Gay and Lesbian Issues in Education* 3: 45–61.

Rankin, Susan R. 2003. *Campus Climate for Gay, Lesbian, Bisexual, and Transgender People: A National Perspective.* New York: National Gay and Lesbian Task Force Policy Institute.

Rankin, Susan, and Genny Beemyn. 2012. "Beyond a Binary: The Lives of Gender Nonconforming Youth." *About Campus* 17: 2–10.

Simmons, Holiday, and Fresh! White. 2014. "Our Many Selves." In *Trans Bodies, Trans Selves: A Resource for the Transgender Community*, edited by Laura Erickson-Schroth, 3–23. New York: Oxford University Press.

Smith, Lance C., Richard Q. Shin, and Lindsay M. Officer. 2012. "Moving Counseling Forward on LGB and Transgender Issues: Speaking Queerly on Discourses and Microaggressions." *Counseling Psychologist* 40: 385–408.

Sue, Derald W. 2010. *Microaggressions and Marginality: Manifestation, Dynamics, and Impact.* Hoboken, NJ: Wiley.

Sue, Derald W., Christina M. Capodilupo, Gina C. Torino, Jennifer M. Bucceri, Aisha M. B. Holder, Kevin L. Nadal, and Marta Esquilin. 2007. "Racial

Microaggressions in Everyday Life: Implications for Practice." *American Psychologist* 62: 271–86.

Thomas, Kecia M., Leigh A. Willis, and Jimmy Davis. 2007. "Mentoring Minority Graduate Students: Issues and Strategies for Institutions, Faculty, and Students." *Equal Opportunities International* 26: 178–92.

Tompkins, Kelley A., Kierra Brecht, Brock Tucker, Lucia L. Neander, and Joshua K. Swift. 2015. "Who Matters Most? The Contribution of Faculty, Student-Peers, and Outside Support in Predicting Graduate Student Satisfaction." *Training and Education in Professional Psychology* 10: 102–8.

Trask, Bahira Sherif, Ramona Marotz-Baden, Barbara Settles, Deborah Gentry, and Debra Berke. 2009. "Enhancing Graduation Education: Promoting a Scholarship of Teaching and Learning through Mentoring." *International Journal of Teaching and Learning in Higher Education* 20: 438–46.

Zimman, Lal. 2009. " 'The Other Kind of Coming Out': Transgender People and the Coming Out Narrative Genre." *Gender and Language* 3: 53–80.

# ELEVEN

# Get over the Binary
## The Experiences of Nonbinary Trans College Students

*Genny Beemyn*

I STARTED WRITING ABOUT and conducting research on trans college students in the early 2000s because I saw that trans students were beginning to come out on college campuses and seeking support, but almost nothing was being published on their experiences and how to address their needs. I had recently come out as trans myself and wanted younger trans people to have an easier time understanding and embracing their identity than I did.

In the years since then, many trans students have come out on their campuses, a small but significant body of research has been published on trans students, and, to varying degrees, many colleges have taken steps to support them. Few studies have yet focused on nonbinary trans students, and they remain an ignored or underserved population on most campuses. This chapter relates the findings of a study I conducted from September 2014 to January 2015, the first national study of nonbinary trans college students. I hope that this research will enable cis faculty and staff in particular to have a greater understanding of the lives of nonbinary trans students and develop policies and practices that better serve their needs.

## THE LIVES OF TRANS PEOPLE AT THE TURN OF THE TWENTY-FIRST CENTURY

In 2011, Sue Rankin's and my book *The Lives of Transgender People* was published based on research we had begun in 2005. We embarked on the work because we were frustrated by the paucity of large-scale studies of trans identity development and the complete lack of studies that considered the wide range of trans people, including trans men, trans women, individuals who have transitioned and who subsequently see themselves primarily as men and women, and people who identify their gender in various nonbinary ways. We sent out a link to an online survey, hoping to recruit 500 participants. We had that many within a few days and had to abandon plans to conduct follow-up phone interviews with all of the interested participants. In the end, we had nearly 3,500 survey participants and more than 400 interviewees, which made it the largest study of trans people in the United States when we published the results.

The main aim of our research for *The Lives of Transgender People* was to examine the processes by which the participants came to understand, accept, and label themselves as trans. We found that regardless of whether the respondents identified as binary (i.e., a trans man/woman) or nonbinary (such as genderqueer, gender fluid, and androgynous), they often experienced similar themes in their identity development, what we referred to as milestones:

- Feeling gender different from a young age and seeking to express this difference through dress and behavior
- Repressing or hiding these feelings in the face of hostility and/or isolation
- Recognizing that there are trans people
- Getting to know about and know other trans people
- Deciding on a specific trans identity
- Overcoming denial and internalized genderism to accept oneself as trans
- Having one's presentation match one's identity
- Deciding whether and when to tell others and developing new relationships after disclosure
- Developing a sense of wholeness within a gender-normative society

Although these were common milestones, not all of the participants experienced each or in this order, or saw every milestone as personally significant to them. In particular, the milestones broke down when it came to age: many of the youngest participants (eighteen to twenty-two) did not experience some of the milestones or did not do so for very long.

Many of the older participants had struggled for years (if not decades) to understand their gender identities; having grown up at a time before the internet was widely available, they often thought that there was something wrong with them and that their experience was unique. Lacking information and role models, many of the older trans women first thought they were crossdressers, and many of the older trans men who were attracted to women first thought they were butch lesbians. It was not until they recognized that they did not simply want to take on gender presentations and roles of a different gender but identified as that gender that they came out and began to transition. The trans women who grew up prior to the 1990s particularly struggled with being able to recognize and accept themselves. None of the trans female interviewees over thirty years old who had expressed their female sense of themselves to their families as youths or who were discovered to be cross-dressing had received a positive response. They were punished, beaten, sexually assaulted, sent to a therapist to be "cured," or institutionalized. As a result, they quickly realized they could not be themselves. Many repressed their feelings, such that close to half of the trans female interviewees had pursued what have traditionally been considered extremely masculine careers and hobbies, including being a firefighter, police officer, truck driver, football player, and street car racer, and a lot had served in the military. In essence, they wanted to hide their female identities not only from others but also from themselves.

In contrast, the trans people in our study who were in their late teens and early twenties, including many of the trans women and the nonbinary individuals who had been assigned male at birth, often received some support from their families when they came out or were recognized by their parent(s) as gender different. The change reflected the increased visibility of trans people in popular culture, as well as the growing availability of the internet, in the 1990s. Our interviews suggested that the younger trans participants benefited from their parents' and their own exposure to online information about trans people. A parent who had questions and concerns about their child's gender identity no longer had to rely on the handful of books that had been published at that time about trans people, many of which portrayed them as mentally ill; they could go online and find information that affirmed trans identities and offered ways to be supportive. Obviously not all parents suddenly began to embrace their trans children, but there was a discernible shift from the ubiquitous rejection narrative.

Our research indicated that trans people also turned to the internet to learn about themselves. Some of the older participants did not realize there were others like themselves until they entered the online world in their forties, fifties, sixties, and even seventies. By comparison, the participants who were eighteen to twenty-two years old were able to be on the internet by their teens and thus often had a much better understanding of their gender identities at a young age and were less likely to be in denial or confused about being trans. Whereas the older participants often experienced their gender identities in isolation for much of their lives, the youngest participants had a virtual community, if not a real-world community, around them and had the opportunity to be talking to other trans people their age from around the world. While many of the younger participants still struggled at times to accept and embrace their gender identities, they could more easily find support.

Another striking generational difference involved how the participants typically viewed and named their gender identities. With few exceptions, the interviewees over thirty identified in binary ways; they were trans men or trans women, or they were male-assigned cross-dressers who identified as having a second, female self. None identified as genderqueer or gender fluid. In contrast, none of the interviewees under thirty referred to themselves as cross-dressers, and many identified their gender as outside a binary. Even some of the younger participants who had or were in the process of transitioning did not see themselves as strictly women or men; they continued to identify as trans, and many chose to be out, even when they had the option of being stealth and being assumed by others to have been assigned a gender at birth that corresponds to how they identify and express their gender today.

## BEYOND A BINARY: THE LIVES OF TRANS COLLEGE STUDENTS TODAY

In the years since we conducted our research for *The Lives of Transgender People*, the number of trans youth identifying as nonbinary has continued to increase, so much so that the majority of trans college students today identify as nonbinary (Beemyn 2016). Despite this change in the makeup in campus trans communities, most research on trans college students remains focused on trans women and men (e.g., Catalano 2015; Goodrich 2012; Jourian 2017; Singh, Meng, and Hansen 2013) or fails to differentiate between binary and nonbinary trans people (e.g., Effrig, Bieschke, and Locke 2011; Seelman 2016). When I began a national study of the experiences of college students who identify outside of a gender and/or sexual binary in 2014, I was surprised to find that no one else had conducted similar large-scale research. I hope that my findings, presented here, will spur further studies on the lives of nonbinary individuals, particularly nonbinary college students.

## METHODOLOGY

### Procedure

To participate in my study, individuals had to identify their gender and/or sexuality as outside of a binary; currently attend a two- or four-year college

in the United States, or have graduated within the past three years; and be between the ages of seventeen and twenty-five. Participants were asked to complete an online survey and encouraged to take part in a follow-up interview.
Because I was interested in seeing whether the colleges that offer more services
and resources for LGBTQIA+ (lesbian, gay, bisexual, transgender, queer, intersex, asexual, and other sexual and gender identities) students are actually
serving the needs of nonbinary students, I focused on the campuses that had
long-standing LGBTQIA+ centers. I emailed study information and a link to
the online survey to the directors of seventy-four of these centers (twenty-nine
in the Northeast, fifteen in the South, fifteen in the Midwest, and fifteen in
the West) asking for their assistance. Fifty-four agreed to help, either directly
by contacting nonbinary students they knew or indirectly by posting an announcement of the research on their center's email discussion list or social
media platforms, such as Twitter and Facebook.

Given that students from other institutions are often a part of a center's
online community and that students often forward or repost material, information about my study quickly spread to students on other campuses, so
ultimately I had a wider range of colleges represented in the research. But reflecting my original aim of documenting students' experiences at the seemingly best colleges for LGBTQIA+ students, the institutions included in my
research were skewed toward the schools rated as the most LGBTQ-supportive.
At the time of the study, fifty-nine of the eighty-four colleges (70 percent) attended by the interviewees were listed on the LGBTQ-Friendly Campus Pride
Index (http://www.campusprideindex.org), with an average rating of 4.4 out
of 5 stars. Twenty-one colleges, or one-fourth of the colleges represented in
the interview sample, had earned five stars.

Participants

The nonbinary survey was available online for almost four months, from mid-
September through late December 2014, and 485 people began the survey
during this time. I removed 125 surveys from consideration because the individuals did not complete the instrument or were outside the parameters of
the study (they were older than twenty-five, they attended a college outside of
the United States or an online college, or they identified their sexuality and
gender within binary categories). The research thus involved 360 students, who
attended 119 different colleges. All of the individuals who provided contact
information were asked if they would participate in a follow-up interview to

provide more information about their experiences growing up and in college. I was able to arrange and conduct interviews with 208 of those surveyed, who attended eighty-four different colleges. The age and racial demographics of the students who completed the survey and those who were interviewed were nearly identical: the average age was 20.4 years in the surveys and 20.3 in the interviews; people of color were 26 percent of the individuals surveyed and 27 percent of the interviewees.

For this chapter, I focus primarily on the 111 interviewees who identified outside of a gender binary. They attended sixty-two different colleges, and the most common identities of these participants were genderqueer ($n = 22$), agender (20), gender fluid (17), nonbinary trans (12), demigender (8), and androgynous (5). Almost all (92 percent) of the nonbinary gender interviewees also described their sexuality as nonbinary. This finding was not surprising, as sexual orientation is typically defined through considering one's gender identity and the gender identity/identities of the individuals to whom one is attracted. If your gender is nonbinary, or if the gender(s) of the individuals to whom you are attracted are nonbinary, then your sexuality is difficult to characterize in binary terms. Most of the nonbinary gender interviewees described themselves as queer, pansexual, bisexual, or asexual.

The vast majority of the participants (87 percent) had been assigned female at birth (AFAB), which is similar to the demographics of other trans research. In both the National Transgender Discrimination Survey (Grant, Mottet, and Tanis 2011) and a study by Laura Kuper, Robin Nussbaum, and Brian Mustanski (2012), AFAB individuals constituted 73 percent of the nonbinary participants, and in *The Lives of Transgender People* (Beemyn and Rankin 2011), they were 87 percent of the nonbinary sample. In the US Transgender Survey (James et. al 2016), the largest survey ever conducted of trans people in the United States, with more than 27,000 respondents, 35 percent of the sample described themselves as nonbinary, 80 percent of whom were AFAB.

Jess, one of the relatively few assigned male at birth (AMAB), nonbinary trans students I interviewed, attributed the scarcity of out individuals like themselves to androcentrism—to masculinity being "rewarded as the default." They elaborated:

> If you present as feminine at all, you will experience transmisogynist violence if you're too "visibly trans," so you have to try and "pass" as a cis woman to be both safe and not gendered as a man.... The experience

of being trans feminine nonbinary can feel pretty much the same as the experience of being a binary trans woman. And when you're forced to choose, you'll usually go for "woman" to avoid violence.

Moreover, when they are not having to be concerned about the likelihood of harassment and violence for being seen as "too trans," AMAB nonbinary people, as well as trans women who cannot or will not be stealth, often have to cope with the opposite reaction: being seen as "not trans enough." Whereas AFAB nonbinary individuals are rarely challenged on their gender expression, transfeminine individuals are frequently critiqued by both cis and other trans people on how well they "do transgender." Specifically, they find themselves in a no-win situation: if they present in conventionally feminine ways, they are viewed as parodying women, and if they are less traditionally feminine, they are dismissed as not "really" women or as "unwomanly." Among the nonbinary AMAB people I interviewed who faced this dilemma was JP; they sought to explore their "transfeminine side," but struggled with the stigma of "not being trans enough."

I was also not surprised that most (82 percent) of nonbinary trans interviewees used nonbinary pronouns to refer to themselves, and of this group, almost all (91 percent) used "they/them/their" for their pronouns. In the past few years, students who want to be recognized as nonbinary have tended to gravitate toward "they/them/their," because it is language that others already have and its usage to describe one person is gaining support in the dominant society. For example, in 2015, singular "they" was added to the style guide of the *Washington Post* and declared the "Word of the Year" by the American Dialect Society (Guo 2016). The handful of students I interviewed who had chosen other pronoun options, specifically "ze/hir/hir," "ze/zim/zir," or "xe/xem/xir," often had difficulty or did not try getting people beyond their close friends to refer to them with these pronouns.

## FINDINGS

### Identifying as Nonbinary Trans

The dominant trans identity narrative today in the media, popular culture, and even among trans people themselves is that individuals recognize themselves as the other binary gender "extreme" from a very young age, identify as trans as soon as they learn this language, and, if they have supportive families, present as that other gender extreme (Beemyn and Rankin 2011; Cordes 2013). Besides erasing the lives of trans women and trans men who begin to self-identify as teenagers or adults, the pervasiveness of this account ignores the very different experiences of nonbinary trans people. In contrast to many binary trans youth, who have a strong sense of themselves as the other binary gender extreme, young people who later identify as nonbinary often do not experience the same degree of gender dissonance. They may not feel entirely comfortable in their assigned gender, but they generally do not have an overwhelming sense of failing to fit into the gender expected of them.

This situation is particularly the case for AFAB youth who present and act in ways that are traditionally read as masculine but do not reject their gender assignment. Typically labeled tomboys, their nonstereotypical feminine behavior is tolerated if not accepted, at least until adolescence, and they likely have friends who are similarly considered tomboys. As a result, they may not feel as socially out of place as someone assigned female who sees themselves as male, and they may not characterize their nonstandard behavior as possibly indicative of a nonfemale identity. For example, Katy, a twenty-one-year-old white college student I interviewed, at first saw themselves as "a different kind of girl" and "chalked [their gender difference] up to being the tomboy archetype and then a bad-ass girl." But in the past few years, as they have learned about nonbinary identities through social media, Katy has begun to identify as a "gender-fluid femme," meaning that "even when [presenting as] masculine, there is still the feminine there," that they are "never completely masculine" in their appearance.

The dearth of images of nonbinary people in the media and pop culture makes it difficult for youth to see themselves as nonbinary. Among the students I interviewed who now identify outside of a gender binary, almost all did not learn about nonbinary trans people until they were teenagers, and most not until they entered college, when they met out nonbinary students or became more active on social media sites. Such was the case with "Randi," a Latinx and white student, who first identified as a trans man in college because that was the only identity they knew. When they learned about other gender options, Randi recognized that describing themselves as "nonbinary transgender" fit better, as they do not feel entirely masculine.

For students of color, identifying their gender as nonbinary can be complicated not only by the lack of images of nonbinary trans people of color but also by the lack of campus spaces that are inclusive of both their race and gender identity. To the extent that Black and Latinx trans people have been visible in the media until recently, it was because of the horrific number of murders annually of trans women of color (Trans Murder Monitoring 2016). In the past few years, the visibility of Laverne Cox and Janet Mock has enabled many young African American trans women to see themselves reflected in popular culture. Consequently, they may be more willing to embrace a trans identity, as they may be better able to imagine a life for themselves as trans women. However, trans women of color of other races, trans men of color, and nonbinary trans people of color remain largely invisible in society, which means that many youth of color still lack role models to help them understand and accept themselves as trans. For example, when Jay, an agender person of color, was beginning to think about androgyny in the eighth and ninth grades, they found that all of the representations of nonbinary identities involved white people, which made it more difficult to take on such an identity themselves.

Jay was one of the participants who indicated that a lack of intersectionality—what they described as "how race, class, ability, etc. interact with gender in platonic, romantic, and sexual relationships on and off campus"—contributed to a less than welcoming institutional climate for them as a nonbinary trans person of color. Similarly, Read, a gender-variant African American demigirl, said that people ignore "how much whiteness is valued in terms of queerness on [zir] campus." Ze reported that white, nondisabled identities remain centralized at zir college and that intersectionality only seems to happen when white leaders are challenged by people of color or when such an analysis is unavoidable, so that it "rarely happens freely." Read is "continually frustrated" by the fact that there are queer and trans comfortable spaces on zir campus, but ones that are racially inclusive. The same situation was faced by Aja, a multiracial gender-fluid student, at their college. They reported that white genderqueer and gender-fluid individuals who were AFAB have a very privileged position on campus that does not get examined. There are not supportive spaces for trans students of color and, to their knowledge, there are not any out trans women of color. Aja's institution is well known as a progressive liberal arts college, but they said that it is progressive only if you are a "white cis gay boy."

The lack of spaces for trans people of color on their campus forced Pau, a gender-fluid Latin@ student, to choose which identities to forefront at any one time and "shape shift in different spaces" because they did not receive support in any one place for all of their identities, including their race, ethnicity, gender, sexuality, and being from an immigrant family. Unable to find a space where they can be all of themselves on campus, Pau turned to social media, particularly Tumblr:

> I consider Tumblr my safe space. It's where I go for comfort from other queer people of color going through the same things as me and also a place where I am in charge of my representation ... Posting selfies on Tumblr has become a very liberating experiences for me. I get to pick the tags, genderfluid, latin@, and there is where I connected with other students who share the similar spelling of Latin@, chican@ [sic], xicanx, queer identity and gender neutral pronouns. Finding selfies in the QPOC [queer people of color] tags was a way to connect with other QPOC blogs and represent an underground catalog of diverse representation—everything I was missing in my groups on campus/immediate life. (email message to author, October 30, 2014)

Because of their lack of familiarity with nonbinary identities growing up and the lack of support for identifying beyond male or female, the average age at which the 111 nonbinary trans students I interviewed began to use their current gender identity label for themselves was nineteen years old, as compared to eighteen for the 16 students in the study who were binary in their gender identity but nonbinary in their sexuality. A study by Rhonda Factor and Esther Rothblum (2008) also found that their binary participants typically began to identify as trans at a younger age than did their nonbinary participants. Of the 166 individuals they surveyed, the trans women came out to themselves on average at 14.2 years old, the trans men at 19.8 years old, and the genderqueer individuals at 20.3 years old.

The nonbinary trans students in my study, who generally had little information about their gender identities before entering college, had a different experience than many of the cis students with nonbinary sexual identities. Although nonbinary sexual identities, such as bisexual, pansexual, and asexual, are represented in the media and popular culture far less than are lesbian and gay identities, there is still greater visibility, particularly of bisexuality, in comparison with nonbinary gender identities. As a result, the students with nonbinary sexualities generally learned about their identities at a younger age and began to self-identify sooner than the students with nonbinary genders. Whereas the nonbinary trans students began to use their current gender identity label at an average of 19 years old, the students with nonbinary sexualities adopted their current sexual identity label at an average of 17.5 years old. An age gap of a year and a half may not seem very large, but the difference between what would typically be a high school senior and a sophomore in college is significant.

### Being Out to a Parent(s): Nonbinary Gender versus Nonbinary Sexuality

The nonbinary trans participants were also less likely than the nonbinary sexuality participants to be out to a parent. Only about half of the nonbinary trans students were open or mostly open about their gender identity to at least one parent, whereas 70 percent of the cis students with nonbinary sexual identities had disclosed their sexual identity to a parent. This difference can partly be explained by the nonbinary trans interviewees coming out to themselves at a relatively later age on average, which meant they had less time to come out to others, including their parents. But more important, for many of these students, identifying to their parents as nonbinary trans was more difficult and involved a greater risk of rejection than identifying as either nonbinary queer or binary trans because of a lack of parental understanding.

Coming out to a parent(s) as sexually nonbinary (e.g., asexual, bisexual, demisexual, pansexual) is often not an easy process because of there are few positive images of nonbinary individuals. Many parents are familiar with and like out lesbian and gay celebrities—such as Ellen DeGeneres, Neil Patrick Harris, B. D. Wong, Wanda Sykes, and Anderson Cooper—and can imagine their lesbian or gay child growing up to be similar to them and living a happy life. But they are largely unaware of out sexually nonbinary individuals, and as a result, they find it more difficult to imagine a bright future for their nonbinary child. For nonbinary students who identify in ways other than bisexual—which is the most well known of the nonbinary sexual identity categories—the process of coming out can be even more daunting because their parents may not be familiar with the terms.

Despite these difficulties in disclosing to parents, many students found it less challenging to come out as nonbinary in their sexuality than nonbinary in their gender. Among the nearly 100 students I interviewed who identified outside of both gender and sexual binaries and who discussed their families in the interview, half were out or mostly out to at least one parent about both identities. But when students were out about only one identity, it was invariably their sexuality. One-third had told a parent(s) about their sexual identity but not their gender identity, whereas just two students had disclosed their gender but not their sexuality. One of the students who was out to their parents about their sexuality but not their gender was Quinn, a white, gender-nonconforming pansexual student. Their father has been accepting of their nonbinary sexuality, while their mother has been less so, claiming that they are too young to really know themselves. But Quinn has not told them that they also identify their gender as nonbinary, because they are afraid that their parents "might do something drastic out of fear."

### Being Out to a Parent(s): Nonbinary Trans versus Binary Trans

At the same time, the nonbinary trans students often found it more difficult to come out to their parents about their gender identity in comparison with the binary trans students. As with the students who are nonbinary in their sexuality, the trans female and trans male respondents rarely found it easy to disclose to parents. However, the parents had a frame of reference for understanding a child who identifies as female or male, which the parents of a nonbinary gender child largely did not possess. This difference was demonstrated by the experiences of the trans participants who had not yet or were not transitioning and who were not out to their parents. Asked why they had not disclosed, both the binary and nonbinary trans students offered some of the same reasons: their parents hold anti-trans attitudes, have conservative religious beliefs, or come from a culture that is intolerant of trans people. But the nonbinary students provided an additional reason not typically given by binary students: that they believe a parent would not get or not take their identity seriously. Many of the participants who expressed this concern reported that their parent(s) would likely see their nonbinary identity as a phase or as not a "real" gender if they came out to them. Some also stated that they thought they would receive support if they identified as a trans woman or trans man because their parent(s) had some knowledge or would become understanding of binary trans identities over time.

Other research has similarly found differences between nonbinary and binary trans individuals in terms of parental disclosure. In Factor and Rothblum's study (2008), the genderqueer participants were much less likely to have come out to their parents than the trans female and trans male participants. Part of this disparity may be explained by the fact that the binary trans respondents were also much more likely to be medically transitioning—to be taking hormones, to have had genital surgery (trans women), and to have had chest surgery (trans men)—than the nonbinary respondents, and thus had less choice about keeping their gender identities a secret from their families. But these results also suggest a greater disregard and dismissal of nonbinary trans identities.

Among the nonbinary trans students in my study who were out to a parent(s) about their gender identity, 40 percent characterized their parent(s) as supportive or very supportive. Although this would seem to be a fairly positive result, especially since many of the students had not been out for very long, and thus their parents had little time to adjust, the figure is disappointing when considering that most of the students who disclosed did so because they expected their parents to be accepting. A few had inadvertently come out to their parents (such as a student who forgot to take off their binder when they went home), but the rest made a calculated decision that it would be better to disclose to their parents than not.

Rather than finding their parent(s) to be supportive, the majority of students described them as nonaccepting or rejecting: 31 percent reported that their parent(s) do not completely get or are uncomfortable with their gender, 15 percent reported that they are completely unsupportive or intolerant, 5 percent reported that they are OK but not great, 5 percent reported that they ignore the issue and will not discuss it, and 4 percent reported that their parents' have different reactions. Many of the participants who indicated that their parent(s) were intolerant or did not understand them said that they use a name and pronouns different from what they were assigned at birth and that their parent(s) do not respect how they identify themselves. Other participants stated that their parent(s) failed to comprehend why they could not accept their gender assigned at birth, but assume a nontraditional gender expression—that is, to be a more "masculine" woman or a more "feminine" man. These parent(s) could not recognize that identifying as nonbinary was more than a matter of gender roles and presentation.

### Affirmation of Nonbinary Trans Identities

Given the overall lack of parental acceptance, it is not surprising that only 4 of the 111 nonbinary trans students indicated that their parent(s) were a principal source of support for their gender identity. But other family members were also not part of their support system. Only 13 percent of the nonbinary trans participants indicated that they received significant support from someone in their family, as compared to 22 percent of the participants who were binary in their gender but nonbinary in their sexuality.

Both the nonbinary trans students and the binary trans students with nonbinary sexualities reported the same main sources of support for their identities: a friend(s) (82 percent versus 75 percent); an LGBTQIA+ group(s) (41 percent versus 37 percent); an online site(s), particularly Tumblr (32 percent versus 27 percent); and a partner or former partner (20 percent for both groups). In addition to the varying degrees to which the participants could turn to their families, there were two other significant differences in levels of support: from a campus LGBTQIA+ center or its director (20 percent versus 35 percent) and from a therapist (7 percent versus 1 percent). Many colleges do not have an LGBTQIA+ center, especially a professionally staffed space, so it could be that fewer of the nonbinary trans students I interviewed happened to be on a campus with such a center than the cis and binary trans students. However, several of the nonbinary trans participants indicated that their campus had an LGBTQIA+ center but that they did not find support there because the space was not inclusive of those with nonbinary gender identities. At the same time, some of the nonbinary trans students of color stated that they did not use their campus LGBTQIA+ center because they saw it as "a white space."

Among all of the students I interviewed, only nine reported that a therapist was a principal source of support. Tellingly, eight of these students were nonbinary trans participants, reflecting how a lack of societal affirmation can take a psychological toll on individuals who identify outside of a gender binary. However, not all of the nonbinary trans students who sought assistance from their campus counseling center indicated finding support there. For example, Kaden, a nineteen-year-old white student, went to the counseling center at their college for help with depression, but rather than receive the aid they needed, they had to educate the therapist about their nonbinary trans identity.

The nonbinary gender students and the binary gender/nonbinary sexuality students also differed in how they first learned and, for some, continue to learn about their gender or sexual identity. More than two-thirds (68 percent) of the nonbinary trans participants explored information about themselves online, compared to less than half (48 percent) of the participants with nonbinary sexualities. Among the nonbinary trans students who specified a website, more than three-fourths (79 percent) mentioned Tumblr, reflecting how reading other people's blogs or sometimes creating their own has become instrumental in shaping the identities of younger trans people today.

Among the participants who relied on Tumblr was "Ray," a white, twenty-one-year-old genderqueer student, who found the site be "a good way to connect with people and learn things if you have social anxiety." Outside of Tumblr, the only other websites that were mentioned by more than one nonbinary trans student were Google ($n = 6$), AVEN (Asexual Visibility and Education Network; $n = 3$), Reddit ($n = 2$), and Wikipedia ($n = 2$).

The interviewees who used gender identity labels for themselves that are fairly common in nonbinary trans communities but much less known outside of them, such as *agender* and *demigender*, were even more likely to have discovered these terms on the internet, typically on Tumblr. The students who had adopted terminology that, at least as of now, is not widely known even among trans people invariably learned it online. For example, Saer, a white, nineteen-year-old participant, identified as nonbinary aliagender (someone who defines their gender as "other," or apart from existing genders) and as a condigirl (someone who considers themselves a girl in certain situations)—both words they found on Tumblr. Saer commented: "A lot of my support comes from Internet outlets, such as Tumblr, where I can find others with open views on gender and sexuality and who investigate all the different myriads of ways to identify and experience" (email message to author, December 3, 2014).

For both the nonbinary gender students and the binary gender/nonbinary sexuality students, meeting a nonbinary person was the second most common way that they learned about their gender or sexuality identity. But meeting others was mentioned more than twice as often by the nonbinary trans than the nonbinary sexuality participants (33 percent versus 14 percent). This difference points to the lack of images of nonbinary trans people in the media and popular culture. Because they do not see nonbinary individuals around them in society, many experienced meeting others who identify their gender as nonbinary as an important educational moment; for those who did not know that nonbinary trans people even existed, it was a revelation. One of the participants for whom being introduced to other nonbinary trans people was transformative was Riley, a white, nineteen-year-old student. He stated that meeting other transmasculine students in college "opened [his] eyes," enabling him to realize that he could identify as transmasculine, too.

The nonbinary trans students less frequently learned about their gender from a friend (20 percent), a college course (8 percent), a partner or former partner (6 percent), or reading a text about a trans person (6 percent). The relatively few participants who gained knowledge about themselves in the classroom reflect how academic fields, including disciplines in the humanities and social sciences, which should especially be inclusive of trans people, continue to be firmly rooted in a gender binary. At the same time, the lack of importance of texts in the participants' identity development process is indicative of the limited number of books and articles that have been written on the lives of nonbinary trans people.

How Colleges Fail Nonbinary Trans Students

All but one of the nonbinary trans students I interviewed stated that their college was not doing enough to support them, even though some attended colleges considered to be among the most "trans supportive" in the country because of their many trans-inclusive policies. The most pressing concerns expressed by the students included the absence of safe and comfortable restrooms, the lack or inadequacy of gender-inclusive housing options, being regularly misgendered in classes, and being unable to use their chosen name and identify outside of a gender binary on campus records. Many of the students indicated experiencing several of these issues.

The lack of gender-inclusive restrooms was the problem most commonly cited by the study participants. Many of the students were able to tell me the exact location of all of these facilities on their campus, because these were the only restrooms that they felt safe and comfortable using, and their college had so few of them. Moreover, the gender-inclusive restrooms that did exist were not always well marked or in convenient locations. Some of the students reported that they made sure to go to the bathroom before they left for classes and planned their day so that they could get back home in time to avoid needing to use gendered facilities, which caused them tremendous stress and personal discomfort. Almost all of the participants stated that their college needed many more gender-inclusive restrooms.

Most of the students also stated that they wished their college offered gender-inclusive housing. A few of the participants indicated that their campus did provide such housing, but in some cases it was not open to incoming students, or they thought it was set up poorly, either requiring a laborious assignment process or being located in an inappropriate facility. Moreover, the colleges that offered gender-inclusive housing rarely made it available in all residence halls and in all types of housing (doubles, suites, and apartments), so the students were forced to choose between housing that supports their gender identity and housing that relates to other aspects of their identities and interests, such as a floor for people in their major, a first-year living-learning program, or an honors residence hall.

Along with issues with facilities, almost all of the participants said that pronouns were not asked by faculty members in any of their classes, including in women's and gender studies courses. As a result, the students who used nonbinary pronouns for themselves frequently struggled with whether they should talk to their instructors or continue to be misgendered. Most did not feel comfortable having this conversation, as they were unsure about how the faculty members would react and were concerned about their grades, so they endured being marginalized and invisible each semester.

Another concern of many of the participants was not being able to have the name they use for themselves and their gender identity included on campus records. More and more colleges are creating a process for students to have their chosen first name (some institutions refer to this as "preferred" name, but it is not a preference) on course and grade rosters, advisee and campus housing lists, online directories, email addresses, unofficial transcripts, and often identification cards and diplomas. But still only slightly more than 200 institutions have taken this step (Campus Pride Trans Policy Clearinghouse 2017a).

At the same time, less than a third of colleges that offer a chosen name also enable students to change the gender marker on their campus records, unless they have changed their gender on legal documents, which in many states requires undergoing gender-affirming surgeries (Campus Pride Trans Policy Clearinghouse 2017a). Moreover, even the colleges that enable students to change their gender marker, it is only from M to F or F to M, which was frustrating to many of the nonbinary trans students I interviewed. Having the gender marker on campus records match one's gender identity is important in cases where gender comes into play at colleges, such as for housing, locker room, and restroom purposes, so that students can be treated in accordance with how they identify.

## IMPLICATIONS

This study demonstrates that nonbinary trans college students often have significantly different identity development experiences than binary trans students and cis students with nonbinary sexualities. As a result, these students may have different expectations and needs from their campuses in terms of support, resources, and policies. But to the extent that colleges provide trans-related services, they rarely recognize any distinctions between nonbinary and binary trans students; instead, they typically take a one-size-fits-all approach that ignores the particular concerns of nonbinary students.

My research indicates that nonbinary trans students tend to recognize their identities at a later age—for many, when they are in college—than either their binary trans or cis/nonbinary sexuality peers. They are also less likely than members of the other two groups to have come out to a parent, and those who are out are less likely to have received what the students characterized as a supportive reaction. Given that many nonbinary college students are both in the process of coming out and cannot turn to their parents for help and encouragement, campuses have an obligation to offer trans-specific support services. Colleges that have counseling centers should train their therapists to be able to work appropriately and effectively with nonbinary trans students and not just the binary trans people they may have encountered in the past. Counseling centers should also hire out trans staff and sponsor a trans support group so that trans students can meet and connect with other people who identify similarly to themselves.

Far fewer nonbinary AMAB individuals feel comfortable embracing and being open about their gender than nonbinary AFAB individuals because of the social stigma associated with someone presumed to be male presenting and acting in ways that are considered feminine. To address this situation, colleges need to conduct outreach specifically to this population, such as through offering a confidential therapy group and events that addresses nonbinary gender identities. While some binary trans speakers are much more well known and will likely attract a much larger audience, colleges also need to bring in nonbinary trans speakers, especially AMAB individuals, so that nonbinary trans students can see themselves reflected in the institution's programming and cis students can learn about a wider range of gender identities. Moreover, if more colleges sponsor nonbinary AMAB speakers, these performers will become more renowned and such events will presumably appeal to more students.

The vast majority (82 percent) of the nonbinary trans students indicated that they received support for their gender identity from their friends; the second most common source of support, which was mentioned by half as many students (41 percent), was a trans or LGBTQIA+ student group. A few stated that they did not need much support for identifying as a nonbinary trans person, and had no interest in getting involved in a campus organization focused on gender identity. Other participants reported that they had sought support from their college's LGBTQIA+ student group(s) but found it unwelcoming because of their gender or other aspects of their identity, such as being asexual or a person of color. Similarly, a lack of inclusiveness also led some participants not to frequent their campus LGBTQIA+ center, but the relatively low rate of receiving support from an LGBTQIA+ center (20 percent) was primarily because many of the students attended a college that failed to provide such a space.

These findings point to the need for colleges to foster groups and spaces that are welcoming to nonbinary trans students, including nonbinary trans students of color. Student Affairs staff should work with students to ensure that campus LGBTQIA+ student organizations are well funded and their leaders, as well as the leaders of other officially recognized student organizations, are well trained on how to run a group, interpersonal dynamics, and social justice issues. If there is student interest, staff members should also support the creation of a trans student group and an LGBTQIA+ student of color group, so that members of these communities can benefit from knowing others who share a similar identity.

Similarly, nonbinary trans students can greatly benefit from having a professionally staffed LGBTQIA+ center on their campus. In addition to offering support to individual students and student groups, center staff members can provide trans-related programming; educate cis students, staff, and faculty about trans people; and advocate for trans-supportive policies. A study I conducted (Beemyn 2010) of campuses with "gender identity" in their nondiscrimination policies speaks to this last point. I wanted to see if having a trans-inclusive non-discrimination policy led to other trans-supportive policies, including offering gender-inclusive housing, requiring gender-inclusive restrooms in all newly constructed buildings, having a private shower/locker room available to people of all genders in a rec center, covering hormones and surgeries for transitioning students under student health insurance, and enabling students to change the name and gender marker on most campus records without having to legally change their name or document a gender transition. Among the eighty-one colleges I surveyed, the institutions that had professionally staffed LGBTQIA+ centers were more likely to have enacted a greater number of these trans-supportive policies. All but one of the twelve colleges that had five or more of these policies in place also had an LGBTQIA+ center, whereas nine of the thirteen colleges that had none of these seven policies also did not have a center. Having an LGBTQIA+ center may indicate that a campus has a more inclusive environment for trans students that makes enacting trans-supportive policies easier, but the colleges with the greatest number of these policies also had LGBTQIA+ center directors who worked diligently to have these policies adopted. The colleges that did not have such a staff person typically had no one who consistently advocated for these policies or it was left to students, who did not have the same access to or standing with senior administrators.

Just having an LGBTQIA+ center is thus not enough; its director has to be a strong advocate in support of trans students who is willing to challenge their college's administration on the students' behalf. Moreover, as shown by the students of color and nonbinary students who indicated that they did not feel comfortable using their campus LGBTQIA+ center, the director, other staff, and volunteers need to be committed to creating an inclusive environment within the space. For example, centers must employ a significant number of staff of color, have working for racial justice at the heart of their missions, and offer programs and services that take an intersectional approach—that is, recognizing the multiple identities of minoritized students and the multiple, overlapping ways in which they experience oppression.

To create a welcoming space for nonbinary trans students, LGBTQIA+ centers must similarly have nonbinary students on staff. They must also not treat staff and visitors as if their gender is binary, and thus should be asking, rather than assuming, people's pronouns. The vast majority (82 percent) of the nonbinary trans students I interviewed used nonbinary pronouns for themselves, and all said that they were rarely given the opportunity to indicate their pronouns. Centers should set an example for other offices and departments by instituting a culture where pronouns are respected and not presumed. Besides asking students what pronouns they use for themselves, center staff can include their own pronouns on nametags and in email signatures.

Colleges also need to have policies in place for students to have the opportunity to indicate their pronouns in classes and noncurricular settings. Some institutions, like the University of Iowa, ask for pronouns on their admissions application; others, like Ohio University, UMass Amherst, and the University of Vermont, give students the ability to add their pronouns to their online student record. Both methods result in the pronouns that are entered appearing on course rosters (Campus Pride Trans Policy Clearinghouse 2017a). In the absence of a means for pronouns to appear on rosters, colleges should encourage instructors who teach small classes to be giving students the ability to indicate their pronouns, such as by going around and having the students introduce themselves with their names and pronouns or passing around cardstock paper and having the students create table tents with their names and pronouns. The aim is for students in classes where they share their names to be able to share their pronouns as well and for other students to respect these pronouns.

In larger classes, instructors are unlikely to learn every student's name and pronouns. In these cases, faculty can simply avoid referring to students by gender. For example, if a faculty member wants to acknowledge something that a student has said, the instructor can refer to the person using "they" ("as they said") or by gesturing to the student and using "you" ("as you said"). A faculty member can also avoid calling on students by gender. For example, instead of calling on "the woman in the back of the room" to ask or answer a question, an instructor can call on "the person in the purple sweater in the back of the room."

Trans students must also have the opportunity to provide their pronouns outside of the classroom, too, so that their gender is not assumed elsewhere on campus. Pronouns should be asked in go-arounds, where people give their names and perhaps other information about themselves, in meetings of student organizations, academic and student affairs committees, and other institutional groups. The check-in forms of health and counseling centers, dean of students offices, and other departments should include the ability to provide pronouns.

Some nonbinary trans students will not want to be out in some contexts, and thus will not want to indicate their pronouns on course rosters, in go-arounds, or on forms. For this reason, it is important that students not be expected or required to state their pronouns. Even though a number of trans students will choose not to be open about their gender in particular settings, they should have the right to make this decision for themselves, rather than faculty and staff members taking away their agency and assuming the power to (mis)gender them.

Along with being frequently misgendered, many of the students I interviewed indicated that their college was failing them as nonbinary trans individuals by not having gender-inclusive restrooms and housing and by not enabling them to change their name and gender marker on campus records. Colleges need to have gender-inclusive restrooms in most if not all academic buildings and stop putting nonbinary trans students into a position of having to choose between possible harassment and violence in gendered restrooms or daily anxiety about finding gender-inclusive facilities. Institutions should immediately degender all single-occupancy women's and men's restrooms by changing the signs to say "restroom" or "all-gender restroom." If this move does not lead to gender-inclusive facilities in most academic buildings, colleges should look to create additional single-user restrooms or convert some multiple-user women's and men's restrooms into gender-inclusive ones. Moving forward, colleges need to commit to having gender-inclusive restrooms in all buildings that are constructed or undergo major renovations.

As with gender-inclusive restrooms, providing safe and comfortable housing for trans students is an ethical imperative. Hundreds of colleges offer gender-inclusive housing, in which students are assigned roommates regardless of gender, but most institutions limit this option to certain floors, buildings, and parts of campus (Campus Pride Trans Policy Clearinghouse 2017b). While having gender-inclusive housing available in some residence halls is an important step forward, it means that most campus housing continues to normalize a gender binary and remains closed to trans students. There is no legitimate reason students should not have the choice to live wherever they want with whomever they want on campus, just as they can do if they live off campus. Many colleges once had separate housing areas based on gender, but in response to student demand, institutions moved to separate buildings and then to separate floors, before enabling most floors in most residence halls to be mixed by gender. It is past time housing officials gave up the vestiges of in loco parentis and allowed all rooms to be mixed by gender on student request.

There is also not a good reason for colleges not to provide a chosen name option. It is legal to do so in all states, and all of the major software systems used by campuses can be modified to accommodate an alternative first name without a significant cost to the institution (Beemyn and Brauer 2015). The best practice is to have two separate processes, so that trans students who are not out to their parent(s) can still have their chosen name used on campus. For example, all students at the University of Massachusetts, Amherst, can enter a chosen name on their online student record, which will appear primarily on course rosters. Efforts are made to prevent mailings sent to them at home from using this name. Trans students who are out to their parent(s) and who may not want to be out on campus can fill out a form with the registrar's office to have their chosen name on most nonlegal documents, including their college ID card. This name will be how they are known throughout the UMass Amherst campus, and email and mail sent to them will use this name.

Colleges likewise have the ability to allow students to indicate their gender identity on campus records without any supporting evidence, such as a letter from a therapist or a gender marker change on other documents. A growing number of institutions give students the option of indicating their gender identity along with their legal sex on the college's admissions form and use this information for housing assignments, as well as to track recruitment and retention rates (Campus Pride Trans Policy Clearinghouse 2017c). Although the federal government and many outside vendors that use higher education data want colleges to report gender as a binary, institutions can still recognize students' nonbinary identities, providing information on their "legal sex" only when required.

An implication that runs through many of the findings of my study is the need for all faculty, staff, and students to be educated about nonbinary trans students. Many of the nonbinary trans students I interviewed suggested that faculty and professional staff members should be required to attend a workshop or take an online course on antitrans discrimination, similar to what many colleges do to address sexual harassment. This training should specifically address antitrans harassment, respect for pronouns and other inclusive classroom practices, and restroom access policies. The respondents also suggested that incoming students should be introduced to these issues at orientation, and students who live in residence halls should be informed about the rights of individuals to use the res hall bathrooms that correspond to their gender identity. The extensive need for education about trans people at all colleges reinforces the importance of well-staffed and well-funded campus LGBTQIA+ centers, which can lead such initiatives.

CONCLUSION

A common adage among faculty and staff is that our students are one step ahead of us. It is inevitable that younger people will be at the forefront of many social and cultural changes to which older people will have to catch up. But in terms of trans identities, faculty and staff are in danger of falling too far behind. Already having a poor understanding of binary trans experiences, many are even less able to grasp the lives of nonbinary students. The central mission of colleges is to educate; they must be doing more to educate cis faculty and staff, as well as cis students, about trans people, while implementing trans-supportive policies and practices that specifically address the needs of nonbinary people. Institutions must stop failing their nonbinary trans students.

WORKS CITED

Beemyn, Genny. 2010. "What Does It Mean Not to Discriminate against Transgender Students?" Presentation given at the annual convention of the American College Personnel Association, Boston, MA.

———. 2016. "Beyond 'LGBTQ': Supporting the Spectrum of Sexual and Gender Identities of Your Students." Webinar presented for PaperClip Communications, April 13.

Beemyn, Genny, and Dot Brauer. 2015. "Trans-Inclusive College Records: Meeting the Needs of an Increasingly Diverse U.S. Student Population." *Transgender Studies Quarterly* 2 (3): 478–87.

Beemyn, Genny, and Sue Rankin. 2011. *The Lives of Transgender People*. New York: Columbia University Press.

Campus Pride Trans Policy Clearinghouse. 2017a. "Colleges and Universities that Allow Students to Change the Name and Gender on Campus Records." https://www.campuspride.org/tpc/records.

———. 2017b. "Colleges and Universities that Provide Gender-Inclusive Housing." https://www.campuspride.org/tpc/gender-inclusive-housing.

———. 2017c. "Colleges and Universities with LGBTQ Identity Questions as an Option on Admission Applications and Enrollment Forms." https://www.campuspride.org/tpc/identity-questions-as-an-option.

Catalano, D. Chase J. 2015. " 'Trans Enough?': The Pressures Trans Men Negotiate in Higher Education." *Transgender Studies Quarterly* 2 (3): 411–30.

Cordes, Drew. 2013. "The Emergence and Danger of the 'Acceptable Trans* Narrative.' " Bilerico Project, March 31. http://bilerico.lgbtqnation.com/2013/03/the_emergence_and_danger_of_the_acceptable_trans_n.php.

Effrig, Jessica C., Kathleen J. Bieschke, and Benjamin D. Locke. 2011. "Examining Victimization and Psychological Distress in Transgender College Students." *Journal of College Counseling* 14 (2): 143–57.

Factor, Rhonda, and Esther Rothblum. 2008. "Exploring Gender Identity and Community among Three Groups of Transgender Individuals in the United States: MTFs, FTMs, and Genderqueers." *Health Sociology Review* 17 (3): 235–53.

Goodrich, Kristopher M. 2012. "Lived Experiences of College-Age Transsexual Individuals." *Journal of College Counseling* 15 (3): 215–32.

Grant, Jaime M., Lisa A. Mottet, and Justin Tanis. 2011. *Injustice at Every Turn: A Report of the National Transgender Discrimination Survey*. Washington, DC: National Center for Transgender Equality and the National Gay and Lesbian Task Force.

Guo, Jeffrey. 2016. "Sorry, Grammar Nerds. The Singular 'They' Has Been Declared Word of the Year." *Washington Post*, January 8. https://www.washingtonpost.com/news/wonk/wp/2016/01/08/donald-trump-may-win-this-years-word-of-the-year/

James, Sandy E., Jody L. Herman, Susan Rankin, Mara Keisling, Lisa Mottet, and Ma'ayan Anafi. 2016. *The Report of the 2015 U.S. Transgender Survey*. Washington, DC: National Center for Transgender Equality.

Jourian, T. J. 2017. "Trans*forming College Masculinities: Carving Out Trans*Masculine Pathways through the Threshold of Dominance." *International Journal of Qualitative Studies in Education* 30 (3): 245–65.

Kuper, Laura E., Robin Nussbaum, and Brian Mustanski. 2012. "Exploring the Diversity of Gender and Sexual Orientation Identities in an Online Sample of Transgender Individuals." *Journal of Sex Research* 49 (2–3): 244–54.

Seelman, Kristie L. 2016. "Transgender Adults' Access to College Bathrooms and Housing and the Relationship to Suicidality." *Journal of Homosexuality* 63 (10): 1378–99.

Singh, Anneliese A., Sarah Meng, and Anthony Hansen. 2013. " 'It's Already Hard Enough Being a Student': Developing Affirming College Environments for Trans Youth." *Journal of LGBT Youth* 10 (3): 208–23.

Trans Murder Monitoring. 2016. "30th March 2016: Trans Day of Visibility Press Release over 2,000 Trans People Killed in the Last 8 Years." *Trans Respect*, March 29. http://transrespect.org/en/tdov-2016-tmm-update.

# TWELVE

# (In)Visibility and Protest

## Trans Men, Trans Women, and Nonbinary Students at New England Women's Colleges

*Shannon Weber*

THIS CHAPTER BEGINS answering a key set of questions: What is the status of trans students at women's colleges in the Northeastern United States? What have their experiences on campus been like at administrative and social levels, and how are women's colleges grappling with their own institutional identities as women's colleges, as they are home to students of diverse genders? In what ways are the campuses becoming more inclusive for trans students, and where is there still room for improvement? Drawing on semi-structured interview research (obtained through snowball sampling) from 2011 to 2014 with current students and recent graduates from two Massachusetts women's colleges (Mount Holyoke and Smith), as well as news articles and media clips, I explore these campuses as spaces that have a complicated relationship to trans inclusion and visibility politics.

On the one hand, in line with my data from LGBQ (lesbian, gay, bisexual, and queer) interviewees at these two campuses, Northeastern women's colleges are often experienced by trans students as spaces where they are able to explore their identities in a safer, more celebratory environment than at many "coed" colleges and universities. As one 2012 trans male graduate of Smith named Jayke told me, "I think [Smith] gave me the freedom to experiment with gender presentation," and then added, "I know a lot of first-years who said they came here because they would feel safe for being trans, genderqueer, or just queer in general ... it is a refuge for a lot of people." Scholar Wendy Schneider echoes this alumnus' sentiment, arguing,

> People who favor making women's colleges accessible and supportive
> for transgender students noted that the climate at these institutions

is built on empowerment and self-expression in a way that most co-educational institutions have not matched. This creates an environment which is conducive to identity development, particularly around gender identity and expression. (Schneider 2010, 102–3)

On the other hand, not all trans students' experiences were positive, and Smith and Mount Holyoke have important differences between them when it comes to reported experiences.

Trans interviewees from both colleges report positive and negative experiences on campus, yet trans men reported having had a more embattled relationship with the administration at Smith, compared with trans men at Mount Holyoke. Although it is true that my snowball sampling yielded more trans participants from Smith than from Mount Holyoke, as I discuss, it is also true that unlike Mount Holyoke, Smith has had multiple highly publicized trans-related administrative controversies that figure largely into the campus politics reported by trans and cis interviewees alike. These controversies dramatically shape how Smith interviewees view the campus administration, and Smith students and alumnae/i overall report more disillusionment and skepticism about the administration than do those from Mount Holyoke.

## TRANS STUDENTS ON CAMPUS: BREAKDOWN BY THE NUMBERS

Out of the fifty-six students and recent alums I interviewed at Smith and Mount Holyoke, eight out of thirty-two (25 percent) of Mount Holyoke interviewees reported currently identifying as some version of non-cisgender. At Smith, the figure was much higher at seventeen out of twenty-four, or approximately 70.8 percent of interviewees. Although only a couple of students at each campus identified as anything other than cis prior to setting foot on campus, a substantial number of my interviewees began to view their gender identities differently after their arrival, whether during the course of attending or after graduation. Taking both sets of data together, roughly 44.6 percent of my interviewees could speak to their experiences as people who fall outside the range of socially sanctioned cis identity. Though my data are statistically not representative of the breakdown of cis and trans-spectrum students at Mount Holyoke or Smith overall, it does indicate the comparatively sizable and vocal nature of trans communities within these close-knit colleges.

To understand the diverse experiences of the interviewees I have grouped as "non-cisgender," it is important to understand the nuances of individuals'

gender identities. It is instructive to think of gender as a constellation of identities, presentations, and experiences with the potential to be as unique as the
individual. As pioneering trans studies scholar Kate Bornstein puts it, "You
get to name your own gender and have it be a real gender. You have the right
to do that, and no one can take that right away from you, because it's always
there in your heart: your gender" (Bornstein 2013, 113). My interviewees'
narratives in many ways mirror this expansive understanding of gender, especially because those I interviewed tended to be steeped in social construc-
tionist understandings of gender through their time at Mount Holyoke and
Smith. This observation holds even for those who did not major in women's,
gender, and sexuality studies. The exposure to queer theory and trans studies,
especially for younger interviewees, no doubt helped form the ways they think
about their own identities and represents a particularly privileged, elite academic vantage point.[1]

    Out of my trans interviewees at Mount Holyoke, two interviewees iden-
tified as trans males at the time of our interviews, one of whom called himself a
"transfag" specifically and indicated throughout the interview that being trans
is a major part of his identity. In contrast, two others identified simply as male;
they foregrounded their maleness and saw their trans status as less defining
or simply as one fact in their medical history. Three other interviewees identified as genderqueer and another identified as both gender-variant and female.

    At Smith, I counted two interviewees who identified as trans males, two
as male, four as genderqueer, and one as gender-variant and female. Beyond
this classification, my data from Smith reflects a somewhat messier breakdown
of non-cis identity labels compared with Mount Holyoke, with two of my genderqueer interviewees respectively identifying as genderqueer and female and
as genderqueer and a trans man.[2] Another Smithie identified as being on the
transmasculine spectrum, another reported being unsure but definitely not cis,
and still another reported her current gender identity as being a "queergirl,"
a complex identity she has come to after a long journey of questioning her
gender identity, pronouns, and presentation and experimenting with different
forms of gendered embodiment. As someone whose experiences depart from
the standard narrative that trans assigned female at birth (AFAB) individuals
are male-identified, and as someone who also has some privilege in currently
using female pronouns and "passing" as a cis woman, this Smithie's narrative
also complicates the idea of a cis-trans binary, showing that there is the possibility for moving across the spectrum of gender to inhabit various identities
at different points.

Importantly, none of my interviewees described themselves as trans women or assigned male at birth. The experiences and needs of trans women and transfeminine-spectrum individuals are therefore not reflected in my interview data, even as I consider a number of questions in this chapter about the inclusion of trans women in a women's college setting. The absence of trans women's voices here is significant when considering the fact that at least one trans woman attended Smith as of 2014 (Merevick and Yandoli 2014), but did not want her name to be known "for reasons of personal safety," according to the *New York Times*. This student wrote in an email to the *Times*, "It's way harder to get your gender stuff lined up for an application to Smith than it is to get it together for a passport change, and that's really saying something" (Feldman 2014).

In another case, at Simmons College, a prominent women's college in Boston, a trans woman who had participated in trans rights activism in high school was admitted with a scholarship and ostensibly celebrated by the college, but in reality the administration realized the student's trans status only after she arrived on campus.[3] From these examples, we can conclude that trans women are already present at women's colleges, but they occupy a tenuous space—far more under the radar than courted by the schools. Although some trans female students may wish to stay under the radar because they identify more as women than as trans women, the threat of institutional rejection is no doubt palpable, given the case of Calliope Wong, a trans woman who strove to apply to Smith in 2012, to which I turn later in this chapter.

TRANS PRESENCE AND ERASURE: A SHORT GENEALOGY

Debates about trans students at women's colleges began publicly simmering at Smith in the mid-2000s, although most of the attention was centered on trans men. Trans male interviewee Roo Azul,[4] who at the time of his application identified as gender nonconforming and genderqueer, told me he had tried to fight for the inclusion of trans women on campus. He did so during his last two years at Smith, from 2004 to 2006, in his capacity as president of a trans student organization. Despite putting pressure on the administration, he laments that "we completely failed on that." In 2004, when Roo Azul gave a workshop titled "Deconstructing Masculinity" and attempted to educate transmasculine students on campus about issues of transmisogyny, he "got a lot of shit for that" from other trans students, who were more focused on the oppression they faced for their gender identities and did not want to turn their critique of gender oppression inward to consider their own male privilege and positionality in hierarchies of gender. Due to the growing visibility of trans men on campus, students mostly focused on trans male experiences and issues. Roo Azul also implicitly ties this focus to the ways that the trans group he was a part of at Smith was "primarily made up of white trans people and allies," as well as students from economically privileged backgrounds; thus, Smith student culture took on an entitled tone of, in Roo Azul's words, "Yes we are [oppressive]—fuck you!"

The Smith administration found itself under the spotlight when, in 2005, the eight-part Sundance documentary series *TransGeneration* chronicled the experiences of student Lucas Cheadle during its exploration of the lives of four trans college students at different campuses across the United States. Cheadle, who had allowed a camera crew to film him as he walked around campus and the local town of Northampton, spoke with family and friends, and advocated his needs to the college, was forced by the Smith administration in the middle of taping to stop using the campus as a filming location, presumably for public relations reasons. In spring 2011, Smith denied trans male student Jake Pecht from acting as an overnight host for prospective students as part of his Gold Key guide duties. Pecht wrote about his experiences in an op-ed in the campus newspaper, *The Sophian*:

> It was insinuated that the real reason I was "inappropriate" was not about a male and a female sharing a room. It was about maintaining Smith's pristine image as a pearls and sweater sets kind of place. The implications were that I cannot host because prospectives should not know about me before they are enrolled and their tuition paid. If I were to host the daughter of an alumnae or a donor, admissions was concerned about potential backlash. (Pecht 2011)

Also in spring 2011, the administration of Wellesley College, located near Boston, Massachusetts, caused a stir when it banned a self-identified transsexual male alumnus from serving as an interviewer for prospective students. Dean of Admission Jennifer Desjarlais explained that they did so on behalf of prospective students, seemingly to stave off the anticipated transphobia of cis female applicants and their parents. Desjarlais also argued that the ban was instituted to ensure that the interviewer had a "very clear understanding of the value of attending a women's college," despite the male alumnus in question plainly stating his commitment to women's education and to Wellesley as an institution (Thulin 2011). In fall 2011, Smith changed its policy on overnight hosts, explicitly asking trans students to refrain from hosting prospective students in accordance with the Honor Code. In their recommendation, the administration emphasized the young ages of prospective students, as well as prospective students' and parents' expectations that the student host at a women's college will identify as a woman (Fitzgibbons and Lynch 2011).

### Invisibility, Visibility, Hypervisibility: Trans Men's Experiences on Campus

For my trans male interviewees in particular, the extent to which others on campus read them as male and validate or question their gender presentations and identities can result in both invisibility and hypervisibility in the women's college space. This tension is evidenced by the experiences of Damon, a Mount Holyoke interviewee from the class of 2015 who applied to college identifying as gender nonconforming and now identifies as male. Damon speaks to the challenges of identifying as male on a campus where students are almost always coded as female. In that type of environment, he explains, it can be difficult to pass as male when female readings of one's body are constantly at play. He provides a humorous story that perfectly captures this tension. He explains, laughing, "At [a specific dorm on campus], there's that one sign on the road that says 'No Passing Zone.' And you see it like as you enter, like when you drive your car like towards campus. It's really funny ... [I was in the car with another trans guy] and I was like 'I can't pass [as male].' We were just in the car driving by, [and] he was like, 'Yeah, look, no passing zone.'"

Despite this alienation, when I asked Damon about his overall experiences with community on campus, he immediately affirmed that his overall experiences with community on campus have been positive. He posited that notions of queer and trans community on campus are likely to be more important to individuals who are still coming to terms with their identities. Given the fact that Damon began identifying as male shortly before arriving at Mount Holyoke, he has not needed to draw on the resources of queer and trans community in the same way some of my other interviewees have.

In other instances, trans men on campus have been rendered invisible and hypervisible at the same time. An extreme example of this can be found in the experiences of Shawn, a 2012 Smith graduate. He describes the humiliation and horror he felt during graduation, when the faculty member in charge of reading graduates' names used his birth name—often referred to by trans individuals as their "dead name"—instead of his chosen name. This occurred despite Shawn taking great pains beforehand to ensure that he would be correctly identified. As he tells the story, the raw emotion of the experience becomes heightened:

I had not legally changed my name yet, but I was very much going by Shawn, and, I really wanted to graduate *as Shawn*. I didn't want that horrible legal name to be announced at my graduation. So I emailed them; I'm like, "Hi, you know, um, is it possible to email in a name that we would like to have read instead of our legal name?" And they're like "Yeah, no problem, just send us the name that you want read and make sure that you tell us how to pronounce it." . . . And um, then I came out to my parents, 'cause I was like, "Hey Mom and Dad, this is what's gonna be happening, and this needs to happen," blah blah blah. And then, um, the day before graduation we have that award thing, you know, where they give out awards—and, and the name was right [at the awards ceremony] ... So I wasn't even worried ... they also warned me that ... the name would be the legal name but that I shouldn't worry because it's just their list so they have to put it on there. So I was like all right, whatever . . . .

And then, I'm at graduation, and, [takes deep breath, palpably upset] all of a sudden this trans kid who had been on T [testosterone] for like, half the year, has the wrong name read? And I'm kinda like, maybe it's 'cause of parents, like, who knows—a lot of these trans guys are just, they're living double lives for most of their time at Smith. And uh, so like all right, [I'm telling myself] it's fine, it's fine. And then it happened again. [Palpably upset] For someone else who had a different name. [Takes a deep breath] And I turned to my friend and I was like, "I hope to God this doesn't happen to me." You know. 'Cause, hey, it can't happen. 'Cause yesterday they didn't mess it up. It can't happen. It can't happen. [I] go up, to get my diploma, and then they say the legal name. And like I was like so shocked, like, I'm glad that I was so in shock because I didn't wanna make a scene—you know it's not just my graduation, it's everybody's. So I didn't wanna make a scene, but I just like, death-glared the president ... and I tried so hard to stay composed, and I walked off-stage, and I just, I totally lost it. I totally was like, "I came out to my *fucking parents* for this; like, you guys lied to me. You lied to me." And I was like, the whole entire day was ruined.

In this moment, Shawn's worst fears came true on arguably the most important day of his time at Smith, forever marring his connection to the school. The act of reinscribing a female gender onto his male person effectively negated his gender identity in front of the entire senior graduating class, friends and relatives of the graduating class, Smith faculty, and his own family.

Shawn adds,

> It would've been fine if—if they had just told me that they couldn't do it, it would've been fine, 'cause I would've been like, I'll just brace myself and just graduate and that'll be that … I walked away from there … I didn't wanna have anything to do with Smith. I was so sick of all their bullshit, you know. It's constantly, all they care about is their fucking money, and their funding, and—you know, their endowed alums who can give them millions of dollars a year; that's all they care about, and they care about their image.

When I asked Shawn if he ever found out whether the other trans male students he referenced had definitively not wanted their birth names read aloud at graduation, he responded that he technically was not sure, but that "it doesn't matter if that's what they wanted or not; they did it to me! And it's just, you know it's one thing to have it happen to one person and you're worried that their parents are there and they need to just get through this last moment … But it happened to *multiple* people and that's why it was kinda like '*What?*' You know? … *Oh man*. It still makes my blood boil."

Shawn's traumatizing graduation experience had a double effect. On the one hand, it rendered him hypervisible as he, taken aback, was forced to walk across the stage clearly presenting as male, and known as male to his peers, to accept a diploma that had been announced under a name socially marked as female, thus presenting a jarring gendered discontinuity. At the same time, this misgendering, regardless of the intent by Smith administrators, marked Shawn as invisible, disregarding his gender identity and presenting him to the Smith community as female, along with the vast majority of his classmates. His correct gender identity was also negated in front of his family, whom he had taken great pains to come out to as trans for this important life milestone. The Smith administration additionally failed to model respectful treatment that arguably may have helped facilitate greater familial comfort with his newly disclosed identity.

As if these damaging acts were not enough for him to contend with, when Shawn later contacted Smith to request a new diploma reflecting his actual name, the registrar at first denied any initial mix-up. The college had apparently retroactively changed all of his records after his name change became legal; according to Shawn, "they have no record of me with my past name 'cause they wanted to cover their asses." The registrar then attempted to make Shawn pay $50 to correct the college's mistake, but agreed to issue him a new diploma for free after he wrote back with a "little rant" about "tak[ing] this diploma without cost as a retribution for all the emotional damages." Shawn's experiences here constitute an attempted erasure by the college of the traumatizing event (graduation), and thus serve as another instance of rendering Shawn invisible—a failed instance, given his assertive refusal to pay the new diploma fee. Under the logic of institutional erasure, if Shawn was always "Shawn" according to official records, then the proof of his dehumanization under a name he rejected could perhaps be rendered invisible as well. Ultimately, whether or not the Smith administration performed any of these invisibilizing maneuvers on purpose, their effect was the same on the Smith alumnus they humiliated and ostracized.

Jayke, mentioned earlier, is another trans male Smithie from the class of 2012—the same class year as Shawn. He reported to me that he had no problems at graduation and had his correct name read aloud. However, he experienced other forms of invisibility and hypervisibility on campus that, similar to Damon's narrative, were bound up in his ability to "pass" as male on an ostensibly all-female campus. He explains that at the beginning of the semester, after he had started to pass as male but before he had gotten to know other students in his dormitory "house," he would get "dirty looks on campus," including when he was using the bathroom in his house (which was designated for use by all house residents, versus an explicitly single-sex bathroom). He also received dirty looks when entering classes due to other students assuming he was not a Smith student and reacting with territorialism against the perceived male "outsider."[5] On the one hand, such reactions indicate that Jayke's maleness is being read correctly, positioning him as hypervisible amid the backdrop of a campus for women that at times exudes discomfort and even hostility toward male students. On the other hand, the invisibility of his identity as a Smithie is palpable. Even when Jayke was correctly read as both male and a member of the Smith community, as occurred during the course of facilitating formal discussions about the status of trans students on campus, he had another student tell him that she did not want him on campus due to his male identification.

Jayke's pleasure in being properly read by others as male was also marred by instances of negativity in the classroom. He explained to me that he had to come out as trans on the first day of class in every course, and that others in the class would give him "weird looks ... including the professor." Although

Jayke identifies some professors as being very respectful about using the correct pronouns and name, he says that other professors would "forget constantly or be adamant on using my birth name." Other professors tokenized his trans status by asking him questions about being trans in inappropriate contexts. He also encountered a Spanish professor who continued to address the entire class using feminine grammar, even after Jayke had spoken to the professor about how to address him, a situation that even now leaves him torn. He acknowledged to me that he understands the perspective that using feminine grammar in a Spanish class is a feminist, woman-empowering act, but that it was also awkward for him to be part of that context and that he could never quite be sure how much transphobia may have been fueling the continued practice.

Jayke also ran into some problems with being misgendered by various institutional systems at Smith, a fact he directly ties to classism. He explains that he tried to change his name and picture on the official rosters distributed to instructors, but because it costs money to take a new photo, he was unable to afford doing so. Despite identifying as coming from an "upper class" background, he says he could not afford having his name legally changed while at Smith, which prohibited him from being able to change his name on his campus ID card, Smith email, transcripts, the student information system, and financial aid documents.[6] He changed his name and photo on Smith internet-based forums, since the forums allow for individual customization, but from his perspective, this was insufficient. He was routinely asked by local businesses in Northampton for secondary ID on presenting his college ID, because they did not believe that he attended Smith and thus deemed him ineligible for student discounts.

The "I Am Smith" public relations campaign was another problematic arena for trans inclusion and (in)visibility among transmasculine Smithies. Used during the 2000s, the I Am Smith campaign displayed biographies of selected high-achieving Smith students on the front of the college website and in promotional and admissions materials in an effort to illustrate the types of diversity and leadership exhibited by Smith women. I use "women" purposefully here, as only (presumably cis) women appeared in the I Am Smith campaign. Indeed, it seems only women of a particular appearance were highlighted. As Jayke describes it, "I was pretty sure I wouldn't see any of my queer friends, my trans friends ... any of my friends who didn't look normative." Although this description forecloses the idea that queerness could "look normative," and thus contributes to femme erasure, it also points to the invisibility of non-female students in the I Am Smith campaign and to the larger institutional invalidation of nonfemale students. Jayke expressed to me, "I hate [the I Am Smith campaign] on so many levels, and not just personally … every single student would be unpierced, very well cleaned up, no shaved hair, no short hair … like one person out of six or a dozen had short hair … So I've gotta look like a woman, have no piercings, no tattoos … all of the things I'm not and my friends aren't, too."

Mount Holyoke interviewees also indicated their frustration with the lack of representation of trans students in promotional materials. Reggie,[7] a Mount Holyoke alum who graduated in 2010, expressed exasperation with the way another alum and dear friend had been treated by the college, indicating that because the alumnus in question was a trans male, his successful science career was not highlighted by the administration:

> [Name of male alumnus] is still intimately involved in all the exciting Mars stuff that … the Astronomy Department is currently doing that Mount Holyoke loves to tout about. But he's never mentioned. And they can get away with it because he's not a [current] student … it's shameful. It's shameful.

Reggie views Mount Holyoke as a place where images of transmasculine-presenting individuals may be featured in advertisements related to the college, which on the surface is a step up from Smith's infamous "cashmere and pearls" public relations atmosphere. Yet when it comes to acknowledging the achievements of nonfemale alumni, the college continues to be strategically silent, effectively promoting the invisibility of trans men even after they graduate.

### Student Activism for Trans Women and Administrative Change

Amid debates about trans men at women's colleges, the needs of trans women wishing to attend a women's college were largely ignored until the fall of 2012, when trans high school senior Calliope Wong attempted to apply to Smith. Wong's experiences with gender identity–based discrimination during the application process, which she documented on her personal blog, led to the issue of admitting trans women to women's colleges being brought to the attention of national media. Wong, who took the time to carefully contact Smith and explain her specific situation, was told by staff that, per the college's "case-by-case" policy of evaluating applications, her application would be considered as long as all of her submitted documents reflected her gender as female. Although all of her high school records and letters of recommendation reflected her gender identity as female, her application was ultimately rejected from consideration in March 2013 because her father had checked off "male" on her Free Application for Federal Student Aid (FAFSA). Chronicling the progress of her application on her blog, Wong wrote, "I cried the day my papers came back. I still feel like crying" (DiBlasio 2013).

Wong's story went viral, gaining coverage in the *Huffington Post* and *USA Today*. As part of the student outcry over this injustice, the Smith group Q&A, said to stand for Queers and Allies or Question and Answer ("Question: Trans women at Smith? Answer: Trans women at Smith!" reads the group's Tumblr page header), sprang up to fight for the right of trans women to attend the college. The group delivered a Change.org petition of over 4,000 signatures to the Office of Admissions in early May 2013, demanding that the college adopt trans-friendly admissions policies for trans women ("Smith College Group" 2013).

In response, the administration slightly changed its admissions policy the following January, so that the FAFSA is no longer used to determine the veracity of an applicant's "consisten[t]" female status (Waldman 2014). (Wong ultimately gave up her quest to join the Smith community and enrolled at a coeducational New England school.) However, the college's continued absence of a concrete policy on admitting trans students and its overall evasiveness on trans issues led to growing tensions on campus and continued to spur student activism.

Smith students protested the following fall, including organizing a demonstration outside the October 2014 Board of Trustees meeting and helping craft a "Pledge of Non-Support," along with other student organizations on campus, to encourage members of the Smith community not to donate to the campus unless demands were met related to the support of trans women, students of color, low-income students, undocumented students, students with disabilities, and students of nontraditional ages (Weber 2016). The organizations gave the Smith administration until May 2, 2015, the date of the last Board of Trustees meeting of the academic year, to address their demands. In the midst of students again protesting outside this meeting, the board voted in favor of a policy considering trans women officially admissible to apply (although they did not take action on a number of the other demands affecting marginalized students). Smith became the fourth of the five remaining prestigious Seven Sisters women's colleges to agree to consider trans women for admission (after Mount Holyoke, Wellesley, and Bryn Mawr; Barnard changed its policy soon after Smith did so).

Trans Hierarchies and Erotic Capital: Nonbinary Students Speak Back

According to my trans male and genderqueer interviewees, white transmasculine students on both campuses have increasingly enjoyed the benefits of a queer student hierarchy that values white masculinity to the detriment of queer femmes, students of color, and queer femmes of color in particular. Trans students have produced their own hierarchies of erotic value and popularity, especially at Smith, where the trans population appears to be larger than at Mount Holyoke (mirroring the larger student population in general at Smith). Some of my Smith interviewees reported feeling alienated and isolated by these tiers of desirability, which are premised in certain normative expectations about identity and behavior.

Scott, a 2010 male Smith alum, describes some trans men on campus as adopting a stereotypically macho demeanor—"moving and sitting in a really specific way"—that he attributes to a desire to "imitat[e] ... cis guys." He had attempted such behavior in the past, which led him to realize that it was "sorta not worth it" because it "sorta makes you look like a jerk." He describes the popular fashion within the trans male community at Smith during this time as "baggy pants, backwards baseball caps, bragging about being players and sleeping with so many girls ... swagger, masculinity, taking up space." As someone who generally felt uncomfortable embodying his gender in such a manner, Scott felt like he did not fit in with other trans men on campus and even received "direct backlash" for not acting macho enough. He identified masculinity, as well as straightness, as a key for success in the trans "clique." Scott also opined that there are multiple queer communities on campus that include the "trans bubble" and the "lesbian bubble," which are separate from each other. According to Scott, the desire of some men on campus to be seen as "male, no trans prefix, just a normal guy" led them to intentionally distance themselves from the queer community. One cis gay-identified Smith alumna from the class of 2012 describes such men as "the trans bro community ... dudey dudes" who alienated some of her trans friends. For these friends, she explains, "The thing that gets called 'the transgender community' is not really a community that has space for them."

Jayke also affirms the idea that heterosexuality was seen by other men as an important component of being male on the Smith campus. Even if not heterosexual, Jayke explains, there was an emphasis on "being a trans man attracted to women ... [or] coming from a lesbian community." This expectation to be attracted to women was hard for Jayke as someone with significant

desires for men. He explains, "I know another gay-identified trans man ...
who was having a really tough time because he was like, 'I'm at a college with
no dating prospects!'"

In these narratives, we see the ways that traditional sexism and heterosexism can sometimes manifest in trans male communities, because so
often the models for what it means to be male are hegemonic constructions of
manhood steeped in entitlement and oppression. The particular hegemonic
construction of white heterosexual manhood acts as an especially entitled form
of maleness on these campuses because the colleges are white-dominated. The
fact that many trans men need to "pass" in a violently transphobic world can
also sometimes mean that attempts at "authentic" manhood reinscribe systems
of oppression. At the same time, these reinscriptions of oppression must be
relentlessly unpacked and reevaluated to cultivate feminist masculinities free
from internalized sexism, racism, homophobia, and transphobia.

At the core of these oppressive enactments of masculinity is a belief in a
rigid gender binary, such that some interviewees express concern for the position of genderqueer and nonbinary students on campus. The trans hierarchy
at Smith had apparently become so talked about in some queer circles that a cis
Mount Holyoke student from the class of 2013 could describe the trans scene
at Smith in detail. She stated:

> Well the thing I've heard about Smith, and I don't really know this,
> personal experience-wise, but I've heard that at Smith, if you are like
> at all genderqueer or gender nonconforming, there's like this big push
> to identify as trans [male] and to start testosterone ... I don't actually
> have any like real evidence for this. I've known people that have done,
> wanted to do research on that. It's a very different environment [from
> Mount Holyoke] in that sense. And I've heard ... that a lot of people
> have then left Smith and *regretted* the fact that they started T, because
> in fact they *don't* wanna look male; they kinda wanted to look an-
> drogynous. And now that's what they did because that's what the en-
> vironment pushed them to.

Although this is clearly a thirdhand account from a non-Smith student, as she
herself acknowledges, it fits into the overall picture sketched by various trans
Smithies of trans communal policing by strongly male-identified students
who have formed a set of implicit gendered guidelines. Another male Smithie
from the class of 2012 also expressed concern at the increased speed at which
younger trans men begin taking testosterone and getting top surgery compared

to the longer process he went through on campus, which might be indicative of the pressure-to-conform culture alleged above or which may simply be the product of differences in comfort and/or the availability of resources between two individuals or cohorts of trans men.

Although not as prominently featured in my interviews with trans Mount Holyoke students, there were also communal expectations about how to be trans at that college. As Reggie puts it, "I think that those [trans social] requirements are dictated by the groups. I think that those requirements are informed by both normative society and also the . . . inverse society that, you know, pervades Mount Holyoke. . . . These . . . pervasive norms . . . still work their way in even into queer spaces. . . . There's the transer-than-thou trope. There's the queerer-than-thou trope." This "transer-than-thou trope" echoes the rigid gender rules experienced by many of my male Smith interviewees within trans circles.

Catia, a self-identified gender-fluid tomboi dyke and junior at Mount Holyoke, reports that there is "a lot of pressure for people to appear androgynous" on their campus. They affirm that there is a queer hierarchy in which femme identity is at "the very bottom," whereas being androgynous or "somehow masculine" is given more value. At the top of the hierarchy, Catia argues, are genderqueer and trans students, specifically trans men. Hinting at the hypervisibility of trans students on campus, they explain, "It's almost impossible to be in the queer community and not know who the trans people are on campus . . . There's a lot of respect and a lot of power given to them that they . . . haven't earned." For Catia, the fact that this power has not been "earned" is indicative of the ease of being desired on campus when presenting as masculine of center.

Catia's description of the erotic premium placed on (white) transmasculine students poses some important questions about the meaning of such a hierarchy. Is the focus on white (trans) maleness in "women's" space problematic? Is this a case of men sexistly taking up too much space and participating in the consolidation of mostly female desire around male bodies? Or does the inordinate "respect" and "power" alleged by Catia arise from students' recognition that trans men's marginalization is all too real, at the campus level and in society at large, and that radical inclusion and celebration is the solution? Can both be true?

Whether one argues that white, male, and/or transmasculine students are at the top of the social pyramid is correlated with the years the interviewee attended college. Older alums, ranging from the class of 2000 to the class of 2005, indicate that trans men were not visible or numerous enough on campus to be considered the most popular. This observation is even more applicable when discussing genderqueer and other nonbinary individuals. Interviewees who readily mention genderqueer people on campus tend to be from the classes of 2013–2017. For example, Shane,[8] a Smith alum from the class of 2005, did not begin to identify as genderqueer until long after they had graduated. Shane's experience testifies to the power of the Smith culture to promote multiple ways to be a woman during their time on campus. Because of this expansive model of what it meant to occupy an AFAB body, it was not until Shane graduated that they came under increased gender policing by non-Smith friends and lovers. Feeling more limited by gender expectations, they increasingly questioned the logic of the gender binary before ultimately rejecting it. The lack of conversation about nonbinary gender identities during Shane's time at Smith (2001–2005) shows how different the climate was on campus, both inside and outside the classroom, compared with later graduates' and current students' experiences. Given the fact that self-identifying as genderqueer has only "taken off" in queer circles in approximately the past five to ten years, it makes sense that the increasing visibility and status of nonbinary identities within campus queer hierarchies are more recent phenomena as well.

Of course, it is important to remember that trans communities are far from monolithic at Smith or at Mount Holyoke, and there are signs that gender diversity is increasing. According to Scott, more students began to come out as genderqueer at Smith in his senior year, from 2009 to 2010. Jayke observes, "There is a large trend towards more genderqueer people" at Smith—"agender, gray zone, wibbly wobbly, bigender, genderqueer." He adds optimistically, "[It's] not just a Smith thing because I'm seeing a lot of that on Tumblr ... social media ... populated by people who are younger than my college generation." The explosion of discussions I have found about nonbinary gender identities across social media platforms and the blogosphere, compared to the dearth of academic scholarship, certainly seems to buttress Jayke's argument. Another recent Smith alum who identifies as genderqueer gives credit to New England's queer-positive environment for the increasing genderqueer presence at Smith. Compared to their rural Southern hometown, where "if you're genderqueer you're ... aesthetically not pleasing and confusing, ... in New England the possibility of transitioning is even there ... [thanks to] the vast gay consciousness" that promotes "tolerance if not acceptance" for people presenting along the "continuum of gender presentations."

At Mount Holyoke, perhaps due to the seeming absence of a trans male clique that enforces rigid gender norms or because my snowball sampling yielded more interviewees of younger ages at Mount Holyoke than at Smith, students from the classes of 2013–2017 described the presence of genderqueer students in even more expansive terms. Similar to Catia, who included genderqueer students as part of the most desirable people on campus at the beginning of this section, the same Mount Holyoke student who voiced her concerns about gender rigidity at Smith described Mount Holyoke as a place where genderqueerness is flourishing:

The genderqueerness is starting to happen younger and younger.... There were not that many visibly genderqueer people in my class as a first-year. There were two trans guys, or sort of questioning gender ... They both came in with "Here's my name, here's what my friends call me, you can use whatever words you want to describe me." ... One of them ... I ended up briefly dating ... It felt like in my year [2013] there were not that many people who were like super genderqueer. And then, the year after that, and the year after *that*, the incoming first-year classes were like *very visibly queer*.... There was this group of like ten girls who all cut their hair the first weekend of college.... They're like the super queer kids, and the genderqueer kids. And they've made up this popular group. That you see at the parties. My friend ... calls them the Fruit Loops ... the popular queer kids on campus ... And I bet if you asked, everyone would name the same like fifteen people. That are like "The Posse." A lot of them are genderqueer.

This student's description, beyond problematically equating gender fluidity and nonconformity with queerness, is also telling for noting the increase in genderqueer students over time and for making the connection between party culture, popularity, and genderqueer identification. For this interviewee, to be genderqueer is in some ways to be seen as a "super queer kid," which at Mount Holyoke is synonymous with cool—a member of "The Posse."

The increasing status of nonbinary students on campus is also perhaps strengthened by the fact that when the Mount Holyoke administration unveiled their updated admissions policies for trans women in 2014, they also explicitly affirmed that trans men and nonbinary students of all assigned sexes are eligible for admission—in short, anyone who is not a cis man is allowed to apply ("Admission of Transgender Students" n.d.). At the time of this writing, Mount Holyoke is the only U.S. women's college to explicitly allow for the admission of all applicants who are not cis men. However, this policy remains controversial for some trans and cis community members, and questions remain as to how well these policies are beginning to be implemented, as more trans applicants apply, accept their offer of admission, and arrive on campus.

### Contemporary Campus Politics and Recommendations

The Mount Holyoke administration has been more publicly trans-inclusive in recent years compared with the Smith administration. For example, during her 2012 convocation speech, newly minted Mount Holyoke President Lynn Pasquerella included the gender-neutral pronoun "zhe" in the midst of discussing diversity on campus.[9] She stated, "Each of us should take it personally when trolls enter [the anonymous Mount Holyoke Internet forum] the Confessional and attempt to undermine the value and worth of any member of our community because of how she, he, or zhe looks, thinks or acts" (Pasquerella 2012). The inclusion of "he" and, in particular, the gender-neutral pronoun "zhe" (also spelled "ze") elicited cheers from the audience as soon as the words had left Pasquerella's mouth. Her speech inspired the Coalition for Gender Awareness (COGA) at Mount Holyoke to post on their Tumblr account, "That absolutely amazing moment when President Lynn 'BAMF' [Badass Motherfucker] Pasquerella says 'she, he, or zhe' in her Convocation Speech." This post was liked and/or reblogged eighty times, with only positive comments, such as "This was a fantastic moment" and "gah I miss Mount Holyoke! The real world sucks" ("That Absolutely Amazing" 2012). Having such a public declaration of gender-inclusive support from the president of a women's college, especially in reflecting an awareness of nonbinary gender identities, may indeed place Mount Holyoke as the first college of its kind to champion such a message. It was certainly a foreshadowing of the college's later groundbreaking admissions policy as the first Seven Sisters institution to accept trans women in 2014 and the only women's college to consider all non-cis male applicants. Indeed, when Mount Holyoke announced their new admissions policy, Pasquerella had led the charge in notifying the trustees of the college that the shift would be taking place, whereas at Smith, the president cited the need for trustee agreement as a reason to defer action on an updated policy.[10]

With respect to Mount Holyoke, however, questions remain as to how to grapple with the idea of being a women's college that does not accept only women, as well as questions about how these admissions policies are put into practice. For example, Mount Holyoke student Emma Podolsky, class of 2018, penned a blog post in October 2015 titled "Mount Holyoke Does Not Care about Trans People," arguing,

> I found out from current first-year students that there were no school-sanctioned activities during orientation centered around support for trans folks on campus. Any dialogue about the trans policy at our school was lead [sic] entirely by student orientation leaders in small groups. Trans students were neglected by the same people who proudly announced their new acceptance at Mount Holyoke College. Several trans-identified first-year students have already had to be put into singles due to threat of safety by roommates who don't understand their gender identity and expression. The classroom experience remains oblivious to any pronouns besides the default she/her we assume of all students at Mount Holyoke.... Our usefulness only goes as far as a publicity stunt to gain more visibility and traction within the currently trendy topic of trans people existing in previously inaccessible institutions. This has happened with all disenfranchised students on campus, from undocumented to international students alike: If there are cameras and reporters, we are thrown in front of them like lifeless ragdolls. When it comes to our humanity at this college, we remain just as invisible as we've always been. (Podolsky 2015)

Invoking the politics of invisibility, Podolsky's scathing analysis indicts the Mount Holyoke administration for using trans students, and students from other marginalized backgrounds, as "lifeless ragdolls" when convenient for public relations purposes, while failing at true inclusivity.

The online comments written in response to Podolsky's blog post mirror many of the discussions I have had with trans and cis interviewees about what it means to be a women's college that accepts applications from those who do not identify as women. One commenter writes,

> The fact that we have trans men attending the college does not change the fact that we are a women's college and I think our trans student body knows that too. What is so wrong with addressing the student body of a women's college as "women"? Don't the majority of the student body attend to attend a women's college? You don't see administrators, faculty, or students address all the other races at a historically black university. Are they shamed and outed for that? No. No they aren't

because all students voluntarily chose to apply and attend a historically black university, knowing that it was one. If they feel uncomfortable of [sic] how they are addressed, or the issued [sic] that are addressed, at the university, then it should be those individuals that should consider transferring, not the whole institution that is beloved by the rest.

This comment speaks to the ongoing debates about the importance of women-centered education and the need for women's educational spaces, balanced with the need of trans people to be recognized as occupying marginalized and legitimate genders.

A few trans interviewees I spoke to at both campuses endorsed modified versions of the term "women's college," such as "historically women's college" or "gender minority college," to denote the complexity of centering women's empowerment while providing a more inclusive space. Other interviewees, in line with most women's colleges that have updated their admissions policies to include trans women but not trans men (and only sometimes AFAB nonbinary people, such as the policy at Wellesley), vocalize that women's colleges should not prioritize the voices of people who do not identify as women. More than one trans male alumnus expressed concerns to me about the idea of a women's college accepting trans men, questioning whether this meant that trans men are not being viewed as "real men" by the administrations of women's colleges. These questions are far from settled, for they represent competing ideas of what the identity of women's colleges should be in the twenty-first century, which gender(s) should be prioritized in a world with multiple forms of ongoing gender-based oppression, and what the historical legacy of a women's college should be.

Regardless of the individual routes various women's colleges take with respect to their institutional identities, it is clear that there is much the campuses still must do to become progressively more inclusive of their student bodies. For those on campus who do not identify as female, regardless of the official admissions policies, students should be treated with respect, which must include an overhaul of the administrative and online systems that continue to misgender and dead name nonfemale students. Although one's legal name is required on official transcripts and one's legal name and legal sex are required on financial aid, employment, and insurance records, all students should have the ability to update their campus-generated email addresses, registrar information, photo identification, and other forms of gender-based data. These changes would be in line with the Departments of Education and

Justice guidelines issued in May 2016 to establish standards for applying Title IX to transgender students. (Although these guidelines were more recently revoked by the Trump administration, and the status of trans students' rights remain precarious and uncertain, the 2016 guidelines provide an important blueprint for securing and improving trans rights moving forward.) Students have the right to be correctly referred to at graduation and all campus events. Faculty and staff should be required to undergo sensitivity training on trans issues, which would include appropriately using male and nonbinary pronouns, challenging ingrained assumptions about students' identities, and fostering trans-inclusive classrooms by asking students their pronouns and incorporating trans-inclusive curricula where appropriate.

For all trans students, and especially trans women, special care must be taken to ensure their physical safety on campus, particularly in dorm life and with respect to roommates, and educational programming about trans women's issues must be incorporated throughout the campus. This education must occur during orientation, alongside initiatives to facilitate conversations and education about other types of difference, and there should be an established contact in the dean's office, ideally connected to offices of diversity and inclusion, should students face any issues with campus safety or bias and hate incidents. Podolsky's reference to the "several trans-identified first-year students" who "have already had to be put into singles due to threat of safety by roommates" speaks to this very real and pressing concern and mirrors the disproportionate rates of violence trans women face in the wider society (Mock 2014; Stotzer 2009), as well as the transmisogyny trans women continually face in women's spaces dominated by cis women (Serano 2007). Given that many women's colleges, like many coeducational institutions, assign incoming students a "common read" that is connected with major lecturers and other programming in their first semester, it would be instructive to assign a text by a trans female scholar and/or activist as a way to bolster support for trans women on campus and promote constructive conversations about the diversity of gender and the human dignity of all trans people.

Women's colleges have the potential to be sites of extraordinarily positive exploration, self-expression, and transformation with respect to gender and sexuality. At the same time, there is much to improve on, even at the most "progressive" Northeastern women's colleges. Although Mount Holyoke and Smith have more inclusive policies than, for example, Hollins University—whose 2015–2016 student handbook misgenders trans male students and states that students transitioning to male are expected to leave the college (Hollins

University 2015)—the narratives presented here illustrate the work that must still be done.

## NOTES

1.  Trans students' educational privilege in conceptualizing gender through social constructionism and postmodernism at an elite private college cannot be overstated, given existing structural barriers that often prevent trans people, especially low-income trans individuals, trans people of color, and low-income trans women of color in particular, from gaining entree to higher education. As Viviane K. Namaste reminds us, "Much social science establishes an opposition between liberated academics who understand the constructed nature of gender and the poor duped transsexuals who are victims of false consciousness" (2000: 37–38). As my interviewees inhabit these particular elite spaces, their own understandings of gender should certainly not be taken to monolithically represent the majority of trans individuals.

2.  Although genderqueer individuals tend to express their genders in terms of not fitting into or moving beyond a binary understanding of "male" or "female," the two individuals referenced in this note use "she/her" and "he/him" pronouns, respectively, to strategically navigate a binary world. In other words, these interviewees do not feel themselves to be strictly female or male, but for survival reasons seem not to have adopted gender-neutral pronouns, as many other genderqueer people do.

3.  This fact was relayed to me by a source in the admissions office at Simmons College who wishes to remain anonymous. Despite the concerningly unintentional roots of this milestone, the Simmons case did provide a blueprint for other women's colleges to admit trans women.

4.  Roo Azul is a pseudonym chosen by the interviewee.

5.  Although it is not unusual for male students from the coed members of the Five Colleges—UMass Amherst, Amherst College, and Hampshire College—to take courses at Smith and Mount Holyoke through the cross-registration system, territorialism and women's college supremacy against off-campus male visitors is a component of campus life that is often acknowledged by students and, at least at Mount Holyoke, even lampooned in college skits. While fostering community among the cis women at Smith and Mount Holyoke, this culture can be understandably alienating for trans male students.

6.  Indeed, with the U.S. Departments of Justice and Education's groundbreaking eight-page "Dear Colleague Letter" in May 2016 that provided

instruction on proper applications of Title IX to transgender students, the refusal to allow a chosen name on some of the documents listed here was for a time considered a violation of Title IX prior to the Trump administration rescinding these guidelines. As the Dear Colleague Letter explains, "Under Title IX, a school must treat students consistent with their gender identity even if their education records or identification documents indicate a different sex.... School staff and contractors will use pronouns and names consistent with a transgender student's identity" (U.S. Departments of Justice and Education 2016, 3).

 7. Reggie is a pseudonym chosen by the interviewee.

 8. Shane is a pseudonym chosen by the interviewee.

 9. Pasquerella served as the eighteenth president of Mount Holyoke from 2010 to 2016.

 10. I thank Genny Beemyn for this insight.

## WORKS CITED

"Admission of Transgender Students." n.d. Mount Holyoke College. https://www.mtholyoke.edu/policies/admission-transgender-students (accessed February 1, 2016).

Bornstein, Kate. 2013. *My New Gender Workbook: A Step-by-Step Guide to Achieving World Peace through Gender Anarchy and Sex Positivity.* New York: Routledge.

DiBlasio, Natalie. 2013. "Smith College Rejects Transgender Applicant." *USA Today*, March 22. http://www.usatoday.com/story/news/nation/2013/03/22/smith-college-transgender-rejected/2009047/.

Feldman, Kiera. 2014. "What Are Women's Colleges For?" *New York Times*, May 24. http://www.nytimes.com/2014/05/25/opinion/sunday/who-are-womens-colleges-for.html.

Fitzgibbons, Sarah, and Clare Lynch. 2011. "Admissions Asks Trans* Students to No Longer Host Prospective Students." *Sophian*, November 8. http://www.smithsophian.com/news/admissions-asks-trans-students-to-no-longer-host-prospective-students-1.2690810#.UIHbIxj3zFe.

Hollins University. 2015. "2015–2016 Student Handbook." Hollins University. https://www.hollins.edu/wp-content/uploads/2014/09/Student-Handbook.pdf (accessed September 15, 2016).

Merevick, Tony, and Krystie Lee Yandoli. 2014. "Smith College Students Continue Fight over 'Discriminatory' Policy on Transgender Applicants."

*Buzzfeed News*, April 21. https://www.buzzfeed.com/tonymerevick/
smith-college-students-continue-fight-over-discriminatory-po.

Mock, Janet. 2014. *Redefining Realness: My Path to Womanhood, Identity, Love
and So Much More*. New York: Atria Books.

Namaste, Viviane K. 2000. *Invisible Lives: The Erasure of Transsexual and
Transgendered People*. Chicago: University of Chicago Press.

Pasquerella, Lynn. 2012. "Taking It Personally." Mount Holyoke College.
Last modified September 4, 2012. https://www.mtholyoke.edu/media/
convocation-2012-lynn-pasquerella.

Pecht, Jake. 2011. " 'I Am Smith' and I Am Male." *Sophian*, April 14. http://
www.smithsophian.com/opinions/i-am-smith-and-i-am-male-1.2270448#.
UIHK6xj3zFd.

Podolsky, Emma. 2015. "Mount Holyoke Does Not Care about Trans
People." *Mount Holyoke Radix*, October 1. http://www.mhradix.org/
blog-queer/2015/10/1/mount-holyoke-does-not-care-about-trans-people.

Schneider, Wendy. 2010. "Where Do We Belong? Assessing the Needs of
Transgender Students in Higher Education." *Vermont Connection: The
Student Affairs Journal of the University of Vermont* 31: 96–106.

Serano, Julia. 2007. *Whipping Girl: A Transsexual Woman on Sexism and the
Scapegoating of Femininity*. Emeryville, CA: Seal Press.

"Smith College Group to Deliver Petition on Transgender Policy to
Administrators." 2013. *MassLive*, May 1. http://www.masslive.com/news/
index.ssf/2013/04/smith_college_group_to_deliver.html.

Stotzer, Rebecca L. 2009. "Violence against Transgender People: A Review of
United States Data." *Aggression and Violent Behavior* 14 (3) (May–June):
170–79.

"That Absolutely Amazing Moment When President Lynn 'BAMF'
Pasquerella Says 'She, He, or Zhe' in Her Convocation Speech." 2012.
*CoGA: Mount Holyoke's Coalition for Gender Awareness*. Last modified September 4, 2012. http://cogamhc.tumblr.com/post/30875237387/
that-absolutely-amazing-moment-when-president-lynn.

Thulin, Lesley. 2011. "Admissions Office Bars Transgender Alumnus from
Interviewing Students." *Wellesley News*, April 27.

U.S. Departments of Justice and Education. 2016. "Dear Colleague Letter on
Transgender Students." May 13. http://www2.ed.gov/about/offices/list/ocr/
letters/colleague-201605-title-ix-transgender.pdf.

Waldman, Katy. 2014. "The Wellesley Man." *Slate*, June 5. http://www.slate.com/
articles/double_x/doublex/2014/06/

transgender_students_at_women_s_colleges_wellesley_smith_and_other s_confront.html.

Weber, Shannon. 2016. " 'Womanhood Does Not Reside in Documentation': Queer and Feminist Student Activism for Transgender Women's Inclusion at Women's Colleges." *Journal of Lesbian Studies* 20 (1): 29–45.

# THIRTEEN

# An Examination of Trans College Students' Sexual Health

*James M. DeVita and Katrin A. Wesner*

THE NEGATIVE CLIMATE FOR TRANS INDIVIDUALS in the United States has been well documented and is associated with individual health concerns (Institute of Medicine 2011; McGuire, Anderson, Toomey, and Russell 2010; Russell et al. 2011). A 2000 report coauthored by scholars from the Gay and Lesbian Medical Association and the Center for Lesbian, Gay, Bisexual, and Transgender Health at Columbia University concluded that "prejudice against transgender individuals is pervasive. There is a long-held view on the part of U.S. medical providers and researchers, as well as the public at large, that transgenderism is pathological. This, in itself, constitutes one of the most significant barriers to care" (Dean et al. 2000, 36). Trans people have historically also faced marginalization within the larger lesbian, gay, bisexual, and trans (LGBT) community, which results in stigmatization, inappropriate conflation of gender identity and sexual orientation, and a lack of information, resources, and training for doctors to meet the needs of trans patients (Dean et al. 2000).

Another considerable obstacle to improved health for trans individuals is that LGBT scholarship, which informs practice, often applies its findings to trans people while including few or no trans participants in its samples (Miner 2009; Rankin 2004; Renn and Reason 2013). This is problematic because gender and sexual orientation are distinct categories of identity, and health-related issues for trans individuals are often different from those of cis LGB people (Dean et al. 2000). The limited research on the health-related issues specific to trans people has largely focused on HIV rates and testing, mental health (specifically depression and suicide), and support services during gender transition (Clements-Nolle, Marx, Guzman, and Katz 2001; Dean et al. 2000; Magee, Bigelow, DeHaan, and Mustanski 2011). Additional research on the health-related concerns of LGBT populations, particularly trans individuals, is greatly needed.

This chapter seeks to contribute to knowledge about the overall sexual health of trans college students through an analysis of data from the American College Health Association's National College Health Assessment (ACHA-NCHA). This national research survey provides insights into the health attitudes, beliefs, and behaviors of college students, enabling health center staff and other student affairs professionals to tailor programs and services to best meet student needs (American College Heath Association 2011). Since NCHA's launch in 2000, it has been administered to over 1.6 million students at more than 775 colleges and universities (American College Health Association 2016). The survey has been updated several times since its inception, and the data used in this analysis was from the second generation, the ACHA-NCHA II.

Studying the sexual health of trans college students is both timely and warranted. Beemyn and Rankin (2011) conducted research on generational differences among trans people and concluded that because of changing norms in society, "this is the first generation of transgender teens who can actually be transgender teens" (1160). Colleges and universities can thus expect many trans students to be out prior to their arrival on campus, while others will come out and transition once they are there, which makes college an especially meaningful time and space for many trans students (Beemyn and Rankin 2011; Lees 1998). College is also an important moment in terms of sexual health. A study by Oswalt and Wyatt (2013) found that "because college is a transitional time when many students begin to examine their own health behaviors and possibly develop life-long health habits, this is a critical time to reinforce low risk sexual behaviors and prevention practices" (1568). Our hope is that a better understanding of trans college students will enable health practitioners and educators to provide services and programs that are more inclusive of the experiences and needs of this population.

LITERATURE REVIEW

As noted already, much of the scholarship on the sexual health of LGBT individuals ignores trans people, and much of the research on trans college students does not consider their sexual health (Rankin 2004; Renn and Reason 2013). Thus, while recognizing the limitations of the literature on the health-related concerns of LGBT youth, we start by reviewing such studies to frame our work. Though not an ideal approach, this discussion serves to indicate what specific information is known about trans youth and demonstrates where research is most needed to understand and address their health-related concerns.

## LGBT Health-Related Concerns

The limited research that exists on LGBT health-related concerns focuses on the prevalence of several health problems among LGBT populations, most notably mental health issues and exposure to risky sexual behaviors (Dugan, Kusel, and Simounet 2012; Fisher and Komosa-Hawkins 2013). Some scholars have linked LGBT-related harassment and victimization to the negative mental and sexual health issues experienced by LGBT individuals (Almeida et al. 2009; Institute of Medicine 2011; McGuire, Anderson, Toomey, and Russell 2010; Russell et al. 2011). For example, a study of LGBT-identified students from eighteen Boston high schools found that the LGBT youth scored significantly higher on a scale of depression than their non-LGBT peers, and the LGBT youth were also more likely than the heterosexual, cis youth to report suicidal ideation and self-harm (Almeida et al. 2009).

Another study of 245 LGBT young adults (ages twenty-one to twenty-five) linked LGBT-related school victimization to mental health risks, as well as to an increased HIV risk from sexual activity (Russell et al. 2011). Although only 8.6 percent of the participants in the study identified as trans, gender was found to be a significant difference among the participants, with "[cis] females report[ing] less LGBT victimization when compared with [cis] males and trans young adults, both male-to-female and female-to-male" (Russell et al. 2011, 226). Gender nonconformity, in particular, was associated with the harassment of cis males and trans individuals:

> Our results show that . . . The stakes of gender conformity are especially high for boys; undoubtedly, much of the LGBT school victimization that they experience is also rooted in a peer culture that demands conformity to masculine gender. In fact, other studies show that adolescent gender nonconformity is a source of significant risk in the lives of young people, particularly for boys and for LGB youth and gender nonconforming LGBT youth. Further research on the link between overall health and gender nonconformity at school is warranted. (228)

While linking LGBT victimization to negative health outcomes, the authors also provide a more hopeful conclusion that through educational and health-related initiatives, the negative effects of this school victimization can be reduced (Russell et al. 2011).

In addition to mental health issues, research has shown that LGBT populations are more likely to engage in risky sexual behaviors, such as having a greater number of sexual partners. For example, in analyzing data from the 2011 National College Health Assessment (ACHA-NCHA II), Oswalt and Wyatt (2013) concluded that among all students who participated in the study, men who identified their sexual orientation as "unsure" reported considerably more partners than did other men, and bisexual women reported more sexual partners than did other women. Oswalt and Wyatt's findings suggest that sexual orientation is correlated with sexual activity among college students.

In this chapter, we extend Oswalt and Wyatt's work to trans college students. Because there could be potential differences across sexual orientation for trans college students, we consider trans students as a whole and trans students grouped by sexual orientation.

## Trans-Specific Health-Related Concerns

Although multiple scholars have confirmed that trans individuals experience depression as a result of a negative social climate (Clements-Nolle, Marx, Guzman, and Katz 2001; Dugan, Kusel, and Simounet 2012; Fisher and Komosa-Hawkins 2013), research that focuses on other trans health-related concerns is limited, especially in the area of sexual health. In a study of 515 trans people from San Francisco, 62 percent of the trans female participants and 55 percent of the trans male participants reported being depressed, while one-third of all of the participants had attempted suicide (Clements-Nolle, Marx, Guzman, and Katz 2001). The researchers also found that 35 percent of the trans women whom they interviewed tested positive for HIV, compared with 2 percent of the trans men. The prevalence of HIV among the trans women in the study is startling and is indicative of the effects of transmisogyny: the bias, harassment, and violence directed against feminine-spectrum trans individuals. The difference in HIV rate by gender also reflects the intersections of transmisogyny with racism, as more than 70 percent of the trans female participants were people of color, compared with one-third of the trans male participants (Clements-Nolle, Marx, Guzman, and Katz 2001).

Oswalt and Lederer (2017) produced the first research that examined trans students' mental health beyond depression and suicide using six years of data from the ACHA-NCHA II. They found that compared to their cis peers, trans students reported higher rates of diagnosis or treatment in the previous year for eleven of the twelve conditions they studied, including anxiety, panic attacks, bipolar disorder, attention deficit hyperactivity disorder, and obsessive compulsive disorder. The only condition for which cis students reported higher rates was insomnia. The researchers concluded that colleges and universities must provide services to respond to these disparities, noting that "Given the high rates of mental health conditions among transgender college students, ensuring that their mental health needs are known and addressed is critical for this population's current and future well-being" (Oswalt and Lederer 2017, 8).

### Potential Supports to Address LGBT Health-Related Concerns

Despite myriad health concerns for LGBT individuals, several studies have identified potential supports that can decrease the risks for negative consequences. Heck, Flentje, and Cochran (2010) found that LGBT youth who attended a high school with a gay-straight alliance (GSA) or similar organization had significantly more favorable outcomes related to school experience, even if they personally never participated in the GSA. The benefits included a greater sense of belonging and connectedness, less alcohol use, and less psychological distress than those students who did not have a GSA or similar organization at their high school. The study did not examine if there were even greater benefits if students were involved in the GSA. Deml (2013), however, found that students who participated in community LGBT youth groups experienced positive mental health outcomes, including fewer suicidal thoughts, lower instances of depression, and a heightened awareness of safer sex practices. In both of these studies, engagement with other LGBT youth was shown to improve the participants' sexual health.

Ryan and colleagues (2010) found that family acceptance had similar positive effects on LGBT people's health, such as enhanced feelings of self-esteem and an improved overall health status. The trans individuals in their study, who represented 9 percent of the sample (*n* = 24), reported significantly lower levels of overall health and social supports when compared with their cis peers and were more likely to have suicidal ideations and to have attempted suicide. But, as for the cis LGB participants, family acceptance was shown to help protect trans participants against depression, substance abuse, and suicidal ideation and behaviors (Ryan et al. 2010).

The positive effects of family acceptance and LGBT school and community groups suggest that initiatives addressing these issues have the potential to improve the health of LGBT people. For example, colleges and universities can create LGBT centers to provide social and educational programming to students, staff, and faculty; to date, more than 200 institutions in the United States and Canada have done so (Consortium of Higher Education LGBT Resource Professionals 2016). Although having such a center does not guarantee that a campus will be welcoming to and inclusive of trans students, the support services and training sessions typically offered by these centers are important steps in creating a trans-affirming campus climate (Beemyn and Rankin 2011; Miner 2009).

## METHODS

### NCHA Data Set

The Spring 2011 data set of the NCHA was the most recent year available when we applied for access from the ACHA. It included 105,781 students from 129 postsecondary institutions (ACHA 2011).

### Sample

To prepare the data set for analysis, we restricted the sample to the respondents who selected "transgender" as their gender identity ($n = 202$). Limiting the data to the respondents who indicated that they were eighteen to thirty years old resulted in 167 participants, and removing surveys that seemed to have unreliable data (e.g., respondents who indicated having sixty-nine sexual partners), gave us a final sample of 161 trans college students. We compared this group to all of the eighteen-to-thirty-year-old non-trans[1] college students ($n = 93,945$).

Because we also wanted to examine how being trans intersects with sexual orientation, we developed new variables that combined the responses to the questions on gender identity and sexual orientation: transgender-heterosexual ($n = 48$), transgender-gay/lesbian ($n = 42$), transgender-bisexual ($n = 40$), and transgender-undecided ($n = 31$).

The nearly equal distribution across sexual orientation was notable and further demonstrates the need to examine the experiences of lesbian, gay, bisexual, and trans people separately and not just as a single group (Miner 2009; Rankin 2004; Renn and Reason 2013).

Data Analysis

Descriptive analyses of the data enabled us to examine the overall sexual health of trans college students. There were seven questions on the survey, four related to behavior and three related to relationships, that we identified as measures of sexual health:

"Within the last 30 days, how often did you have oral sex? Vaginal intercourse? Anal intercourse?"

"Within the last 12 months, with how many partners have you had oral sex, vaginal intercourse, or anal intercourse?"

"Within the last 12 months, have you experienced any of the following when drinking alcohol: Someone had sex with me without my consent? Had sex with someone without their consent? Had unprotected sex?"

"Have you ever been tested for Human Immunodeficiency Virus (HIV) infection?"

"Within the last 12 months, have you been in an intimate (couple/partnered) relationship that was . . .

- emotionally abusive (e.g., called derogatory names, yelled at, ridiculed)?
- physically abusive (e.g., kicked, slapped, punched)?
- sexually abusive (e.g., forced to have sex when you didn't want it, forced to perform or have unwanted sexual act performed on you)?"

(American College Health Association 2011)

For each of these questions, we calculated the means, standard deviations, and proportions of responses (percent). We present the findings in tabular format and discuss the meaningful relationships we found in the data.

FINDINGS

The variables in the NCHA data set allowed us to examine two aspects of sexual health: sexual behaviors and relationships. The results in these areas revealed troubling patterns for trans college students, including an increased likelihood to engage in risky sexual behaviors and to experience multiple forms of abuse in personal relationships.

Sexual Behaviors

When compared to the non-trans students surveyed, the students who identified as trans were more likely to engage in sexual activity in the last month, reported higher numbers of sexual partners in the past year and were more likely
to engage in risky sexual activity while under the influence of alcohol. The one
encouraging finding was that the trans students were more likely to be tested
for HIV than were their non-trans peers; however, when we examined the data
by sexual orientation, we found that the highest risk groups (i.e., gay and bisexual respondents, regardless of gender identity) were less likely to be tested.

As stated, the trans students reported slightly higher rates of sexual activity in the past month than did non-trans students. Although the trans and
non-trans respondents engaged in oral sex (53.6 percent versus 44.7 percent)
and vaginal intercourse (50.0 percent versus 48.3 percent) at similar rates in
the past thirty days, 18.2 percent of the trans students engaged in anal intercourse, as opposed to only 4.8 percent of the non-trans students (Table 13.1).
This finding suggests that trans students may be more likely to engage in anal
intercourse and, as a consequence, need to be provided with safer sex information that specifically addresses this form of sex. The results also suggest differences in sexual activity among trans students. Those indicating that they
were undecided about their sexual orientation reported the highest rates of
sexual activity in the past month in all of the categories, which suggests that
not being sure of one's sexuality may lead to more sexual experimentation.

TABLE 13.1 Sexual Activity in the Last 30 Days

|  | Oral Sex | | Vaginal Intercourse | | Anal Intercourse | |
|---|---|---|---|---|---|---|
|  | N | % | N | % | N | % |
| Non Transgender | 41,712 | 44.7 | 45,004 | 48.3 | 4,436 | 4.8 |
| All Transgender | 89 | 53.6 | 83 | 50.0 | 30 | 18.2 |
| Transgender Heterosexual | 23 | 47.9 | 26 | 54.2 | 6 | 12.8 |
| Transgender Gay/Lesbian | 23 | 54.8 | 17 | 40.5 | 9 | 21.4 |
| Transgender Bisexual | 19 | 47.5 | 20 | 50.0 | 5 | 12.5 |
| Transgender Undecided | 21 | 70.0 | 18 | 60.0 | 9 | 30.0 |

Similar patterns emerged from our analysis of the numbers of sexual partners in the past twelve months. On average, the trans students reported twice the number of sexual partners as their non-trans peers ($M$ = 2.88 versus 1.44) in the past year (Table 13.2). Among the trans respondents, the heterosexual students indicated having the fewest number of sexual partners on average in the last year, whereas those who were undecided about their sexual orientation had the most (2.04 versus 3.70). These findings again demonstrate that trans people cannot be treated as a monolithic group and that sexual health materials need to be targeted to reach different segments of the trans population.

TABLE 13.2 Partners in the Last 12 Months

|                           | Mean | SD   | N      |
|---------------------------|------|------|--------|
| Non Transgender           | 1.44 | 2.05 | 93,945 |
| All Transgender           | 2.88 | 4.42 | 167    |
| Transgender Heterosexual  | 2.04 | 2.74 | 48     |
| Transgender Gay/Lesbian   | 2.93 | 4.30 | 42     |
| Transgender Bisexual      | 2.93 | 3.83 | 40     |
| Transgender Undecided     | 3.70 | 6.36 | 31     |

Trans students reported higher rates of having sex without getting (3.6 percent) or giving (7.3 percent) consent due to alcohol use than did their non-trans peers (0.3 percent and 1.7 percent, respectively; Table 13.3). These results suggest that trans students are especially vulnerable to being victimized and to victimizing others when alcohol is involved. The findings are also in line with other research showing that trans people in general experience high rates of sexual assault. For example, 47 percent of the respondents to the United States Transgender Survey (James et al. 2016), the largest study to date of trans people in the United States, reported that they had been sexually assaulted at some point in their lives, and 10 percent indicated that they had been sexually assaulted in the previous year. Similar results were reported by the Association of American Universities (AAU) study of sexual assault on college campuses, which found that 39 percent of the trans seniors reported experiencing nonconsensual sexual contact at least once during their time at college, and three-fourth of all of the trans undergraduates indicated experiencing sexual harassment. The rates of sexual assault and misconduct were highest among the students who identified as trans, genderqueer, gender nonconforming, questioning, or another identity not listed in the AAU study (Cantor et al. 2015).

In terms of sexual orientation on the NCHA survey, the trans students who were undecided about their sexual identity reported the highest rates of sex without getting (10.0 percent) or giving (16.7 percent) consent as a result of alcohol use. These rates are alarming and support the finding that being uncertain about their sexuality may lead some students to engage more often in risky sexual behaviors.

The trans students who were undecided about their sexual orientation were also the most likely group to have unprotected sex while under the influence of alcohol, but not significantly greater than the trans respondents from the other sexual orientation categories. The rates of unprotected sex as a result of intoxication for the trans and non-trans students were similar (16.4 percent versus 13.0 percent), demonstrating that all students need information and resources about safer sex practices, particularly in relation to alcohol use.

TABLE 13.3  As a Result of Alcohol

|  | Unprotected sex | | Sex without getting consent | | Sex without giving consent | |
|---|---|---|---|---|---|---|
|  | N | % | N | % | N | % |
| **Non Transgender** | 12,086 | 13.0 | 314 | 0.3 | 1,561 | 1.7 |
| **All Transgender** | 27 | 16.4 | 6 | 3.6 | 12 | 7.3 |
| **Transgender Heterosexual** | 7 | 14.6 | 0 | 0 | 1 | 2.1 |
| **Transgender Gay/Lesbian** | 8 | 19.5 | 2 | 4.8 | 3 | 7.3 |
| **Transgender Bisexual** | 5 | 12.5 | 1 | 2.5 | 3 | 7.5 |
| **Transgender Undecided** | 6 | 20.0 | 3 | 10.0 | 5 | 16.7 |

One encouraging finding was that the trans respondents, who reported higher rates of sexual activity and risky activity as a result of alcohol use also reported higher rates of being tested for HIV (37.3 percent versus 25.9 percent; Table 13.4). The trans participants who were undecided about their sexual orientation were found to have the lowest rate of being tested (22.6 percent), which is particularly troubling because this group also had the highest rate of sexual activity, highest number of partners in the past thirty days, and highest rates of sex without giving and getting consent as a result of alcohol use. The groups with the highest rates of being tested were the bisexual trans students (57.5 percent) and the lesbian and gay trans students (40.5 percent). These findings may reflect a greater awareness of HIV/AIDS among LGB individuals and the success of testing outreach efforts directed at LGB communities by campus health and LGBT centers and local HIV/AIDS organizations.

TABLE 13.4  Ever Tested for HIV

|  | N | % |
| --- | --- | --- |
| Non Transgender | 24,097 | 25.9 |
| All Transgender | 62 | 37.3 |
| Transgender Heterosexual | 14 | 27.1 |
| Transgender Gay/Lesbian | 17 | 40.5 |
| Transgender Bisexual | 23 | 57.5 |
| Transgender Undecided | 7 | 22.6 |

Relationships

Trans individuals are also at an increased risk for negative mental and physical health consequences in relationships (e.g., Heintz and Melendez 2006; James et al. 2016). Heintz and Melendez (2006) found that among the trans people included in their study, 40 percent had experienced sexual violence (i.e., forced sex with a partner), 60 percent had never used safer sex protections (e.g., condoms) during sex with an abusive partner, and that requests to engage in safer sex practices resulted in verbal, physical, or additional sexual abuse. The authors connected intimate partner violence directly to an increased risk for sexually transmitted diseases and other negative health outcomes.

The NCHA data set allowed us to examine reported rates of intimate partner violence. We found that the trans students were more likely than their non-trans peers to indicate having been in emotionally, physically, and sexually abusive relationships, and as with the results related to sexual behaviors, we discovered differences by sexual orientation. The lesbian and gay trans students

reported the highest levels of emotional, physical, and sexual abuse in relationships, but all of the trans groups experienced considerable rates of abuse.

In terms of emotionally abusive relationships, the trans students were
nearly twice as likely as their non-trans peers (18.2 percent versus 9.7 percent)
to indicate that they had been in such a relationship (Table 13.5). The contrast
was especially pronounced between the lesbian and gay trans students and the
heterosexual trans students (36.6 percent versus 8.3 percent). More research
is needed to better understand the intersections between gender identity and
sexual orientation, but because of internalized homophobia and anti-trans
prejudice among LGB people (Dean et al. 2000), it is not surprising that trans
people might experience abuse in relationships with lesbian/gay individuals.

TABLE 13.5  Emotionally Abusive Relationships

|                          | N     | %    |
|--------------------------|-------|------|
| Non Transgender          | 9,033 | 9.7  |
| All Transgender          | 30    | 18.2 |
| Transgender Heterosexual | 4     | 8.3  |
| Transgender Gay/Lesbian  | 15    | 36.6 |
| Transgender Bisexual     | 7     | 17.5 |
| Transgender Undecided    | 4     | 12.9 |

As with the individuals who had been in emotionally abusive relationships, the trans students were much more likely to experience physically
abusive relationships than were their non-trans peers (9.0 percent versus 2.2
percent, Table 13.6). Although the heterosexual trans respondents again had
fewer experiences with abusive relationships than did other trans groups, bisexual trans respondents actually had the lowest rate of reported physically
abusive relationships (6.3 percent versus 5.0 percent).

Given that many physically abusive relationships are also sexually abusive,
we were not surprised to discover that the rates reported for sexually abusive
relationships were only slightly less than those for physically abusive relationships: 8.4 percent for the trans students and 1.6 percent for the non-trans students
(Table 13.7). These findings highlight the need for institutions to address intimate
partner violence and promote healthy relationships and for these efforts to be
inclusive of all types of relationships and individuals of all sexual orientations.

TABLE 13.6 Physically Abusive Relationships

|  | N | % |
| --- | --- | --- |
| Non Transgender | 2,047 | 2.2 |
| All Transgender | 15 | 9.0 |
| Transgender Heterosexual | 3 | 6.3 |
| Transgender Gay/Lesbian | 6 | 14.6 |
| Transgender Bisexual | 2 | 5.0 |
| Transgender Undecided | 4 | 12.9 |

TABLE 13.7 Sexually Abusive Relationships

|  | N | % |
| --- | --- | --- |
| Non Transgender | 1,471 | 1.6 |
| All Transgender | 14 | 8.4 |
| Transgender Heterosexual | 2 | 4.2 |
| Transgender Gay/Lesbian | 5 | 12.2 |
| Transgender Bisexual | 4 | 10.0 |
| Transgender Undecided | 3 | 9.7 |

DISCUSSION

The purpose of our project was to examine the overall sexual health of trans college students to gain a better understanding of this population and enable college health educators and other health practitioners to provide more directed, inclusive programming. We are troubled by the patterns that emerged from the analyses, which revealed that trans college students were more likely than their non-trans peers to be sexually active, engage in risky sexual behaviors, and be emotionally, physically, or sexually abused in an intimate relationship. All of these findings suggest that trans students would benefit from specialized support services at colleges and universities that would help them develop more positive sexual health outcomes. The one positive finding was that the trans students were more likely than their non-trans peers to have been tested for HIV, but the testing rate was relatively low (approximately 37 percent), given the sexual risks revealed by their other responses.

The high rates of negative sexual health outcomes among trans students are not surprising, as research also shows that trans students disproportionately experience negative mental and physical health outcomes (Clements-Nolle, Marx, Guzman, and Katz 2001; Dean et al. 2000; Dugan, Kusel, and Simounet 2012; Fisher and Komosa-Hawkins 2013). Besides demonstrating that trans students face a number of sexual health issues, our study offers insights into how they can be targeted in sexual health outreach efforts. For example, our finding that trans students have higher rates of anal sex than their non-trans peers suggests that educational programming on safer sex practices needs to be trans-inclusive and directed specifically toward trans students.

Differences by sexual orientation within the trans sample illustrate the heterogeneity of trans communities, but these distinctions are often missed when LGBT people are considered as a single entity (Beemyn and Rankin 2011; Miner 2009). Our analyses revealed some important differences between trans groups: the heterosexual trans students were the lowest risk trans group in nearly every category and were the most similar to their non-trans peers; the trans students who were undecided about their sexual orientation reported the highest rates of sexual activity, were the most likely to engage in risky sexual behaviors as a result of alcohol use, and were the least likely to be tested for HIV. The lesbian and gay trans students indicated the highest rates of intimate partner violence, with more than one in three reporting emotional abuse in a relationship, one in seven reporting physical abuse, and one in eight reporting sexual abuse. These differences demonstrate the importance of considering the intersections of gender identity and sexual orientation in examining the sexual health of trans students.

We recognized two implications from our research findings:

### Implication 1: More Research Is Needed on the Sexual Behaviors and Identities of Trans College Students

Researchers have noted that topics related to trans students are often ignored in the literature on LGBT people in higher education (Rankin 2004; Renn and Reason 2013), which means that their specific experiences are frequently not addressed. Moreover, when trans students are considered, they are typically treated as a homogeneous group. Our findings reveal significant differences between trans students based on sexual orientation and between trans students and their non-trans peers.

Although our results are notable, our conclusions are limited by the relatively small sample of trans respondents and the data being from a single year more than five years ago. Another limitation of the data set results from the restricted identity categories offered on the survey. Gender included only three options (male, female, and transgender), and sexual orientation included only four (heterosexual, lesbian/gay, bisexual, and undecided). These weaknesses point to the need for a more LGBT-inclusive data set on college students that addresses health-related issues, so that the sexual health experiences of trans students and differences across identity groups can be better understood.

The results of our research could be used to develop qualitative studies that would help identify the factors that contribute to the negative outcomes we uncovered and their implications. For example, the finding that trans students report higher rates of emotional, physical, and sexual abuse in intimate relationships could be a starting point for considering the effects of abusive relationships on the health, well-being, and success of trans college students.

### Implication 2: Institutions Should Provide Specialized Support Services for Trans Students That Consider Differences by Sexual Orientation

Campus health services should collaborate with their campus LGBT resource center or diversity office to collect information from and provide services specifically to trans students. Materials and services aimed at supporting the LGBT community as a whole are not sufficient, as trans students have unique health needs that are typically overlooked in general outreach efforts. For example, the trans students in the sample who identified their sexual orientation as "undecided" were the most likely group to engage in risky sexual behaviors and the least likely to be tested for HIV. Although the survey did not allow the respondents to explain what they meant by "undecided," we can infer that at least some of the people selected this option because their sexuality did not align with the limited choices provided (i.e., heterosexual, gay/lesbian, bisexual). Institutions must move away from the traditional "trinary" of sexual orientation categories if they are to recognize and respond to the sexual health concerns of many of their trans (as well as non-trans) students today.

Other steps that colleges and universities must take to address the sexual health needs of trans students include offering a professionally led trans support group; regularly training counseling, health services, and crisis intervention staff on the experiences of trans students; and providing trans-inclusive health-related materials, resources, and programs. Because these changes are far-reaching and ongoing, campus administrators must be strongly committed to these efforts if they are to succeed.

CONCLUSION

Trans students deserve a college experience that is safe and supportive (Beemyn and Rankin 2011; Lees 1998). Much more research is needed on how best to create such an affirming environment, including how campus health services can best support this population. This chapter has highlighted some sexual health disparities for trans students. These and other areas of sexual health should be further investigated and addressed. Campus health services and health educators should develop resources, materials, programs, and services tailored to trans students, paying particular attention to the ways that gender identity and sexual orientation intersect.

ACKNOWLEDGMENTS

We would like to acknowledge and thank the American College Health Association for access to the NCHA II Spring 2011 data set for the analysis reported in this study.

NOTES

1. Because the survey asked gender identity only as male, female, and transgender, with the ability to select only one option, some of the respondents who marked male or female might actually identify as trans men or trans women. For this reason, we do not characterize the participants who indicated male or female as "cis" but as "non-trans," while keeping in mind that some of these individuals might also identify as trans if given more than one option for their gender identity.

WORKS CITED

Almeida, Johanna, Renee M. Johnson, Heather L. Corliss, Beth E. Molnar, and Deborah Azrael. 2009. "Emotional Distress among LGBT Youth: The

Influence of Perceived Discrimination Based on Sexual Orientation." *Journal of Youth Adolescence* 38: 1001–14.

American College Health Association. 2011. *American College Health Association—National College Health Assessment II: Spring 2011 Data Set.* Hanover, MD: American College Health Association.

———. 2016. "Participation History." http://www.acha-ncha.org/partic_history.html.

Beemyn, Genny, and Sue Rankin. 2011. "Introduction to the Special Issue of 'LGBTQ Campus Experiences.' " *Journal of Homosexuality* 58: 1159–64.

Cantor, David, Bonnie Fisher, Susan Chibnall, Reanne Townsend, Hyunshik Lee, Carol Bruce, and Gail Thomas. 2015. "Report on the AAU Campus Climate Survey on Sexual Assault and Sexual Misconduct." AAU, September 3. https://www.aau.edu/Climate-Survey.aspx?id=16525.

Clements-Nolle, Kristen, Rani Marx, Robert Guzman, and Mitchell Katz. 2001. "HIV Prevalence, Risk Behaviors, Health Care Use, and Mental Health Status of Transgender Persons: Implications for Public Health Intervention." *American Journal of Public Health* 91: 915–21.

Consortium of Higher Education LGBT Resource Professionals. 2016. "Find an LGBTQ Center." http://http://www.lgbtcampus.org/find-an-lgbtqa-camp us-center.

Dean, Laura, Ian H. Meyer, Kevin Robinson, Randall L. Sell, Robert Sember, Vincent M. B. Silenzio, Deborah J. Bowen, Judith Bradford, Esther Rothblum, Scout, Jocelyn White, Patricia Dunn, Ann Lawrence, Daniel Wolfe, and Jessica Xavier. 2000. "Lesbian, Gay, Bisexual and Transgender Health: Findings and Concerns." *Journal of the Gay and Lesbian Medical Association* 4: 101–51.

Deml, Michael. 2013. "An LGBT Youth Group's Role in Building Social Support and Implications for Risk Behavior." *UW-L Journal of Undergraduate Research* 16: 1–20.

Dugan, John P., Michelle L. Kusel, and Dawn M. Simounet. 2012. "Transgender College Students: An Exploratory Study of Perceptions, Engagement, and Educational Outcomes." *Journal of College Student Development* 53: 719–36.

Fisher, Emily S., and Karen Komosa-Hawkins. 2013. *Creating Safe and Supportive Learning Environments: A Guide for Working with Lesbian, Gay, Bisexual, Transgender, and Questioning Youth and Families.* New York: Routledge.

Heck, Nicholas C., Annesa Flentje, and Bryan N. Cochran. 2011. "Offsetting Risks: High School Gay-Straight Alliances and Lesbian, Gay, and Transgender (LGBT) Youth." *School Psychology Quarterly* 26: 161–74.

Heintz, Adam Jackson, and Rita M. Melendez. 2006. "Intimate Partner Violence and HIV/STD Risk among Lesbian, Gay, Bisexual, and Transgender Individuals." *Journal of Interpersonal Violence* 21: 193–208.

Institute of Medicine. 2011. *The Health of Lesbian, Gay, Bisexual, and Transgender People: Building a Foundation for Better Understanding.* Washington, DC: National Academies Press.

James, Sandy E., Jody L. Herman, Susan Rankin, Mara Keisling, Lisa Mottet, and Ma'ayan Anafi. 2016. *The Report of the 2015 U.S. Transgender Survey.* Washington, DC: National Center for Transgender Equality.

Lees, Lisa. J. 1998. "Transgender Students on our Campuses." In *Working with Lesbian, Gay, Bisexual, and Transgender College Students: A Handbook for Faculty and Administrators,* edited by Ronni L. Sanlo, 37–46. Westport, CT: Greenwood Press.

Magee, Joshua C., Louisa Bigelow, Samantha DeHaan, and Brian S. Mustanski. 2011. "Sexual Health Information Seeking Online: A Mixed-Methods Study among Lesbian, Gay, Bisexual, and Transgender Young People." *Health Education and Behavior* 39: 276–89.

McGuire, Jennifer K., Charles R. Anderson, Russell B. Toomey, and Stephen B. Russell. 2010. "School Climate for Transgender Youth: A Mixed Methods Investigation of Student Experiences and School Responses." *Journal of Youth and Adolescence* 39: 1175–88.

Miner, Jack. 2009. "How to Make Your Office and Institution More Transgender Friendly." *College and University* 84: 69–72.

Oswalt, Sara B., and Alyssa M. Lederer. 2017. "Beyond Depression and Suicide: The Mental Health of Transgender College Students." *Social Sciences* 6: 1–10.

Oswalt, Sara B., and Tammy J. Wyatt. 2013. "Sexual Health Behaviors and Sexual Orientation in a U.S. National Sample of College Students." *Archives of Sexual Behavior* 42: 1561–72.

Rankin, Susan R. 2004. "Campus Climate for Lesbian, Gay, Bisexual and Transgender People." *Diversity Factor* 12: 18–23.

Renn, Kristen A., and Robert D. Reason. 2013. *College Students in the United States: Characteristics, Experiences, and Outcomes.* San Francisco: Jossey-Bass.

Russell, Stephen T., Caitlin Ryan, Russell B. Toomey, Rafael M. Diaz, and Jorge Sanchez. 2011. "Lesbian, Gay, Bisexual, and Transgender Adolescent School Victimization: Implications for Young Adult Health and Adjustment." *Journal of School Health* 81: 223–30.

Ryan, Caitlin, Stephen T. Russell, David Huebner, Rafael Diaz, and Jorge
    Sanchez. 2010. "Family Acceptance in Adolescence and the Health of
    LGBT Young Adults." *Journal of Child and Adolescent Psychiatric Nursing*
    23: 205–13.

# FOURTEEN

# Microfoundations of Trans Academics' Experiences

## A Sense of Paranoia and Hypersensitivity

*Erich N. Pitcher*

Living as we did—on the edge—we developed a particular way
of seeing reality. We looked both from the outside in and from
the inside out. We focused our attention on the center as well as
the margin. We understood both.

—bell hooks (1984)

SYSTEMS OF DOMINATION AND SUBORDINATION require oppressed individuals to develop new ways of seeing, as hooks (1984) and Hill Collins (2000) have previously described. Part of the view of outsiders within (Hill Collins 2000), and margin/center frameworks (Hill Collins 2000; hooks 1984; Spivak 1993) more broadly, is the adverse effects that facing oppression has on individual people and groups (Sensoy and DiAngelo 2012). An example of the effects of living within a system of subordination was provided by Joy,[1] a white, male-to-female transsexual who is a full professor in the humanities at a private research university in the Eastern United States. In speaking to me about not having had her recent grant application funded, she said, "Structural oppression creates this kind of general sense of paranoia and hypersensitivity." Joy's reaction is reflective of the experiences of many minoritized academics (Bulhan 2004; Fanon 2005; Stanley 2006). Joy further explained,

> Part of the problem is if you're a minority, you can't actually be sure
> that this or that person is oppressing you. . . .The truth is most people
> who submitted [grant] proposals weren't accepted and none of them
> were trans. I submit a lot of things that are not accepted, so there is no
> guarantee that [being trans was the reason for not receiving the grant]
> is true . . .

For Joy, a nagging question lingers in the notification of the grant proposal: was this because I am trans? Although Joy may be experiencing gender-based oppression, it is difficult to ascertain when, if, and how this form of oppression affects her.

In this chapter, I focus on how small, everyday occurrences create the sense of paranoia and hypersensitivity that Joy felt. As such, I responded to the following research question: How do within-organization processes (or micro-foundations or inequality regimes) shape trans academics' experiences? The answers to this question arrived out of an analysis of situations like the one that Joy described. In particular, I examined the participants' interview transcripts for evidence of how having a minoritized identity (or multiple minoritized identities) and corresponding systems of structural oppression led them to be aware of when and how oppression pressed, molded, and created contours within their experiences. In short, I looked for indications of genderism[2] and other systems of oppression in the lives of the participants. Genderism emerged through small, everyday processes, in much the same ways that racism, sexism, classism, ableism, and heterosexism manifest (Sensoy and DiAngelo 2012).

## STUDY DESCRIPTION AND METHODS

Building on the incident Joy described about not having a grant application funded, I highlight how within-organization events and conditions shape trans academics' experiences. In my larger qualitative inquiry (Pitcher 2016), I invited thirty-nine trans academics to participate in two interviews and respond in writing or verbally to a narrative prompt. In this chapter, I draw on all three data sources to respond to the research question above. The answers derive from a thematic analysis (Ayres 2008; Miles and Huberman 1994; Miles, Huberman, and Saldaña 2013), in which I developed story matrixes for the participants' key stories. Then I "selectively stacked" (Miles, Huberman, and Saldaña 2013, 108) the data related to the various relevant experiences into a single document.

In the larger study, I engaged participants in an interpretative practice (Holstein and Gubrium 1995), wherein they and I explored organizational events and their meaning (Rubin and Rubin 2011). To ensure the accuracy, trustworthiness, and credibility of this inquiry, I triangulated the data (i.e., drawing on multiple sources of data) and member checking (Creswell 2009). Member checking occurred in three ways: checking for understanding directly within interviews, the participants reviewing their transcripts, and the participants providing feedback about the emergent themes. I also used rich, thick descriptions of the findings (Creswell 2009) and an analytic triangulation (ThễNguyịn 2008) process involving a small group of peer debriefers to enhance the trustworthiness and credibility of the conclusions (Guba 2004; Leech and Onwuegbuzie 2008; ThễNguyịn 2008).

## THEORETICAL GROUNDING

I draw on two aspects of the conceptual framework from the larger study: inequality regimes (Acker 2006) and microfoundations (Powell and Colyvas 2008). Briefly, inequality regimes are within-organizational processes that contribute to and exacerbate social inequalities (Acker 2006). Related to inequality regimes are microfoundations, or "institutional forces [that] shape individual interests and desires, framing the possibilities for action and influencing whether behaviors results in persistence or change" (Powell and Colyvas 2008, 277). Together inequality regimes describe the outcomes of organizational microfoundations. By examining the microfoundations evident within organizational events, I seek to connect within-organizational processes to larger social structures.

Within microfoundations, there are different kinds of "building blocks" (Powell and Colyvas 2008, 278), of which sensemaking is one (Weick 1995). Sensemaking is the micro-process of how individuals decide to take action based on the meanings derived from organizational action (Weick 1995). The notion of sensemaking was especially evident in the participants' descriptions of exercising agency over identity disclosure, which I discuss in more detail later.

In this chapter, I argue that there is no singular trans experience, nor a singular academic experience, and therefore there is no singular trans academic experience. Instead, there are some partially shared contours of experiences, because trans academics work within institutions marked by persistent genderism (Bilodeau 2009). Although genderism shaped all participants' experiences to different degrees and in different ways, I seek to highlight the various ways that small organizational processes are enactments of systems of oppression.

## ANALYTIC CONCEPTS: ADDITIONAL LABOR, THE WALL, AND TENSION

I use three analytic concepts to describe how genderism affected participants: additional labor, the wall, and tension. Two instances where these metaphors were present involved Tobey and AJ. Tobey, a white transmasculine administrator and adjunct professor, described how the demand to perform identity-related work manifested in his experiences. In response to my question about whether he has been treated differently than cis colleagues, he said, "Because I'm constantly educating people about my [gender] identity, I think I *am* treated differently because that's not something everybody has to do." Instead of being recognized as needing to perform identity-related work, Tobey was ultimately punished for it, because the "extra" labor was seen as taking time and energy away for his job responsibilities. At the time of our interviews, Tobey had been recently notified that his contract would not be renewed, at least in part because of how his identity was taken up in the workplace (e.g., having to educate others about being trans).

Other minoritized scholars likewise perform certain kinds of "extra" labor for different reasons (e.g., dispelling myths about competency that derive from white supremacy and anti-Black racism). The extra labor that minoritized scholars, in this case trans academics, perform is often in service of retaining one's dignity, humanity, and ability to feel whole (Croom and Patton 2012; Ford 2011; Stanley 2006). I use the notion of additional labor to describe how trans academics are subject to demands that non-trans academics are not.

AJ, a tenure-track assistant professor at a private women's liberal arts college, described genderism as a constant obstacle: "That gender binary system is always there. It's always something to navigate around." Particularly at a women's college, genderism shaped every aspect of the institution. "It affects the way we structure spaces like restrooms and changing facilities.... It affects everything." AJ has been involved in various efforts to support trans faculty and students at the institution but acknowledged that

> we're just constantly hitting that wall. And *I can't imagine* any workplace where everybody is on board with this stuff [disrupting the gender binary] and [where] it's easy for trans scholars. I just don't think we're there yet in our society, especially with people who are outside of the binary, like me, in my identity.

In using the image of "hitting that wall," AJ is describing the cumulative effects of attempting to loosen the grip genderism has on one particular academic institution. This characterization is similar to how diversity workers describe hitting the wall in their attempts to unsettle racism within higher education organizations (Ahmed 2012). "The wall" and "hitting the wall" are important metaphors for understanding the limits placed on minoritized bodies because of the systems of oppression endemic to higher education.

The final analytic concept is tension. Through these everyday practices and processes that instantiate genderism, AJ alludes to a tension between pushing for change and being unable to enact significant change because the wall prevents movement beyond a certain point. Other participants also described how the tensions of operating within a genderist environment affected their experiences in academe. The genderism they encountered was manifested in three primary ways that I discuss below: misgendering, hypervisibility and invisibility, and identity disclosure. These tensions[3] lead me to conclude that trans academics, like many minoritized scholars, are "professionally *other.*"

## MISGENDERING: INTERPERSONALLY AND DIGITALLY

One of the key features of genderism is forced social labeling into a binary gender system, which results in all bodies being read and typically categorized as either male or female and then referred to by the pronouns associated with that gender, "he/him" or "she/her" (Bilodeau 2009). Several narrators faced difficulties in getting others to use their correct pronouns, which I call interpersonal misgendering, or digital misgendering when this happened through online systems (e.g., course management software). Although the sources of misgendering differed, the effects on the participants were similar: they felt invisible, marginalized, and disrespected.

Before I describe the various ways that two narrators, Westley and Mary, experienced interpersonal misgendering, I want to note that it is important to temper these findings by their experiences of racial privilege. While the sting of misgendering is painful, both participants also have privileged racial identities that make them more at home in the academy than scholars of color. For example, participants of color, including Susan, an African American retired adjunct professor; Martina, a Latina full professor; and Max and Nick, both academic librarians of color, navigated genderism and racism (and in some cases also transmisogyny[4]). Because of how systems of oppression and privilege intersect and overlap (Hill Collins 2000; Sensoy and DiAngelo 2012), it is important to remember that white trans academics navigate a majoritized racial identity and minoritized gender identity, and trans academics of color navigate minoritized racial and gender identities. The misgendering experienced by Westley and Mary has to be seen within this larger context.

Westley identifies as a white trans boy. He served as an adjunct instructor in the humanities at multiple community colleges in the South and then in West at the time of our interviews. Westley has a feminine gender presentation and others did always recognize him as "he," in part because of assumptions rooted in genderism (Bilodeau 2009).

Westley described working for a community college that was "quite pleased to have trans faculty, even if [his] pronoun was not necessarily known or respected in most situations." Although his immediate supervisor and the dean of the college got his pronouns right, he reported that "almost every other faculty person got my pronoun wrong." These faculty members "were all really nice about it if I corrected them, but I had a fair amount of anxiety around [correcting them] because lots of folks didn't know me or . . .get my pronouns right. There was no. . .training, talking with any other faculty about, 'Hey, you need to get this right.' " Westley felt that while "some folks tried real hard," his not "being read as male . . . all of the time I taught there" meant that he had to "constantly assert" his pronouns and was rarely properly gendered outside of his interactions with his dean and supervisor.

Westley's difficulties with pronouns demonstrate how informal inter-actions can enact genderism. The mislabeling of Westley occurred through schemas and assumptions about the sex/gender binary (Bem 1981), which re-flect how the microfoundations of gender operate (Powell and Colyvas 2008). Westley faced the consequences of genderism in having to remind people con-stantly of his correct pronouns and experienced anxiety as a result.

Mary, a white woman in the sciences at a research university in the West, also had trouble within her department with interpersonal misgen-dering. Following a successful bid for tenure, she decided to move forward with gender transition. While other colleagues "had her back," two people in her department refused to call her "Mary" and use "she/her" pronouns. Mary explained one of these situations as follows:

> [A] faculty member, who over the space of five years would use the wrong pronouns, and it didn't happen all the time, because not every conversation has pronouns, or he'd use my old name "Mark" which I identify as male. And so, I finally had enough. I tried to work with him on it. . . . I had to officially ask a request of my chair to help resolve the issue. It wasn't about punishment. I just wanted it to stop.

When Mary asked the department chair to help resolve the issue, an official complaint was filed and the college's office of equity and inclusion launched an investigation. Because of the length of time the investigation took, Mary felt that "they didn't seem to take my accusation very seriously." The hold-up in the investigation was the need for Mary and the department to provide "sufficient proof that it [misgendering] [caused] substantial harm," and obtaining this documentation was difficult because the inappropriate behavior often occurred in private conversations. The breakthrough in the case occurred when "this guy . . . referred to me as 'he' during a faculty meeting, at my department faculty meeting," which "tilted the decision" in Mary's favor. Eventually, he was "physically moved to a different place. His committee assignments in the department were ended to just minimize contact . . . It was just to separate us so that he couldn't do any harm."

Thinking that the situation was finally resolved, Mary was devastated when she received notice that her colleague was appealing the decision to remove him from the department. She said:

> That letter was prepared by a local lawyer, . . . and it was just horrible . . . very transphobic accusations, speculating about whether I really am a woman or not, if I've had surgeries or not . . . And so I had to wait for, god, another six months over the summer, last summer (2014). It finally resolved last November (2014) where I had to actually testify and I rebutted all these things at the faculty appeals board and everything was upheld.

Mary's experiences reveal the additional labor demanded of her to get some of her colleagues to recognize her name and pronouns. She had to file a complaint and deal with the appeals process simply to be treated as herself. Unlike most cis female/woman-identified academics, transfeminine academics who transition on the job must contend with other's expectations of what constitutes a "real" woman—an enactment of transmisogyny.

Online systems also confer gender, and several participants encountered digital misgendering. I focus here on the experiences of Jackson, a white male graduate student instructor and doctoral candidate in the social sciences at a research university in the Midwest at the time of our interviews. He gender transitioned at the beginning of his graduate program and, beyond his first semester, faced virtually no issues with interpersonal misgendering. However, he did experience misgendering through online data systems. He explained:

> On [course management software] I am "Miss Jackson" and it will not change even though my gender marker is changed in every other system on campus. My birth certificate has been amended, my driver's license is changed, and I'm still "Miss Jackson" when I email my students from [the online system]. And I'm out, so that's fine, but I'm not out to them when I'm emailing them before their class starts!

Part of the reason that other people properly gender Jackson relates to his masculine gender expression and having medically transitioned. As a person "who
has the privilege of having had hormone replacement and also chest surgery,"
Jackson is recognized as a man by others now. At the start of his doctoral
program, that was not the case, a circumstance that disheartened him. Early
in his medical transition, Jackson had a professor who refused to use his name.
He described the situation as follows:

> My name wasn't changed on documents yet, but he refused to call me
> Jackson all semester. Then the chair of my department called him on
> the phone in front of me and said, "this stops today." Then it never hap-
> pened again and it was just taken care of, not a problem. That was really
> awesome, so that kind of thing ... interactional problems ... that shit
> is shut down, like people put a stop to that immediately.

By preventing the kinds of invalidation that other trans people may experience,
Jackson's department chair erected a different kind of wall, one that disallowed
interpersonal misgendering.

This small interaction reveals something else about how misgendering
operates. Specifically, Jackson benefited from having moved from one gender
extreme to another and identifying solidly within the gender binary as a man.
His legal name change was already in process, which cued others to use the
correct name, and his access to testosterone, which made him quickly look like
other men, prompted the use of the correct pronouns. His identity was thus
afforded a kind of authority and legitimacy. For the participants who did not
pursue legal name changes or medical intervention, being misgendered was
more common, and addressing it was often more complicated than simply advocating for correct name and pronoun usage.

Like Jackson, Cassidy, a Native American female who teaches on an adjunct basis in the humanities at a research university in the West, recounted
times when others spoke out against her being misgendered. In one instance,
a colleague at a graduate student research colloquium advocated on her behalf.
She explained:

> I never made any secret of being trans, or my identification as a woman.
> So when one of the other grad students, and there are all, obviously
> defining this along the gender lines as a binary, and the student says
> that there are eight women and nine men or something like that [in the
> room] and I realize at that one instantaneous moment, for whatever

reason I was being counted as a man. The woman that was sitting next to me stopped [this misgendering]. . . . She said, "wait a minute, that's not my count." She went around and named the women in the class, and I was named as another woman, that made me feel so good, that another woman would recognize me as my identified self. And then, of course, the person who made the original comment kind of stuttered and stammered a bit and didn't know where to go with that. . . . But I felt that [experience] will always remain with me.

Cassidy reveals one of the actions that advocates and accomplices to trans individuals can take to challenge misgendering. The relatively small gesture of correcting the labeling of Cassidy as "not woman" was a particularly powerful moment for her, one that has stuck with her for many years.

## HYPERVISIBILITY AND INVISIBILITY

Some participants actively countered others' misgendering, and this made their trans-ness hypervisible. In a context where trans is created as an impossible category of identification (Enke 2012; Namaste 2000; Spade 2011)—that is, where the larger framework for understanding gender precludes the possibility that one could be trans or some gender other than man or woman—trans-ness can become hypervisible when it is made visible. Connor, a white trans postdoctoral researcher in the social sciences at a research university in the West, described feeling simultaneously hypervisible in moments when he corrected someone about their inappropriate pronoun use and invisible when he was misrecognized as not a man.

Other participants, like Gabe, an assistant professor in the humanities, and Mike, a tenured academic librarian, seemed troubled by other people forgetting about their being trans. Still other participants, such as AJ, were made invisible by others' expectations about what a trans person looks like. Hypervisibility and invisibility present a variety of tensions for trans scholars, including when and how to disclose one's gender identity for those who are not seen as trans. The decisions about disclosing one's trans-ness, in addition to the identity-related work performed because of genderism, is another manifestation of the kinds of extra labor in which trans academics must engage.

Seemingly small, everyday occurrences, such as written and spoken comments, can also make trans-ness invisible or hypervisible. Tobey, a white, trans man/transmasculine administrator and adjunct instructor in the social sciences at a regional comprehensive university in the East, described how "hearing 'you guys' all the time when talking about big groups, [and] hearing things like 'ladies and gentlemen' " made him feel invisible. At other times, though, he felt hypervisible because of his trans-ness and his views about trans issues. Tobey recounted one such event in his narrative response. He wrote,

> I received my teaching evaluations recently for a class I taught . . . I was reading the comments sections, in which students are encouraged to free write about their thoughts on the class, anonymously. One student had some particular complaints about the organization of the class, and some of the content, and also stated that I, as a professor, pushed my views about "transgenders" onto the class. When reading this comment, I became saddened and scared about how suddenly vulnerable I was even when in a position of power over this student. In one comment, the cisgender student felt able to question my very identity (and those like me). I was struck because I had decided to specifically not come out as transgender in that class, and I can afford not to because I have passing privilege. Despite my decision to not share my personal history or identity as a trans person, this student still managed to intuitively "pick up on" my "values" related to trans identities.

Tobey's narrative reveals that even if someone does not come out as trans, the potency of social accountability for adhering to cis norms is ever present. It is worth noting how language practices leave Tobey feeling invisible in one instance and hypervisible in another because of his teaching about trans issues.

Building on the notion of ephemeral moments, or microfoundations, where trans-ness is hypervisible, I share a story from Cassidy. She described a situation in which a street preacher proselytizing on campus called attention to her: "I've had occasion to walk by . . . and I'd hear them say, 'the queers and the trans people.' . . . They were very obviously directing their comments at me." As a six-foot, two-inch Native American woman, Cassidy recognizes that she is "always going to be clocked" by others (read as not a cis woman), but if anyone disrespects her, she will "turn it right back in their face very hard." Cassidy's experience indicates that simply not fitting into cis appearance norms can make one's trans-ness hypervisible. She also demonstrates a kind of labor of resistance, which some trans academics use to counter the negative effects of hypervisibility.

Sometimes a trans academic might become hypervisible because of another aspect of their identity. Max, a Black trans man who works as a librarian for a community college in the Midwest, indicated that with respect to his trans identity, his work environment has "been good," but that he has had to deal with anti-Black racism and hypervisibility in the form of surveillance of his work by his white female supervisor. Max said:

> when I first got here, when I was using Prezi, or PowerPoint or whatever, for some of my [teaching] sessions, I noticed that my department chair wanted to look through them and approve them before I would teach, which wasn't happening with my other [white] colleagues.

He cited another example:

> I noticed that when I did a women's history month display . . . I had books from our collection, and then I also had a PowerPoint that accompanied it . . . my colleague [the department chair] was like, "There aren't enough white women in this display." And so she went through it with a fine-tooth comb, and my response to that was like, "Well, there's six white women, six Black women, five Latina women." I broke down [the demographics]. White women were not centered, and I think that white people aren't used to seeing things in which white women aren't centered.

In requiring him to have his presentations approved and criticizing the number of women of color in the display, Max's department chair is symbolically policing him and his identities, thus making his Blackness hypervisible. At the same time, the supervisor's desire to center white women in the display also serves to make people of color less visible in his workplace. Max noted that "race is . . . a touchy topic with this particular person," which is presumably what led the department chair to subject him to various means of surveillance. As demonstrated by Max's experiences, racially minoritized trans academics often must perform additional labor to navigate both racism and genderism.

Although some of the study participants felt hypervisible at times because of their gender, or in Max's case, because of his race, others felt more invisible because their colleagues "forget" about their trans-ness. One of these participants, Gabe, is a white male tenure-track assistant professor in the humanities at a regional comprehensive university in the Midwest. Because most of the other out trans people on his campus identify as nonbinary and are more readily identified as gender nonconforming, Gabe often feels overlooked as one of the few trans men. He said:

> It's very hard for me to show up as trans because people forget I'm trans
> here. It's like because I'm passable [read as a cis man] and because I'm
> far along in transition and pretty normatively gendered, I have to work
> pretty hard to get people to think about the fact that I might be having
> experiences that are difficult. Because when they look at me, it's easy
> for them, like I don't make them uncomfortable mostly. When I get
> pushback is when I say things they don't want to hear. I haven't had
> anyone treat me badly because of how I look or because of my docu-
> mentation or anything like that. It's weird to feel like, asked to be the
> token to speak about trans issues, but then also have very little recog-
> nition that, maybe I should be protected or maybe people should be
> worried about how I'm running into invisible barriers . . . I don't see a
> lot of concern about those things.

Because Gabe is presumed to be just another white cis heterosexual man, his
experiences as a queer and trans person are invisible, except when others recognize that they can use his trans-ness by having him speak at events, like the
Trans Day of Remembrance.

Some participants, including AJ and Will, raised the issue of how others'
assumptions about what a trans person looks like influenced their visibility.
Gender attribution, or forced social labeling, is one of the microfoundations of
genderism that contributes to the inequality regimes (Acker 2006) that trans
academics experience. AJ addressed this issue, commenting:

> For most people in the US society, it's a two, and only two, gender
> system. Even with the increasing visibility of trans people like Caitlyn
> Jenner and Laverne Cox, people see, "Okay, male to female, okay."
> So, even if they are accepting of that, it still fits into the binary
> framework.

The myth that there is a singular way to be trans—to transition from male to
female or female to male and to identify as binary—pervaded many of my conversations with participants about visibility and their lives as trans academics.
Having to contend with others' assumptions about trans people seemed to influence when and how some participants disclosed their trans identity. For instance, Will described the tensions inherent in coming out as trans. Will is a
white man who is a non–tenure-track instructor in the social sciences at a research university in the Midwest. When I asked him why he did not disclose
his identity, he said,

Because it is very strange to come out at this point. I feel like I need to convince people. Or they've known me for seven years and then, "Oh, why is it I've never talked about it?" I feel like people might go, "Oh, so you cross dress at night? You put on dresses?" No. There's a little bit of convincing that needs to go on, or people just don't get it.

Will addresses the precise problem that AJ described about the current visibility of trans people. Public opinion situates trans people as either transitioning to female/woman or male/man, rendering gender nonbinary individuals invisible. Often transitioning to male/man is less understood, so in Will's case, because he is currently perceived as a cis man, his colleagues would assume he would transition toward a female/woman identity. Will's comments reflect how trans academics exercise agency in deciding whether to disclose their trans identities within a context of invisibility.

EXERCISING AGENCY IN DISCLOSING TRANS IDENTITY/STATUS/HISTORY

Within this study, some of the participants expressed a strong desire to exercise agency over whom and how they tell people about their trans identities. The notion of exercising agency was especially salient for those who are not readily identifiable as trans by others. Not all of the participants view their trans-ness as part of their gender identities; instead, they identify as men or women. Trans academics may use different language for themselves, employ a variety of identity/status/history disclosure tactics, and have differential abilities to exercise agency over telling others about their gender; yet each contends with a social milieu marked by genderism. Genderism creates a context that can make trans identities inaccessible and impossible (Bilodeau 2009; Enke 2012; Namaste 2000). Exercising agency for trans academics is about having the ability to set the terms of social engagement and maintain some level of control over how and whom one tells about their identity.

Will was in a position to exercise a tremendous amount of agency over not revealing his trans status, but this also meant he had to be more guarded in social interactions. When I asked Will what it was like not to disclose at work, he said,

I have to be very careful with my language, especially with pronouns, and especially with thinking about, "Oh, when I was seventeen and I had a boyfriend, blah, blah, blah." I think if I said that [having had a boyfriend at seventeen] it would be confusing … so I just have to be careful when I'm talking.

In having to be "very careful with my language," Will engaged in additional labor in anticipation of potentially negative events, a kind of minoritized stress (Pitcher 2017) and sensemaking (Weick 1995). He further explained, "I am very careful at disclosing information because I am under the assumption that in general people are more likely than not to be like discriminatory, or be transphobic."

Like Will, Arun, a multiracial/multiethnic white, Middle Eastern, Jewish male in the social sciences, described the importance of exercising agency over telling his colleagues about his trans history. When Arun served as a visiting professor at a liberal arts college in the West, he recounted a situation with a colleague where the person asked about Arun's motivation to teach on trans topics. He said,

> It seemed like [the colleague] was trying to ask me if I was trans. That was sort of the real question but he was sort of phrasing it in a round-about way that seemed to be just academic curiosity. That was awkward. That was the one thing in my whole year with the department that ever really sort of sent up a red flag or sort of made me feel uncomfortable.

When I asked Arun to elaborate about this kind of experience, he said,

> When I've been asked that question of why I do work with trans people, I always sort of feel like … I always sort of freeze up a little bit. I have to decide in that very moment which answer I am going to give. I have my two answers. I have my answer where I say, "Well I am trans and so I think it is important," but then I have my academic answer, "People aren't working on this and we can learn x, y, and z from working with trans people." I feel like I have to kind of assess which question the person is really asking. I feel like usually the question is sort of "Why do you care about trans people?" or "Why would you even think to study trans people?" and they are looking for the "Because I am trans" answer. I guess the way that he responded, I ended up telling him. I gave him both answers together, basically. I did tell him that I was trans. His re-action after that seemed like he didn't quite know how to talk about that, or how to respond, or whether or not it was okay to ask something else or say something else about that. That is what makes it awkward.

I think he just really didn't know how to talk to me about those topics but really wanted to for really good genuine reasons of wanting to get to know me and to know more about my work and that kind of thing.

Arun's comments here are indicative of the experience of many trans academics, who have to struggle with how to answer questions about their identity and the interrelationship it might have with their work. Certainly all scholars must provide a rationale for the work they perform, but when that work aligns with one's identity, such questioning strikes closer to one's personhood. The decision making Arun described is a microfoundational process that aligns with sensemaking (Weick 1995). Through sensemaking, Arun is performing additional labor that ultimately creates an inequality regime (Acker 2006) for him, as it does for other trans academics in a similar situation.

In addition to contexts where they were directly asked about their trans identity, some study participants felt the need to talk about their identity in certain spaces. They often performed additional labor to disrupt the cis assumptions present within and beyond higher education environments. Skeeter, a Jewish trans associate professor in a social science at a large public research university in the West, characterized the classroom as an important space for identity disclosure. When I asked Skeeter about what it means to Skeeter to be a trans academic, Skeeter stated,

> I've found though that when I'm in a classroom with my students and LGBT work comes up, it's like I all of a sudden go in to "trans academic mode." That's where I am very aware and I have to kind of toe the line. I usually come out but it's a matter of context . . . I always think, "Is this the moment that I'm going to come out? Am I going to demonstrate that I am the first tenured person in my field?" I don't even know if my [undergraduate] students would understand that. My doc students would. So I would say that's really where I feel it.

For Skeeter, the classroom, especially when LGBT topics come up, is the time that Skeeter's trans identity becomes even more salient and there is a desire to discuss trans-ness. Skeeter also experienced being in "trans academic mode" when writing and during faculty senate meetings, where there are "queer people present, but none of them are trans." Skeeter then has some agency, but feels a sense of responsibility to "toe the line" about disclosing.

Having described the various ways individual exercise agency through the sensemaking process (Weick 1995), I now complicate this microfoundational process (Powell and Colyvas 2008) by discussing the experiences of Susan, an African American trans adjunct instructor (now retired). Susan taught for thirty years in the social sciences at a historically Black liberal arts college in the South, and even though she recognized herself as trans during that time, she did not transition until after retiring. When I asked her if she wished that she had been more out as trans when she was still teaching, she said:

> Yeah ... I would have because I would have liked to have interacted with more trans students than I have. To help them when they were going through that to teach them when they're nineteen, twenty, twenty-one. To be able to talk to somebody who is forty-five to fifty, almost sixty now. Because I've had a couple of students and they were having those issues and they came to me and we talked about it. Ultimately I did help them out. It would have been nice but at same time, it would have been difficult.

Susan's desire to have been more visible is thus less about her own needs than about wanting to have been better able to support younger trans people. When she and I talked about how or why she felt it was not possible for her to gender transition while in her teaching role, she said:

> To be honest, *I can't even imagine.* I can tell you that ... [I didn't disclose] because the administration would be upset. They probably wouldn't let you be involved with anything dealing with the public. They would probably want you to teach your class and go. They would worry about if you were trans, then the students that might be trans but they can't [be turned trans]. The students [would] probably [be] supportive of you but also from the standpoint that it helps them.

Susan highlights how agency is unevenly distributed across institutional types and contexts. Her sensemaking about her organizational context led her to recognize that being trans at the college was utterly impossible. She felt that if she told her students or colleagues that she was trans, "It would be a problem."

The anti-trans climate at Susan's school should not be seen as indicative of all historically Black colleges but as reflective of the institutional mindset on her campus. She described the various financial difficulties that her former institution faced, which led the school to want to avoid anything that could detract from its image or hinder its ability to recruit top students. Sadly, the college administration apparently considered visible trans people to be a potential liability, rather than an asset, in these efforts.

All of this competition and institutional precarity results from the institutional logics of the market and corporation (Thornton, Ocasio, and Lounsbury 2012). Within her specific department, she said, "we're a corporate department. We deal with large corporations, a lot of fundraising. It's tough enough trying to get a job in corporate America being an African American male, but that [being gender nonconforming] adds another variable to it." To be seen as a positive representative of the college, one must adhere to the expectations of corporate donors and employers, which typically include being visibly gender conforming. Susan's department works to place graduates in these corporations, so her role was also to inform students about the gender expectations that African American men in corporate America would face. Thus, the relative impossibility of being trans at Susan's former institution stems from the precarious market position of the school (e.g., the institution needed corporate donors to keep the college open) and not exclusively from an underlying transphobic sentiment. Susan's experiences demonstrate that institutional context can play a significant role in how much agency a trans academic feels they have to disclose their identity.

For some, exercising agency about their identity is not possible because they are publicly known as a trans person, were hired in part because they are a trans person, or because someone else removed their agency by disclosing their identity. For example, Stanley, a white FTM/genderqueer librarian, Ph.D. candidate, and graduate student instructor, recounted an experience where someone else publicly revealed that he is trans. He described the situation as follows:

> At the end of my first year in the Ph.D. I wound up filing a discrimination complaint against one of my professors ... I identify as male and have a beard and have a relatively deep voice so I don't get misgendered that often anymore thanks to physical transition. So, I'm not out to everyone in my program. I use my agency to determine when and if I disclose to people. So what wound up happening was one of my instructors outed me to the class when I wasn't in the room. Basically, he misgendered me when talking about my research so that was kind of awkward. That was a really shitty way to end my first year. And so I filed a grievance and we had a mediated hearing with the faculty member and there were these next steps put into place but I have no idea if he ever did any of them.

Stanley's physical transition made him invisible as trans until his professor took away his agency and made him hypervisible. Thus, for Stanley and some other trans academics, agency and visibility are interrelated processes shaped by the genderist environment. The professor also reinforced the stereotype that trans people are not really the gender they say they are, but are make-believers (Bettcher 2007).

Taken together, the experiences of Will, Arun, Skeeter, Susan, and Stanley illuminate the complexity of agency with respect to trans identity/status/history disclosures. Although identity disclosure was influenced by context, others' assumptions about what a trans person looks like, and one's sensemaking, agency was not evenly distributed among the study participants. In addition, there were anticipated negative consequences for individuals like Will and Arun, who are not readily identifiable as trans.

### BEING AND BECOMING PROFESSIONALLY *OTHER*

I encapsulate the major themes described in this chapter with the concept of "being and becoming professionally *other*." This phrase references a quote from Joy, who described how her workplace gender transition made her professionally *other* and the difficulties that resulted in her life.

To be and/or become professionally *other* entails being subjected to demands of performing certain kinds of labor that people who do not share your identities and/or who adhere to established norms do not have to perform. In the case of trans academics, this means managing one's identity through complex processes of visibility, logics of possibility and impossibility about trans identities, and navigating the various tensions associated with genderism (e.g., misgendering). At the beginning of this chapter, I argued that there is no singular trans academic experience, but there are some partially shared contours of experiences. The shared tensions experienced by trans academics are the common thread that "being and becoming professionally *other*" articulates.

Although trans academics may face unique forms of oppression, they are not alone in being "outside in the teaching machine" (Spivak 1993, 294). In my own theorizing, I have imagined the central core of the institution as holding certain norms (e.g., masculine, whiteness) and identities (e.g., white, man, Christian). Spivak (1993) would eschew the use of identity, particularly in its more essentialized forms, and focus instead on processes of normalization. Thus, I follow the notion that machines derive meaning through how they work and what they plug into and what plugs into them (Deleuze and Guattari 1988). The center of the teaching/research/service machine has a set of norms related to social systems (e.g., heterosexism) but also values that are covert ways to communicate that same system (e.g., valuing linearity and rational thinking). My use of the phrase "outside in the teaching machine" is about the complex relations of power that occur within academia and how these relations manifest in the experiences of trans academics (Spivak 1993). Through being and becoming professionally *other*, trans academics are simultaneously margin/center; they are inside, but not of, the institution, at least in terms of gender.

Given that trans academics are professionally *other*, it behooves them to develop coalitions and exercise coalitional politics with other minoritized academics to address the ways institutional norms create margins and centers in the first place. Thus, I call for a coalitional politics that builds on the work of individuals and groups already combating racism, sexism, ableism, and heterosexism within the academy. The notion of being and becoming professionally *other* led me to the conclusion that there are many working "in" institutions of higher education, including trans academics, who are not "of" the institution in a variety of ways. They are "outside in the teaching machine" (Spivak 1993).

## NOTES

1. Some (but not all) participants selected pseudonyms for this study.

2. Genderism is endemic to higher education (Nicolazzo 2016) and is a system of oppression that holds the underlying assumption that there are two and only two genders, which are essential to one's assigned sex at birth (Bilodeau 2009; Jourian 2014).

3. In this, I use "tension" in two ways. First, tension is mental or emotional strain. Second, tension refers to being stretched tight, tautness. In describing each of the tensions that participants' experience, I enumerate the mental and emotional consequences, as well as the ways in which bodies and lived experiences are stretched tight by systems of oppression.

4. *Transmisogyny* is a term for negative attitudes, hatred, and violence directed at trans women and feminine-spectrum individuals.

## WORKS CITED

Acker, Joan. 2006. "Inequality Regimes: Gender, Class, and Race in Organizations." *Gender and Society* 20 (4): 441–64.

Ahmed, Sara. 2012. *On Being Included: Racism and Diversity in Institutional Life*. Durham, NC: Duke University Press.

Ayres, Lioness. 2008. "Thematic Coding and Analysis." In *The Sage Encyclopedia of Qualitative Research Methods*, edited by Lisa Given. Thousand Oaks, CA: Sage Publications.

Bem, Sandra L. 1981. "Gender Schema Theory: A Cognitive Account of Sex Typing." *Psychological Review* 88 (4): 354.

Bettcher, Talia Mae. 2007. "Evil Deceivers and Make-Believers: On Transphobic Violence and the Politics of Illusion." *Hypatia* 22 (3): 43–65.

Bilodeau, Brent. 2009. *Genderism: Transgender Students, Binary Systems and Higher Education*. Saarbrucken, Germany: VDM.

Bulhan, Hussein Abdilahi. 2004. *Frantz Fanon and the Psychology of Oppression*. New York: Springer Science and Business Media.

Creswell, John W. 2009. *Research Design: Qualitative, Quantitative, and Mixed Methods Approaches*, 3rd ed. Thousand Oaks, CA: Sage.

Croom, Natasha, and Lori Patton. 2012. "The Miner's Canary: A Critical Race Perspective on the Representation of Black Women Full Professors." *Negro Educational Review* 62/63 (1–4): 13–39.

Deleuze, Gilles, and Félix Guattari. 1988. *A Thousand Plateaus: Capitalism and Schizophrenia*. London: Bloomsbury.

Enke, A. Finn. 2012. "The Education of Little Cis: Cisgender and the Discipline of Opposing Bodies." In *Transfeminist Perspectives in and beyond Transgender and Gender Studies*, edited by Anne Enke, 60–77. Philadelphia: Temple University Press.

Fanon, Frantz. 2005. *The Wretched of the Earth*. Translated by Richard Philcox. New York: Grove Press.

Ford, Kristie A. 2011. "Race, Gender, and Bodily (Mis) Recognitions: Women of Color Faculty Experiences with White Students in the College Classroom." *Journal of Higher Education* 82 (4): 444–78.

Guba, Egon G. 2004. "Authenticity Criteria." In *The SAGE Encyclopedia of Social Science Research Methods*, edited by Michael Lewis-Beck, Alan Bryman, and Tim Liao. Thousand Oaks, CA: Sage.

Hill Collins, Patricia. 2000. *Black Feminist Thought: Knowledge, Consciousness, and the Politics of Empowerment*. New York: Routledge.

Holstein, James A., and Jaber F. Gubrium. 1995. *The Active Interview*. Thousand Oaks, CA: Sage.

hooks, bell. 1984. *Feminist Theory from Margin to Center*. Boston: South End Press.

Leech, Nancy L., and Anthony J. Onwuegbuzie. 2008. "Debriefing." *The SAGE Encyclopedia of Qualitative Research Methods*, edited by Lisa Given. Thousand Oaks, CA: Sage.

Miles, Matthew B., and A. Michael Huberman. 1994. *Qualitative Data Analysis: An Expanded Sourcebook*. Thousand Oaks, CA: Sage.

Miles, Matthew B., A. Michael Huberman, and Johnny Saldaña. 2013. *Qualitative Data Analysis: A Methods Sourcebook*, 3rd ed. Thousand Oaks, CA: Sage.

Namaste, Viviane K. 2000. *Invisible Lives: The Erasure of Transsexual and Transgendered People*. Chicago: University of Chicago Press.

Nicolazzo, Z. 2016. *Trans\* in College: Transgender Students' Strategies for Navigating Campus Life and the Institutional Politics of Inclusion*. Sterling, VA: Stylus.

Pitcher, Erich N. 2016. "Being and Becoming Professionally Other: Understanding How Organizations Shape Trans\* Academics' Experiences." PhD diss., Michigan State University.

———. 2017. " 'There's Stuff that Comes with Being an Unexpected Guest': Experiences of Trans\* Academics with Microaggressions." *International Journal of Qualitative Studies in Education* 30 (7): 688–703.

Powell, W. W., and Jeannette Colyvas. 2008. "Microfoundations of Institutional Theory." In *The SAGE Handbook of Organizational Institutionalism*, edited by Royston Greenwood, Christine Oliver, Roy Suddaby, and Kerstin Sahlin-Andersson. London: Sage.

Rubin, Herbert J., and Irene S. Rubin. 2011. *Qualitative Interviewing: The Art of Hearing Data*, 3rd ed. Thousand Oaks, CA: Sage.

Sensoy, Özlem, and Robin J. DiAngelo. 2012. *Is Everyone Really Equal?: An Introduction to Key Concepts in Social Justice Education*. New York: Teachers College Press.

Spade, Dean. 2011. *Normal Life: Administrative Violence, Critical Trans Politics and the Limits of Law*. Brooklyn, NY: South End Press.

Spivak, Gayatri Chakravorty. 1993. *Outside in the Teaching Machine*. New York: Routledge.

Stanley, Christine A. 2006. *Faculty of Color: Teaching in Predominantly White Colleges and Universities*. San Francisco: Jossey-Bass.

ThếNguyịn, Thu Su'o'ng. 2008. "Peer Debriefing." In *The SAGE Encyclopedia of Qualitative Research Methods*, edited by Lisa Given. Thousand Oaks, CA: Sage.

Thornton, Patricia H., William Ocasio, and Michael Lounsbury. 2012. *The Institutional Logics Perspective: A New Approach to Culture, Structure and Process*. New York: Oxford University Press.

Weick, Karl. 1995. *Sensemaking in Organizations*. Thousand Oaks, CA: Sage.

# FIFTEEN

# From "My Absolute Worst Nightmare" to "I Couldn't Ask for Anything More"

Trans Individuals' Interactions with College Administrators, Professors, and Others Representing Institutional Power

*Kristie L. Seelman*

UNTIL VERY RECENTLY, scholars have widely overlooked the experiences of trans people in college settings (Effrig, Bieschke, and Locke 2011; Nicolazzo 2016; Renn 2010). However, with an increase in media attention to the lives of trans people in the past decade, a wider segment of society is being exposed to the reality that trans people live in all parts of the country and can be found in all spheres of life, including within higher education. There is a sizable amount of research documenting issues related to the campus climate for trans and gender-nonconforming students, including experiences of discrimination, microaggressions, harassment, and violence (Bilodeau 2007; Grant, Mottet, and Tanis 2011; Rankin 2003; Rankin et al. 2010; Seelman, Woodford, and Nicolazzo 2017) and exclusion from gender-segregated spaces, such as bathrooms and housing (Bilodeau 2007; Seelman 2014b). Furthermore, previous work has detailed best practices for including trans individuals in college settings (Beemyn 2005a; Beemyn, Curtis et al. 2005; Beemyn, Domingue et al. 2005; Rankin et al. 2010; Seelman 2014a) and campus policy recommendations (Beemyn, Curtis, et al. 2005; Rankin et al. 2010; Seelman et al. 2012).

However, research is scant regarding trans people's interactions with those who represent the institution's power—people who hold explicit institutional status and influence as part of their role. Such positions include those who are supervisors, administrators (presidents, provosts, deans, etc.), professors (in relation to students), and staff with a high degree of influence over a key campus process, such as admissions or student health and counseling services. This chapter details a community-driven research project that studied the interactions of trans students, staff, and faculty with those who represent institutional power in college settings, how these interactions have influenced trans people's experiences of higher education, and how such exchanges could be improved.

## LITERATURE REVIEW

Campus administrators and staff have the power to positively affect the lives of trans individuals, but to achieve that goal, "they will need to reconsider many of their assumptions about gender and the structure of higher education" (Beemyn 2005b, para. 10). The marginalization of trans people is often institutionalized, reproduced in a college's norms, values, behaviors, and communications about what the institution stands for and who belongs (and who does not belong) in the campus community. When such norms and values systematically marginalize trans people, this population is negatively affected in many ways, from being ignored to being denied access to a bathroom, being unable to change their name on campus records, being denied admission or a job, and being subjected to violence, harassment, and bullying (Bilodeau 2007; Grant, Mottet, and Tanis 2011; Rankin et al. 2010; Seelman et al. 2012). Given that people in roles representing institutional power are often the "face" of the college, are actively involved in funding and policy decisions at the highest levels of the institution, and determine many of the campus procedures and rules that affect trans people, the actions and nonactions of this group are critical to efforts to counteract trans marginalization.

However, little previous research has examined trans individuals' interactions with people in roles representing institutional power and whether these authority figures tend to contribute to or challenge the institutional marginalization of trans people. Some general themes have been documented, including an overall lack of knowledge about trans experiences and a lack of trans curriculum content (McKinney 2005; Rankin 2003; Seelman et al. 2012), blatantly transphobic actions and words (Bilodeau 2007; Case et al. 2012; Seelman 2013), entrenched cis-normative beliefs (Case et al. 2012), struggles with getting professors to use correct names and pronouns for trans students (Bilodeau 2007), and resistance to efforts to address the harassment, bullying, and violence targeting trans people on campuses through policy change (Case et al. 2012). Little is empirically documented about the hiring, promotion, and other employment experiences of trans staff and faculty (for an exception, see Bilodeau 2007). Trans faculty in particular remain an understudied subgroup in higher education literature (Renn 2010). Research is also scant about the day-to-day actions of administrators that may be experienced as supportive or unsupportive by trans and gender-nonconforming individuals.

The present study aims to address these gaps in the knowledge base. The research question is: How do trans and gender-nonconforming students, staff, and faculty in higher education describe their interactions with people in positions of institutional power (e.g., supervisors, staff, administrators, professors)?

## METHODOLOGY

This study was completed as part of a mixed methods dissertation (Seelman 2013). The focus here is on a qualitative portion of the dissertation, which was based on a project conceptualized and carried out by Colorado Trans on Campus (CTOC). CTOC was an informal coalition organized by the Colorado Anti-Violence Program (now called Survivors Organizing for Liberation) in 2009. CTOC was composed of students, staff, and faculty at universities in Colorado, as well as community advocates and volunteers, who were dedicated to improving the lives of trans and gender-nonconforming people (Seelman et al. 2012).

### Procedure

Interviews were conducted with thirty students, staff, and faculty between 2009 and 2010. All participants were over age eighteen, had worked or studied at a Colorado institution of higher education in the previous twelve months, and either identified as or were frequently perceived by others as being trans or gender variant. Announcements of this study were distributed to offices of student services, LGBTQ centers, relevant email lists, and other contacts at college campuses in Colorado. All interviews were face to face and took place in locations chosen by participants that allowed for private conversation. After completing the interview, participants filled out a pen-and-paper demographic survey. The thirty anonymous transcripts (or interviewer notes) and participant demographics were shared with the author for secondary data analysis as part of dissertation research (see Seelman 2013).

### Sample

More than a third of the participants (40 percent, $n = 12$) identified their gender when on campus[1] as being genderqueer, nonbinary, androgynous, or another nonbinary term; 23.3 percent ($n = 7$) identified as a man, trans guy, or another identity on a transmasculine spectrum; 13.3 percent ($n = 4$) identified as a woman, trans woman, or another identity on a transfeminine spectrum; and 23.3 percent ($n = 7$) used a combination of identity terms that spanned these different categories—such as identifying as both genderqueer and a trans guy. This sample ranged in age from 18 to 45 years old, with an average age of 29.8 years (standard deviation = 8.42) and mode of 20. More than two thirds (70 percent, $n = 21$) of the participants identified as white, 16.7 percent ($n = 5$) identified as Latinx (including those who identified as both white and Latinx), 6.7 percent ($n = 2$) selected "Other" and wrote in Jewish, and 6.7 percent ($n = 2$) identified with some other race/ethnic identity or with multiple identities.

Nearly two thirds of the sample (63.3 percent, $n = 19$) were students, 10 percent ($n = 3$) were faculty, 10 percent ($n = 3$) were staff, and 16.7 percent ($n = 5$) were in multiple roles on campus. Length of time affiliated with a campus ranged from just one month to more than eight years. Participants represented a variety of departments and offices, including the social sciences, humanities, natural sciences, professional degree programs (law, medicine, etc.), and campus administration. Ten different college/university campuses in Colorado were represented in this sample. The campuses ranged in size from having fewer than 2,000 students to having over 20,000 students. Most (70 percent, $n = 7$) were public institutions. Eighty percent ($n = 8$) of these campuses were four-year institutions, and 20 percent ($n = 2$) were two-year institutions.

## RESULTS

A total of six themes emerged from the research question, each of which will be reviewed here.

### Theme One: Refusing to Use or Having Difficulty Using Correct Names and Pronouns

This first theme focused on participants' stories of how people in positions representing institutional power either refused to use correct names or pronouns when referring to a trans individual or had a lot of difficulty doing so. This included instances where people made incorrect assumptions about a person's gender and first name or did not believe the person's claimed identity. Such experiences affected participants across all gender identity groups, regardless of whether individuals used male, female, or gender-neutral pronouns for themselves.

Most instances of name/pronoun misuse in academic settings occurred within the classroom and involved an instructor. One common classroom practice that led to misnaming was the class roll call. A number of participants said they dread the moment when a professor reads through a class roster to take attendance because their college does not give students the ability to have a name other than their birth name (what trans people refer to as their dead name) in campus systems. As a result, they have to ask professors to use their correct name, which can be a struggle, as demonstrated by one participant's experience:

> I knew that it said [masculine birth name] on [the class roll], and I just recently decided to start going by [correct name] ... and I wanted to ... let [my professor] know [my correct name]. ... At first she reacted the same way that most people do, which is ... that pause, and then that eyebrow raise, and then, "[Correct name]?" ... or "How do you spell that?" ... She goes, "Well, I'll try to remember that, I can't make any promises." And then the next [class] day ... she was reading off roll, and she called [incorrect] name and ... I kind of raised my hand and I said, "[Correct name]," and she goes, "Oh that's right ... I'm really going to try and remember that." ... After class, I introduced myself and I said ... "The reason that I want to go by [correct name] is because I'm currently going through—" and I used the term "gender transition" because I didn't want to explain all the minutia. ... The point that I was trying to make was ... this is important to me ... And she seemed standoffish to me when I was explaining that, and I think that she thought that I was attacking her for not remembering, when in reality I was trying to say ... "I'm just not trying to be cute ... This is the reason why I want that," ... and she said, "Oh okay, well, like I said, I'll do my best to remember." And in parting, I was like, "Well why don't you just mark it on your thing there, just erase those last letters, and that's all it'll take?"

There are a number of important issues to note in this example. First, the professor had to be reminded on multiple occasions by the student of zir correct name, to the point that the student suggested the simple solution of making a note on the roster. Second, class rosters often only include a student's legal name, so that trans and gender-nonconforming individuals who go by a different name have to tell their instructors that their name is incorrectly listed if they want to avoid being misnamed and possibly misgendered. When an instructor simply reads through the class roster, there is a risk of unintentionally outing a trans student.

In other cases, participants described scenarios where it was clear that a faculty member was purposefully addressing them by their dead name or incorrect pronouns. A genderqueer student shared how professors at zir school have sometimes tried to justify not using gender-neutral pronouns by citing their feminist political beliefs:

> I have had a few professors who I think do refuse to use gender-neutral pronouns. . . . I think it comes from a belief that, in using gender-neutral pronouns, I think everyone should use gender-neutral pronouns, and I don't believe that at all. The example that was actually given to me by a professor was, "If you say *he* raped *her*, you know that there's a power relationship there. That's something that we can work with in society to challenge gender-based oppression, right? But if you say *ze* raped *ze*, you have no idea what that power relationship is, and you destroy any chance of challenging sex- or gender-based oppression, harassment, discrimination, all these sorts of things." . . . And therefore . . . [this professor] refuse[s] to use gender-neutral pronouns . . . so that has been frustrating.

In this example, the professor failed to differentiate between engaging in a theoretical debate about gender oppression as part of classroom learning and respecting a trans individual's choice of personal pronouns.

Another academic case where a trans individual might have their name challenged is in relation to classroom assignments and exams. A student in a natural sciences program told of such a situation:

> [The professor is] handing tests back at the end of class, and she calls names out, which is my absolute worst nightmare: instructors who like to stand at the front of the stadium and call each individual person's name out and have them walk down the stadium stairs and take your paper and walk back to your desk. So . . . it's our first test . . . I'm ready for the [first letter of my last name] so that I can just grab my paper . . . Totally feeling anxious. She calls my name, I walk up . . . and I reach for my paper, and she says, "No, [participant's first name]." And I say, "Yeah, that's me." . . . And she says, "No . . . you're not [participant's first name]." . . . And at that point, I rip my paper out of her hand, and I just walked out of the room. . . . She's calling after me, she's trying to stop

me because ... I'm some nut case who's running off with somebody's paper ... And then she gives up and she says ... "Oh, pffft! Whatever!" And then you hear students laughing.

This professor made a snap judgment about how the student should look based on her legal first name and wrongly concluded that the student claiming the test was not the "correct" person. This encounter was made more embarrassing for the student because it happened in front of a classroom of peers who laughed.

The trans and gender-nonconforming participants who were employed on college campuses also encountered situations where supervisors refused to use or had difficulty using their correct names and pronouns. Several of those interviewed discussed such scenarios, which sometimes occurred even after other employees had been informed of the appropriate name and pronouns or after the person had been hired with assurances that the campus was affirming of trans people. One faculty participant described how he encountered a lot of "mispronouning" (being referred to with incorrect pronouns) in his work department:

> The first two months that I worked here, I hadn't done any physical transitioning, and a lot of people in the [department] called me "she" even though they knew better. I mean, they'd all been informed otherwise. [They] were people who were ... involved in the interview ... my fellow faculty members, [and the fact that they] were mispronouning me was frustrating, and I never found out, I still don't know how many people I work with ... were informed [that I prefer male pronouns], or how they were informed, before I started working here. My boss claims she doesn't know ... And my [upper level administrator] called me "she" in a team meeting, and it was all just horrible.

One subtheme related to being misnamed or misgendered by people in power on campuses was the degree to which a trans or gender-nonconforming person was read by others as female or male (sometimes referred to as passing) or was farther along in a transition process. Although individuals who are perceived as trans are not the only ones who are frequently addressed with incorrect pronouns or names, several participants attributed such experiences to the fact that they are not regularly read as a binary gender or have not yet completed their transition. A genderqueer individual, who used a mixture of gendered and gender-neutral pronouns for zirself, said, "I think that how I get seen in the context of language of particular pronouns, my students do a far better job than any of my colleagues around either mixing them up ... I almost feel like I have to take testosterone before I get seen [by colleagues], which seems really screwed up to me." Educating cis members of a campus about the need to ask everyone for their pronouns, regardless of a person's gender expression, would be one method for creating an environment where all gender identities are respected.

### Theme Two: Marginalizing Me or Treating Me and My Community as Invisible

People in positions of power on campuses often either deliberately ignored the presence and needs of trans and gender-nonconforming people or failed to see this population. In some cases, institutional officials pressured trans people not to focus on trans-related issues in their work, teaching, or research or acted in ways that minimized or dismissed the unique challenges faced by trans people on college campuses.

A powerful way this theme was manifested was in how university officials, particularly upper-level administrators, did not speak about issues or concerns of trans people, even when naming and supporting other minoritized populations on their college campus. A staff person at a public university offered:

> Our [university's lead administrator] talks about all kinds of different people and still leaves out folks around sexuality and gender identity and expression.... There's no institutional accountability or ownership for the ways in which transphobia ... shows up on campus daily, and I think very few things will change until the university as a whole starts to have that conversation with itself.... If things don't shift on the top, very few things are going to change where I am.

This participant highlights how, if a university truly wants to be committed to supporting diversity and contributing to the visibility of minoritized populations, leaders need to do their part to acknowledge such populations in their public speeches, policy initiatives, and everyday interactions.

Another way that marginalization occurred on campuses was related to supervisors discouraging trans individuals from focusing on trans-related topics in their work, teaching, or research. One faculty participant described such a situation:

> I meet with my [upper-level administrator] because we have annual evaluations.... My research interests tend to be about queer stuff. She

really does not like this.... Last year, I told her about how I had wanted to do research following a participatory action model involving people [using our work department] disclosing as transgender and asking for resources, and then analyzing what type of assistance they received.... And, so I told my [upper-level administrator] about this ... and then she said ... I should do research about something that relates to my job. So, yeah, it definitely felt like I was being shut down.... So, I worry that the type of research and work that I do isn't going to be okay because she doesn't support it, which would then mean I probably won't get promoted.

Part of the resistance that this individual received from the administrator was around his research proposal not being "related to his job," which was experienced by the faculty member as having his research interests "shut down." At the same time, the administrator did not acknowledge or affirm the value of such research for trans people on campus or how this topic may be particularly meaningful for the faculty member, who himself identifies as trans.

Other participants spoke about cases of being marginalized or treated as invisible in terms of how campus staff or administrators responded to their requests for assistance or reports of discrimination and harassment. One student participant, who experienced multiple instances of being harassed and having property in his residence hall room damaged, discussed how housing staff ignored and minimized his reports: "I started getting harassed by someone on campus. They broke into my room, wrote on some of my shit. I talked to the [housing staff] and they basically said, 'I'm sorry, it's not my problem,' and it just kind of continued." This student's attempts to seek help and address problems of harassment were insensitively and improperly handled by housing staff, leaving the person to feel unheard and unsafe.

Theme Three: Displaying or Promoting Transphobia or Lacking Education about Trans People

This theme concerns how people in positions representing institutional power on campuses failed to learn more about how to work with trans and gender-nonconforming people (even when such opportunities were provided on their campus), actively communicated pejorative misinformation about trans people, or openly opposed and ridiculed trans people and their concerns.

Transphobia was displayed through disgust, fear, or discomfort toward trans and gender-nonconforming people and was encountered within the classroom, in hiring and employment situations, within on-campus health care centers and student services offices, and in daily interactions with other people. The participants were confronted with transphobic reactions that ranged from somewhat implicit to very blatant.

Some of the most blatantly hostile encounters were experienced by students in classrooms, where faculty members openly insulted and encouraged fear and hatred of trans people. One student, who identifies as a transsexual woman, shared a story of coming out in a class and being subsequently maligned by her professor:

> [The professor] was talking about testosterone and its connection to sex drive. Then I spoke up and said, "As a transsexual, I think I have something important to offer on this." The professor responded with, "We always seem to have weird people in here." Then, later in another class session, trans [issues] got brought up again. And the professor asked, "Wouldn't you feel like beating up your wife if she was once a man?" Students started agreeing and just expressing disgust about trans people, and the professor didn't challenge it. I had to leave that space because it was so uncomfortable for me.... So that was a really negative experience with disclosing [my transsexual identity] ... After he brought that up in class, I stopped being that open. I didn't want to be a spectacle! So I don't really share my identity in classes anymore.[2]

Other participants spoke of transphobia occurring in employment-related interactions. Several discussed grappling with an apparent level of discomfort among their coworkers, and others described a general lack of follow-through among staff and administrators in learning more about how to competently serve and support trans employees. Still others encountered transphobia and seeming discomfort with someone's gender identity or expression among those involved in campus hiring. For example, the following situation was described by a faculty participant:

> I had applied for a position here that I didn't get, and in processing that ... I can't rule out that my gender presentation wasn't part of the reason I didn't get the position. I think that the ... lead decision maker was really uncomfortable with my gender, and it was my understanding after the process that I was close to the unanimous choice of

the search committee, but the [administrator] didn't hire me, and so I remember having that thought in the interview because I definitely didn't connect with him.... I remember thinking like, "We're not, we're not connecting and I don't know what's going on here." And so when I didn't get it ... I had that thought like, "Maybe he's not ready to have someone be that visibly queer in his department and all that came with that" ... and I can't affirmatively say that that's what it was.... There's certainly no way to prove someone's general discomfort with someone else's gender presentation ... but in hindsight, I wish there was a way to have that conversation.

This faculty member's experience reflects how difficult it can be to know if someone's actions are motivated by prejudice and, if so, whether it is conscious or unconscious bias. Regardless of whether transphobia is blatantly or implicitly expressed, it has very real consequences for trans people's livelihoods and well-being.

Among the student participants, an area where they frequently experienced transphobia was in health care. Many students are forced to use their campus health center because of their insurance coverage or the lack of other, nearby options. But these settings can be hostile places for trans students, especially when medical staff are ignorant about and antagonistic toward trans patients. A student shared this story:

I had bronchitis or something, so I had to go in [to the campus student health center] ... [And the health provider said,] "So, you're on testosterone and you have had a double mastectomy?" And I was like, "I'm transgender." She's like, "What's that?" So I had to explain that, and she just kept ... making all these expressions of kind of shock and disgust and making me repeat things, and saying, "Well, I don't really understand." ... And I felt terribly self-conscious about having to lift up my shirt because there were these scars that were pretty visible at that time ... So I left, I'm like, "I never want to see her again."

When trans and gender-nonconforming individuals who disclose their identities are met with expressions of "shock and disgust" and basic questions about what trans means by their medical providers, they are likely to become fearful of seeking follow-up care and may avoid it altogether. They are also likely to share their negative experience with other trans people, furthering alienating the trans community from medical professionals.

### Theme Four: Privileging Binary Systems of Gender

Many participants recounted experiences where people in positions representing institutional power acted in ways that privileged binary systems of gender and ignored trans oppression. These instances included when people in these roles tokenized trans people on campus, expected them to educate cis people about "the trans experience," asked them inappropriate personal questions, or treated being trans (or transitioning) as the root of all of a trans person's problems. Another aspect of this theme involved people in positions of power acting as if success was solely in the hands of the trans individual, thereby ignoring the role of systemic barriers.

A number of participants shared that they were regularly expected or asked to educate cis people on campus about the "trans experience," as if they could speak for all trans and gender-nonconforming people. For example, a student in the social sciences said: "I was in a class . . . and the teacher would continually say, 'I'm not sure if I'm explaining this right. [Name] can you explain it for us?' " Even if not maliciously intended, when professors, supervisors, or administrators regularly defer to a trans person to speak about their experience and teach others, they are tokenizing the trans individual while also excusing themselves from learning about trans people and how to be an ally to the trans community.

Regardless of their role on campus, participants reported being asked personal questions by their supervisors, administrators, staff, or faculty. These personal questions were on topics such as their body or genitals, whether they had undergone transition(s), how they understood or expressed their gender, and the status of their relationships with family members after coming out as trans. Such questions were asked by people who did not need this information to do their job; in the few cases where such information was relevant, the questions were asked in a very insensitive manner. One student, who was twenty-two years old, noted that she has found it traumatic to be repeatedly expected to answer personal questions about her financial independence from her parents, even though she recognizes that the financial aid staff are not trying to cause her harm: "I mean, there are a lot of raw wounds that hadn't been healed yet . . . and I have to go through [those financial independence questions] again and again and again." Although it may be necessary for financial aid officers to ask very personal questions to students about their families as part of determining financial need, staff should be aware that trans and gender-nonconforming students and others who have been rejected by their families of origin may find the experience to be very painful. Personal questions should be asked in a way that acknowledges and respects this reality for students.

Personal questions may come from anyone on campus, even from people within the LGBTQ community, who one might expect to be more culturally competent and sensitive. A faculty member encountered such a scenario when he first started teaching on his campus:

> I've had [faculty colleagues] ask me all kinds of horrible questions when I tell them I'm genderqueer ... I don't know if that's faculty thinking, "Oh well, I'm [LGBTQ], too, so I can ask you those things." It's kind of like that if you meet another minority, "Oh, I'm a minority, too, so I know what you're feeling. I know what it's like." And it's like, "Maybe you have an idea, but we're different people. We have different backgrounds. Just cause we're both minorities doesn't mean you're going to understand everything about me."

Again, part of the pattern at work here was that faculty members seemed to believe that they were entitled to this personal information—"I'm queer, too, so I can ask you those things." These were pressure-laden interactions for the participant, especially because he was a new faculty member. He emphasized that he was not comfortable sharing these details, and that just because these other faculty members identified as LGBTQ does not mean that they will "understand everything about me."

People in positions representing institutional power often ignored or minimized the systemic barriers that trans people face that can impede their success on campus. Such "blindness" to structural oppression contributes to the problem of inequality precisely because there are documented disparities in how institutions treat trans people compared with cis people. This theme was expressed by a thirty-year-old student who was relatively new to her degree program:

> It takes a lot to be ... vulnerable and walk in [to a professor] and say ... "Here's what I need as a student in your course, what would be helpful to me." And I don't ever feel that I'm asking for anything above and beyond.... I had one professor, her reaction to me was, "Well, situations are what we make of them, and we can only be responsible for ourselves. And, in the end, if you want to be successful, you will be." ... If this were truly [a situation where] ... my success rests squarely on my shoulders, then that would be an entirely different story, but I'm

not sure that that's really how it really goes down ... I have yet to reach a point where I come clean and reach out to a professor and have what feels like a ... validating experience.

By expecting the student to succeed on her own, the professor ignores the very real threats of discrimination, harassment, and institutional barriers that confront trans and gender-nonconforming people.

### Theme Five: Punishing Me for Gender Nonconformity

This theme focused on participants' experiences with people in positions representing institutional power acting in ways that punished them for being trans or gender nonconforming. Such punishment included requiring trans people to jump through hoops that are not expected of cis people, such as showing identification; publicly shaming or teasing trans people about their name, pronouns, gender identity, or gender expression; firing or not hiring a person because of their gender identity or gender expression; and outing a trans person. While all of these topics are represented in the data, I cover just a few exemplars here.

An example of shaming and setting up additional barriers for trans people came from a student who was looking to take a make-up exam for a course in which the faculty member did not recognize all of his students due to the size of the class. The participant recounted:

And so I show up to take my test [at the professor's office], and he's got a student in his office ... And, [the professor] looks at me and he's like, "Who are you?" and I said, "I'm [feminine-sounding first name], we had emailed, you said I could come in and take my exam." He said, "You're not [first name]." And I said, "Yes, I am ... Here's my ID." And he looks to the [other] student and he says, "[First name]'s a girl's name, isn't it? ... He's not a woman ... do you know him?" ... So in my head, I'm starting to go into a total meltdown.... He finally gave in, but he made me sit in his office while he was talking to the student, and then afterwards he asked me to see my ID again, actually made a copy of my student ID and stapled it to my test.... In his mind, he still wasn't convinced ... That was a really shitty experience ... But it's pretty typical—having interactions with professors who assume I'm a guy. I'm not.

Other students in the course were not required to show an ID to take the exam, but this student was forced to do so because of the professor's judgments about what a woman should look like.

Another example of "punishment" occurs when people in positions of power out a trans person to others. Being outed can result in severe emotional, academic, or job-related consequences for a trans person, not to mention the risk to personal safety. An example was shared by a faculty member:

> What happened is that—this is before I started hormones—and I guess [was presenting] kind of ambiguous[ly], and people would ask [human resources staff person] if I was a he or a she. And she would tell them, but then she would explain why.... So I was very upset when I heard about that.... Once I'd calmed down a little, I went and told my boss who said that this person was just trying to be helpful and she didn't mean anything by it. And I'm like, "I don't care if she didn't mean anything by it, it's still violating my confidentiality and my privacy."

If someone chooses to keep their trans identity private, this information should only be shared on a need-to-know basis. In settings where administrators, staff, and faculty are inexperienced in working with trans populations or fail to understand the importance of not outing people, a training session should be required to help create a campus culture that values, affirms, and respects trans individuals.

### Theme Six: Supporting, Listening to, and Affirming Me and Other Trans People

Not all of the themes identified in the data reflected negative interactions with people who represented institutional power. In fact, several interviewees made clear that they have experienced very positive and supportive interactions with people on campus in administrative, faculty, and staff roles. Examples are further detailed here.

Responding with Support and Affirmation When a Trans Person Discloses Their Gender Identity.   Participants noted that choosing to disclose one's gender identity or status as trans can be a moment of incredible vulnerability. Having this disclosure greeted with affirmation and encouragement by a supervisor, faculty member, staff person, or administrator was often a surprising yet important moment of support. A natural sciences student shared:

> I disclosed to my [natural science department] teacher first this [term] ... and she ... was pretty responsive.... She had a lab notebook one day with a male name in it and didn't know if it was someone who was in that class because she wanted the names of all the men in the classroom,

and she asked me as well as every other man in the room, which was
pretty cool because most other students wouldn't gender me that way,
and she did it without being awkward or obvious. . . . It was pretty cool.

This student felt validated by this interaction because the professor respected
and affirmed his gender identity and treated him like "every other man
in the room."

A minority of participants shared examples where an administrator, staff
person, faculty member, or supervisor respected a person's request to be addressed by a particular name or pronouns; corrected their own mistakes in
misnaming or misgendering an individual, on realizing they made an error;
or checked in with a trans person about how to refer to them. One positive
example was offered by a faculty member in relation to going through a university's hiring process:

When people from the search committee were checking my references,
my two standard references, to whom I wasn't out yet at the time, used
female pronouns for me . . . and then my friend here . . . called me "he"
. . . because she knew I identified as male. . . . One HR person in the [de-
partment] apparently put two and two together, and called me at work
. . . and asked me what pronouns I preferred. . . . I really appreciated her
asking because she'd prefaced it with wanting me to be comfortable
interviewing.

Recognizing That Trans and Gender-Nonconforming People May Have Some Unique
Needs and Challenges. Participants felt affirmed when administrators and
faculty members recognized that trans and gender-nonconforming people may
face challenges and have specific needs within the campus environment that
differ from those of cis people. Supportive actions recognized the humanity
and dignity of the person, while acknowledging the existence of transphobia
and structural barriers for trans people and the need for cis people to educate
themselves about trans lives and create positive change.

For example, a student shared how his faculty supervisor recognized that
he would be experiencing some physical changes and additional stressors while
starting hormones in the next term and offered to have the student work behind
the scenes, rather than in front of a classroom, early in the transition process:

[Faculty member is] somebody that I have talked about the whole trans
issue, and since I hope to be starting hormones before next [term]

... we decided that it'd be great if I didn't have to teach and his class doesn't require recitations. And so, he's like "I'll just ask for you as my [teaching assistant], and then I won't have to worry." Yeah ... so on that level, employment has been great. I couldn't ask for anything more ... I think his support, probably first and foremost, gave me the ability to even approach the idea of coming out to people.

Some of the students discussed affirming experiences using campus health centers. One student participant stated:

And [the health care provider] even said, she even went through logistics. "If you don't want to wait in the women's waiting room, we'll find another room for you.... We will work with you on this." ... I had asked her if she could write me a carry letter, which is the letter that ... I can keep in my wallet, so if my ID gets rejected, I can say, "Hey, this is why I don't look like my ID." She even wrote that up for me. And she's been working on other things in my file. She put on a specific flag and stuff that says I'm trans, so extra care with my file.

Gender-segregated spaces, such as a waiting room for a women's health clinic, can be particularly difficult for trans people to navigate, especially for those in the process of transitioning to male or who identify as nonbinary. This health care provider recognized such a barrier for the student and expressed a willingness to find solutions. She also understood the need for a carry letter (which describes a person's gender identity and process of transitioning), should the student's ID be challenged by the police or security officials, and for the student's correct name and gender to be on his health file.

*Acting with Kindness and Not Tokenizing Me for Being Trans or Gender Nonconforming.* Participants discussed how some people who represented institutional power on campus simply treated them with kindness. These administrators, staff, and faculty did not exoticize them, call unnecessary attention to their trans identity, or expect them to speak for all trans people. A quote that epitomized this theme came from a student interviewee:

I think [one place of support that surprised me] in general ... [was] the nonchalance about it that I'd experienced when I'd disclose to professors, where they like take a minute to get it ... They're like, "Oh, oh okay, that's cool," and it's over, and they're not about to ask me a ton of questions or like make me explain.

*Attempting to Correct an Individual's Records and Email Address to Reflect the Person's Correct Name and Gender.* Participants who sought to change their campus records to reflect their correct names and gender identities frequently encountered resistance and bureaucratic hurdles. Therefore, when campus representatives went out of their way to assist trans individuals in changing these records, their actions were perceived as extremely supportive. Participants said that simply the act of trying to help them on this issue was affirming, even if the campus bureaucracy and information systems ultimately did not allow changing these records. One student recounted such an experience:

> When I called the [LGBTQ student services office] . . . I said . . . "What do I do for all this stuff?" And [the guy I spoke to said], "Okay, here's the name of someone at the registrar, here's the name of someone at all the different places who is either queer or an ally." . . . So the woman at the registrar's office was like, "Okay, we can use your initials. That's all we can do. We can use your initials and then you can say, 'Hey, there's a mix-up. This is my name.'" . . . The woman who worked for [the IT department] was really great with the email. And she erased my other name and made it all switch to just my initials.

In this case, the student was not able to change all of his campus records. But staff communicated the precise issues in respectful, clear language and described a feasible (albeit imperfect) workaround.

*Educating Themselves about Trans and Gender-Nonconforming People and Their Needs.* In some circumstances, people in positions of institutional power were proactive in learning about trans people and how to best serve this population, even if they had yet to knowingly encounter a trans person. These administrators, faculty, and staff may have informally educated themselves or previously attended trainings, workshops, or conferences that contributed to their ability to competently serve trans and gender-nonconforming people. Such proactive education on the part of campus leaders and officials generally led to more positive interactions. One student shared the following:

> Part of a really supportive thing is just when . . . professors are already familiar with what I'm talking about and then take the next step of providing me with suggestions or ideas. Not only do I not have to explain myself to them, but they actually have sort of a complex understanding of me that then enables them to give nuanced advice. . . . I just feel really seen by some of the people who've been really supportive. . . . They don't

need a lot of explanation. . . . They just sort of hear me, and then they're excited to take the next step instead of getting stuck in, like, "No wait. Could you explain your gender identity one more time?"

For this student, interacting with professors who are already familiar with trans issues results in feeling seen and heard, an experience that contributes to the student's sense of belonging.

Additional Methods of Support. There were several other types of support described by participants; however, each of these topics was mentioned by only a small minority of the thirty people interviewed. These additional methods included apologizing for mistakes (such as incorrectly labeling a person's gender) and correcting one's actions, allowing employees to dress according to their gender identity, and advocating for trans-supportive campus policies.

Participants were appreciative when administrators, professors, or other people in positions of power recognized that they had done something that negatively affected trans people and apologized. A student talked about such a situation:

> [Staff person] came back to the interaction that we had initially had [where she misread my gender and said some racist remarks toward me]. And she said, "I've thought a lot about it, and I just want to say that I'm sorry. I still don't know entirely where I went wrong, but I want to figure it out, and my job is to support all students on campus, and so if you need anything at all . . . please come back [to this office]." . . . There's something that feels genuine. . . . The positive interactions are those [that] largely come from people who don't make it my problem . . .—that somebody would actually kind of take that on: "Whoa! I fucked up! I am sorry to YOU!"

This is an example of how recognizing the negative impact of one's actions and apologizing for making mistakes, as well as changing one's actions in the future, can have a reparative effect on relationships with trans campus members.

Another participant shared an example where an upper-level administrator advocated for gender-inclusive bathrooms and locker rooms:

> [Our campus has] the only recreation center that I know [which] has put—for every pair of gendered bathrooms—a gender-inclusive restroom, as well as gender-inclusive locker rooms—and not at my behest, but at the [upper-level administraaaaator]'s, that was all [her

doing] ... I would say that actually [upper-level administrator] is actually part of my support network ... She's amazing because she was just like, "This is the right thing to do," and I'm like ... that makes me extraordinarily happy!

Although there were few stories shared by participants in this study about upper-level administrators who proactively changed college policies to reflect best practices, such efforts can have a profound, positive effect on trans campus members' well-being.

## DISCUSSION

This community-initiated study aimed to address a gap in the research literature about the interactions of trans students, staff, and faculty members with people in roles representing institutional power in higher education. The inclusion of trans staff and faculty in this study is a step toward documenting trans experiences on campuses beyond those of students. The data highlighted a multitude of experiences with a lack of knowledge among administrators and supervisors about how to support trans people and a lack of initiative to build such knowledge. People in roles of institutional power frequently used incorrect names and pronouns in referring to trans individuals. They typically relied on institutional records to determine what name or pronouns to use for a person, rather than asking the person directly. Trans identities were often made invisible and marginalized on campuses, and transphobic beliefs were voiced to trans people with regularity. In addition, administrators, faculty, and staff frequently regarded cis identities as preferable, normal, and healthy and assumed that someone was cis unless the person was visibly gender nonconforming; they also sometimes singled out trans people for sanctions or required them to jump through extra hoops, such as having to show ID to take an exam when cis people were not required to do so. Such actions contribute to a climate that treats trans people as outsiders who are abnormal and not welcomed. Counteracting these norms often takes a great deal of thoughtful reflection, awareness of what transphobia looks like on campuses, and a commitment by people in authority to unlearn transphobic beliefs and behaviors.

This broad range of negative experiences is in line with the work of other scholars who have examined trans people's interactions with cis administrators and faculty on college campuses (Bilodeau 2007; Case et al. 2012; McKinney 2005; Rankin 2003). Furthermore, other scholars have documented similar patterns affecting other marginalized communities, such as being asked to "speak for" all of a minority population (Lindsay 2010; Molina 2008), being taught from curricula that do not contain content on their identities (Ballan 2008; Lindsay 2010; Quaye and Harper 2007), and being blamed for the problems they encounter (Schiele 2007). Trans people were often tokenized, asked inappropriate personal questions, and treated as if identifying as trans was the root of a person's challenges on campus.

People in administrative, faculty, and staff roles contributed to the invisibility and marginalization of trans and gender-nonconforming people by never speaking about them in public speeches, ignoring trans people when encountering them on campus, and discouraging trans people from studying topics or doing research about being trans. Such anti-trans biases demonstrate the need for those in administrative and leadership roles to receive trainings about what it means to be trans, what this population may need on campus, and why explicitly referring to this population in speeches, policies, and mission statements is important for creating an inclusive environment. The findings indicate that staff, faculty, and administrators often discriminated against trans people in various ways. Campus personnel need to be trained on why these behaviors are unacceptable, how to identify and stop such forms of prejudice, and how to treat trans people with the same respect and dignity as cis people.

This study also contributes to knowledge about the types of behaviors exhibited by people with institutional power that were experienced as supportive by trans and gender-nonconforming students, staff, and faculty. Some of the study participants who had positive interactions with an administrator or a faculty or staff member believed that the person in authority had previous experiences with trans people, had participated in trainings about supporting trans individuals, or experienced their own marginalization (gender-related or otherwise) that may have created an ability to empathize. Regardless, supportive actions reflected respect for every person on campus, inclusivity, and a commitment to unlearning and challenging transphobia.

Implications for Higher Education

The results of this project demonstrate how administrators, faculty, and staff can take steps to welcome and affirm trans people at their colleges and universities. Here are some specific recommendations stemming from this study.

### One-to-One Interactions

- Respond with affirmation and tact when a trans or gender-nonconforming person discloses their gender identity. Maintain confidentiality related to identity disclosure, sharing such information only when necessary as part of your job.
- Do not ask a trans person inappropriate personal questions (including about their body); rather, educate yourself about the trans community through attending trainings and presentations, reading trans literature, and so on.
- Acknowledge the unique needs and challenges that trans people face on college campuses.
- Do not assume that a person uses their legal first name; always present an opportunity for people to tell you the name they want to use on campus. Do not assume you know a person's pronouns; err on the side of asking people to tell you what pronouns they would like to have used for themselves.
- Apologize for mistakes (such as incorrectly labeling a person's gender) and work to correct your actions in the future.

### Campus Policies

- Enable students to have a chosen name on all nonlegal records and documents, including course rosters, ID cards, online directory listings, email addresses, advisee lists, unofficial transcripts, diplomas, and in all software systems that do not need their legal name.
- Give students the ability to change the gender marker on their campus records on request (i.e., without a letter from a therapist or doctor and without the need to change other documents first) and indicate their pronouns for course rosters.
- Educate the campus community that people have the right to use the gendered facilities that match their gender identity and that it is inappropriate to challenge someone's access to a restroom, locker room, or residence hall based on their gender identity or gender expression.

### Public Relations

- Emphasize policies that support and protect trans people and clearly articulate that acts of anti-trans discrimination and harassment are unacceptable on campus and will be quickly and thoroughly addressed.
- Openly discuss a commitment to gender inclusivity in public speeches and public relations efforts.

### Academic Settings, Curricula, and Faculty Support

- Encourage faculty to take class attendance by allowing students to indicate their names and pronouns, rather than relying on the names listed on course rosters.
- Offer trainings and ongoing support for faculty about how they can effectively instruct trans and other minoritized students and incorporate trans issues into curricula.
- Support, encourage, and reward faculty who act as allies to trans people and develop curricula that incorporate works by and/or about trans people.

### Recruitment and Retention

- Create, promote, and fund trans-inclusive spaces on campus, such as an LGBTQ center, where trans people can find support and community.
- Provide information to new students and employees about trans-related resources on campus and in the local community.
- Offer mentorship programs and support teams that can help trans people navigate difficult bureaucracies and feel welcomed on campus. Provide one-to-one mentorship opportunities when possible.
- Provide information on how trans students and others can change their names or gender markers on campus records and how they can obtain a legal name change, if desired.
- Allow employees to dress according to their gender identity.
- Offer scholarships that support trans students and cis allies who are advocates for this population.

### Student Health Services

- Train campus health center staff about how to sensitively and effectively serve trans and gender-nonconforming students.
- Advertise the presence of trans-competent health center staff in health-related materials and brochures. Be prepared to refer students to community resources when there is not someone on campus who is knowledgeable about serving the health-care needs of trans individuals.
- When medical services are targeted to one gender (such as a women's health clinic), train the staff to be able to serve trans patients and others who have bodies that are different than what they may expect.

## ACKNOWLEDGMENTS

This study would not have been possible without the work of Colorado Trans on Campus, particularly N. Eugene Walls, Kelly Costello, Karly Steffens, Kyle Inselman, Hillary Montague-Asp, and Sarah Nickels. I also give thanks to Nicole Nicotera, Walter LaMendola, the member check participants, and the thirty people who shared their stories as part of this study.

## NOTES

1. Because the CTOC study was primarily concerned with how campuses can better support trans people, the focus is on participants' gender identities on campus.

2. This interview was not audio recorded, and therefore this quote is a paraphrase based on the interviewer's notes.

## WORKS CITED

Ballan, Michelle. S. 2008. "Disability and Sexuality within Social Work Education in the USA and Canada: The Social Model of Disability as a Lens for Practice." *Social Work Education* 27: 194–202.

Beemyn, Brett Genny. 2005a. "Making Campuses More Inclusive of Transgender Students." *Journal of Gay and Lesbian Issues in Education* 3 (1): 77–87.

———. 2005b. "Trans on Campus: Measuring and Improving the Climate for Transgender Students." *On Campus with Women* 34 (3). http://www.aacu. org/ocww/volume34_3/feature.cfm?section=2.

Beemyn, Brett [Genny], Billy Curtis, Masen Davis, and Nancy Jean Tubbs. 2005. "Transgender Issues on College Campuses." *New Directions for Student Services* 111: 49–60.

Beemyn, Brett Genny, Andrea Domingue, Jessica Pettitt, and Todd Smith. 2005. "Suggested Steps to Make Campuses More Trans-Inclusive." *Journal of Gay and Lesbian Issues in Education* 3 (1): 89–95.

Bilodeau, Brent Laurence. "Genderism: Transgender Students, Binary Systems and Higher Education." PhD diss., Michigan State University, 2007.

Case, Kim A., Heather Kanenberg, Stephen Erich, and Josephine Tittsworth. 2012. "Transgender Inclusion in University Nondiscrimination Statements: Challenging Gender-Conforming Privilege through Student Activism." *Journal of Social Issues* 68 (1): 145–61.

Effrig, Jessica C., Kathleen J. Bieschke, and Benjamin D. Locke. 2011. "Examining Victimization and Psychological Distress in Transgender College Students." *Journal of College Counseling* 14 (2): 143–57.

Grant, Jaime M., Lisa A. Mottet, and Justin Tanis. 2011. *Injustice at Every Turn: A Report of the National Transgender Discrimination Survey*. Washington, DC: National Center for Transgender Equality and the National Gay and Lesbian Task Force. http://www.thetaskforce.org/static_html/downloads/reports/reports/ntds_full.pdf.

Lindsay, William G. 2010. "Redman in the Ivory Tower: First Nations Students and Negative Classroom Environments in the University Setting." *Canadian Journal of Native Studies* 30 (1): 143–54.

McKinney, Jeffrey. 2005. "On the Margins: A Study of the Experiences of Transgender College Students." *Journal of Gay and Lesbian Issues in Education* 3 (1): 63–76.

Molina, Kristine. 2008. "Women of Color in Higher Education: Resistance and Hegemonic Academic Culture." *Feminist Collections: A Quarterly of Women's Studies Resources* 29 (1): 10.

Nicolazzo, Z. 2016. " 'It's a Hard Line to Walk': Black Non-Binary Trans* Collegians' Perspectives on Passing, Realness, and Trans*-Normativity." *International Journal of Qualitative Studies in Education* 8398 (August): 1–16.

Quaye, Stephen John, and Shaun R. Harper. 2007. "Faculty Accountability for Culturally Inclusive Pedagogy and Curricula." *Liberal Education* 93 (3): 32–39.

Rankin, Sue R. 2003. *Campus Climate for Gay, Lesbian, Bisexual, and Transgender People: A National Perspective*. New York: National Gay and Lesbian Task Force Policy Institute. http://www.thetaskforce.org/static_html/downloads/reports/reports/CampusClimate.pdf.

Rankin, Sue, Genevieve Weber, Warren Blumenfeld, and Somjen Frazer. 2010. "Executive Summary: State of Higher Education for LGBT People." Charlotte, NC: Campus Pride. http://issuu.com/campuspride/docs/campus_pride_2010_lgbt_report_summary/19?e=0.

Renn, Kristen A. 2010. "LGBT and Queer Research in Higher Education: The State and Status of the Field." *Educational Researcher* 39 (2): 132–41.

Schiele, Jerome H. 2007. "Implications of the Equality-of-Oppressions Paradigm for Curriculum Content on People of Color." *Journal of Social Work Education* 43 (1): 83–100.

Seelman, Kristie L. 2013. "A Mixed Methods Examination of Structural Bigenderism and the Consequences for Transgender and Gender Variant People." PhD diss., University of Denver.

———. 2014a. "Recommendations of Transgender Students, Staff, and Faculty in the USA for Improving College Campuses." *Gender and Education* 26 (6): 618–35.

———. 2014b. "Transgender Individuals' Access to College Housing and Bathrooms: Findings from the National Transgender Discrimination Survey." *Journal of Gay and Lesbian Social Services* 26 (2): 186–206.

Seelman, Kristie L., N. Eugene Walls, Kelly Costello, Karly Steffens, Kyle Inselman, Hillary Montague-Asp, and Colorado Trans on Campus Coalition. 2012. "Invisibilities, Uncertainties and Unexpected Surprises: The Experiences of Transgender and Gender Non-Conforming Students, Staff, and Faculty at Colleges and Universities in Colorado." Denver, CO. https://portfolio.du.edu/ewalls2.

Seelman, Kristie L., Michael R. Woodford, and Z Nicolazzo. 2017. "Victimization and Microaggressions Targeting LGBTQ College Students: Gender Identity as a Moderator of Psychological Distress." *Journal of Ethnic and Cultural Diversity in Social Work* 26 (12): 112–25.

# SIXTEEN

# Rising like a Phoenix
## One Institution's Journey through Trans and LGBTQIA Inclusion

*Matthew Antonio Bosch and Dana Pursley*

WITH GROWING INTERNATIONAL VISIBILITY, awareness, and celebration of a variety of gender identities and sexual orientations, many institutions of higher education are making advances in welcoming, supporting, educating, and communicating across a diversified student body with regard to LGBTQIA inclusion. This chapter follows the journey of Elon University through multiple stages of inclusion, citing examples where LGBTQIA and specifically trans-identified students, faculty, staff, and alumni benefited from these growing inclusion efforts. We hope that by detailing how Elon uses collaborative partnerships, leadership across the university, and institutional strategic planning with dedicated resources to improve services and programs for LGBTQIA students, we can serve as a model for other colleges, particularly other private and Southern colleges.

## INSTITUTIONAL CONTEXT

Founded in 1889, Elon University is a selective, midsized, private liberal arts university with a historical connection to the United Church of Christ. Known for an institutional model that integrates academic, residential, and engaged learning experiences, Elon has four hundred full-time faculty members who teach in more than sixty departments and approximately 6,000 undergraduate and 750 graduate students from all fifty states and over fifty countries.

Elon is located in a politically conservative county in North Carolina, and one quarter of the university's students are from the state. The majority of Elon's student population hails from the Northeast and Mid-Atlantic. With many students coming from regions of the United States with more visible

LGBTQIA populations and greater protections under LGBTQIA rights laws, Elon has been pushed by students to become more LGBTQIA-supportive, and the university has responded in the past few years by seeking to address the needs of LGBTQIA people as part of a greater institutional emphasis on diversity and inclusion.

Elon University's emergence as a nationally recognized institution was the result of a series of ambitious strategic plans. In 2009, the university's board of trustees approved the current strategic plan, the Elon Commitment, which is set to guide the institution through 2020 (Lambert n.d.). The Elon Commitment is organized around eight themes, the first being the university's commitment to diversity and global engagement. The goal is to foster an environment in which there is diversity in thought, perspective, history, and background (Elon University n.d.).

To achieve this goal, Elon has taken swift action to double the institutionally funded need-based financial aid budget, reconfigure merit-based financial aid awards, provide new endowed scholarships to make study abroad accessible to every student, and expand support for students from minoritized communities by strengthening and expanding the roles of the campus multicultural center and multifaith center. Although addressing the needs of LGBTQIA students was not explicitly included in the 2010–2020 plan, a collective student response to anti-LGBTQIA state laws and a sense of growing marginalization in North Carolina ultimately led to the development of resources, programs, and support services for Elon's LGBTQIA community.

RECENT HISTORY OF LGBTQIA INCLUSION

Elon's nondiscrimination policy, which includes gender identity and sexual orientation, applies not only to students and employees but also to all individuals associated with the university, such as vendors, contractors, and guests. The intentionality for explicitly encompassing anyone who sets foot on campus was vital to establishing the expectation that the institution is committed to inclusion, including LGBTQIA inclusion.

Prior to 2000, the majority of LGBTQIA inclusion efforts arose from Spectrum, Elon's queer–straight student alliance, which was founded in the mid-1990s. During this time, faculty and staff often served as key mentors to students and organized events focused on gender and sexuality. However, there was not a unifying effort or a movement for LGBTQIA voices to be valued and heard across students, faculty, staff, and alumni.

In addition, until 2000, Elon's mascot was the Fighting Christian. Given the university's renewed commitment to diversity and inclusion, along with an increasing enrollment of non-Christian students, Elon made the decision to change its mascot to the Phoenix in 2000 (Keller 2004). The Phoenix makes reference to Elon rising from the ashes following a 1923 fire that destroyed most of the campus. Some alumni have remained resistant to the mascot change, holding closely to the ideals of the former Fighting Christian culture, which had impeded the creation of an LGBTQIA-inclusive environment.

In the 2010s, a number of contentious state and national issues caused Elon to reconsider its stance on LGBTQIA inclusion and take a more supportive and celebratory position. In 2011, a state constitutional amendment, Amendment 1, was proposed to ban same-sex marriage in North Carolina; during an off-cycle election, the amendment passed in 2012. Students were actively involved on all sides of the marriage equality debate, but a majority seemed to oppose the amendment (Haney 2013).

During this time, Chick-fil-A's presence on Elon's campus was also contentious, as many students, faculty, and staff banded together to protest the company's funding of organizations that actively lobbied for marriage bans and discrimination against LGBTQIA people. Despite the Student Government Association's support for removing the Chick-fil-A franchise from campus, the board of trustees voted to keep it on the recommendation of the Vendor Policy Committee, which is charged with reviewing policies regarding vendor contracts. However, Chick-fil-A was relocated from the center of campus within the Moseley Center student union to a less convenient dining hall (McGovern 2013).

In 2011, an LGBTQIA resource room was created and staffed by a faculty coordinator and an undergraduate student worker. While people celebrated the establishment of this first officially dedicated space for LGBTQIA people at the university, many felt that its placement in a building on the edge of campus, rather than in a central location, perpetuated the notion that LGBTQIA people are seen as marginal at Elon. Donations from LGBTQIA alumni and employees, along with a startup grant from a local nonprofit, provided funding for resources, including books, media, and educational materials on the experiences of LGBTQIA people.

In 2012, Elon University hosted a groundbreaking LGBTQIA Summit. Forty faculty, staff, students, and alumni met to address LGBTQIA community building on campus and make recommendations for increased resources and support for LGBTQIA community members (Simonetti 2012). That May, Elon

hosted its first Lavender Graduation to honor and celebrate the accomplish-
ments of the out LGBTQIA seniors who had persisted, despite the harmful
effects of the Amendment 1 and Chick-fil-A campus debates (Olsen 2012).

## CREATION OF THE GENDER AND LGBTQIA CENTER

With growing activism and growing momentum for LGBTQIA visibility, the
administration moved forward with a recommendation from the LGBTQIA
Summit to create Elon's first LGBTQIA center. In July 2013, Elon University
hired its first full-time LGBTQIA center director and changed the name of the
unit from the LGBTQ Office to the Gender and LGBTQIA Center to emphasize
both the intersections across sexual orientation, gender identity, and gender
expression and the inclusion of trans male, trans female, and nonbinary gender
students. The "Q" stands for "questioning" and "queer" identities, while the "I"
and "A" were added to include intersex and asexual identities.

With the transformation of the LGBTQ Resource Room into the Gender
and LGBTQIA Center, its location was moved into the central Moseley Center
student union building. The center currently contains four rooms, including a
social space, resource rooms for students, and the director's office. The director's office has an additional door into the hallway, which is useful for closeted
and questioning students, who may want to discuss their gender identity or
sexual orientation without being seen by their peers.

The director's position was strengthened by a dual reporting structure
to both student affairs, through the assistant vice president for student affairs,
and academic affairs, through the associate provost for academic and inclusive
excellence. The dual reporting structure was important because the center included directives not just for affecting LGBTQIA student life but also to serve
as a liaison and central unifying voice for faculty, staff, and alumni.

## PRESIDENTIAL LGBTQIA TASK FORCE

With the hiring of the center director in August 2013, University President Leo
M. Lambert appointed a group of fourteen faculty, staff, alumni, and students
to a newly created Presidential LGBTQIA Task Force. This group was charged
with creating and implementing a report that would make recommendations
to advance LGBTQIA inclusion in Elon's policies and practices. The end result
was a three-year institutional strategic plan that focused on four main goals
to improve the campus climate:

Goal 1: Support: Improve campus resources and services for current LGBTQIA students, staff, faculty, and alumni, especially through collaborative partnerships.

Goal 2: Welcome: Create a more welcoming educational, living, and working environment for LGBTQIA students, staff, faculty, and alumni.

Goal 3: Educate: Enhance LGBTQIA education and allyship across campus.

Goal 4: Communicate: Convey strong and supportive institutional messages across the campus for LGBTQIA community members.

Within each goal were six to ten subgoals, and within each subgoal were specific strategies for each year. The plan also included a year 0 in each category to track progress already made.

## LGBTQIA IMPLEMENTATION AND ASSESSMENT TEAM (PHASE II OF THE TASK FORCE)

Upon completion of the task force's report, a new LGBTQIA Implementation and Assessment Team (IAT) was appointed in summer 2014 to layout a framework and timetable to begin implementing the task force's recommendations. This team included five of the original fourteen members from the Presidential LGBTQIA Task Force, along with new faculty and staff members. Each year, the membership rotates to involve emerging faculty and staff advocates and reinvolve original task force members.

An important first step for the IAT was deciding to divide the group into specific subcommittees, which held individual meetings with departments. The subcommittees compiled the recommendations for each area and met with the directors and key staff members from that area. In these meetings, IAT members discussed the recommendations, answered questions, heard concerns, brainstormed timelines for improvements, and in some cases learned that some of the plans were already in progress. Some departments offered to speed up timelines for implementing changes in their areas.

Originally, a number of IAT members pondered whether our colleagues would first need to be educated on terms like *transgender, gender pronouns,* and *LGBTQIA* before they could understand the strategies we were asking them to implement. But departments were readily supportive, and many of the requested changes had already been considered, just not pushed through to completion. The changes had remained at a lower priority level, but departmental advocates frequently offered to make them higher priorities. Many departments wanted to be allies, and many understood the necessity for changes, such as new pronoun fields on student records and class rosters, or reasons for asking and tracking LGBTQIA demographic information on our admissions applications and college fair inquiry cards.

These departmental meetings showed those of us who identify as LGBTQIA that we can hold biases of our own at times about cis and heterosexual people's level of understanding about LGBTQIA people. We were fortunate to have allies across the university who wanted to help and who turned to the IAT for guidance.

## SUCCESSES IN POLICIES AND PROCEDURES

Through collaborative partnerships, Elon University has advanced LGBTQIA inclusion in multiple ways. The following areas are listed in alphabetical order. This is not an exhaustive list of all advances, and there will likely be a need for more changes in the future that are currently unforeseen. Many of the changes relate to improving the campus experience of trans students because that was where the most work was needed.

## ACADEMICS

The academic inclusion of LGBTQIA identities is paramount to students feeling validated and valued in the classroom. After recognizing the prevalence of LGBTQIA topics across the Women's and Gender Studies curriculum, a group of faculty members joined together to request a name change to Women's, Gender, and Sexualities Studies (WGSS) to be explicitly inclusive of people and topics across the different gender and sexuality spectrums. Nearly 100 courses count toward the WGSS minor, and WGSS seniors are honored annually at a special banquet.

We have also created a searchable diversity course database through the Center for the Advancement of Teaching and Learning. If a student wants to search for all academic courses addressing a particular area of diversity (e.g., gender identity, sexual orientation, race, faith), they simply click on that topic in a drop-down menu, and a list of relevant courses will pop up. Faculty members self-report the diversity areas of their courses to avoid any uncertainty.

Gender and LGBTQIA ally trainings have been implemented for the president's senior staff, including all academic deans. Hot topics at these sessions have included the hiring, promotion, and tenure of LGBTQIA faculty and how to create inclusive environments within classrooms and departments. These discussions are vital because Elon's academic deans are responsible for a large portion of hiring and determining curricula that align with the university's commitment to building an inclusive academic community.

ADMISSIONS

A university's admissions office is crucial to creating a welcoming impression well before students are accepted to the institution. Because of this, Elon's Office of Admissions readily agreed to implement recommendations regarding the inclusion of an optional LGBTQIA identity question on the application for enrollment and on the prospective student inquiry card, which is given out at recruitment events, including college fairs and high school visits. The question asks: "Do you consider yourself part of the LGBTQIA community?"

If a student checks the box to indicate "yes," they are sent a letter from admissions that highlights LGBTQIA campus resources, including the Gender and LGBTQIA Center, the Gender and Sexuality Living Learning Community, and the WGSS academic program. We hope prospective LGBTQIA students will feel welcomed and included by the university and will benefit from having this information all in one place, rather than having to search for it in the sea of college admissions material.

In addition to the LGBTQIA question, students can describe their gender identity on the admissions application through an optional question that asks if they identify as a man, woman, or "self-identify." If they click on "self-identify," a text box appears in which the student can write in their gender. Since this question was added to the form in 2015, several students have used this option to indicate identities beyond male and female.

The admissions office has also expanded their Phoenix Fusion Weekend, formerly known as Multicultural Weekend, to intentionally include LGBTQIA students. This weekend pairs admitted students with hosts who share similar identities, such as being LGBTQIA students of color. The admissions staff members work with trans and gender-nonconforming admitted students to try to pair them with a host of the gender identity they wish.

ADVANCEMENT AND ALUMNI ENGAGEMENT

We created an LGBTQIA Alumni Network to bring together LGBTQIA Elon graduates, whether for social connections, job networking opportunities, or meeting current students. The leaders of the group come to campus each semester to connect with and publicize the network to LGBTQIA students. To draw in LGBTQIA alumni, the network hosts an annual leadership gathering and social mixer in an area with a large alumni chapter, such as in Washington, DC.

One key area where our alumni have helped advance inclusion is around our new gender pronoun ribbons. In the Elon colors of maroon and gold, these adhesive ribbons attach to people's nametags for LGBTQIA-related events. The gender pronoun ribbons say "My pronouns are . . .," and underneath in a larger font is "they/them," "she/her," or "he/him." When people arrive for events, they are encouraged to take both a nametag and a pronoun ribbon. By having the ribbon separate from the nametag, it avoids any awkwardness around trying to find someone's pronouns on a small nametag amid what might be a lot of other information (e.g., title or class year). The ribbons have helped decrease the misgendering of attendees at events.

Elon's LGBTQIA alumni, along with supportive employees, have helped our LGBTQIA fund grow steadily. This fund supplements gender and sexuality inclusion efforts and programming that may be sponsored by the Gender and LGBTQIA Center, the WGSS academic department, or any affiliated student organizations. This fund also annually awards about fifteen scholarships to LGBTQIA students who have demonstrated a strong commitment to LGBTQIA inclusion and achievements in research, leadership, service, activism, or academic performance.

## ATHLETICS AND CAMPUS RECREATION

We have had great success in providing LGBTQIA educational trainings for Athletics and Campus Recreation, including all professional staff members and NCAA sports team captains. We are supported by LGBTQIA-identified staff in each of our three main athletics areas: coaching staffs, athletic trainers, and academic support. In these areas, the LGBTQIA-identified staff members serve as important mentors to both out and closeted student athletes. In addition, we have had a number of out LGBTQIA student athletes featured in student media coverage. For example, in April 2016, Elon's student newspaper, *The Pendulum*, included a cover story about two athletes who are partners (Simon 2016).

Campus Recreation, which encompasses intramurals and club sports, has added pronoun fields to its participant forms and altered its policies regarding hotel and overnight rooming assignments to enable trans and gender-nonconforming students to be housed with whom they feel most comfortable, regardless of gender identity. All single-day club sport tournaments were converted from "coed" to "open" competition, thereby allowing students to play without needing to identify specifically as a male or female player. Students also now have the option to play intramurals and club sports on a team aligned with their gender identity.

## CAREER SERVICES

Our career services area is known as the Student Professional Development Center (SPDC). The entire division attended an LGBTQIA ally training, where we discussed topics specific to LGBTQIA people in the workplace, including dress codes, pronoun usage, microaggressions, and helping students who decide to come out on their résumé or during the interview process. The SPDC has received a "gold ranking" from Out at Work's Career Center Certification Program, a nationally recognized assessment of LGBTQIA inclusion and support in career services.

## FACILITIES AND PHYSICAL PLANT

Elon currently offers over 100 gender-inclusive restrooms for students, faculty, staff, and campus visitors. The signage displays the words "Universal Restroom," along with Braille and a wheelchair access symbol, as all of our universal restrooms are also ADA-compliant. We use "universal restroom," rather than "all-gender restroom" or "gender-neutral restroom," because we have found that these gendered phrases can be confusing to some nonfluent English speakers looking for restroom facilities. All campus buildings constructed in the future will include universal restrooms. Many of these restrooms will also have baby-changing tables, which are important for everyday usage and our larger events like move-in, homecoming, and commencement.

## FRATERNITY AND SORORITY LIFE

Individual chapters within our Pan-Hellenic Council, Interfraternity Council, and National Pan-Hellenic Council have participated in LGBTQIA educational sessions. Every January during sorority recruitment, the Gender and LGBTQIA Center trains all forty-five of the Pi Chi sorority recruitment leaders, who act as orientation leaders for the rush process. Important elements of these sessions include creating welcoming environments through inclusive language and iconography and challenging the heteronormativity and gender normativity associated with pledging a fraternity or sorority.

We have had several chapters change their policies to be more inclusive of LGBTQIA people. Some now allow out trans-identified people to pledge, and some have removed restrictions that required students to bring members of another gender as dates to their events. In April 2015, Elon's student newspaper ran a feature article on being LGBTQIA within fraternity/sorority life, in which students shared their experiences, both positive and negative, in pledging and being part of a fraternity or sorority (Canada 2015).

## HEALTH, WELLNESS, AND COUNSELING

The staffs of our Medical Health Services, Health Promotions, and Violence Response areas and Counseling Center meet each semester with the staff of the Gender and LGBTQIA Center to discuss issues facing our student population, whether related to academic stresses, coming out, gender identity exploration, or social anxieties. The entire health, wellness, and counseling division staffs have participated in several LGBTQIA-related trainings, including a session with a medical professional who specializes in trans health care. As a result of these trainings, our health staffs have updated the student health intake forms to include gender pronouns and LGBTQIA identity terms. Our medical health record system has likewise been changed to include a pronoun field and a student's chosen first name, along with their legal name. Counseling staff members also keep up with LGBTQIA-related trends by being active in professional organizations, including the Association for LGBT Issues in Counseling and the American College Health Association.

## HOUSING AND RESIDENCE LIFE

Elon University offers many options for students to live in mixed-gender housing. Students of any gender identity can live with one another in our apartments, suite-style living areas, and four-person pods across several of our residential neighborhoods. An intentional decision was made not to group all of the mixed-gender housing in one area, as that would have made the housing less desirable or inaccessible to some students. In addition, Housing and Residence Life staff members are open to meeting with individual students who may have specific housing requests related to their gender or sexual identity.

In fall 2014, a Gender and Sexuality Living Learning Community was created for students interested in exploring LGBTQIA-related topics. This community shares a floor with a social justice–themed community and is linked directly to our WGSS academic program via faculty advisers. Students in the community engage in monthly dinner discussions about events, speakers, and hot topics on campus and about current events in the news.

## HUMAN RESOURCES

In fall 2013, an LGBTQIA Employee Resource Group was created with funding and support from Human Resources and the Office for Leadership and Professional Development. This group provides a wide array of opportunities for faculty, staff, and administrators, including connecting new and returning employees socially to build community and helping employees work together to improve the campus climate. The group plans an annual gathering for the president's senior staff and LGBTQIA employees to celebrate successes, discuss opportunities for growth, and take the overall pulse of the workplace community.

## POLICE, SAFETY, AND SECURITY

All of our public safety officers, police squads, and dispatchers participated in an LGBTQIA ally training session. These workshops address same-sex domestic violence, such as the need to recognize that an altercation between two men or two women could be intimate partner violence. We also cover the need to ask and use the gender pronouns desired by the person and how to handle situations in which the gender marker, name, or photo on a driver's license does not match the gender identity or expression of the person to whom they are speaking. We included an honest discussion about why trans people, and LGBTQIA people in general, might be fearful or skeptical of police officers, given the history of police harassment and mistreatment of LGBTQIA communities, which includes being misgendered, physically and sexually assaulted, and subjected to violence as a result of being put in a jail or holding area with others based on their sex assignment, rather than their gender identity.

Our campus police have also visited Spectrum meetings to listen to LGBTQIA students discuss their experiences involving police and safety officers. The officers have asked questions and gained valuable insights from these meetings. For their part, the officers thoroughly review and explain our online bias incident reporting system, as well as Elon's LiveSafe App, which enables students to request assistance or indicate suspicious activity.

## UNIVERSITY RECORDS MANAGEMENT

With an increasing presence of out trans and gender-nonconforming students on Elon's campus, it became evident that students were not having their gender identity reflected in and affirmed by university records. This was the result of a number of disparate systems not talking to one another. Students were seeing their "preferred name" in some records, while other systems were still using their legal first name (dead name). In fall 2016, Elon replaced the term "preferred name" with "campus name," following a recommendation made by Genny Beemyn (2016). For many trans and gender-nonconforming students, neither their pronouns nor their name are preferred, which implies that other people have a choice in which to use. Someone's name and pronouns *are* their name and pronouns, and they should only be referred to by them.

The addition of a campus name field in university systems now ensures that this name will be used for a student all over campus, including their residence hall door decoration, the label on a package to mail services, the login screen for class selection, and their records at health services. In the past, these were all places where Elon trans students were disrespected and outed by having their dead name appear. The Registrar's Office staff believes it is worth fixing 3,000 name mismatches to ensure that our trans students feel supported and included. Creating a campus name option has not only benefited trans students; it is also widely used by students who have a nickname. More than 2,000 students are currently listed by a first name other than their birth name in campus records, except for their transcripts and employment and financial aid records, which are considered legal documents and must use a student's legal name.

### Diplomas

Starting in May 2014, graduating seniors could elect to have their chosen name read aloud at graduation and printed on their paper diploma, as we want diplomas to reflect who students are and for students to feel proud showcasing them. The Registrar's Office staff meets with all seniors to ensure that they have completed graduation requirements; as part of these meetings, they ask each student how they want their name to appear on their diploma. We also allow trans alumni to request a new paper diploma with their chosen name. In May 2015, Elon began providing students with a certified electronic copy of their paper diploma, which they can send to employers and graduate schools. The electronic diploma likewise uses a student's chosen name.

### Email Changes

Elon uses the first letter of a student's first name and their full last name for their email address. As a result, a student who had established a campus name with the university would have a mismatch with their email address, if their new first name started with a different letter. Since 2015, students have been able to request an email address that incorporates their campus name and have any email sent to their former address forwarded.

### Pronouns

Since 2015, trans students have had the option of providing their gender pronouns to the Registrar's Office, which put this information on faculty course rosters. In fall 2016, a pronoun field was added to students' online profiles, so that they could directly and more easily indicate their pronouns for course rosters, and first-year students were encouraged to add their pronouns to their profiles during orientation. The pronoun options are "they/them," "she/her," and "he/him," and students receive a reminder every semester during the class registration period to update this information, if needed. With the introduction of pronouns on course rosters, faculty members have had discussions about implementation in departmental and all-faculty meetings.

### CHALLENGES AND NEXT STEPS FOR INCLUSION

We continue to see an expansion in the number of students who are declared minors or enrolled in WGSS courses. However, it is currently not an academic major, which means that faculty members in other departments must cross-list their courses so that they count toward the minor. Similar to many universities, a number of our courses across the curriculum address LGBQ topics and people, but few courses focus on trans and gender-nonconforming people.

Expanding our LGBTQIA Alumni Network presents ongoing challenges for a number of reasons. Alumni may be unaware of the recent LGBTQIA-supportive changes, and some might not have been out while at Elon. Moreover, we have only asked whether students identify as LGBTQIA in the past few years, so we are unable to use this data yet to track LGBTQIA alumni. For some of our trans alumni, connecting back to Elon could mean connecting back to a time and place before their gender transition, when they were not their whole selves. Therefore, trans alumni may not be nearly as excited to re-engage, despite recent campus efforts and advances toward trans inclusion.

More voices are needed, both from LGBTQIA-identified students and cis, heterosexual students, to advance conversations about inclusion in more heter-onormative or gender-binary activities, including athletics, campus recreation, and fraternity and sorority life. Systems need to be in place in these areas that can fully support LGBTQIA students, so that they feel comfortable being themselves and can come out, if they choose to do so. To improve the climate for LGBTQIA people and the overall athletic experience, athletics has implemented a new diversity com-mittee, which includes student athletes, coaching staff, athletics administrators, and diversity center staff. Both athletics and fraternity and sorority life are inter-ested in implementing LGBTQIA ally campaigns, which would include creating visible iconography, like an ally button using Greek letters, or getting further con-nected with #BeTrue, the Athlete Ally pledge, OutSports.com, or other organiza-tions that advance conversations about LGBTQIA people in sports.

Although our university has a policy affirming that students may use the gendered facilities that align with their gender identity, we currently only offer men's and women's locker rooms in our athletics and campus recreation buildings. Within these buildings, we have converted several larger universal restrooms into changing areas by adding benches and hooks to hang clothes and by installing new signs that say "Changing Room." We also do not have multistall universal restrooms on campus, but we are looking to learn more about how some universities have begun creating them.

In March 2016, North Carolina passed legislation known as House Bill 2 (HB2), which includes a provision requiring people in the state to use the restrooms and locker rooms in public schools and colleges and in public buildings that correspond to the gender on their birth certificates. Even though Elon is a private university, and thus not directly affected by HB2, and it has publically reaffirmed its commitment to LGBTQIA inclusion (Anderson 2016; Hamzik 2016; Lambert 2016), the law has had negative effects on our students, faculty, staff, and community. Despite the university's inclusive stance, some admitted students subsequently indicated that they were not attending Elon or any other North Carolina university because of this law. Even though the law was modified, many LGBTQIA students will probably not apply to Elon or other NC schools because many other states are considered much more supportive of LGBTQIA rights. The law may also affect our ability to recruit and retain LGBTQIA faculty and staff members.

Another obstacle we face is that because Elon does not offer any student health insurance plans, the university cannot assist trans students who are seeking access to long-term counseling, hormones, or gender-affirming surgeries. They must rely on plans connected to family members or the Affordable Care Act. Our human resources department is reviewing options for employees to have transition-related procedures covered under staff health insurance plans.

Within a university's publications, it can be difficult to offer authentic representations of different minoritized groups, rather than tokenism. It is especially difficult to show images of individuals who are unambiguously queer or trans. University Communications, Elon's public relations department, is working to increase inclusion of students in photos who represent a variety of sexual orientations and gender identities and expressions.

Although we have expanded our gender-inclusive housing options for students in apartments and suites, where students of different genders may live separately within the same unit and share a bathroom or common area, our traditional first-year and sophomore residence halls do not offer students of different gender identities the ability to live together in a double room. There have been conversations about making this change, but there is currently not a timeframe for doing so.

We will continue to educate faculty and staff about using "they/them" and other nonbinary pronouns. Faculty members have begun conversations, but more education is needed to ensure a smooth application of gender pronouns beyond "she/her" and "he/him."

Finally, a newly created group of students, faculty, and staff known as the Trans Inclusion Squad has created a list of recommendations for advancing support for trans and gender-nonconforming people in the areas of facilities, curriculum and pedagogy, human resources, records management, and student life. These suggestions will be reviewed by Elon's senior administration and then executed by the LGBTQIA Implementation and Assessment Team.

CONCLUSION

Elon University has made substantial advances toward trans inclusion and LGBTQIA inclusion more broadly. We have been honored to receive recognition for our efforts, including making Campus Pride's "Top 25 Best of the Best

Colleges and Universities" list in 2015, its "Best of the Best Top 30 List of the LGBTQ-Friendly Campuses across the Nation" in 2016, and its "Best of the Best Top 25 LGBTQ-Friendly Colleges and Universities" in 2017 (Campus Pride 2015, 2016, 2017). We continue to strive to improve our support for LGBTQIA students. The greater LGBTQIA inclusiveness of our programs, policies, and practices will positively affect our students, but it can take time to change campus culture. Moreover, this work requires ongoing attention and action. At Elon, we are committed to creating a campus environment in which our LGBTQIA students feel valued and validated.

## WORKS CITED

Anderson, Dan. 2016. "Elon Statement Regarding NC Legislative Action." Elon University. March 25. http://www.elon.edu/e-net/Article/129694.

Beemyn, Genny. 2016. "College Students with Non-Binary Sexual and/or Gender Identities." Presentation at the annual meeting of the American College Personnel Association, Montreal, Canada, March 6–9.

Campus Pride. 2015. "Campus Pride 2015 Top 25 Best of the Best Colleges and Universities." https://www.campuspride.org/2015-top-25.

———. 2016. "Campus Pride Releases Annual 'Best of the Best' Top 30 List of the LGBTQ-Friendly Campuses across the Nation." August 22. https://www.campuspride.org/campus-pride-releases-annual-best-of-the-best-top-3 0-list-of-the-lgbtq-friendly-campuses-across-the-nation.

———. 2017. "Campus Pride's 2017 Best of the Best Top 25 LGBTQ-Friendly Colleges and Universities." https://www.campuspride.org/campus-pride s-2017-best-of-the-best-top-25-lgbtq-friendly-colleges-universities/.

Canada, Kady. 2015. "Students Who Come Out as LGBTQIA within Greek System Face Additional Challenges." Pendulum, April 8. http://www.elo npendulum.com/article/2015/04/students-who-come-out-as-lgbtqia-with in-greek-system-face-additional-challenges.

Elon University. n.d. "The Elon Commitment: Engaged Minds. Inspired Leaders. Global Citizens." https://www.elon.edu/e-web/administration/ president/strategicplan2020/default.xhtml.

Hamzik, Tommy. 2016. "Elon Faculty Issues Resolution against HB2." Elon News Network, April 11. http://www.elonnewsnetwork.com/article/2016/04/ elon-university-faculty-resolution-hb2-lgbt-bathroom-north-carolina.

Haney, Adrianne. 2013. "Elon Campus Members Speak Out against Amendment One." YouTube, March 14. https://www.youtube.com/ watch?v=0WgUsE4g6HA.

Keller, George. 2004. *Transforming a College: The Story of a Little-Known College's Strategic Climb to National Distinction*. Baltimore, MD: Johns Hopkins University Press.

Lambert, Leo M. 2016. "Letter: Discriminatory State Law Is Stunning and Disappointing." *Times News*, March 31. http://www.thetimesnews.com/opinion/20160331/letter-discriminatory-state-law-is-stunning-and-disappointing.

———. n.d. "Statement of President Leo M. Lambert on Diversity and Global Engagement." Elon University. http://www.elon.edu/e-web/administration/president/strategicplan2020/diversity/president_statement.xhtml.

McGovern, Brennan. 2013. "Chick-fil-A to Remain at Elon." *Elon News Network*, April 25. http://www.elonnewsnetwork.com/article/2013/04/vendor-policy-committee-votes-in-favor-of-chick-fil-a-at-elon-university.

Olsen, Kristen. 2012. "University Honors Graduating LGBTQ Community during First Annual Celebration." Elon News Network, May 7. http://www.elonnewsnetwork.com/article/2012/05/university-honors-graduating-lgbtq-community-during-first-annual-celebration.

Simon, Alex. 2016. "LGBTQIA Athletes Find Match at Elon." *Pendulum*, May 3. http://www.elonpendulum.com/article/2016/05/lgbt-athletics-jess-farmer-aly-quintana.

Simonetti, Kristin. 2012. "Elon Alumni Association Holds First LGBTQIA Summit." *E-Net News*, December 3. https://www.elon.edu/E-Net/Article/60216.

# A GUIDE TO TRANS TERMINOLOGY

AGENDER PEOPLE: Individuals who identify as not having a gender. Agender people may identify as genderless, gender-neutral, or neutrois, having an unknown or indefinable gender, or deciding not to label their gender.

BIGENDER PEOPLE: Individuals who experience their gender identity as two genders at the same time or whose gender identity may vary between two genders. These genders may be masculine and feminine or may include non-binary gender identities.

BINARY TRANS PEOPLE: Individuals who identify as trans women or trans men.

CHOSEN NAME: The name that someone uses for themselves. The term "preferred name" should not be used because the name that a trans person goes by is not a preference.

CIS OR CISGENDER PEOPLE: Individuals who identify with the sex that was assigned to them at birth (i.e., people who are not trans).

DEAD NAME: The first name assigned at birth to a trans person that they do not use for themselves.

DEMIGENDER PEOPLE: Individuals who feel a partial connection to a particular gender identity. Examples of demigender identities include demigirl, demiboy, and demiandrogyne.

FEMININE OF CENTER PEOPLE: Individuals assigned male at birth who tend toward the feminine in their gender identity/expression.

GENDER BINARY: The social system that sees only two genders and requires everyone to be raised as a man or a woman according to the sex assigned to them at birth.

GENDER-FLUID PEOPLE: Individuals whose gender varies over time. A gender-fluid person may at any time identify as male, female, agender, any other non-binary gender identity, or as some combination of gender identities.

GENDER IDENTITY: An individual's internal sense of their gender, which may be different from or the same as the person's sex assigned at birth.

GENDER-INCLUSIVE OR GENDER-EXPANSIVE FACILITIES: Bathrooms, restrooms, and locker rooms that are open to people of all genders. They may be single- or multiple-user facilities.

GENDER-INCLUSIVE HOUSING OR GENDER-EXPANSIVE HOUSING: Residence hall rooms that are assigned regardless of gender, so that a student can have a roommate(s) of any gender. Sometimes "gender-neutral housing" is used, but this term is increasingly seen as inappropriate because it implies that the concept of gender is being neutralized or erased, rather than being expanded and embraced.

GENDERISM: The societal, institutional, and individual beliefs and practices that assume that there are only two genders and that gender is determined by one's sex assignment at birth or by specific sex characteristics. Genderism privileges cis people and leads to prejudice and discrimination against trans and gender-nonconforming people.

GENDER-NONCONFORMING PEOPLE: Individuals who do not adhere to the traditional gender expectations for appearance and behavior of people of their assigned sex. Some identify as trans, but others do not.

GENDERQUEER PEOPLE: Individuals who identify as neither male nor female (but as another gender), as somewhere in between or beyond genders, or as a combination of genders.

MASCULINE OF CENTER PEOPLE: Individuals assigned female at birth who tend toward the masculine in their gender identity/expression.

NONBINARY TRANS PEOPLE: An umbrella term for people who do not fit into traditional "male" and "female" gender categories. Nonbinary people include those who identify as agender, bigender, gender fluid, genderqueer, pangender, and various other genders.

PANGENDER PEOPLE: Individuals whose gender identity is numerous, either fixed (many at once) or fluid (moving from one gender to other genders).

PERSONAL PRONOUNS: The pronouns that someone uses for themselves. The phrase "preferred pronouns" should not be used because someone's pronouns are not a preference.

SEX ASSIGNED AT BIRTH: Sex designation given at birth, typically based on one's genitals. Most people are assigned female at birth (AFAB) or assigned male at birth (AMAB).

TRANS OR TRANSGENDER PEOPLE: An umbrella terms for individuals whose gender identity or expression is different from the gender assigned to them at birth. Among individuals who might identify as trans include binary trans people (trans women and trans men) and nonbinary trans people (those who identify as agender, androgynous, demigender, gender fluid, genderqueer, and other identities that go beyond traditional gender categories).

TRANSFEMININE PEOPLE: An umbrella term for individuals who were assigned male at birth but who identify with femininity to a greater extent than with masculinity.

TRANSMASCULINE PEOPLE: An umbrella term for individuals who were assigned female at birth but who identify with masculinity to a greater extent than with femininity.

TRANS MEN: Men who were assigned female at birth.

TRANSMISOGYNY: The unique discrimination experienced by trans women and transfeminine individuals, who face a combination of anti-trans and anti-women beliefs and practices.

TRANS WOMEN: Women who were assigned male at birth.

# CONTRIBUTORS

KASEY ASHTON is the associate director of the Women in Science and Engineering (WISE) Village at North Carolina State University (NCSU). She earned her M.Ed. and Ed.D. in higher education administration with a specialization in student affairs at NCSU.

GENNY BEEMYN, Ph.D., is director of the Stonewall Center at the University of Massachusetts, Amherst, and the coordinator of Campus Pride's Trans Policy Clearinghouse. They are the author of *A Queer Capital: A History of Gay Life in Washington, D.C.* (Routledge, 2014) and, with Sue Rankin, *The Lives of Transgender People* (Columbia University Press, 2011). Genny is currently working with Mickey Eliason on *Campus Queer: Addressing the Needs of LGBTQ+ College Students* for Johns Hopkins University Press.

C. RAY BORCK, Ph.D., is assistant professor of sociology and cocoordinator of gender and women's studies at Borough of Manhattan Community College (BMCC), City University of New York (CUNY). His research interests are epistemology, pedagogy, and gender. He lives in Flatbush, Brooklyn, with his dog, Rudy Huxtable, and cat, Tuxedo Mustache.

MATTHEW ANTONIO BOSCH serves as director of the Gender and LGBTQIA Center at Elon University in Elon, North Carolina. With six years on the American College Personnel Association Governing Board, he served as chief diversity officer for North Hennepin Community College, where he was chosen for Top 25 Latino Leaders in Minnesota by the Hispanic Chamber of Commerce. A first-generation college attendee, this graduate of Harvard University and Cornell University brings humor, authenticity, and intersectional identities across race, class, gender, and sexuality to discussions of inclusion and leadership on college campuses.

Active feminist, trans activist, and proud mama ANNABELLE TALIA BRUNO holds master's degrees in Japanese literature and linguistic theory but styles herself as a world-wise educator. Southern born and bred, Annabelle lives in Lexington, Kentucky, with her brilliant son, Luke, and her two sweet puppies, Arya and Sansa.

CADEN J. CAMPBELL graduated from Sweet Briar College in 2013 with a B.A. in English language and literature. His honors thesis, "A Witch? Who Is Not? Gender Instability and the Monstrosity of the English Renaissance Witch," received highest honors. Today, he and his wife, Jennifer, live in Eureka Springs, Arkansas, where he is the stewardship writer for Turpentine Creek Wildlife Refuge. Caden will be starting seminary as a postulant for Holy Orders in the Episcopal Church in fall 2018.

JAMES M. DEVITA, Ph.D., is assistant professor of educational leadership and program coordinator for the M.Ed. in Higher Education at the University of North Carolina, Wilmington (UNCW). His research interests include scholarship on teaching and learning, theory and practice in higher education graduate programs, and marginalized and targeted populations in higher education, particularly LGBTQ+ students.

ABBIE E. GOLDBERG is associate professor of clinical psychology at Clark University in Worcester. Her research focuses on sexual and gender minorities' experiences within various contexts (e.g., families, schools, and broader communities). She is the author of over eighty peer-reviewed articles, fifteen book chapters, and two books, and the editor of two books, including the *SAGE Encyclopedia of LGBTQ Studies*.

KEI GRAVES, M.H., has worked in higher education since 2013, doing a variety of jobs from advising to teaching. Kei also serves as the founder and co-chair of their college's Sexual Orientation and Gender Equity Committee, which focuses on LGBTQ+ advocacy, policy, and programming on campus. They hope that in sharing their story, a greater understanding and awareness of nonbinary individuals working at the community-college level of higher education will be garnered.

ALANDIS JOHNSON earned their doctorate at Miami University (Ohio) in educational leadership: student affairs in higher education with a graduate certificate in women, gender, and sexuality studies. Their scholarship focuses on nonbinary trans students within higher education.

LISA N. JOHNSTON is a college librarian who early in her career started the first GLBTQ organization at Sweet Briar College. She is an active member of the GLBT Round Table of the American Library Association and has served as chairperson of the Stonewall Book Awards. Lisa is director of library services at Eckerd College in St. Petersburg, Florida.

ERICH N. PITCHER, Ph.D., currently serves as the program lead for adult and higher education in the College of Education at Oregon State University. Erich uses organizational perspectives to understand equity, diversity, and inclusion within higher education, with a particular focus on the lives of trans academics and minoritized students' success.

DANA PURSLEY serves as the associate director of the Center for Leadership at Elon University in North Carolina. She received her bachelor's degree in child and adolescent psychology from Heidelberg University and her master's degree in higher education and student affairs from Ohio State University. Dana's higher education career includes working in residence life, leadership development, and gender and LGBTQIA education.

YULONDA RIOS (cover artist) is a self-taught artist who creates paintings that reflect her perception of the human condition as she envisions it. She is a native Californian and currently resides in Palm Springs with her two dogs, Patty and Babes.

KRISTIE L. SEELMAN, Ph.D., MSW, is an assistant professor of social work at Georgia State University's Andrew Young School of Policy Studies. Her research focuses on ways of improving policy, educational settings, and social services for LGBTQ+ populations. Kristie's work has been covered by media outlets such as the *Washington Post, Newsweek, Inside Higher Ed*, and *The Academic Minute* (NPR).

JACKSON WRIGHT SHULTZ is the author of *Trans/Portraits: Voices from Transgender Communities* and a regular contributor to *Conditionally Accepted*, a publication of *Inside Higher Ed*. He is an administrator of TRiO student support services at Everett Community College and an adjunct professor at Granite State College. He also serves as the education director of TEACH Alliance, a trans advocacy nonprofit organization.

S. SIMMONS, Ph.D., is the interim director of the Gender and Sexuality Center and an adjunct instructor at the University of Illinois at Chicago. S.'s interests and passions include advocacy, education, and research that extend the power of marginalized people. S. works to create spaces in scholarship and practice that center the voices and experiences of people of color, LGBTQIA+, low-income, and first-generation students, faculty, and staff in higher education.

SHANNON WEBER is a researcher, content writer at The Body Is Not An Apology, and scholar of LGBTQ studies. Shannon holds a Ph.D. in feminist studies and has held teaching positions in gender studies at Tufts University, Brandeis University, Northeastern University, the University of California, and Wellesley College. Read more about her current projects at www.shannonweberphd.com and say hello on Twitter @ShannonWeberPhD.

TRE WENTLING, assistant professor in women's and ethnic studies at the University of Colorado, Colorado Springs, is a first-generation college graduate. He earned his doctorate in sociology from Syracuse University's Maxwell School of Citizenship and Public Affairs and a certificate of advanced studies in women's and gender studies from Syracuse's College of Arts and Sciences. Along with Abby Ferber (University of Colorado, Colorado Springs) and Kimberly Holcomb, Tre coedited the anthology *Sex, Gender, and Sexuality: The New Basics* (Oxford University Press, 3rd ed., 2017).

KATRIN A. WESNER, Ed.D., is the director of student health services at the University of North Carolina, Wilmington (UNCW). Her research interests include emergency preparedness and response in higher education, health care literacy, and trans student success. Katrin is a fellow of the American College Health Association.

# INDEX

www.ingramcontent.com/pod-product-compliance
Lightning Source LLC
Chambersburg PA
CBHW021119270326
41929CB00009B/959